Harriet Martineau and the Birth of Disciplines

One of the foremost writers of her time, Harriet Martineau established her reputation by writing a hugely successful series of fictional tales on political economy whose wide readership included the young Queen Victoria. She went on to write fiction and nonfiction; books, articles and pamphlets; popular travel books and more insightful analyses. Martineau wrote in the middle decades of the nineteenth century, at a time when new disciplines and areas of knowledge were being established. Bringing together scholars of literature, history, economics and sociology, this volume demonstrates the scope of Martineau's writing and its importance to nineteenth-century politics and culture. Reflecting Martineau's prodigious achievements, the essays explore her influence on the emerging fields of sociology, history, education, science, economics, childhood, the status of women, disability studies, journalism, travel writing, life writing and letter writing. As a woman contesting Victorian patriarchal relations, Martineau was controversial in her own lifetime and has still not received the recognition that is due her. This wide-ranging collection confirms her place as one of the leading intellectuals, cultural theorists and commentators of the nineteenth century.

Valerie Sanders is Professor of English at the University of Hull, UK.

Gaby Weiner is Visiting Professor at the University of Sussex, UK.

The Nineteenth Century Series

Series editors
Vincent Newey
Professor Emeritus, University of Leicester, UK
Joanne Shattock
Professor Emeritus, University of Leicester, UK

The series focuses primarily upon major authors and subjects within Romantic and Victorian literature. It also includes studies of other nineteenth-century British writers and issues, where these are matters of current debate: for example, biography and autobiography, journalism, periodical literature, travel writing, book production, gender and non-canonical writing.

Recent in this series:

Harriet Martineau and the Birth of Disciplines

Nineteenth-century intellectual powerhouse

**Edited by Valerie Sanders
and Gaby Weiner**

LONDON AND NEW YORK

First published 2017 by Routledge

2 Park Square, Milton Park, Abingdon, Oxfordshire OX14 4RN
52 Vanderbilt Avenue, New York, NY 10017

Routledge is an imprint of the Taylor & Francis Group, an informa business

First issued in paperback 2018

British Library Cataloguing in Publication Data
A catalogue record for this book is available from the British Library

Library of Congress Cataloging-in-Publication Data
A catalog record for this book has been requested

ISBN: 978-1-4724-4693-0 (hbk)
ISBN: 978-0-367-17580-1 (pbk)

Typeset in Times New Roman
by Apex CoVantage, LLC

Contents

Figures

Contributors

Sharon Connor was awarded her PhD thesis by the University of Liverpool in 2014. Titled 'Retrieving the Husbandless Woman: Single Women in Victorian Fiction', her thesis explores the Victorian novel as a powerful tool of resistance to the dominant ideology surrounding women and marriage. Through the novels of Harriet Martineau, Charlotte Brontë and Margaret Oliphant, the different categories and experiences of the lone woman are shown to be of greater complexity than has been previously recognised.

Iain Crawford is Associate Professor of English at the University of Delaware in Newark, Delaware. His current book project is a study of the long and complex professional relationship of Charles Dickens and Harriet Martineau, focusing upon its implications for the development of the Victorian press and the emergence of the nineteenth-century professional woman of letters. His essay, "Harriet Martineau, Charles Dickens, and the Rise of the Victorian Woman of Letters," is forthcoming in *Nineteenth-Century Literature*, and he has contributed chapters on Dickens and Martineau to the collections *Charles Dickens and the Mid-Victorian Press, 1850–1870* (University of Buckingham Press, 2012) and *Dickens and Massachusetts: The Other America* (under review at University of Massachusetts Press).

Alexis Easley is Associate Professor of English at the University of St. Thomas in St. Paul, Minnesota. Her first book, *First-Person Anonymous: Women Writers and Victorian Print Media*, was published by Ashgate in 2004. Her second book, *Literary Celebrity, Gender, and Victorian Authorship*, was published by Delaware UP in 2011. Her most recent publications appeared in three 2012 essay collections, *Women Writers and the Artifacts of Celebrity, Women in Journalism at the Fin de Siècle*, and *Centenary Essays on W. T. Stead*. She also serves as editor of *Victorian Periodicals Review*.

Keiko Funaki is a Post-Doctoral Fellow of Musashi University Research Center and lecturer in the History of Economic Thought and the History of Social Thought at Musashi University and Otsuma Women's University in Tokyo, Japan. Her doctoral thesis, completed in 2002, was entitled 'J. S. Mill's View of Nature: an Approach from *Three Essays on Religion*'. She is particularly interested in economic thought and the religious views of the Victorian age and in the relationship between the idea of women's emancipation and classical political economics. She has written 'The role of political economics in feminism of the Victorian age' (Chapter 3 of *The Rise of Feminism in the Victorian Age*, Ochanomizushobo, Tokyo 2012, in Japanese). She has continued to write articles on Harriet Martineau for the annals of Musashi University Research Center. She has been a keen member of the Martineau Society, and looks forward to further examination of the works of Harriet Martineau.

Michael R. Hill holds earned doctorates in geography and sociology from the University of Nebraska-Lincoln (UNL). He has taught courses in geography, design studies, landscape architecture, urban planning and sociology during appointments at Iowa State University, the University of Minnesota-Duluth, Albion College, the University of Notre Dame and UNL. He currently edits *Sociological Origins* and is a senior tutor in the UNL Department of Athletics. Hill is the author/editor/co-editor of eleven books, including: *Archival Strategies and Techniques* (1993), *Harriet Martineau: Methodological and Theoretical Perspectives* (2001), Harriet Martineau's *How to Observe Morals and Manners* (1989) and Harriet Martineau's *An Independent Woman's Lake District Writings* (2004). Most recently, he edited a collection of Charlotte Perkins Gilman's writings on *Marriages, Families and Children* (2011). Hill received the American Sociological Association's Section on the History of Sociology Distinguished Scholarly Career Award in 2003 and two Distinguished Scholarly Book Awards, in 2002 and 2005, respectively.

Susan Hoecker-Drysdale is Emerita Professor of Sociology, Concordia University, Montreal. She has taught at The University of Kentucky and The University of Iowa and was Scholar in Residence at American University, Washington DC. She was Visiting Fellow, Institute of Historical Research and at the School of Advanced Study, University of London. Among her publications are *Harriet Martineau: First Woman Sociologist* (1992); co-editor, *Harriet Martineau: Theoretical and Methodological Perspectives* (2001); editor, *Harriet Martineau: Studies of America, 1831–1868*, 8 volumes (2004), "Harriet Martineau," in *Fifty Key Sociologists: The Formative Years*" (2007), as well as chapters and articles on Martineau, other women sociologists and the history of sociology. Current projects include *The Feminist Tradition in Sociology*, in progress.

Deborah A. Logan (PhD, University of North Carolina, Chapel Hill) is professor of English at Western Kentucky University, where she teaches Victorian Literature and World Literatures, and is editor and general manager of *Victorians Journal* (formerly *The Victorian Newsletter*). She is the author of three monographs: *Harriet Martineau, Victorian Imperialism, and the Civilizing Mission* (Ashgate 2010), *The Hour and the Woman: Harriet Martineau's "Somewhat Remarkable" Life* (Northern Illinois University Press, 2002) and *Fallenness in Victorian Women's Writing* (University of Missouri Press, 1998). She has edited twenty volumes of Martineau's work, including six volumes of letters.

As a result of a Fulbright-Nehru Senior Research Scholarship (Jadavpur University, Kolkata, West Bengal, 2012), Logan has just completed a two-volume study of *The Indian Ladies' Magazine*.

Valerie Sanders is Professor of English and Director of the Graduate School at the University of Hull. Her doctorate on Harriet Martineau was published as *Reason Over Passion: Harriet Martineau and the Victorian Novel* (Harvester, 1986); and she subsequently edited Martineau's *Selected Letters* for the Clarendon Press (1990) and a reissue of *Deerbrook* for Penguin Classics (2004). Recent monographs include *The Brother-Sister Culture in Nineteenth-Century Literature: From Austen to Woolf* (Palgrave Macmillan 2002) and *The Tragi-Comedy of Victorian Fatherhood* (Cambridge University Press, 2009). Besides publishing on women's autobiography and anti-feminist Victorian women writers, she has edited two volumes of nineteenth-century women's childhood autobiographies with Ashgate (2000 and 2012). She has also edited and co-edited four volumes of Pickering and Chatto's *Selected Works of Margaret Oliphant*, including most recently Oliphant's 1883 novel *Hester* (2015).

Lesa Scholl is the Dean of Academic Studies at Emmanuel College, University of Queensland. She was awarded her PhD from Birkbeck College, University of London in 2008, supervised by Professor Hilary Fraser. The monograph derived from her dissertation, *Translation, Authorship and the Victorian Professional Woman: Charlotte Brontë, Harriet Martineau and George Eliot*, was published by Ashgate (September 2011). Her other publications include articles and book chapters on Harriet Martineau, George Eliot, Christina Rossetti, Henry Mayhew and pedagogical approaches to translation theory and literature. Her research interests extend to literature as cultural history, forms of translation and economic fictions. Current projects include literary representations of hunger 1800–1940, and an international collaboration, *Place, Progress and Personhood in the Works of Elizabeth Gaskell*.

Beth Torgerson is an Associate Professor of English at Eastern Washington University in Cheney, Washington. Her book, *Reading the Brontë Body: Disease, Desire, and the Constraints of Culture*, was published by Palgrave (2005; paperback 2010). Her chapter "Gift-Giving and Community in Cather's *The Song of the Lark*" is included within Debra Cumberland's edited collection of *Willa Cather's* The Song of the Lark (Rodopi, 2010). She has published in *Victorian Review*, *Nineteenth-Century Literature*, *The Martineau Society Newsletter*, *The Brontë Messenger* and *Disability Studies Quarterly*.

John Vint is Emeritus Professor at Manchester Metropolitan University (MMU) and Honorary Professor at Perm State University, Russia. He was formerly Head of Department of Economics at MMU, and he has taught at universities in the UK and North America. His research interests lie in the history of economic thought and this has drawn him to the question of the popularisation of economic ideas and the work of Harriet Martineau. In 1993 he won the Joseph Dorfman Prize for the Best Dissertation in the History of Economic Thought and published a monograph based on his doctorate entitled *Capital and Wages* in 1994. For eighteen years up to 2012 he was the editor of the *History of Economic Thought Newsletter.* He is at present researching and writing on classical political economy and Harriet Martineau, and is currently Chair of the Martineau Society.

John Warren, formerly Senior Lecturer and subject leader in history at Birmingham City University, was awarded his D.Phil at the University of Oxford on Harriet Martineau's early fiction and its relationship to Martineau's intellectual and local context. His publications include *History and the Historians* (2000), *Elizabeth I: Meeting the Challenge* (2008) and a chapter on the Rankean impact on English historical writing in Stefan Berger et al., *Writing History Theory and Practice* (2010).

Ruth Watts is Emeritus Professor of History of Education at the University of Birmingham. Her research interests are in the history of education and gender and she has published much on these, including articles on Harriet Martineau and education. She is honorary life member of both the History of Education Society and the International Standing Conference for the History of Education, President of the Martineau Society and a member of the Women's History Network.

Gaby Weiner has worked at various universities in the UK (Open University, London South Bank University) and Sweden (Umeå University) and is currently Visiting Professor at Sussex University, Visiting Professorial Research Fellow at Manchester Metropolitan University and Academic Consultant at Umeå University. She has written and edited a number of publications on gender and social justice in education, including *Just a Bunch of Girls* (1985, reprinted 1987, 1988 and 1989), *Feminisms in Education* (1994) and *Closing the Gender Gap* (1999, with Madeleine Arnot and Miriam David). Her most recent book is entitled *Deconstructing and Reconstructing Lives* (2011, with Lucy Townsend). It draws on early publications on Harriet Martineau, including editorship of Virago reprints of Harriet Martineau's *Autobiography* and novel *Deerbrook* (both in 1983), and a doctoral thesis completed in 1991 entitled 'Controversies and Contradictions: Approaches to the Study of Harriet Martineau' (1991). She has been an active member of the Martineau Society and has published several articles arising from presentations to Society members.

Acknowledgements

This collection grew out of the 2013 annual meeting of the Martineau Society in Liverpool. One of the key questions at such meetings is how best to show to the wider world the depth and breadth of Harriet Martineau's intellectual scholarship and legacy. Because she has been claimed in recent years as a foremother of disciplines such as Political Economy, Sociology and Literature, and also as important to such sub-disciplines as Life Writing, Women's Studies and Travel Writing, it was decided to try to encapsulate her literary output in the form of chapters based on the range of disciplines and fields of knowledge to which she contributed. We also realised that several of the main Martineau scholars were at the meeting, so it provided the opportunity to recruit them to the project on the spot, as it were. We have also to thank the Martineau Society for allowing individual chapter authors to test out their ideas to the highly informed and knowledgeable Martineau Society audience. For that, we thank the Society and its members, without whom this book would not have been published.

We also thank the following people for their support in this venture: Ann Donahue, our-ever supportive editor at Ashgate, whose enthusiasm for the project and sound advice saw us through all the usual challenges of publishing an essay collection; Ashgate's anonymous reader, whose report offered the perfect balance of encouragement and specific suggestions; Beth Torgerson for her strenuous and determined search for fitting illustrations; and David Hamilton, who helped with our discussion on the origin of the disciplines.

For permission to include images from their collections we gratefully acknowledge the following: the US National Library of Medicine, The Master and Fellows of Trinity College Cambridge, and the Wellcome Library, London.

Introduction

The disciplines and Harriet Martineau

Valerie Sanders and Gaby Weiner

> While our science is split up into arbitrary divisions; while abstract and concrete science are confounded together, and even mixed up with their application to the arts, and with natural history; and while the researches of the scientific world are presented as mere accretions to a heterogeneous mass of fact, there can be no hope of a scientific progress which should satisfy and benefit those large classes of students whose business it is, not to explore, but to receive.[1]

At first sight, this statement from Harriet Martineau's Introduction to her translation of Comte's *Positive Philosophy* forms a surprising start to an essay collection making claims for her mastery of multiple disciplines. What she describes here is a state of disciplinary muddle: of science distracted by the arts, and miscellaneous information mixed up with serious scientific research. The very notion of interdisciplinarity is presented as a nightmare from which Comte's carefully constructed hierarchies of the sciences are designed to rescue us. Yet by 1853 when this work was published, Martineau had gained public recognition as a populariser of political economy, a sociological traveller, a contemporary historian, a domestic novelist, a philosophical invalid, a defender of mesmerism and an author of children's stories. Far from requiring her interests to be as scrupulously segregated as this declaration implies, she had become a living embodiment of interdisciplinarity and its possibilities. She had also become an expert in each of the disciplines in its own right.

Harriet Martineau wrote in the middle decades of the nineteenth century, at a time when new disciplines and fields of knowledge were being established. It was a time of considerable optimism that the world would be improved through knowledge of newly understood scientific laws applicable both to nature and society. She was particularly interested in exploring the application of scientific laws to human behaviour. In so doing, she was not only a key intellectual force of her time but also an influence on emerging disciplines and fields of study such as sociology. Much of her work was in fictional form though in her later years she was primarily a journalist for the *Daily News*. Her writing on behalf of women and the vulnerably sick and against slavery gave her a role in social reform and political activism, while her written works on education and childhood, and the pedagogic stance of much of her general writing, led her to assume the title of 'Popular Educator'. She thus wrote on subjects and issues that were of interest in her space and time, namely Victorian England, primarily over four decades, 1820s to 1860s.

Yet, her corpus of writing also reflects Martineau as an individual woman, bodily, socially and intellectually. For her, like many writers of the nineteenth century, the knowledge she drew on and promulgated was a unitary 'science', even though later commentators would connect her work to different disciplines, for example, political economy, sociology, history and newly emerging work on the mind. She could write on these disparate topics because what was known as science or knowledge had not yet been organised into the disciplines and fields we recognise today. As Hall[2] points out, Martineau's writing could be innovative because this was a period which allowed women as well as men to experiment with writing forms.

So how was it that her different writings could reflect her own wide interests yet also be recognised as formative to the newly emergent disciplines of the nineteenth century? Following Stichweh,[3] this was because many disciplines were taking shape over the period of Martineau's writing career: 'The scientific discipline as the primary unit of internal differentiation of science is an invention of the nineteenth century'.

Martineau could write as she did, with power and authority on a wide range of topics, for several reasons: her undoubted wish to be heard or, as she put it, 'need of utterance' and her extraordinary ability and drive, and also because of the times she lived and worked through, when 'truths' were being challenged and knowledge was reconstituting into disciplines.

The use of the word 'discipline' as a concept and practice has a long history. In its original sense, *discipline* meant the systematic instruction intended to train a person, sometimes called a *disciple*, in a craft, trade or other activity, or to follow a particular conduct or order. *Disciple* is here derived from the Koine Greek word *mathétés* (from *math*, or mental effort needed to think something through), to mean a pupil or apprentice (to a master craftsman). Alternatively its origins have been traced to the Latin *discere* meaning learning, and later, *disciplina*, meaning the ordering of knowledge for educational purposes. *Disciplina* has a more pedagogical focus on the means of inculcating knowledge as opposed to *doctrina*, which emphasises the codification of beliefs or body of teachings.[4]

Disciplina is also associated with moderation in behaviour, as in the twelfth-century bishop's household, where the bishop was entreated to avoid extremes of 'austerity and frivolity, cruelty and laxness' and instead provide a model of behaviour for his household in the service of church and state.[5] For Hugh of St Victor, a leading medieval theologian and writer, discipline was the process of 'learning virtue'. However, as Jaeger points out, this diverged from the more conventional sense of *disciplina* at the time which equated *ars* and *disciplinae* with 'the disciplines'. So, here we have different interpretations of discipline: as the systematic training of a *disciple*, as virtuous behaviour and as a body of knowledge.

From the Renaissance onwards *disciplina* came to be associated with systems rather than units of knowledge, alongside increasing use of classification systems and encyclopaedic compilations. Predominant during this Early Modern period was a disciplinary concern to preserve and archive what was known to be true.[6]

People of knowledge such as philosophers, scientists and other scholars were in the main generalists, able to disseminate their ideas in a range of all-purpose publications. The first two scientific journals appeared in the same year, 1655: the *Journal des sçavans* in France initially contained obituaries of famous men, church history and legal reports, while the London-based *The Philosophical Transactions of the Royal Society* published letters that scientists wrote to one another, mostly in the first person.[7] The aim of such publications was to provide a general forum for discussion.

In the latter decades of the eighteenth century, however, the expansion of knowledge frontiers made it necessary to concentrate on smaller *fields* of scientific activity. This reflected developments in education systems, and the 'close coupling of the emerging disciplinary structures in science and the role structures of institutions of higher education'.[8]

In a parallel shift, early modern Europe witnessed a slow movement away from regarding the main task of scholarship and learning so as to uncover and preserve the truth, towards an increased interest in experimentation and invention. Knowledge remained based on four traditional disciplines, Theology, Medicine, Law and Arts, inherited from the middle ages, but from the mid- to late nineteenth century, secularization and the expansion of university education led to the inclusion of new subjects such as non-classical languages and literatures; social sciences such as political science, economics, sociology and public administration; and natural science and technology disciplines such as physics, chemistry, biology and engineering. These were joined in the early twentieth century by education and psychology, and in the 1970s and 1980s, by new disciplinary fields such as women's studies, black studies and disability studies derived from contemporary social movements.

So, at the time of Martineau's birth in 1802, what it meant to study and learn was at a critical point: scholarship aimed at identifying knowledge considered to be true was being challenged by scholarship which questioned previously held truths and understandings. Following this, scientific studies morphed into research disciplines aimed at understanding newly identified laws perceived as governing both the physical and social worlds.

These intellectual shifts saw parallels in Martineau's own development as a writer. When she began to write in the 1820s, her first book, on prayers and hymns in 1826, was devotional rather than critical. However, the questioning environment of her Unitarian childhood and youth and the opening up of intellectual horizons beyond the home, provided what we would now call a discursive space in which she could offer her own challenges to taken-for-granted truths such as the so-called natural inferiority of girls and women. Thus, two of her earliest articles, 'Female Writers on Practical Divinity' (1822) and 'On Female Education' (1823) in the Unitarian periodical the *Monthly Repository*, emphasised the importance of women as social agents, including presumably her young self. She wrote regularly and prolifically for the *Monthly Repository*, so much so that Francis

Mineka identified more than 89 articles by her published in the two years between 1829 and 1831, ranging from parables and tales, to review essays on celebrated Nonconformists.[9]

Later, as the nineteenth century and her own writing matured, she was able to branch into more worldly subjects such as political economy and taxation, albeit through the interpretive lens of fiction. She also tinkered with the new genre of the realist novel (*Deerbrook*, 1839; *The Hour and the Man*, 1841; *The Playfellow* series for children, 1841) but there is a sense that Martineau preferred what she felt to be more serious work on cutting-edge topics, such as the state of America or Ireland or India.

Much of Martineau's corpus of work was the consequence of commissions arising from public interest. For example, she wrote her first travel book *Retrospect of Western Travel* (1838) at the request of her publishers, and *Guides to Service* (1838–40) came about at the behest of the Poor Law Commissioners. Her *History of the Thirty Years' Peace* (1849–51) was undertaken at the bidding of Charles Knight who had himself written the first chapters and was then unable to proceed further.

Her methodological book *How to Observe Morals and Manners* (1838) was wanted, again by Charles Knight, for a new 'How to Observe' series, of which the opening volume was Henry De la Beche's *How to Observe Geology*. de la Beche (1796–1855) was a geologist and palaeontologist, first director of the Museum of Practical Geology and of the Geological Survey of Great Britain, and an early advocate of geological survey methods. Martineau's was the second volume in the series. Thus, both authors could be said to be pioneers in observation techniques and fieldwork methodologies.

Martineau's removal to the Lake District in 1845 and her long-term employment as journalist for the *Daily News* from 1852 onwards freed her from the day-to-day pressures of metropolitan life and simultaneously gave her a regular income which meant thereafter, that she could exert greater choice in her written output. As well as her daily journalism, she wrote philosophical works, histories, books about her travels to the East, descriptions of the surrounding beauty of the Lake District and how she farmed her small estate. She re-published *Daily News* obituaries as biographical sketches of the eminent in 1869 when she was stretched financially and wrote scholarly articles about girls' and boys' education (1832, 1864), the employment of women (1859) and the British military (1859). Her translation of *Philosophie Positive* in 1853 was the outcome of a 'fascination' with Comte's positivism and a 'dream' of translating it so that it would be read by people unlikely to see the original. And near the end of her life, in 1869, she published four letters in the *Daily News* in support of Josephine Butler's struggle to repeal the Contagious Diseases Acts which had legalised medical inspections of women in military towns. In so doing, Martineau fired an early shot in one of the most important British feminist campaigns of the nineteenth century. Her extraordinarily wide range of writing, her boldness and certainty, and her ability to connect with public concerns meant that she was accorded great recognition and respect throughout her lifetime, even if she also, at times, attracted controversy and criticism.

As she assumed the authority of public *savant*, moves were afoot to restrict what she and other generalists could say. Thus, while her publication of *Life in the Sickroom* (1844) brought her experience of sickness into the public arena to general acclaim, the volume was disparaged by the nascent medical establishment as indicating a case of 'nervous exhaustion' for which the treatment prescribed was 'unconditional submission'.[10] As Winter argues, Martineau's 'authoritative portrayal of invalidism' challenged the growing confidence of medical practitioners as trained experts able to subject the patient 'to the healthy influence of medical discipline'.[11]

A similar pattern is evident in her treatment by economists. Political economy was already a powerful discourse when she began writing about it in the 1830s. Scottish philosopher, Adam Smith, is often cited as the 'father' of modern economics for his treatise *The Wealth of Nations* which appeared in 1776 on the eve of the Industrial Revolution, with associated major changes in the economy. Successive political economists provided intellectual responses to rapid shifts in class relations following the Napoleonic Wars, resulting, within a space of fifteen years, in the 1832 Reform Act, the 1834 Poor Law and the Repeal of the Corn Laws, all of which were much influenced by arguments derived from economics.[12] Martineau held that political economy was a science hardly known, and that if there was a case for reform, it should be based on economic principles. Her series *Illustrations of Political Economy* (1832–4) sought to illuminate these principles through fictional tales based on James Mill's four sets of economic operations: Production, Exchange, Distribution and Consumption.

She thus introduced and popularised political economy in the 1830s. However, contemporary political economists such as John Stuart Mill were unsympathetic to her efforts at economic education, accusing her of reducing laissez-faire to 'an absurdity'[13] and she was further ridiculed for poor quality of writing, misplaced reform zeal and lack of femininity.[14]

Excepting contemporaries, furthermore, Martineau's economic works subsequently received little attention from economists as we shall see later in this volume. The main reason for this, as Mike Sanders suggests, was because Martineau was a lone woman in the nineteenth century, apart from Jane Marcet, in writing on political economy.[15] Both wrote primarily as popularisers of established economic theories, interpretative and illustrative of, rather than challenging to, established orthodoxies. Consequently, though Martineau wrote more extensively and provided more detail than Marcet, both were dismissed as serious economists, and accorded little more than a footnote in the history of the discipline.

Likewise, Martineau's translation and interpretation of Comte's *Philosophie Positive*, acknowledged as a founding text of modern sociology, and her pioneering sociological texts, *Society in America* and *How to Observe Morals and Manners* were ignored by university academics in the process of establishing sociology as a university discipline from the 1850s onwards. And it is only relatively recently that her foundational sociological work has gained recognition.[16]

There have been two principal motivations for recent increased attention to Martineau's life and work. The first has been the discovery of new sources, for example, R.K. Webb's identification of Martineau's 'something under' 1,500 leaders and articles in the *Daily News*[17] and the more recent digitisation of many of her publications as well as the collection and publication of her letters, all of which has made Martineau's writing more readily available. A second motivation for increased interest in Martineau as well as other women intellectuals, social activists and notables, first at the end of the nineteenth century and then from the 1980s onwards, has been feminism in its various forms, and particularly its wish to restore women to their rightful place in history, society and culture. Nineteenth-century feminists tended to concentrate on Martineau's role as innovator and female role model – for example, Florence Fenwick Miller's biography published in 1884[18] – but more recently the focus has been on the different kinds of contribution she has been seen to make, as writer, novelist, sociologist, political economist and so on. And it is from this latter body of scholarship that this volume draws.

The essays included in this collection were commissioned to provide the first fully comprehensive overview of Harriet Martineau's contribution to the disciplines, both within her own lifetime, and subsequently, into the twentieth and twenty-first centuries. There has to date been considerable scholarly disagreement as to exactly which discipline(s) and fields of knowledge Martineau most influenced and best represents. Was she primarily a populariser of political economy or public educator? Should she be more permanently remembered as an early feminist, the 'first woman journalist' and founder of modern sociology or for her travel writing or letters? For example, Caroline Vernon, eponymous heroine of Martineau's contemporary, Charlotte Brontë's (1839) Angrian novelette, sees her primarily as a travel writer: 'a lady who must have been the cleverest woman that ever lived. She travelled like a man, to find out the best way of governing a country'.[19]

Given Martineau's own shifting concerns, which kept pace with the rapid intellectual developments of her half-century of professional activity, it might be more accurate to say that her engagement with knowledge and the disciplines changed emphasis from decade to decade. Starting out as a populariser of classical economic theory, she quickly broadened her range, feeling compelled to speak up for vulnerable and oppressed groups, especially black slaves in the southern states of America, and the sick and disabled. Characters with disabilities emerged in her fiction, which also tackled the plight of governesses and single women, while her travels in America turned her into a nascent sociologist as well as a political and cultural commentator. Women's issues of all kinds were the staple of her journalism, though this, in turn, embraced topics as varied and apparently unconnected as industrial processes, Irish politics, the health of the nation, the condition of domestic servants, Salem witchcraft, the future of the West Indies, the Royal Family and 'Female Dress.' An apparently compulsive educator of others, Martineau turned both inwards and outwards, drawing on her own experiences to develop new theories of sickroom management, a passionate defence of mesmerism, useful tips on cow-keeping and a religion-free philosophy for the end of life. The great and small claimed her attention equally. Her voluminous correspondence with the high-profile people of her day as well as her friends, relatives and neighbours, responded to everything from local gossip to affairs of state. All that happened to Martineau and in the wider world of her purview, she saw – without systematically designing it – as potential 'copy' for her multifarious publishing purposes. The danger of this stance was her dismissal by scholars, as a generalist too closely tied to her times, and therefore at risk of being quickly written out of history. Addressing ephemeral issues as a self-educated expert, Martineau's ability to turn her hand to all kinds of writing worked against her, inviting distrust and scepticism from an academic culture which increasingly valued specialisms and painstaking training in a single discipline, rather than a cheerful and pragmatic openness to opportunity where it arose.

The inspiration for this essay collection was in fact the difficulty of categorising and explaining Martineau's lasting significance. Overlooked for many years, from the time of her death in 1876 until the 1950s, she is now enjoying an upsurge of attention. As Ella Dzelzainis and Cora Kaplan, editors of a recent Martineau essay collection, argue, 'Since she specialized neither as novelist, nor economist, nor journalist, nor historian, and deliberately – and successfully – sought the widest audience of readers that contemporary literacy could provide, she has, in the past, been too easily categorised simply as a populariser, even by the modern feminist scholarship that has played such an important part in reviving her reputation.'[20] Our collection overlaps with Dzelzainis and Kaplan's in that we share some of the same contributors and similar topics (e.g., Deborah Logan on Martineau's correspondence), and they too acknowledge her interdisciplinary, or rather 'pre-disciplinary', interests;[21] but there are also significant differences in our approaches. Whereas their collection arose out of a conference, and organises its essays around three headings – 'Authorship and identity,' 'Political economy, technology and society,' and 'Empire, race, nation' – with an emphasis on the 'contradictory trajectories' (p. 9) of Martineau's writing and ideas, ours was prompted by a wish to focus specifically on the disciplines with which her name has been associated. As Dzelzainis and Kaplan argue, 'No critical consensus has emerged on the historic significance of the positions Martineau took or what they represented in the genealogy of liberal thought' (p. 7). While this remains a key issue with Martineau, we have shifted this debate specifically to the different disciplines with which we see her as engaging, and attempt in our 'Afterword' to decide which of them should be regarded as most directly 'hers', whether in terms of lasting impact, or quite simply the one with which she deserves to be most closely associated.

Initially a disadvantage the recent promotion of interdisciplinary scholarship has served Martineau well, as have new directions in cultural and feminist history which highlight the problematic status of women as public figures and voices of authority. Alison Winter, for example, in her study of Martineau as a celebrated invalid, examines the process by which the 'isolated invalid became, in Martineau's vision, the truly authoritative commentator on public life',[22] a position that also intrigued Susan F. Bohrer. Martineau's prolonged illness of 1839–44, which took her out of public life, created, claims Bohrer, the 'contradictory status of a woman who has taken to bed but retains public stature'.[23] It is partly this paradoxical position between public and private that makes Martineau's role as (at least partly) authorised educator of the nation so innovative yet so difficult to evaluate in terms of its lasting impact. Was she primarily a public figure with a voice of authority, whose views were disseminated by some of the period's establishment journals, or a private householder, who for the last thirty years of her life deliberately removed herself from public engagement in the personal sense, while continuing to broadcast her views on every aspect of Victorian life? How was she understood by her various publics? To what extent is her writing relevant today?

This essay collection confronts the issue which has pervaded Martineau studies and downplayed her lasting influence: if she was essentially a populariser of ideas – as in her early work on political economy – could she be seen to be in any sense an originator? If she was largely a mouthpiece for the ideological conflicts of her own times, to what extent was her writing foundational to specific disciplines? And to what extent did the positions she adopted on, for example, slavery, women and disability enhance or diminish her historical and disciplinary importance?

The contributors to this collection have each been asked to chart Martineau's involvement in, and lasting impact on, a specific 'discipline' or field. We have avoided following a strict chronological order, given Martineau's often simultaneous activity in different areas. We begin with chapters that indicate the foundational characteristics of her work: her autobiographical writing and her role as public educator. Both these aspects thread through her entire oeuvre. These are followed by chapters which illustrate her contribution to a variety of disciplines and fields of knowledge, culminating in a focus on her informal correspondence. As Deborah Logan argues, letters provided Martineau with a form of 'rehearsal space', where she could debate current concerns with her correspondents, and capture controversies in their initial, inchoate form, as their full implications were worked out. The final chapter of the volume draws together the various claims and arguments made in preceding chapters to provide a tentative evaluation of Martineau's disciplinary legacy.

For Lesa Scholl, in the opening chapter, the *Autobiography*, published posthumously in 1877, maps extensively Martineau's entry into the disciplines of history, psychology, literary criticism and philosophy, and shows the extent to which she created a new understanding of them: for example, by realizing on reading Jane Marcet's *Conversations on Political Economy* (1816), that she had been 'teaching it unawares'.[24] As Martineau progressed through life, testing other human experiences on her own mind and body, she inserted herself into the broader narrative of national progress. Martineau's life was thus an extending of human experience to encompass the troubles of many who were completely unlike her, but with whose political and social needs she developed both a private and a public empathy.

Her lifelong mission was to inform the public about what she regarded as the most important issues of the day; so her continuing, often self-appointed role as an educator was the natural consequence of her success with the *Illustrations*. Ruth Watts, in Chapter 2, however, reminds us that Martineau was just as keen to acquire knowledge as to disseminate it, and far from being a passive conduit for other thinkers' ideas, she questioned traditional assumptions on many matters, ranging from women's education to orthodox Christian belief. Convinced that *education* was responsible for most of the differences between people, she argued that a good rational education should be extended to all, in particular those who were generally excluded from it. Why is Martineau not better known as an educational theorist? Ruth Watts answers this question by exploring her key educational principles, which though enlightened, were never concretised in action. Her impact on education was therefore somewhat muted, even if her educational ideas speak out to us over the ages.

The second section of the book explores Martineau's contribution to specific disciplines and fields of knowledge. It opens, in Chapter 3, with a critical examination of Martineau's positioning in the discipline which first made her famous, that of political economy. As John Vint and Keiko Funaki point out, the theories of Adam Smith, James Mill and the other classical economists were already known, at least to the educated classes, in the early part of the nineteenth century. Martineau herself had no difficulty accepting their validity, and in launching her *Illustrations* was determined to show her readers how these seemingly dry concepts of supply and demand, production and population, would impact on imagined, but realistically conceived, communities. The chapter considers the fundamentals of *political economy* driving this early phase of Martineau's publishing life. The authors not only capture and critique the kind of political economy Martineau promoted, but also explore why she was so determined to popularise what was known as the 'dismal science'. While Martineau would have been the first to acknowledge there was nothing in the discipline of political economy, or its popularisation that she invented, she nevertheless stands out as the only nineteenth-century writer to gain celebrity status for the dissemination of economic theory through a series of tales set in different countries, classes and historical moments. Something of a cross between Hannah More's 'moral tale' and the 'social problem novel' of succeeding decades, the *Illustrations* were Martineau's own invention, albeit an unlikely source of instant popularity which continues to puzzle critics today.

In contrast, Martineau's reputation as a founder of the discipline of *sociology* has been more extensively acknowledged, initially through the activities of the Harriet Martineau Sociological Society on Mackinac Island, Lake Huron, in 1997. Michael Hill, a founding member of this group, asserts, in Chapter 4, that Martineau's impact on the discipline, through respectively her small volume *How to Observe* (1838), her range of acute social observations of communities and systems in America, the Middle East, Ireland and England, and her translation and condensation of Auguste Comte's *Philosophie Positive*, constituted a significant reformation of sociological principles and methods. Her interdisciplinary approach, claims Hill, played a key part in what she was able to achieve, thus making her one of the earliest and most influential practitioners of what is now championed as 'public sociology'. Today's sociologists, he suggests, would benefit from a better understanding of Martineau's contribution to the discipline.

Susan Hoecker-Drysale, in Chapter 5, offers a complementary perspective on Martineau's sociology to that of Michael Hill. She focuses on Martineau's theoretical and methodological projects on the subject of work, a theme running throughout Martineau's lifelong research and writings. Martineau's approaches to, and her studies of, work are explored against the economic, social and structural transformations of the time, when work was a central focus for women writers and for sociological thinkers.

Martineau's contribution to some disciplines was less as a 'founder member' than as an innovator in some aspect of a field already populated by others. Although she was by no means the first female historian, Alexis Easley argues, in Chapter 6, that it was unusual for a nineteenth-century woman to write a comprehensive national *history*, especially a contemporary history, as Martineau did with her *History of England during the Thirty Years' Peace 1816–46* (1849–50). Nor was this her first attempt at narrative history, as she had already incorporated an historical perspective into her studies of American culture and 'Eastern Life'. Easley proposes that while Martineau's *History* is clearly situated within the conventions of nineteenth-century Whig historiography, her contribution to the field is innovative insofar as Martineau inflects her narrative with a 'proto-feminist sensibility', which reinforces the historicity of women's lives, and makes the status of women a measure of social evolution and a moral indicator of national advancement.

As already noted, disabled characters feature frequently in Martineau's *fiction*, the best-known being the lame governess, Maria Young, in *Deerbrook* (1839), which Sharon Connor, in Chapter 7, sees as a novel unique in Martineau's output. Her enmeshing of public social issues with the personal concerns of her characters, Connor argues, gives rise to a new form of female writing later described by the poet Dora Greenwell as reflecting and exploring 'the secret of a woman's heart'.[25] Although Martineau writes rather awkwardly about women's dawning awareness of romantic feelings, she was experimenting with this in a decade (the 1830s) when emotional subtlety in fiction was arguably less finely nuanced than it became in the hands of Elizabeth Gaskell and George Eliot some years later. Martineau never repeated the experiment of a full-length novel of domestic realism, moving on to a fictional biography of the Haitian leader Toussaint L'Ouverture in *The Hour and the Man* (1841), but *Deerbrook* remains an intriguing novel in which the lame governess, Maria Young, comes to represent the plight of all women faced with the need to work or marry in order to achieve economic stability. At the same time Martineau's unease with women's self-absorption and emotionalism clearly surfaces in *Deerbrook*, and Connor questions whether marriage – so closely explored in this novel – necessarily offers a more secure emotional future than that of resilient independence, no matter how unpromising the single woman's prospects.

The roots of *psychology* provide the context for Beth Torgerson's examination, in Chapter 8, of Martineau's contribution to the new Victorian sciences of the mind. Torgerson traces Martineau's interest in Mental Physiology, mesmerism and phrenology, as a means of placing her within the longer disciplinary history of psychology. For example, after writing of her own experience and that of her maid of the curative effects of mesmerism, or hypnosis, not only does

Martineau endorse mesmerism as a therapeutic agent for healing, but also she famously challenges medical men and scientists to focus their scientific skills on exploring mesmerism to the full, and its force for good or otherwise. Torgerson shows that Martineau was present during the birth pains of psychology even though she was limited, as a woman and non-physician, in respect of what she could achieve.

The third section of the book considers Martineau's standing in various sub-disciplines or fields of knowledge. Her interdisciplinarity was such that each of her interests appears to segue smoothly into the others, for example, her sociological interests stimulated partly by what she observed of the *treatment of women* around the world. In reviewing Martineau's writings on women, and overall impact as an early feminist thinker, in Chapter 9, Gaby Weiner inevitably engages with many of the other causes Martineau adopted, such as the 'political non-existence of women,' as Martineau calls it in relation to American society, and in Britain the campaign against the Contagious Diseases Acts of the 1860s. While it is problematic to apply the anachronistic term of 'feminist' to nineteenth-century public figures, not least because of their own often self-contradictory stance on women's issues, Weiner demonstrates not only the breadth of Martineau's scholarship on women, and also her attention to a wide range of social injustices affecting women of all classes and many nationalities, but also her theoretical clarity in seeking reasons for, and solutions to, women's lowly status.

As we have already seen, *travel writing* was an established field when Martineau made her foray into it, via her two-year American 'sabbatical', which took her through the southern slave states as well as to dangerous anti-slavery conventions in the North. But here too she achieved something new, diverging from the approach of her immediate predecessors Alexis De Tocqueville (*Democracy in America*, 1831) and Frances Trollope (*Domestic Manners of the Americans*, 1832). Iain Crawford, in Chapter 10, examines Martineau's ethnographic methodology as a travel writer, as set out in *How to Observe Manners and Morals* (1838) before exploring her later work, *Eastern Life, Present and Past* (1848) in the context of her sociological and political interests. Crawford's argument is that Martineau used her travel writing to discuss intellectual issues central to British public discourse in the late 1840s. As her career as a journalist developed, she further exploited opportunities to incorporate what she had learned from her travels into her public discussion of other urgent contemporary issues.

Martineau's career in *journalism* was lifelong, and underpins much of what she achieved, from her tentative debut in the Unitarian *Monthly Repository* at the age of twenty, to her final contributions to the *Daily News* and the *Edinburgh Review* in her sixties. Her compulsion to speak out made her a 'natural', and her fluent, rapid style, and air of homely common sense admirably suited the requirements of at least eighteen different periodicals, enabling her to range freely over the full gamut of nineteenth-century issues. Even here, however, as Valerie Sanders indicates in Chapter 11, Martineau's contribution is far from straightforward. Like other of her female contemporaries she disguised both voice and identity, while taking her argument in often unpredictable directions. Sanders's analysis of her response to the Great Exhibition of 1854, for example, shows her initial neglect of the exhibits of the Crystal Palace to focus on the people milling around the stands. Her deafness notwithstanding, she eavesdrops on 'ignorant' conversations, and observes people incongruously eating their sandwiches before going to see the 'savages and beasts'. The whole experience becomes for her yet another exercise in ideologically-driven social observation which allows her to plead for Sunday opening of the exhibition, for Saturdays to be set aside for the 'workers', and Mondays for the 'aristocrats', and also for the reconfiguration of the exhibits to 'change a heterogeneous collection of objects into a philosophical whole.'

Much of Martineau's writing drew closely on her personal experiences as already noted, and in regarding her life as 'somewhat remarkable'[26] she mined it constantly for anecdotes and exemplary stories. For example, her novel *Deerbrook* includes talkative and boisterous children in many of its scenes, reflecting Martineau's long-term interest in child psychological development, in common with many other nineteenth-century writers and commentators. John Warren's recuperation of Martineau's *childhood* domestic experiences in Chapter 12 first addresses the mixed influences of Associationism and Wordsworthian romanticism on her construction of childhood before demonstrating how treatment of the child was for her a litmus test for the moral quality of households – much as Alexis Easley suggests was the case with women by their societies, as shown in her *History*. Martineau's notion of the child, as reconstructed by Warren, reveals its complex nuances, inflected by what he sees as her own 'craving for justice' and her unflinching revelation of corrupted households and brutalised scenarios in her manual of family life, *Household Education* (1849). Martineau's inspiration for these stories came from her own, often miserable, childhood experiences in what appeared to others an enlightened and educated Norwich manufacturer's household of the first twenty years of the nineteenth century.

Martineau used another form of life writing, her voluminous *correspondence*, in lieu of drafting her arguments to correspondents on both sides of the Atlantic. Logan shows how Martineau's correspondence – even the most ostensibly private – resonates with writing intended for publication. She highlights the idea that correspondence as authorial practice is, for Martineau, the most spontaneous, authentic form of expression, and that its clarity and purity are essential to the quality of her most polished published works.

The final section of this collection on Martineau's legacy goes beyond reappraisal of Martineau's 'relevance' in the twenty-first century or reassessment of her contribution to the abolition of slavery, the Contagious Diseases Acts and so on. Indeed, many of her most hard-fought campaigns and concerns have long been overtaken by history and the inevitability of social and political change. Valerie Sanders and Gaby Weiner in their Afterword, draw on the preceding chapters of the book to argue that Martineau's main legacy is her impact on the professionalisation of the variety of disciplines and fields of knowledge to which she contributed. The dominant task of Martineau's working life was to observe human culture and society in the mid-nineteenth century, during which the influence of the gentlemanly amateur gradually declined in favour of the trained professional.

Martineau seems at first glance the epitome of this vanishing culture: a provincial woman of idiosyncratic opinions, who – naively, perhaps – accepted the challenge to address not just the nation's ills, but also those of the wider world. However, she also embraced modernity and scientific progress, and displayed a thirst for knowledge and for what was new in her era theoretically, politically and socially. Moreover, her letters show the enormous professionalism and commitment which she brought to her writing. It is argued that the essays in this collection together and separately, make sense of Martineau's apparently fragmented career and recuperate her for a number of 'disciplines' and fields. Moreover, they show that her originality lies, not only in her fictionalisation of economics, innovative work in sociology, political and social campaigns and so on, but also in the writing genre she pioneered, of observation and reportage, which rendered accessible to the masses, ideas and debates that had been hitherto exclusive to the elite.

Notes

1 *The Positive Philosophy of Auguste Comte, Freely Translated and Condensed by Harriet Martineau*, 2 vols. (London: John Chapman, 1853), Vol. I, p. vii.

2 Catherine Hall, 'Writing a history, writing a nation: Harriet Martineau's history of the peace.' In: Ella Dzelzainis and Cora Kaplan (eds.), *Harriet Martineau: Authorship, Society and Empire* (Manchester: Manchester University Press, 2010), pp. 231–53.

3 Rudolph Stichweh, 'Scientific disciplines, history of.' In: Neil J. Smelser and Paul B. Baltes (eds.), *International Encyclopedia, of the Social and Behavioural Sciences* (Oxford: Elsevier Science, 2001), pp. 13727–31, pp. 13727.

4 Op. cit.

5 C. Stephen Jaeger, *The Envy of Angels: Cathedral Schools and Social Ideals in Medieval Europe 950–1200* (Philadelphia, PA: University of Pennsylvania Press, 1994), p. 242.

6 Stichweh.

7 John Swales, *Genre Analysis: English in Academic and Research Settings* (Cambridge: Cambridge University Press, 1990).

8 Stichweh, p. 13728.

9 Francis E. Mineka, *The Dissidence of Dissent: The Monthly Repository1806–1836* (Chapel Hill: University of North Carolina Press, 1944).

10 'Life in the sickroom,' *British and Foreign Medical Review* 18 (1844), pp. 472–81.

11 Alison Winter, 'Harriet Martineau and the reform of the invalid in Victorian England,' *The Historical Journal*, 38:3 (September 1995), pp. 597–616; pp. 600 and 608.

12 Simon Dentith, 'Political economy, fiction and the language of practical ideology in nineteenth-century England,' *Social History*, 8:2 (1983), pp. 183–99.

13 Letter from John Stuart Mill to Walter Coulson, November 22, 1850. In Lord Robbins *The Evolution of Modern Economic Theory* (London: Macmillan, 1970), p. 125.

14 J. W. Croker, 'Miss Martineau's monthly novels,' *Quarterly Review*, 49 (April, 1833), pp. 136–52.

15 Mike Sanders, 'From "Political" to "Human" economy: The visions of Harriet Martineau and Frances Wright,' *Women: A Cultural Review*, 12:2 (2001), pp. 192–203.

16 Alice S. Rossi, 'The first woman sociologist: Harriet Martineau 1802–76.' In: A. S. Rossi (ed.), *The Feminist Papers: From Adams to De Beauvoir* (New York: Bantam, 1974), pp. 118–24; Paul L. Riedesel, 'Harriet Martineau and the birth of sociology,' *Free Inquiry in Creative Sociology*, 8:1 (1980), pp. 61–62; Michael R. Hill, 'Preface to the sesquicentennial edition.' In: Harriet Martineau (ed.), *How to Observe Morals and Manners* (New York: Transaction Publishers, 2002), pp. xi–xiv.

17 Robert K. Webb, 'A handlist of contributions to the *Daily News* by Harriet Martineau 1852–1866,' (1959).
18 Florence Fenwick Miller, *Harriet Martineau* (London: W.H. Allen, 1884).
19 Charlotte Brontë, 'Caroline Vernon.' In: Heather Glen (ed.), *Charlotte Brontë: Tales of Angria* (Harmondsworth: Penguin, 2006), p. 370.
20 Dzelzainis and Kaplan, p. 1.
21 Ibid., p. 2.
22 Winter, 1995, p. 607.
23 Susan F. Bohrer, 'Harriet Martineau: Gender, disability and liability,' *Nineteenth-Century Contexts*, 25:1 (2003), pp. 21–37; p. 23.
24 Harriet Martineau, *Autobiography* (1877); rept. ed. Linda Peterson (Peterborough, ON: Broadview Press, 2007), p. 123.
25 Dora Greenwell, 'Our single women,' *North British Review*, 36 (1862), p. 63.
26 *Autobiography*, ed. Peterson, p. 34.

Part I
Foundational characteristics

1 Mapping the intellectual self

Harriet Martineau's *Autobiography* and the role of life writing in defining disciplines

Lesa Scholl

Harriet Martineau's *Autobiography* (1877) has been celebrated as radically trans-forming the autobiographical genre, most particularly in regard to the nineteenth-century female autobiography. The self-shaping that autobiographical writing involves, alongside the agency of the author to narrate their own tale, provides a powerful space for articulating individual and social identity. Most critics have read the *Autobiography* as a continuation of Martineau's conviction that it was her duty to teach the nation, as well as further evidence of her desire to maintain control over her public persona. Linda Peterson, in her introduction to the *Autobiography*, emphasises Martineau's deliberate self-shaping, from her 'interdicting the publication of her letters and asking friends to burn private correspondence', to writing her own obituary in the third person, arguing that she 'in effect prevented others from shaping her life story, and thus . . . maintained the power to tell it her own way.'[1] Similarly, Lucy Bending writes that Martineau's *Autobiography* came out of her 'desire to put forward her own case, to represent herself in a way that was not inflected by the interpretations of others whose desire for Martineau to be what they expected her to be was at times overwhelming,'[2] while Jill Ker Conway observes that 'Martineau, a woman who had become one of the leading educators of her society on social and economic matters . . . wanted the world to know how she had become such a phenomenon.'[3]

It is within this context of Martineau as a social and cultural phenomenon, and her desire to control the expression of the nature of her impact, that this chapter is positioned. I argue that her impact as a public intellectual is mapped autobiographically through her intricate engagement across a variety of academic disciplines and through her formal learning and scholarly work, as well as her encounters with leading figures of those intellectual fields. Valerie Sanders humorously recounts that 'George Eliot was filled with a renewed sense of horror at the indignities of self-exposure' upon reading Martineau's *Autobiography*;[4] but most importantly, Sanders remarks on Martineau's deliberate move away from a conventional feminine autobiography, which even shied away from using the generic term, to the more masculine approach of presenting 'a history of [her] life and opinions.'[5] Indeed, Sanders suggests that Martineau was the 'only female autobiographer of the nineteenth century to give anything like "her own intellectual history".'[6] Ironically playing on the knowledge that female autobiographers who 'emphasised the pleasant and entertaining aspects of their lives . . . got a better press',[7] Martineau facilitates this feminine mode to some degree in the way she discusses her encounters with intellectual figures, ultimately subverting the private, social setting by transforming it into an interdisciplinary space of ideas.

Martineau's position within the context of female autobiography has received a great deal of critical discussion, with some scholars accentuating the feminine qualities of her work, such as Conway drawing out the way in which the opening chapters focus on Martineau's inner life and religious turmoil, 'religious sensibility' being a conventional feature of female memoirs,[8] while others, like Sidonie Smith, have argued that Martineau wrote her autobiography in a 'manly' manner: 'Harriet Martineau . . . assumes the role of the "manly" woman, appropriating the prerogatives and privileges of male selfhood.'[9] Conway circumvents some of the masculinisation of Martineau by claiming it was the fact that she was seemingly on her deathbed that allowed her to 'throw away many concerns about privacy and modesty', yet by Conway's own admission, Martineau had been 'one of the leading educators of her society on social and economic matters', and so it seems unlikely that she would have felt constrained to speak because of her gender.[10] Indeed, as Sanders points out, the women 'who were bold enough to call their work "autobiography" were generally women who had already flouted convention, and drawn attention to themselves by their participation in controversial campaigns', for which Martineau was famed.[11]

Other assessments have been more willing to embrace the hybrid nature of Martineau's style in terms of gendering. Sanders observes that Martineau 'may have written more self-consciously as a woman in some parts of the book than in others', but '[b]y the end. . . . Men and women have been subsumed into a mystical conception of "Man".'[12] This melding of gender aligns with Peterson's observation that Martineau was deliberately confronting 'a dominant male tradition' by 'insist[ing] upon gender-free patterns of human development', and suggesting that women 'should adopt universal patterns of interpretation, systems that apply to all humankind.'[13] It is in this reference to human development – one might say, human *intellectual* development – that Martineau's autobiography fuses as a critique both of the genre of female life writing and the ways in which education and learning are conceived within her Victorian society. David Amigoni draws on Peterson's observations on the hybridity of female autobiography to suggest that its 'generic instability and hybridity' should be considered 'the basis for exploring the "diversity of forms"' inherent in life writing.[14] This 'diversity of forms' resonates powerfully with the way in which Martineau engages intellectually with the world around her, and is reflected in her hybrid (both in terms of gender and intellectual disciplines) literary productions.

Martineau's resistance to external definition has made her notoriously difficult to categorise as a writer. As Alexis Easley states later in this volume, Martineau's unwillingness to 'tie herself down to another multi-volume history writing project' reflects her deliberate attempts to defy categorisation. However, the unfortunate result of this defiance is that for much of the twentieth century Martineau was defined as a 'miscellaneous' writer, thus 'trivialising her achievement in multiple fields of discourse, including her important work as a historian.'[15] This chapter therefore examines the *Autobiography* as Martineau's intellectual self-shaping, and thus her statement of the role her decades of intellectual productivity had in forming not just her own understanding of intellectual disciplines, but also the role of the disciplines in the fabric of British cultural heritage. I begin by look-ing at the role of interdisciplinarity in Martineau's narrative. The conversations between disciplines are fundamental to her accounts of her personal intellectual development. The categorising and re-categorising of the disciplines enables her to construct her identity on her own terms, but within the legitimisation of those established disciplines. I go on to examine the layering of Martineau's categorisa-tion techniques, from mapping, to hierarchies and disciplinary evolution along the lines of Comtean positivism, to, again, a hybrid approach that encompasses these maps and structures with the narrative of life writing. This section then flows into the more specific focus on the foundation of, not just theology, but theological modes, in Martineau's intellectual rationalisation. While engaging in the tradi-tionally female mode of religious exploration, Martineau goes further in reveal-ing how the theological method of apologetics influenced the organisation of her intellectual space. It then follows that Martineau's personal intellectual develop-ment is broadened into the national narrative, as autobiography is viewed as his-torical material. For Martineau, however, this material is produced consciously, as she deliberately seeks to take an active role in continuing to shape Britain's intellectual culture after her death.

While engaging with Martineau's personal life, it is significant that her account only reveals the personal insofar as it furthers the understanding of her intellectual progress. Conway suggests that as a genre, autobiography brings together discrete disciplines, providing access to questions of history, psychology, literary criticism and philosophy.[16] In this vein, Harriet Martineau, as an interdisciplinary writer (as many nineteenth-century public intellectuals were), uses her *Autobiography* to tease apart the disciplinary threads, providing a canvas for their interconnec-tions and progress. Her map reflects the influence of Auguste Comte's positiv-ist approach to the scientific disciplines, but extends this structure to incorporate the humanities as well, authenticating them by bringing them underneath the sci-entific banner. As Easley has argued, Martineau thus reasserts herself into the broader narrative of national progress.[17] Between the boundaries of self and self-construction, Martineau's *Autobiography* seeks to establish the intellectual dis-ciplines necessary to Britain's intellectual development, facilitating Martineau's own life narrative to model the pathway of progress.

Autobiography and intellectual development

Interdisciplinarity is enjoying a resurgence of currency, yet it is often framed as an innovation of scholarship. Thomas Scheff argues for 'researchers to become gener-alists after their initial training in a discipline or subdiscipline', for 'the most physi-cal science progress has been made when separate disciplines or subdisciplines have combined.'[18] He bases his argument on the conviction that where the physical

sciences have learnt to become interdisciplinary, the social sciences and humanities are lagging behind. However, the establishment of discrete divisions, or at least
the segregation of scholars to particular specialisations, is relatively new: Harriet
Martineau, like most nineteenth-century public intellectuals, was what Scheff
would describe as a generalist, engaging across fields, bringing them into conversation with each other in order to speak to the social, political and economic issues
that concerned her. Thus the researchers promoting interdisciplinarity are returning
to a scholarly openness that was indicative of Victorian intellectual engagement.

The division of academic or intellectual disciplines creates a myth of order
and organisation. In reality, however, disciplines are most relevant and active
when flowing in and out of one another, entering into conversation. Discrete disciplines, therefore, standing alone, are inherently unstable in a way that reflects
Bending's assessment of Martineau's *Autobiography*, referring to the 'profound
instability of many of Martineau's own terms of description, as she puts forward
what initially seems to be a consistent position.'[19] In looking at the connections
Martineau makes between the development of intellectual disciplines and her personal life story, it is important to acknowledge that development rarely occurs in a
neat, seemingly consistent way. It is only in looking back that an imaginary sense
of order can be imposed. Autobiography becomes, then, a provocative space in
which to explore the dynamic nature of intellectual disciplines, for the diversity
and flow of disciplines reflects the 'chaotic ebb and flow of experience' that is
imperfectly translated into 'a narrative form with a beginning, a middle and an
end' – imperfect because an autobiography gives a false sense of an ending to a
life that is not yet over.[20] This desire to create narrative stability is essential to the
fabric of Martineau's life writing, her early need to categorise displayed through
her childhood account of making books in order to record her favourite maxims,
as well as her compulsion to order biblical vices and virtues.[21] Martineau recalls
laying aside this compulsion as ultimately fruitless; the seeming instability that
Bending notices, then, can be seen as Martineau's acknowledgement that such
order or consistency is impossible in the context of development and progress.

In line with ideas of development and progress, autobiographies are essentially
about transformation. In discussing the recurring theme of childhood isolation
in female Victorian autobiographies, Sanders speaks of the writers 'transforming
dislocation into distinction',[22] in a similar vein to Smith's reading of Martineau's
Autobiography as the 'evolutionary story of selfhood as it traced the curve of individual experience from a tormented childhood to the autumnal years of personal
satisfaction and social integration.'[23] However, a more intellectual focus is found
in regard to the male autobiographers whom Martineau emulated:

> Where the author had undergone several changes of belief, a stage-by-stage
> account of his philosophical evolution formed an essential part of his public
> act of self-justification, as it did for a small number of women, especially
> Harriet Martineau; but there is a sense too, that male autobiographers felt
> they owed their audiences a special insight into the way their careers devel-
> oped and their books were written.[24]

It is evident that as much as Martineau indulges in her personal trauma, thereby shocking George Eliot, she values this experience as the catalyst for her intellectual transformation. In *Autobiography: Narrative of Transformation* (1998), Carolyn Barros argues for four 'types of transformation' that are central to the Victorian autobiography – 'religious, philosophical, scientific, and literary' – making a strong case for the vital connection between personal and intellectual development, as well as the relationship between the individual thinker and the broader nation: '[t]hese narratives also manifest the values, beliefs, and attitudes of the culture in which they are inscribed and to which they are addressed. Thus autobiographies both conform to and speak against their cultures.'[25]

Martineau's conviction of the importance of these specific areas of religion, philosophy, science and literature (or hermeneutics) – which could be termed as meta-categories of intellectual disciplines – is made particularly evident in her account of her acquaintance Miss Kelty's autobiography, *Reminiscences of Thought and Feeling* (1852). She refers to Kelty's work as 'a painfully impressive biography', and goes on to relate the philosophical and religious chasm between them:

> Systems of religion and philosophy are evidently something very different to her from what they are to me; and I cannot lay open, or submit to controversy, the most solemn and severe subjects of all, when they can be made a means of excitement, and a theme of mere spiritual curiosity.[26]

It would seem that Martineau denotes the autobiography as 'impressive' in the vein of conventional female autobiographies (perhaps with an ironic tone of derision), as it is included in a section that looks at several other female writers. Important in this account is that she indirectly suggests her own vision of how autobiographies should be written: intellectual development and ideas are at the centre, but should be dealt with in a way that provokes sincere thought and critique, rather than sensationalism. Life writing itself becomes a science, one that should resist trivialising anecdotes and take seriously the development of thought in a positivist, empirical fashion.

Sanders notes the way in which W. H. Davenport Adams, in the *Child-Life and Girlhood of Remarkable Women* (1883), 'warn[ed] his impressionable young readers' against the example set by Harriet Martineau, stating that while Adams 'attempts to show that achievement is not necessarily incompatible with a pleasant temperament', he also 'underlines the moral dangers of intellectual confidence.'[27] In fact, the intellectual agency that Martineau displays in her *Autobiography* is crucial. It is much quoted that she thought it her 'duty' to present the world with her autobiography, to provide a map of her intellectual journey for posterity, as her final act of teaching the nation, and indeed, teaching the world. Conway observes that '[w]henever someone tells her story straight and in an authoritative voice we know she has developed her own sense of agency and can sustain it despite nagging cultural doubts.'[28] Martineau's career was marked by this authority and determination, not just in relation to any of her own doubts, but the criticism of her public. Nevertheless, the confidence that threatened readers such as Adams was instrumental in elevating her across the globe, and the *Autobiography* is the ultimate form of 'capitalizing on celebrity culture as a way of ensuring her own enduring fame as a woman of letters.'[29] Martineau's motivation for writing her intellectual map, however, goes deeper than a vain desire to be remembered on her own terms. Toward the end of the *Autobiography*, she writes of her childhood idols passing away – Dr. Follen, Dr. Carpenter – as well as lifelong friends including Lord and Lady Durham, Lord Sydenham, Thomas Drummond, Lord Henley and Dr. Channing. The effect of this overwhelming series of loss of mentors who had helped shaped Martineau's views not only made Martineau intimately aware of her own mortality, with the 'departure of these and many more [keeping] the subject of death vividly before [her]',[30] but also of the tenuous nature of knowledge – without ideas being written down, ordered and organised, knowledge could easily be lost or corrupted, particularly given the shortness of the human lifespan. Knowing that her mind was in print and mapped out, and that it would survive her, created a form of immortality for Martineau in light of her uncertainties over life after death.[31]

Self-engineering through intellectual engagement

Conway makes a point of noting, however, that not only physically, but '[i]ntellectually, Martineau lived into a vigorous old age, her life a combination of Franklin-like self-engineering and Rousseauistic emotional Sturm und Drang.'[32] Self-engineered through deliberate, independent intellectual engagement, in one sense Martineau's *Autobiography* reflects other nineteenth-century women's autobiography in that she 'prefer[s] to evolve [her] own form, rather than adopt the forms established by [her] male contemporaries.'[33] This idea of evolution is useful in addressing Martineau's construction and understanding of the disciplines, and her relationship to them. Through her cross-disciplinary writing, she constantly teases apart and re-categorises genre and discipline, revealing the progress through them as well as their interconnections. Easley notes that '[r]eading Martineau's *History* [*of the Thirty Years' Peace*] in tandem with the *Autobiography* and other auto-biographical texts reveals the ways that she worked across genre';[34] yet even more crucially, the cross-referencing of the *History* that Easley observes throughout the *Autobiography*[35] even more powerfully invites cross-disciplinary engagement – one discipline reinforces the other.

The *Autobiography* is structured around the ways in which disciplines are connected to one another. The *History* is connected closely to economics, as Martineau comments on the reviews of the *History* 'notic[ing] more emphatically' the chapter on 'the speculations, the collapse, and crash of 1825 and 1826.'[36] Economics is then blended with moral and political science, with Martineau's introduction to the work of Jane Marcet.[37] Then, when she recounts Robert Owen asking her to read Shakespeare's *Hamlet* through the lens of Necessarian doctrines, Martineau's political and moral economy connects back to her childhood obsession with literature, poetry and even theology. The continual convergence of disciplines, especially in the first half of the *Autobiography*, creates an image of the various intellectual disciplines connected to one another like a web, rather than a kind of linear progression or scientific hierarchy. There becomes more of a sense of linear progression, however, later in the *Autobiography*, reflecting Martineau's own path, in which she became influenced by Auguste Comte and his 'glorious hierarchy of the sciences.'[38] Yet Martineau again exhibits her independence, and translates Comte's method to incorporate all disciplines, including the humanities, in her map. In this way, the humanities are elevated to a commensurate objective level with the sciences, according to Comte's positivist vision. We return to this theme in the last chapter of the book.

While Martineau's positivist approach to the disciplines is not purely Comtean, his vision infuses her memory of her early obsession with patterns and categories. Sidonie Smith argues that 'the pattern-making, or hermeneutical, propensity that characterised her early response to life' is crucial to understanding Martineau's intellectual development: '[p]atterns provided a means of control, making life more coherent and tractable, less chaotic and threatening.'[39] In this sense, Martineau's fusion of mapping, hierarchy and evolution in understanding the relationship among disciplines can be seen as redesigning the canon of disciplines. Her specific mention, though, of 'mapping out moral qualities' in the *Autobiography*,[40] shows her rudimentary understanding of learning as being able to be mapped and ordered, therefore understood, albeit from the reflections of adulthood. Smith argues that Martineau's exposure to Comte moves her account beyond a typical autobiographical bildungsroman, as 'the specific characteristics of her journey derive their definition from the epistemological categories Martineau adapted from Auguste Comte';[41] yet Martineau goes beyond Comte, partly through the 'unusually distinct awareness of human development theory' that she gained from him.[42]

Closely related to positivism, evolutionary theories were also influential in Martineau's memory of her intellectual journey. Smith asserts that this influence, 'especially . . . the belief that the environment is central in shaping individual destiny', is fundamental to the structure of Martineau's recount of her childhood and its 'relationship to her later intellectual development.'[43] This idea draws out the importance Martineau saw in a dual vision that looked both at the individual and the broader society or culture. The dialogue she experienced between the individual and society begins as early as her account of learning Latin and French both from masters and her older siblings,[44] and flows through to her reflections on how to observe appropriately as a traveller.[45] The *Autobiography* in this sense delivers a powerful message of the importance of understanding what we know (or *can* know) and how we know it (according to the intellectual disciplines), with a practical purpose of using that understanding to engage with the wider world. For Martineau, understanding the patterns of her learning enables her to position herself internationally, as well as to speak effectively on international platforms.

Navigating the distinction between the knowable and the unknowable is intricately connected to comprehending the discreteness of the disciplines. Following a Comtean progression, Martineau travels intellectually from the theological, through the metaphysical, to the scientific or positivist perspective. However, it is important to note that she does not actually leave behind the earlier stages in the way that Comte would suggest is necessary, but rather she positions them as permanent foundations for progress. Her earliest recollections of astronomy, for example, are tied up in the tall tale of her grandfather's barber, who tells the seven-year-old Harriet, in explanation for his lateness, that 'a star had fallen in the night', made of 'the beautifullest and clearest crystal', and that it was blocking a road. The believing child was anxious to visit the lane and collect some of the crystal herself, but found 'not a single spike of the crystal was left' by the time she arrived.[46] Martineau recalled, 'my early notions of astronomy were cruelly bewildered by that man's rhodomontade.'[47] There is a sense of fusion among religion, fairytale, myth and science in this introduction to astronomy in a way that reinforces the importance of metaphysical enquiry that leads to the scientific; and although this anecdote recounts a tall tale, it serves as a reminder that human myth exists as undiscovered science. While Comte determined that intellectual thought should be restricted to what can be known, Martineau does not entirely dismiss the unknowable. She speaks of 'how contentedly [she] went on, . . . floating and floundering among metaphysical imaginations' as she studied a variety of philosophers, and makes a point that this process was necessary to her development; although she says it 'would no doubt have been a fine thing' for her 'if a teacher had been at hand to show [her] the boundary line between the knowable and the unknowable', she acknowledges that in looking back she is possibly 'supposing herself sooner capable than [she] really was of practically distinguishing between a conception and a conviction.'[48] She concludes that gradually learning the connection between 'physical and moral science' – which can be termed as the science that can be known and the science that cannot be known in an empirical sense – 'by [her] own forces, and for [her] own use' was a more valuable way to come to understanding the divisions of knowledge. In other words, despite Comte's positivist vision, the metaphysical remains an essential element in human understanding.

Although I agree with Smith's assessment that 'Martineau found Comte's developmental categories the most powerful hermeneutical tool for understanding the world and herself',[49] it is evident that Martineau did not adhere to his dismissal of what could not be known empirically. Hermeneutics remain key: unlike Comte, who refused, for example, to read any other scientific or philosophical work in order to preserve his 'cerebral hygiene',[50] Martineau was too aware of the nuances of culture on a global scale to hold the conviction that all knowledge worth knowing could be reduced to empiricism. For this reason, Martineau maintains her respect for theology and poetry, two disciplines (although I use the term loosely here in regard to poetry) that were fundamental to her education, rather than dismissing the humanities for the apparently more coherent and tangible world of science. For her, the intellectual disciplines are to some extent equalised, not hierarchical, and interdependent, like her meritocratic version of political economy. This approach is justified through the scope of different types of truth, knowing and interpretation that the hermeneutical disciplines open up, and the understanding that empirical science can only know the world – past, present, and future – in a finite way. Within her emphasis on intellectual 'steadiness, consistency, and progressiveness',[51] the

Martineau who is writing from what she believes to be her deathbed, is struck by the understanding that 'it is possible that we human beings, with our mere human faculty, may not understand the scheme, or nature, or fact of the universe!'[52] Therefore, although she concludes the *Autobiography* with the ideal that '[w]hen scientific facts are established, and self-evident truths are brought out of them, there is an end of conflict',[53] Martineau is very aware that this kind of absolute knowledge is out of the reach of humanity: there will always be gaps in understanding, and therefore there will always be conflict. However, this conflict is what enables continual intellectual progression.

Approach to disciplines – apologetics

Given that Comte positions theology at the beginning of his positivist progression – as the most rudimentary level of human intellectual development – it is appropriate that Martineau, writing in a positivist mode, begins her autobiographical intellectual map with her exposure to theology. Her construction of books of maxims, mentioned earlier as a sign of her foundational need to categorise knowledge, is significantly connected to her exposure at the very early age of one and a half to the Methodist influence of Mrs Merton in Carleton: 'I believe this was my first effort at book-making. It was probably what I picked up at Carleton that made me so intensely religious as I certainly was from a very early age.'[54] Martineau's apocryphal account of this visit (although there are no doubts about her precocity) sets the stage to connect her intellectual approach intrinsically to theological methods. Sanders observes that '[a]utobiography is traditionally an apologetic mode' and that even male authors 'felt the need to apologise for obtruding themselves and their concerns on the public.'[55] I argue that Martineau takes the idea of apology even further, adopting, in the recount of her intellectual development, the theological mode of apologetics – most commonly a sub-discipline of Christian theology, a form of rhetoric defined by the OED as a 'defensive method of argument', designed to provide a systematic defence of an intellectual or moral position. Given the interest Martineau had in the connection between moral and physical science, as well as her appreciation of rhetoric as taught in Mr Perry's day school, her *Autobiography* can be seen as an apologetics for her map of intellectual disciplines, which is a crucial departure from Comte; for unlike Comte, Martineau returns to theology repeatedly, including at the end. There is even the potential to see theology as the centre of Martineau's map – a central starting point, as opposed to Comte's linear model in which theology is a beginning to be left behind.

Martineau's changing response to theology underpins the entirety of her intellectual development. However, rather than adhering to the conventional equated divisions of secular/theological and science/philosophy, Martineau reorders these disciplines:

> But there is an essential point, – the most essential of all, – in regard to which the secular and theological worlds seem to need conviction almost equally: viz., the real value of science, and of philosophy as its legitimate offspring. . . .

It is, of course, useless to speak to theologians or their disciples about this, while they remain addicted to theology, because they avowedly give their preference to theology over the science with which it is incompatible. They, in the face of clear proof that science and theology are incompatible, embrace theology as the foundation of wisdom, goodness and happiness. They incline, all the while, to what they call philosophy; – that is, to theologico-metaphysics, from which they derive, as they say, (and truly) improvement of intellectual power, and confirmation of their religious faith in one direction, nearly equivalent to the damage inflicted on it in the other. The result must be, when the study is real and earnest, either that the metaphysics must dwindle away into a mere fanciful adornment of the theology, or the theology must be in time stripped of its dogmatic character, exhausted thereby of its vitality, and reduced to a mere name and semblance.[56]

Crucially, Martineau does not dismiss theology, even at this late stage of her career and life. Rather, she challenges the tendency of theologians to ignore the necessary interactions with other disciplines, namely science. She does not suggest that theology and science are entirely incompatible, but she criticises theologians for holding onto their old ideas even when other disciplines disprove their perspective. In this way, she pre-empts the twentieth-century philosopher of science Alfred North, who argued that a 'clash of doctrines is not a disaster – it is an opportunity. . . . In formal logic, a contradiction is the signal of defeat; but in the evolution of real knowledge it marks the first step in progress.'[57] Rather than polarising the disciplines, Martineau suggests that they must speak to one another, and the older theology must respect the emerging knowledges of science, rather than responding to science as a threat. Thus she does not reject theology *per se*, merely the *addiction* to theology: when every discipline is subsumed under the theological, there cannot be progress. Indeed, even the study of philosophy becomes a 'mere fanciful adornment' to theology, rather than a disciplinary force in its own right. It is not that Martineau is asserting that science has every answer, but speaking to her mid-Victorian audience, she points out that neither is human theology all-knowing, or capable of standing apart from other intellectual pursuits.

Martineau's interest in theology feeds into her professional writing from her first articles on female devotions, but of particular interest here is her autobiographical account of the three essay competitions she won in 1830–31, in which she was essentially required to write a Unitarian apologetic directed first to Catholics, and then to Muslims and Jews.[58] During her travels to the East in particular, Martineau takes this vision further, fusing theological apologetics with history to reveal the common ancestry of Judaism, Christianity and Islam in the ancient Egyptian mythologies. This approach contains an air of science, as it suggests an evolution of religion. She recounts telling one of her travel companions, '[m]y book will illustrate the genealogy, as it appears to me, of the old faiths, – the Egyptian, the Hebrew, the Christian and the Mohammedan,' and recalls, '[t]he result of the whole, when reconsidered in the quiet of my study, was that I obtained clearness as to the historical nature and moral value of all theology whatever, and attained that view of it which has been set forth in some of my subsequent works.'[59] The method of disciplinary fusion influences her other intellectual activities as well, as she connects, for example, the development of her ideas of political economy to the study of geography and literature.[60] The interconnectedness of the disciplines and the conversations among them create relevance for Martineau, making them pertinent to the world around her in the same way that the dialogue she creates between theology and history connects the present cultural milieu to the past. Even more importantly, if the disciplines can speak to one another and find agreement, this interdisciplinary dialogue becomes the evidence in proof required of the apologetic mode.

Writing for the three apologetic essay competitions was crucial in shaping Martineau professionally – the prize money enabled her to take the time to begin writing her Political Economy series that would make her internationally famous – but it also revealed her strength in writing in the apologetic vein. This approach, with its theological foundations, gives Martineau's otherwise intellectual autobiography a flavour of the Victorian spiritual autobiography. However, the decidedly intellectual focus prevents Martineau from being marginalised as a female autobiographer in this sense. As Linda Peterson suggests, Martineau believed that 'women . . . should adopt universal patterns of interpretation, systems that apply to all humankind';[61] and in this way, it is evident that Martineau elevates her autobiographical work above personal self-reflection to an apologetic that encompasses the nation's culture and understanding.

Intellectual development of the nation

Martineau's ambitious project to set forth an apologetic that would shape the nation through her personal intellectual journey is an extension of the idea of autobiography as 'a historiographical document capable of capturing the essence of a nation or the spirit of an age.'[62] Like Smith, Alison Booth brings autobiography into the scope of the 'proliferated collections of memorial tributes to enhance national heritage' within nineteenth-century Britain.[63] The difference with Martineau, however, is that her *Autobiography* is not an unconscious example of the spirit of the age expressed through a deliberate writing of self. Instead, she deliberately sets herself the task of defining the nation through her *Autobiography* by creating a national heritage of Britain's cultural engagement through the intellectual disciplines. She uses life writing to examine the disciplines together: rather than reading biology, botany and philosophy separately, autobiography takes on the grand vision to address the 'entire span of humanistic inquiry about what it means to be human, how the individual is shaped by society, whether she or he ever has free will, what shapes the imagination, what talents are valued and what misunderstood', and then, to extend further, 'how great political figures are formed and how they resonate with their followers.'[64] After giving anecdotes throughout of her encounters with national and international leaders, as well as business people, scholars and intellectuals, toward the end of her *Autobiography*, Martineau lays out a summary of her own intellectual development that flows seamlessly into showing the impact of her education on British intellectual culture by referring to the proliferation of published work that came of her studies. She states '[i]t has been a leading pleasure and satisfaction of mine, since I grew up, to compass some one department of knowledge at a time, so as to feel a real command of it, succeeding to a misty ignorance',[65] but also emphasises spontaneity in such a way that, as an established traveller, she mirrors the explorer following a general map, but discovering new wonders along the way. The literary is important at this point, as the imagination is fundamental to discovery in all fields of thought.

Martineau's position as a lionised public intellectual justifies placing her autobiographical work alongside that of other 'Victorian literary figures [who] also assumed a prominent place in the English imagination, redefining as they did the way human beings situated themselves in relationship to God, to nature, to history, and to each other.'[66] Specifically, though, her *Autobiography* 'tells a story of the development of a new idea of Englishness: the emergence of reform-minded sensibilities that had transformed the nation.'[67] Easley argues that Martineau seeks to 'authorize herself as a contemporary historian and literary celebrity', which 'demonstrate[s] her desire to integrate women's stories and experiences into the broader narrative of British history.'[68] Easley further argues that Martineau asserts that 'women not only had a place in literary history but a role in the moral history of the nation as well.'[69] However, through her close engagement across an array of intellectual disciplines, it is evident that Martineau's vision incorporates but goes beyond the moral or the literary to encompass the broader scheme of human understanding. As Smith suggests, '[h]er story is the story of civilization's advancement.'[70] Thus the intellectual map that Martineau provides in her *Autobiography*, humanised and brought to life through the accounts of her London and Ambleside coteries, creates a pointed vision of Martineau's plan of progress for the British Empire after her demise.

Notes

1 Linda H. Peterson, Introduction to *Harriet Martineau's Autobiography* (Toronto: Broadview Press, 2007), p. 8.
2 Lucy Bending, 'Self-presentation and instability in Harriet Martineau's *Autobiography*.' In: Ella Dzelzainis and Cora Kaplan (ed.), *Harriet Martineau: Authorship, Society and Empire* (Manchester: Manchester University Press, 2010), pp. 63–73, p. 63.
3 Jill Ker Conway, *When Memory Speaks: Reflections on Autobiography* (New York: Alfred A. Knopf, 1998), p. 88.
4 Valerie Sanders, *The Private Lives of Victorian Women: Autobiography in Nineteenth-Century England* (New York and London: Harvester Wheatsheaf, 1989), p. 17.
5 Sanders, *Private Lives*, p. 11.
6 Sanders, *Private Lives*, p. 79.
7 Sanders, *Private Lives*, p. 7.
8 Conway, *When Memory Speaks*, p. 88.
9 Sidonie Smith, *A Poetics of Women's Autobiography: Marginality and the Fictions of Self-Representation* (Bloomington and Indianapolis: Indiana University Press, 1987), p. 123.
10 Conway, *When Memory Speaks*, p. 88.
11 Sanders, *Private Lives*, p. 6.

12 Sanders, *Private Lives*, pp. 130, 134.

13 Linda Peterson, *Victorian Autobiography: The Tradition of Self-Interpretation* (New Haven and London: Yale University Press, 1986), p. 153.

14 David Amigoni, Introduction to *Life Writing and Victorian Culture* (Aldershot: Ashgate, 2006), p. 1.

15 Alexis Easley, 'Rewriting the past and present.' In: *Harriet Martineau and the Birth of Disciplines: Nineteenth-Century Intellectual Powerhouse* (Aldershot: Ashgate, 2016?), pp. 101–20.

16 Conway, *When Memory Speaks*, p. 17.

17 Alexis Easley, 'Harriet Martineau: Gender, national identity, and the contemporary historian,' *Women's History Review*, 20.5 (2011): pp. 765–84, p. 767.

18 Thomas Scheff, 'Getting Unstuck: Interdisciplinarity as a New Discipline,' *Sociological Forum*, 28.1 (2013): pp. 179–85, pp. 181, 179.

19 Bending, 'Self-presentation and Instability,' p. 67.

20 Conway, *When Memory Speaks*, p. 3.

21 *Autobiography*, ed. Peterson, p. 41.

22 Sanders, *Private Lives*, p. 70.

23 Smith, *Poetics of Women's Autobiography*, p. 124.

24 Sanders, *Private Lives*, p. 11.

25 Carolyn A. Barros, *Autobiography: Narrative of Transformation* (Ann Arbor: University of Michigan Press, 1998), viii.

26 Martineau, *Autobiography*, p. 323.

27 Sanders, *Private Lives*, p. 8.

28 Conway, *When Memory Speaks*, p. 88.

29 Easley, *Literary Celebrity*, p. 69.

30 Martineau, *Autobiography*, p. 459.

31 Of life after death, Martineau writes: 'As to death and the question of a future life,—I was some time in learning to be faithful to my best light, – faint as it yet was. I remember asserting to a friend who was willing to leave that future life a matter of doubt, that we were justified in expecting whatever the human race has agreed in desiring.' (*Autobiography*, p. 460).

32 Conway, *When Memory Speaks*, p. 91.

33 Sanders, *Private Lives*, p. 79.

34 Easley, *Literary Celebrity*, p. 97.

35 Easley, 'Harriet Martineau,' p. 777.

36 Martineau, *Autobiography*, p. 117.

37 Martineau, *Autobiography*, pp. 123–24.

38 Martineau, *Autobiography*, p. 617.

39 Smith, *Poetics of Women's Autobiography*, p. 129.

40 Martineau, *Autobiography*, p. 57.

41 Smith, *Poetics of Women's Autobiography*, p. 131.

42 Sanders, *Private Lives*, p. 134.

43 Smith, *Poetics of Women's Autobiography*, p. 129.

44 Martineau, *Autobiography*, p. 79.

45 Martineau, *Autobiography*, p. 330.

46 Martineau, *Autobiography*, p. 53.

47 Martineau, *Autobiography*, p. 54.

48 Martineau, *Autobiography*, p. 104.

49 Smith, *Poetics of Women's Autobiography*, p. 131.

50 Throughout Comte's letters to Mill, there are repeated references to, and a preoccupation with, maintaining his 'cerebral hygiene' by abstaining from reading other intellectuals' work. See Oscar A. Haac (ed. and trans.), *The Correspondence of John Stuart Mill and Auguste Comte* (New Brunswick and London: Transaction Publishers, 1995).

51 Martineau, *Autobiography*, p. 104.

52   Martineau, *Autobiography*, p. 459.
53   Martineau, *Autobiography*, p. 647.
54   Martineau, *Autobiography*, p. 41.
55   Sanders, *Private Lives*, pp. 6–7.
56   Martineau, *Autobiography*, p. 558.
57   Alfred North Whitehead, *Science and the Modern World* (New York: Macmillan, 1962), pp. 266–67.
58   See Martineau, *Autobiography*, pp. 131–35.
59   Martineau, *Autobiography*, pp. 520–21.
60   Martineau, *Autobiography*, p. 80.
61   Linda H. Peterson, *Victorian Autobiography: The Tradition of Self-Interpretation* (New Haven and London: Yale University Press, 1986), p. 153.
62   Smith, *Poetics of Women's Autobiography*, p. 3.
63   Alison Booth, 'Men and women of the time: Victorian prosopographies.' In: David Amigoni (ed.), *Life Writing and Victorian Culture* (Aldershot: Ashgate, 2006), pp. 41–66, p. 41.
64   Conway, *When Memory Speaks*, p. 17.
65   Martineau, *Autobiography*, p. 497.
66   Smith, *Poetics of Women's Autobiography*, p. 125.
67   Easley, *Literary Celebrity*, p. 96.
68   Easley, *Literary Celebrity*, p. 95.
69   Easley, 'Harriet Martineau,' p. 773.
70   Smith, *Poetics of Women's Autobiography*, p. 132.

2 Harriet Martineau and popular education

Ruth Watts

Harriet Martineau was a lifelong educator. She wrote much on education and she was proud of teaching in a Mechanics' Institute in the 1850s and '60s; she strongly supported national education for all when this did not exist; she supported many educational developments, especially with regard to girls and women. She was a foremost British feminist intellectual of the nineteenth century, speaking to and leading on many crucial issues of the day, both national and international. In all her prolific and widely read publications, including her journalism, she remained cheerfully optimistic that great social reform and change could be secured if only every person, female and male, poor and rich, were rightly educated. Her own life was dominated by the quest both to educate herself through reading, study, travel and active engagement in social, economic, political and religious issues and to educate the public by publishing in a range of literature, the scientific answers she believed she had found to questions on these issues. This chapter argues that it was in these ways that she contributed to the discipline of education in the sense of *disciplina* given in the Introduction which has both a 'pedagogical focus on the means of inculcating knowledge' and of moderating behaviour. Yet Martineau's writings and views on education were also underpinned by attention to the psychology and philosophy of education in a way that heralded an emergent discipline in the more modern academic sense. Through such writings she may be regarded as a public educator, but this chapter also attempts to show why she has been neglected as such.

Because all of Martineau's writings had an educative purpose, it has been necessary to be selective and just a few examples from her prolific output have been chosen which are particularly pertinent to education.

Educational philosophy and psychology

Many of Martineau's own beliefs and attitudes stemmed from her Unitarian upbringing, with its lively intellectual and cultural life. Briefly, modern Unitarianism emerged from 'Rational Dissent' in the second half of the eighteenth century, Rational Dissent being the closest form of Christianity to Enlightenment thinking in Britain. Rational Dissenters fervently promoted free enquiry in religion for all people and sought to apply reason to everything. Characterised less by spirituality than a desire for moral order and perfection, their beliefs encouraged a wide range of thinking, although generally they rejected both the Trinity and original sin. The consequence of the latter particularly, fostered their hopes in what humanity could achieve and become, beliefs further underpinned by their educational philosophy and psychology. Many Unitarians of the late eighteenth and early nineteenth century were deeply affected by the educational philosophy of their radical and dynamic leader, Joseph Priestley, who in turn was profoundly influenced by the associationist psychology of David Hartley (1705–1757). Priestley reissued Hartley's *Observations on Man* in compressed form and joyfully argued for his premise that because all knowledge is derived in the first place from external impressions, everything must be part of a chain of cause and effect leading back to a first cause or God. This 'necessarianism' was not accepted by all Unitarians but they and other progressive educationalists welcomed the emphasis on environment and circumstance rather than innate character or divine intervention in forming people from birth; while the stress on thinking for oneself and learning through enquiry, experiment and experience suited their enthusiastic exploration for scientific explanation and methods in all matters, including education. In sum, they postulated that interconnected, correct, intellectual, moral and physical education from birth could lead people not only to happiness and knowledge, but also to virtue and love of God.[1]

The psychological basis of the educational philosophy propounded by Priestley and other progressive educationalists such as the Edgeworths and William Godwin – influenced by his and Hartley's writings – was the beginning of education as a science according to the educational historian Brian Simon. Seeing humans as the product of their circumstances and associations, they affirmed that an enlightened education, planned scientifically to develop desired moral and intellectual powers, was the most vital of those circumstances.[2]

For Unitarians, such beliefs made them ardent educators of both middle and working classes. This included girls and women since associationist psychology held no negative intellectual assumptions about anyone. Their educational philosophy, encouraging active and experiential learning and teaching in all areas of education and promoting 'modern' subjects such as science, history and English, was at the heart of their yearning to create an 'enlightened', democratic society of liberal, humane, thinking beings who would eschew the superstitious and ignorant ways of the past. Richard Price, another leading thinker in Rational Dissent, stressed that all people were given the opportunity by God to use their reason to create a reformed and wise society.[3]

Some Unitarian chapels became centres of liberal thought. Despite, however, Unitarianism's appeal to men and women of the middle and artisan ranks in urban, commercial and industrial areas, the community was never numerous.[4] Harriet Martineau herself later professed atheism, yet the educational heritage she had imbibed affected her all her life. Not least, she was convinced that all people, including women and all those of the working classes, could, and should be, educated to think accurately and independently for themselves. Only then, she was sure, could people achieve virtue themselves and a better life for all. She was deeply influenced by both Priestley and Dr Lant Carpenter who taught her to revere Priestley's edition of Hartley when she spent 15 months at her Aunt Kentish's school in Bristol and got to know him as her aunt's neighbour and Unitarian minister. Carpenter himself had a well-reputed school run according to the educational principles of Hartley and Priestley which he promoted in his 1820 book, *Principles of Education.*[5]

Harriet Martineau was chiefly educated at home, although besides her time in Bristol, she enjoyed two years from the age of eleven receiving a grammar school education in a local mixed school. Early on she had a passion for translating Latin and Italian and studying the Bible and philosophy. Although she complained that young women had to hide their learning, she also learned much in her twenties within her familial and liberal circles in Norwich and elsewhere. For example, she was deeply affected by visits to Newcastle and Scotland and other places like North Wales and the Lake District which bred in her a lasting, almost spiritual love of natural beauty and poetry, especially Wordsworth. From childhood, she was very fond of the lovable, liberal educationalist, the Rev. William Turner of Newcastle, whom she met through visiting relatives.[6] From him and other leading Unitarian educators she internalised the idea that women too, as Hannah Greg said, should be educated 'in the notion of their being individual and rational and immortal beings'. At the same time, a liberal education which created women of greater understanding should enable them to be better mothers, companionable, supportive wives and the centre of cultured, intellectually lively, socially concerned homes.[7] Deeply versed in secular and religious literature, Martineau remained a voracious reader, learning all her life both from other thinkers and her own experiences. The latter included visits to exhibitions and public lectures and was punctuated for many years by travels which took her to both the new and the ancient worlds. She became part of vibrant intellectual, literary and social networks, maintained and extended through prolific correspondence, yet, as a nineteenth-century woman she kept within certain social proprieties. For example, she never accepted social invitations except 'where my acquaintance was sought, as a lady, by ladies' and she was critical of what she perceived as silly women spoiling the meetings of the British Association for the Advancement of Science because they seemed more intent on amusement than science.[8]

Educating the public

Non-fictional texts by women on the many subjects deemed to be 'masculine' were unusual in the early nineteenth century, but, encouraged by the liberal attitudes of the Unitarians, Martineau began publishing early. Among her early writings, she demonstrated a strong desire, evident in all her work, to clear the irrationalities and additions that had crept into traditional assumptions. In 1831, for example, she examined the Bible as a text like any other and in the light of its context, history and geography. Such an undertaking, although radical for the period, was to become a hallmark of Unitarian Biblical scholarship, albeit mostly undertaken by men. These essays, proffered by Martineau to make known the 'truth' of Unitarian Christianity to the Roman Catholics, Muslims and Jews, respectively, as we saw in the previous chapter, won prizes and were published by the Unitarians, thus illustrating their ease with women discussing such matters. Educational treatises in themselves, these texts demonstrated the pattern of intensive rapid research and clear, penetrating writing which became characteristic of her work.[9]

Other writings of her twenties exemplified Martineau's debt to both Hartley and to Unitarian ideals on education, freedom of thought and human progress and her wish to impress such ideas on others. As early as 1823 she supported equal education for women in *The Monthly Repository*, a Unitarian journal. She adroitly brushed aside the usual objections, by emphasising that women could not perform their appointed duties and employments, including their vital role in bringing up children, as well as they should unless their minds were fully developed and they became rational, thinking persons. The noble influence of intellectual women such as Anna Barbauld and Elizabeth Carter exemplified the private and public good of allowing woman to claim her 'privileges as an intellectual being', a point Martineau had made implicitly in 1822 in her articles on 'Female writers on Practical Divinity'.[10]

Among further articles for the same journal, Martineau explicitly recalled Hartley when she attempted to teach the art of thinking clearly and accurately to those who were unlikely to learn this elsewhere, a clarion call to rational thinking for all men and women that was the basis of her thoughts on education. In 'Essays on the Art of Thinking', she expounded and exemplified how people could learn to form habits of accurate thought and observation which would then infuse their thinking, teach them the complexity of the origins of ideas and compel them to base their arguments on evidence. 'By the law of association', she argued,' every idea entertained in the mind introduces other ideas, which, in their turn, bring in more. This law we cannot suspend; but it is in our power to controul [sic] its operation and to make choice of the mode in which our ideas shall be combined.'[11] Thus rational thought on a range of ideas should be encouraged early. In wanting all people to have a useful education and to understand the many subjects which affected their lives, she opposed narrow learning, both that of most girls and the classical focus of boys' schools. Similarly, she derided those who read without reflection, deducing that illiterate cottagers, who had habits of quick and accurate observation and had worked out their opinions from experience, were wiser than insatiable readers who did not think clearly about what they had read. Having reached such a state of rational understanding people could advance ideas and become able to deduce and apply general principles from observed facts. In such ways 'enlightened' intellects could be created which, in turn, could invigorate moral sensibilities (although 'learning is not wisdom, any more than conviction is truth'),[12] and half the evils which affected humanity might be removed. She wondered why, when so much moral strength was wasted by the infirmity of people's mental faculties, the power of a sound mind was not better appreciated.[13] Thus she saw such mental education as the foundation of personal and national intellectual and moral well-being. In arguing in these ways she was reiterating the educational ideas of leading Unitarian educationalists in a readable series of short articles in the most popular Unitarian journal of the day.

From 1828 Martineau attributed her own personal intellectual progress to working with the editor of the *Monthly Repository*, the radical Unitarian minister William Johnson Fox.[14]

Keeping to the gendered proprieties of the day, it was only when her family's business failed that she was freed to turn to writing professionally. Having already proved she could write well, her avowed aim from the start was to enlighten the public in knowledge she believed it needed. For her first major undertaking, this appeared to her (as depicted elsewhere in this volume), to be the 'truths', of political economy, the 'science' which allowed people to understand how they might acquire and enjoy prime objects of their lives – 'the necessaries and comforts of life'. She decided that it was time to stop what she considered to be an all-important moral and political *science* being the preserve of a few and to convey it to all readers. As already noted, to do this, she developed the fictional methods of a former popular writer on political economy, Jane Marcet: 'we have chosen this method not only because it is new, not only because it is entertaining, but because we think it the most fruitful and the most complete.'[15] In this vein she adopted what had become predominantly a female form of dealing with serious subjects; except that her twenty-five novelettes, *Illustrations of Political Economy*, published monthly 1832–4, were not dialogues or letters as had previously been the norm but full stories with their economic summaries drawn up at the end. Her instant fame, with a wide range of people, including politicians and civil servants eagerly seeking her advice and support on political, economic and social matters, indicated that her educational task had an impact and was popular at least with the middle classes, although not necessarily with the mass of people as she had desired. According to Martineau, MPs sent so many Parliamentary 'blue books'[16] to Norwich, that the postmaster could not deliver them unless in a barrow.[17]

This, indeed, seemed to be the work of an enlightened educator offering enlightenment to others in society. Martineau wanted to include political economy in a 'democratic' education so that working people would accept its 'science' and understand the need for 'free' labour and the iniquities of taking strike action, but this was a stance which won her little approval from the working classes. She 'earnt' some praise for her depictions of poverty and working-class life and she certainly did not lack sympathy for those in the 'lower' classes. Later, indeed, she described 'the position of the well-conditioned artisan [as] the most favourable that society affords' for developing the best human beings.[18] Yet she followed much contemporary Unitarian and Utilitarian thinking in her acceptance of the benefits of capitalism.

Martineau's underlying aim, from the 1830s, was to teach people how to cooperate in productive communities where everyone had enough to live on and could obtain the best education possible. A fine example of this can be found in her tale *Briery Creek*, in which, to teach about productive consumption, she describes an American settlement where the humane Dr Sneyd (modelled on Priestley) and his family provide a field which can be used as both a cricket pitch and a bleaching area for the women. Miss Sneyd helps to establish a school which Dr Sneyd and his son keep light and warm in the evenings so that it can be used as a museum and library – an interesting gendered division of interests but women can attend in the evening as well, albeit so that they can use the candlelight to sew. The whole settlement is intended to enjoy, alongside other activities, music and dancing so that properly organised 'social mirth' could dispel vice, loneliness and misery.[19]

Martineau was eager to prove that the lack of useful, liberal, rational knowledge prevented both poor and rich alike from developing morally and intellectually and thus they made wrong choices in life, possibly even turning to evil. In one of her subsequent *Tales of Taxation, The Scholars of Arneside*, Martineau stressed that everyone needed access to the right type of knowledge if there was to be a prosperous, contented country. In depicting how the illiterate people of Arneside were deprived of knowledge, although some eagerly sought it, she raged both against unsound taxes (especially indirect ones) and the privileged who wanted to keep knowledge to themselves: God, she stated, 'did not make his beautiful world that one might walk abroad on it, while a thousand are shut into a dark dungeon. . . . Does the sun shine more brightly when a man thinks he has it all to himself?' Mechanics' Institutes, despite inadequacies, she argued, did more for the mass of people than the Universities of Oxford and Cambridge.[20]

Not all of Martineau's middle-class readers appreciated such views: for example, her Malthusian over-population themes outraged many, particularly because they came from a young woman. Her discussion of 'masculine' topics and refusal to 'simply endorse patriarchal ideologies'[21] or methods brought charges of unfemininity as well as upsetting those who opposed her views.[22] Similarly, she shocked many readers on both sides of the Atlantic and won many admirers in her efforts to educate the public on the real consequences of slavery. One of her political economy tales, *Demerara*, shrewdly portrayed slavery as an economically disastrous system which corrupted everyone in it, both slaves and their owners alike. Through using the strategy of narrating the return of a brother and sister to Demerara in Guyana, after being educated in England for fourteen years, Martineau was able to contrast the views of the enlightened, well-educated Alfred with those of his father, Mr Bruce, who, though a well-meaning slave owner, was inevitably corrupted by the system. His overseer and other local slave owners and their white servants and even his little daughter were equally, sometimes more, corrupted. Alfred counters his father's complaints and arguments about profits by insisting that the latter could only lastingly be made in a system based on humanity rather than bad institutions and owning people. Martineau also perceptively shows that slaves too were corrupted by their circumstances. Even a good man like Cassius deliberately pretends to be lazy, in order to depress the price for his freedom, so that one day he might be able to buy it. Other slaves have learned cruelty through seeing it in action so often. Throughout the story Martineau illustrates how everyone would profit if the slaves were freed. She depicts the mental, emotional and physical cruelties of slavery, including the perpetual miserable unease and fear of the slave owners. She prophesied the potential intelligence and nobility of free slaves, emphasising at the same time that potential could not be truly known until black people gained their freedom.[23]

This tale was written before Martineau had seen slavery for herself, although she researched well before writing it.[24] It was widely read and praised in England and sufficiently well known in America for her to be courted by abolitionists and upholders of slavery alike, anxious to persuade her of their views, when she went to America from 1834 to 1836.[25] In contrast, *The Hour and the Man: A Historical Romance* (1841), was written after her American trip. Most unusually for the period, it had a black man, Toussaint L'Ouverture, as hero. Martineau's account of how this ex-slave expelled the French and later the Spanish from what became known as Haiti, incorporated both a passionate hatred of slavery and the environmentalist educational ideas which she had imbibed from her upbringing. For her, L'Ouverture was able to rule intelligently and in an enlightened manner, partly because of his good fortune in having been permitted to read and gain access to classical works, especially those of Epictetus and Fénélon, which taught him to be a stoic. He also discovered how to conduct troops and battles from Marshal Saxe's *Military Reveries*. L'Ouverture is portrayed as inspired by the struggles of the ancient Greeks for liberty, although he had neither seen liberty in action nor had he the power of appropriately exercising the virtue in which he gloried.[26]

Martineau's somewhat overblown, didactic narrative was accompanied by an appendix of nearly 60 pages at the end to show her evidence[27] and that the aim was worthy. Martineau tried to prove that black people, even brutalised slaves, could overcome their circumstances, given the right education and opportunities; for they had as much potential as Europeans to show intelligence, humanity, love and virtue. In the same way, Europeans could be corrupted by living in the unjust brutality of a slave state. Thus she tried to depict the class distinctions and enmities in both white and black communities once L'Ouverture was able to establish black rule. L'Ouverture, and his wife and daughters especially, portrayed the dignity, intelligence and beauty of black people, once they were 'unhardened by degradation, undebased [sic] by ignorance, unspoiled by oppression . . .'[28] L'Ouverture (so called because he made an opening for black people in Martineau's interpretation)[29] proved to be a wise ruler, teaching his people to have self-confidence and encouraging a thriving economy and educated people, an ideal state where former oppressors are forgiven.[30]All this, however, was lost when Bonaparte re-established slavery and overthrew L'Ouverture.

Martineau was not the first woman to write against slavery, nor the first to become a leading voice against it: Elizabeth Heyrick was a notable example of one who had already done so.[31] But Martineau's originality lay firstly in showing the economic disadvantages of the slave system as depicted in *Demerara* and secondly adopting the format of the novel to show up the iniquities of the system and the benefits of its opposite. Eleven years before Harriet Beecher Stowe's *Uncle Tom's Cabin* (1852), Martineau used fiction to educate the public on the matter.

Martineau exulted in the fact that *The Hour and the Man* sold so well despite the initial misgivings of her publisher,[32] Moxon. Such concerns were hardly unusual. More unusual was to portray a black man as hero. Heroes like Ira Aldridge, the black actor, were rare.[33] While praise for the book from people such as Maria Edgeworth and even Florence Nightingale might have been expected, Thomas

Carlyle's depiction of black people as lazy, 'superstitious . . . excitable and impulsive', an inferior, effeminate 'race' who should get accustomed to the whip, was not seen as extraordinary in the virulent debates of the day about slavery, colonization and the treatment of subject people.[34] In contrast, Martineau portrayed L'Ouverture's realization both of the 'freedom and rights of his race' and that 'the rule which the free man has over his own soul, over time and eternity, – subject only to God's will – is a nobler authority than that of kings', as demonstrating that the 'negro race' [sic] could be redeemed' by liberty, whereas oppression had 'put out the eyes of their souls, and withered its sinews'.[35]

Martineau was in the company of many of the liberal urban intelligentsia such as John Stuart Mill and the scientist Mary Somerville, besides many Unitarians and Quakers, in claiming that black and white were unequal, not innately, but in education and circumstances and in her assumptions of 'superior' Western culture which needed to be learned by all – including not only blacks and browns but also women and the working class.[36] Yet she articulated such messages in a readable, dramatic form. In various more conventional writings too, especially on India, she had much to say about how Britain should govern its empire, trying to stimulate concern for the disadvantaged and understanding of the differences of cultures and the double standards of the colonials. And in *How to Observe Morals and Manners* (1838), she wrote the first methodological treatise on qualitative research. Even so, her positive ideals concerning equality and respect for other cultures did not lose sight of the 'enlightened' education she so deeply wished to uphold.

Such concerns fed into her fiction, for example, *The Scholars of Arneside* mentioned above and her novel *Deerbrook* (1839), a love story, but also an exploration of the struggles of a middle-class apothecary – another unfashionable hero – when faced with an epidemic in a village where the people are too ignorant to understand his scientific and hygienic solutions. Martineau used her story to indicate the growth of professional medicine and how it was hampered by the general lack of understanding of the need for scientific knowledge and public hygiene. Once again an enlightened education of all was called for.[37]

Education of the working classes

Increasingly, Martineau expressed herself less in fiction, as depersonalised texts on scientific matters generally superseded more familial forms in the nineteenth century.[38] '[E]nlightening the heathens back home' only began in the early nineteenth century, pronounced Martineau in her *History of the Peace . . . a History of England from 1816–1854*.[39] Even then, she argued, the instruction in the monitorial schools was poor, there was a 'miserable pretence of learning' and the use of the Bible as a class book meant that children became sick of it. Arguing for an education to awaken minds, enable labourers to read and take part intelligently in their living and working lives, Martineau unstintingly promoted education for all. She was frustrated alike by the quarrels between Dissenters and the Church which thwarted the emergence of a national system of education and by governments who appeared to prefer an 'ignorant, dependent and wretched' people rather than an 'enlightened' one. Thus were lost opportunities to educate those who most needed it but were 'least capable of demanding it, desiring it, and even conceiving of it'.[40]

Martineau herself provided such an education to her poorer neighbours when she had settled in Ambleside, embarking on a series of lectures which began by chance but quickly grew in popularity. Soon, despite her deafness, she was lecturing regularly to 'a large body of working men and women, domestic servants, master builders etc . . . '. There were so many they had to extend the room but she made sure that the local gentry were excluded, those 'rich men and women who exact enormous rents for stinking, undrained cabins'.[41] To help solve the problem of the latter, and after a series of lectures on health, sanitation and drainage, she established the Windermere Permanent Land, Building, and Investment Association which, with its clean, dry, affordable model cottages for the working poor proved to be a great success. This, indeed, was a practical enlightened education in action.[42]

Thus it is little wonder that Martineau praised the earlier spread of Mechanics' Institutes, in many places established by Unitarians. She realised, however, that people could learn little from lectures at the Institutes if they could not follow these up by reading. Thus she spoke well of the Society for the Diffusion of Useful Knowledge in the 1820s which provided affordable pamphlets on a wide range of useful knowledge for working people, although she thought its failure to publish on political and ethical issues short-changed its recipients. For Martineau, as we have seen, education for democracy was a prime requisite of popular education and she admired those who tried to provide this, such as William Cobbett.[43] She desired the enfranchisement of working men, particularly the most intelligent, but she was confused by their continuing support for trade unionism and convinced that otherwise intelligent men were being pressured by their peers who in turn were seduced by the phony arguments of self-interested leaders. In 1859 her detailed arguments in the *Edinburgh Review* on the 'Secret Organisation of Trades', opposing what she saw as the malignant growing power of trade unionism, were ably opposed by the very kind of intelligent worker she desired. Her opinions were also refuted by a report in 1860 from the National Association for the Promotion of Social Science (NAPSS), a society much admired by Martineau, whose mass of evidence included reports from cooperative trade unionists, demonstrating both their moderation and respectability. Such findings, paradoxically, were to help the Liberals under Gladstone support the extension of the franchise which Martineau supported.[44]

For Martineau the best type of education available included stimulating methods of learning, science, enjoyable educational activities both practical and literary and an absence of corporal punishment and rote learning. Thus she welcomed Pestalozzi's ideas on child development, as she did John Pyke Hullah's successful spur to the popular recreation of good music. Martineau enthusiastically welcomed the 'virtual education' provided by museums, art galleries and exhibitions in large towns – as we shall see in Valerie Sanders's discussion of her visit to the Crystal Palace at Sydenham – and thought this would improve popular taste as would the knowledge of other cultures through the influx of foreign immigrants. Her desire for interesting and enjoyable education extended to demanding proper public institutions for all 'lunatics' so that they too could benefit from liberty, fresh air, sunshine and amusement. She held that educators were becoming more respected by the middle class, although professional training for both elementary schoolteachers and governesses was needed if they were to gain 'honour and independence'.[45] Such views were significant as from the 1830s Martineau was a very well-known author and from the 1850s a prominent journalist and thus her opinions mattered at the time.

Education of women

Martineau showed great respect for governesses, as exemplified in her sympathetic portrayal of Maria Young, the governess in *Deerbrook*, as we also see in Sharon Connor's analysis in Chapter 7. Martineau recognised Maria's ambivalent position, her loneliness, her wish that she could *educate* her charges properly without interference. When Maria got this chance, her Socratic methods were admired as was her self-education in German earlier.[46] One of Martineau's strongest beliefs, reiterated from her earliest writings, was the need and the right for women to receive the best education conceived. She was glad of her own education both literary and practical, unlike many of the period, seeing no conflict between the two.[47] She declared in her one book with education in the title – *Household Education* – that 'on no subject is more nonsense talked . . . than on that of female education, when restriction is advocated'. She derided the usual barring of women from learning classics on the grounds they were similarly excluded from those professions which required them when, simultaneously it was argued that boys needed to study them 'to improve the quality of their minds'. She gave examples of good female mathematical and classical scholars to demonstrate that women were capable of abstract thought and argued that since women already learned French and arithmetic, they were equally able to learn Greek and mathematics. If there was any truth in the often-repeated charge that women were shallow and frivolous, knowledge of deep subjects would change that. Such a full, enriching education would not prevent women being 'womanly'. Moreover, like the well-known scientist Mary Somerville who, she said, was an excellent housekeeper, other well-educated women performed their *proper* occupations better; they did not neglect them. Indeed, they were better wives, mothers and teachers of the young because of their education:[48]

> Men do not attend the less to their professional business, their counting-house or their shop, for having their minds enlarged and enriched and their faculties strengthened by sound and various knowledge; nor do women on that account, neglect the work-basket, the market, the dairy and the kitchen. If it be true that women are made for these domestic occupations then of course they will be fond of them. . . . For my part, I have no hesitation in saying that the most ignorant women I have known have been the worst housekeepers; and that the most learned women I have known have been among the best, – whenever they have been early taught and trained to household business, as every woman ought to be.[49]

Martineau claimed never to have liked pedantry – something intellectual women were often accused of and of which she herself contradictorily accused the blue-stockings of the eighteenth century. Even Jane Marcet, whose example she had built upon when writing her political economy tales, could not escape her criticisms. She had no room for Mary Wollstonecraft because she let herself be ruled by her passions, but Martineau truly admired true intellectuals such as Anna Barbauld and Mary Somerville, who were moral and had well-run homes.[50] She was sure that home was actually the place where most people were educated morally and intellectually, with families cooperating together in lifelong learning. Mothers were at the centre of this so their moral and intellectual education was vitally important. She said elsewhere:

> Every woman who can think and speak wisely, and bring up her children soundly, in regard to the rights and duties of society, is advancing the time when the interests of women will be represented, as well as those of men.[51]

Martineau's detailing of such education and the way it should materialise in homes in *Household Education* was but one of her many discussions of the subject. For example, an article, 'What women are educated for', written for *Once a Week* in 1861, was part of the early campaign to provide access to higher education for women. She ironically observed how even men who thought themselves liberal in allowing young women to receive a good education at Queens' College in Harley Street, thought its whole purpose was merely to fit women to be 'companions to men' and 'mothers of heroes'.[52] She said she knew many women had to support themselves and welcomed opportunities for women to use skills of sewing, nursing and running a home in a more professional and lucrative way. This could be helped, she argued, by new inventions such as the sewing machine which could allow women to do less exhausting and nerve-racking work, those 'occupations now kept from them by men'.[53] Similarly, she enthusiastically championed Florence Nightingale's nursing reforms and the scientific, practical and moral education women thus needed to become professional nurses, an education which called for proper schools and 'a new department in children's schools'. Rejoicing that such developments would allow fit and able women to leave 'overstocked' female industries while lifting the standards of nursing, she commented darkly that there was 'as much trouble with [untrained] floating saints and virgins on the one hand, as with grovelling mercenaries [who only wanted payment] on the other'.[54] This aspect of Martineau's work is examined in more detail by Weiner in Chapter 9.

Ever deeply conscious of the importance of hygiene, Martineau became a collaborator of Florence Nightingale (also from a Unitarian background), when Nightingale chose Martineau to popularise the significance of her findings on poor sanitation in the military. Martineau campaigned for women to be allowed to train as doctors – a controversial topic from the 1860s as it was tied up with other debates on higher education for women and possible admission to professional work hitherto reserved to men.[55]

In addition, as we see again in Weiner's chapter, Martineau publicly supported the growth of women's rights (which was taking place somewhat slowly), and such ground-breaking Acts of Parliament as the Infant Custody Act of 1839 and the Married Women's Property Bill of 1853, and she was an ardent campaigner against the Contagious Diseases Acts of the 1860s. A supporter of the Women's Movement of the 1850s and '60s and especially of those who used the National Association for the Promotion of Social Science to promote their educational and legislative struggles, she found it absurd that a taxpayer and influential writer like herself had no vote.[56] Thus, this experienced and widely read writer used her talent to stir people into new ways of thinking about gender matters.

A public educator

As we have seen, Martineau was not afraid to challenge contemporary thinking. Having already upset both the medical world and religious believers, the horror provoked by her announcement of atheism was compounded by the publication of *Eastern Life, Present and Past* (1848). In challenging ecclesiastical authority and doctrine she was not alone in mid nineteenth-century Britain, but what was unusual is that she published her ideas in a popular travel book. Furthermore, while seeking to untangle myth and historical truth, her openly expressed admiration of the civilization of ancient Egypt challenged Victorian supremacy. In such ways she sought to educate the public in easier approaches to 'truths' which she believed she had discovered and which they ought to understand.[57]

Martineau thought it imperative that she should think for herself and then speak out, provided she had evidence to prove her points. As a historian, she used a wide range of sources and, like Joseph Priestley in the eighteenth century, she insisted that social and cultural, as well as political, history was essential to the overall understanding of history. In her *History of the Peace*, for example, as we shall see in Chapter 6, she linked literature, history and biography to show that educational, industrial and scientific developments shaped both culture and modern society.[58] She was a significant figure in social science as Michael Hill and Susan Hoecker-Drysdale show later in this volume, and her translation and dissemination of Comte's ideas in Britain and then back to France was another example of public education.[59] Practical in local life and health reforms, she was, above all, a public educator whose prolific output of books, articles, newspaper leaders and letters was underpinned by her deep desire to use the experiential, environmentalist education of her youth to promote liberal, humane and active citizenship for all people.

Conclusion

Harriet Martineau has become known in recent times as an influential woman who succeeded in a patriarchal intellectual context, and as embedded in the culture of her day, yet also subversive.[60] She was influential in her own time as a popular educator. Her support was constantly requested by those who wished to publicise their stance on a variety of questions from the 1830s to the end of her life, for example, taxation, abolition of slavery, sanitary reform and the campaign against the Contagious Diseases Acts and for higher education and rights for women. From her early writings such as 'Essays on the Art of Thinking' to her last book, *Biographical Sketches* (1868), her writings are littered with references to education, both directly on types, structures and educators and indirectly in promoting ways of thinking about different issues. She employed a variety of genres of writing to educate others and her success in doing so brought her personal fame and independence. Yet her abundant output on so many issues and the very way she worked militated against her legacy as an educator and she has rarely been featured in standard books on the history of English education. Her educational ideas, indeed, are mostly referred to when writers are discussing other matters, such as women's history and 'emancipation' in the nineteenth century in particular. Martineau wrote no great work of philosophy or psychology on education, she founded no educational institutions nor was she employed in an educational capacity excepting her informal lectures in Ambleside. She was not directly involved with the establishment of schools; she did not lead any great reform of education. Her newspaper and journal articles on education were clearly important yet, by their nature, were generally ephemeral, asking for response and revision. Fictional tales were used as educational treatises, of which Thomas Day's *Sandford and Merton* is a prime example. But this did not happen to any of Martineau's tales nor did fictional writing win respect in 'scientific' education as time went on. *Household Education* was superseded by the very changes in national and girls' education which Martineau desired. Martineau's economic views particularly fell from favour for many years.

Nevertheless, Martineau saw herself as a popular educator and national instructor and she was. She was widely read and her support counted in her day because others realised that she had the gift of clarifying and expressing difficult, abstract (sometimes abstruse), arguments in accessible ways. Florence Nightingale's invitation to help publicise her work on sanitation is an example of this, especially as Nightingale was no inexperienced author herself. Furthermore, in her articulation of how people should learn, who should be educated and the moral, social and political arguments why, her specific arguments for particular reforms and her deliberate use of a variety of ways to educate the public, Martineau can be celebrated as at the forefront of both *disciplina* and the emergent discipline of education in the nineteenth century. As such she is deserving of greater study. Her writings and ideas have undergone a revival in the past thirty years, partly because of some of the authors in this book. I would argue that Martineau as an educator needs no less recognition.

Notes

1 Drawn from Joseph Priestley's works as follows: *An Essay on the First Principles of Government*, XXII. 1771; *An Essay on a Course of Liberal Education for Civil and Active Life; A Syllabus of a Course of Lectures on the Study of History; The Plan of*

44   *Ruth Watts*

the Course of Lectures on the History of England. XXV. Published with *Miscellaneous Observations Relating to Education*, 1780; 1st ed. 1765; *Disquisitions Relating to Matter and Spirit; The Doctrine of Philosophical Necessity Illustrated* III. 1782; 1st ed. 1777; *Introductory Essays to Hartley's Theory of the Human Mind Works*, III. 1790; and *Lectures on History and General Policy*, XXIV. Philadelphia, 1803, 1st ed. 1788.

2 Brian Simon, *The Two Nations and the Educational Structure 1789–1870* (London: Lawrence and Wishart, 1974), pp. 44–50.

3 Priestley, 1761; 1762; 1767; 1798; 1803; Ruth Watts, *Gender, Power and the Unitarians in England, 1760–1860* (London: Longman, 1998); Ruth Watts, 'Rational dissenting women and the travel of ideas,' *Enlightenment and Dissent*, 26 (2010), pp. 1–27.

4 Watts, *Gender, Power*, pp. 4–5.

5 Harriet Martineau, *Autobiography*, ed. Linda Peterson (Peterborough, ON: Broadview Press, 2007), pp. 94–6, 102–3; Lant Carpenter, *Principles of Education* (London: Hurst, Bees, Orme and Brown, 1820).

6 Martineau, *Autobiography*, p. 54.

7 Peter Spencer, *Hannah Greg (Nee Lightbody) 1766–1828* (Styal: Quarry Bank Mill Trust, 1985; 1st ed.), p. 20, passim; Harriet Martineau, *Household Education* (London: Edward Moxon. 1849); Watts, *Gender, Power*, pp. 66–70, 88–9, passim.

8 Martineau, *Autobiography*, p. 255; pp. 424–5.

9 Harriet Martineau, *The Essential Faith of the Universal Church Deduced from the Sacred Records* (London: Printed for the Unitarian Association, 1831); Martineau, *Autobiography*, pp. 131–7.

10 [Harriet Martineau], 'On female education,' *Monthly Repository*, XVIII (1823), pp. 77–81; [Harriet Martineau], 'Female writers on practical divinity,' *Monthly Repository*, XVII (1822), pp. 593–6; pp. 746–50.

11 [Harriet Martineau], 'Essays on the art of thinking, IV,' *The Monthly Repository* New Series 3 (November 1829), pp. 745–57; p. 751.

12 'Essays on the art of thinking, VI,' *Monthly Repository* New Series 3 (December 1829), pp. 817–22; p. 818.

13 'Essays on the art of thinking,' *Monthly Repository*, New Series Vol. III (January–December 1829), pp. 521–6, 599–606, 707–12, 745–57, 817–22.

14 Martineau, *Autobiography*, pp. 124–5.

15 Harriet Martineau, *Illustrations of Political Economy*, 9 vols. (London: Charles Fox, 1832–4). No.1 *Life in the Wilds* 1832, iii–xiii; Martineau, *Autobiography*, pp. 123–4; Lana L. Dalley, 'Domesticating political economy: Language, gender and economics in the illustrations of political economy.' In: Ella Dzelzainis and Cora Kaplan (eds.), *Harriet Martineau: Authorship, Society and Empire* (Manchester: Manchester UP, 2010), pp. 103–17, 104–8, 103–17, 104–8.

16 Parliamentary or Privy Council reports, issued in a blue cover.

17 Martineau, *Autobiography*, p. 150.

18 Harriet Martineau, *Household Education* (London: E. Moxon, 1849), pp. 45–6.

19 Harriet Martineau, *Briery Creek* (London: Charles Fox, 1833), p. 105.

20 Harriet Martineau, *The Scholars of Arneside: Illustrations of Taxation* (London: Charles Fox, 1834), pp. 110–13; p. 129, passim.

21 Caroline Roberts, *The Woman and the Hour: Harriet Martineau and Victorian Ideologies* (Toronto: University of Toronto Press, 2002), p. 25.

22 [William Empson], 'John Hopkins's notions of political economy and illustrations of political economy,' *Edinburgh Review*, LVIII (April 1833), pp. 1–39; [G. Poulett Scrope], 'Miss Martineau's monthly novels,' *Quarterly Review*, 49 (April 1833), pp. 136–52; 'Miss Martineau's tales,' *The Christian Remembrancer*, II (1841), pp. 178–84; Martineau, *Autobiography*, pp. 166–72.

23 Harriet Martineau, *Demerara* (London: Charles Fox, 1833).

24 Martineau, *Autobiography*, p. 161.

25 Martineau, *Autobiography*, pp. 334ff.

26 Harriet Martineau, *The Hour and the Man: A Historical Romance*, 3 vols. (London: Edward Moxon, 1841), pp. 68, 90, 120–21, 123.

27 Ibid., III, pp. 247–304.

28 Ibid., p. 210, 228–35, 284–5.

29 Because he exploited openings in the defences of the opposition in the battles of 1793, according to the historical record.

30 Martineau, *The Hour*, pp. 194, 216–27, 260–8.

31 Clare Midgley, 'The dissenting voice of Elizabeth Heyrick: An exploration of the links between gender, religious dissent and anti-slavery radicalism.' In: Elizabeth J. Clap and Julie Roy Jeffrey (eds.), *Women, Dissent and Anti-Slavery in Britain and America, 1780–1865* (Oxford: Oxford University Press, 2011), pp. 88–110.

32 Martineau, *Autobiography*, pp. 439–40.

33 Jan Marsh (ed.), *Black Victorians: Black People in British Art* (Aldershot/Hampshire: Lund Humphries, 2006), pp. 86–7, 154–55, 187–8.

34 Susan Hoecker-Drysdale, *Harriet Martineau: First Woman Sociologist* (Oxford/New York: Berg, 1992), pp. 80, 90 n.1; Catherine Hall, *White, Male and Middle Class. Explorations in Feminism and History* (Oxford: Polity Press, 1992), pp. 270–3.

35 Martineau, *The Hour*, pp. 130–2, 138, 146.

36 Hall, pp. 254–5, 264–89; Angela Woollacott, *Gender and Empire* (Basingstoke, Hampshire: Palgrave Macmillan, 2006), pp. 7–8, 46–50.

37 Felicity James, ' "Socinian and political-economy formulas": Martineau the unitarian.' In: Ella Dzelzainis and Cora Kaplan (eds.), pp. 74–87.

38 Ann Shteir, *Cultivating Women, Cultivating Science: Flora's Daughters and Botany in England 1760–1860* (Baltimore and London: Johns Hopkins University Press, 1996), pp. 145, 150–69, 220–7, 237.

39 Deborah Logan (ed.), *Harriet Martineau's Writing on British History and Military Reform*, 6 vols. (London: Pickering and Chatto, 2005), Vol. I, p. 358.

40 Logan, I, pp. 358–9; II, pp. 252–4; V, p. 61, pp. 100–01, pp. 127–8.

41 Barbara Todd, *Harriet Martineau at Ambleside* (Carlisle: Bookcase, 2002), pp. 166–8.

42 Todd, pp. 168–71, 175–7.

43 Logan, II, pp. 58–60, 89–92, 252–4; III, pp. 171–4.

44 Logan, V, pp. 100–1, I passim; Mark Curthoys, " 'Secret organisation of trades': HM and 'free labour.' " In: Ella Dzelzainis and Cora Kaplan (eds.), pp. 138–50, 140–50; Cadbury Research Library, University of Birmingham, Harriet Martineau Papers, MSS 3/i HM on strikes 1859, 1321–37.

45 Logan, III, pp. 183, 191–3; V, 105–6, 316–18; Valerie Sanders (ed.), *Harriet Martineau Selected Letters* (Oxford: Clarendon Press, 1990), pp. 75–6, 80, 148, 200, 227, 243, 255, 259.

46 Harriet Martineau, *Deerbrook* (1839 rpt. ed. Valerie Sanders Harmondsworth: Penguin, 2004), p. 313.

47 Martineau, *Autobiography*, pp. 50–1.

48 Martineau, *Household Education*, pp. 221, 223–4, passim.

49 Ibid., pp. 221–2.

50 Gayle Graham Yates (ed.), *Harriet Martineau on Women* (New Brunswick, NJ: Rutgers University Press, 1985), pp. 101–3; Harriet Martineau, *Biographical Sketches 1852–1868* (London: Macmillan and Co., 1870, 1st ed.1868), p. 388.

51 Martineau, *Autobiography*, p. 305.

52 Yates 97–8; the full text is 97–107.

53 *Household Education*, pp. 224–6, pp. 283–7.

54 Logan, VI, pp. 163–9.

55 Logan, VI, pp. 161–202, 240–7, 258–91, 295–312, 315–17; III, 62; Ruth Watts, *Women in Science: A Social and Cultural History* (London: Routledge, 2007), pp. 122–4, 127–31.

56 Yates, pp. 51–83, 216–24 and 239–67, passim.

57 Joan Rees, *Writings on the Nile: Harriet Martineau, Florence Nightingale, Amelia Edwards* (London: The Rubicon Press, 1995), pp. 19–45, passim.
58 Logan, I, pp.xv–xxv.
59 Lesa Scholl, 'Provocative Agendas: Martineau's Translation of Comte.' In: Ella Dzelzainis and Cora Kaplan, pp. 88–99.
60 Hoecker-Drysdale, *First Woman.*

Part II
Contribution to disciplines

3 Harriet Martineau and classical political economy

John Vint and Keiko Funaki

Harriet Martineau is widely regarded as the most successful populariser of classical political economy. While she went on to greater success and recognition as a journalist and writer, however, interest in her views on theoretical political economy waned. Current attention to her work within economics is confined to those interested in the history of economic thought, dating back to the publication in 1958 of Mark Blaug's book *Ricardian Economics: A Historical Study* in which he devoted a chapter entitled 'Political Economy to be Read as Literature'.[1] This has been followed by work by others on Martineau's popularisation of political economy, her impact on popular debates and her role in the struggle for the hearts and minds of Victorian middle and working-class readers.[2]

This chapter explores Harriet Martineau's understanding of, and application of, classical economics in her early work – the *Illustrations of Political Economy* 1832–34 and *Poor Laws and Paupers Illustrated* 1833–4.[3] It examines her work through key mid nineteenth-century concepts derived from classical theorists. We begin with the origins of her framework derived from James Mill, and then explore the use made by Martineau of key ideas from the work of Adam Smith on natural law and harmony of interests, Thomas Malthus on population, poverty, the Poor Laws and approach to industrial conflict and David Ricardo on the Corn Laws, before reflecting on contemporary reactions to Martineau's political economy and her contribution to the discipline.

The political economy framework

As already noted in the Introduction, the framework Martineau used for the stories in the *Illustrations* followed the general approach and structure of James Mill's *Elements of Political Economy*. Both authors shared similar pedagogical aims, that is, the belief that certain kinds of knowledge are cumulative and that students of the subject should only move on to the next stage when earlier stages are completed. As Mill put it in his *Preface*:

> My object has been to compose a school-book of Political Economy, to detach the essential principles of the science from all extraneous topics, to state the propositions clearly and in their logical order, and to subjoin its demonstration

to each. . . . They who are commencing the study ought to proceed slowly, and to familiarize themselves with the new combinations of ideas.[4]

Mill made it clear that he would not make any claims of originality and that he would not hinder the learner's concentration by mentioning any authorities. Martineau wrote in similar vein in the *Preface* to volume one of the *Illustrations*:

> We trust it will be found that as the leading principles come out in order, one after another, they are so clear, so indisputable, so apparently familiar, that the wonder is when the difficulty is to come, – where the knotty points are to be encountered. We suspect that these far-famed difficulties arise, like the difficulties of mathematical and other sciences, from not beginning at the beginning and going regularly on.[5]

Mill's *Elements* was a simplified version of Ricardo's more complex *Principles of Political Economy* published in 1817, and had been the outcome of his tuition of his son John Stuart Mill.[6] At the age of thirteen in 1819, the younger Mill began a course of instruction on Ricardo's work while walking with his father, and took notes which formed the basis for the *Elements*. This is where Martineau learnt Ricardo's economics, and although we cannot be sure, it is likely that she never read Ricardo's *Principles* in the original.

In her *Autobiography* Martineau recalls that during her negotiations with Charles Fox concerning publication, he told her that he had met James Mill, who had convinced him that Martineau's 'method of exemplification could not possibly succeed'. Fox therefore wanted her to change her plan and 'issue my Political Economy in a didactic form'.[7] Perhaps Mill had been favourably influenced by Marcet's *Conversations* which used that format or he might have been impressed with the peripatetic dialogues with his son.[8] Martineau refused and this turned out to be a life-changing decision.

In terms of structure, Martineau used Mill's categories – Production, Distribution, Exchange (Interchange in Mill's terminology) and Consumption, although she added other topics, such as slavery and poverty.[9] There are twenty-five tales in the *Illustrations* series, each, apart from the last, with a summary of the key points usually at the end. Sometimes these closely reflect the points made in the story – at other times they do not.

The last tale, *The Moral of Many Fables*, is a grand summary of the whole series, and in the *Preface* to this tale Martineau presents, like Mill, her reflection on the intellectual debt she owed to other people and with the aid of a typically earthy parable:[10]

> It must be perfectly needless to explain what I owe to preceding writers on the science of which I have treated. Such an acknowledgment could only accompany a pretension of my own to have added something to the science – a pretension which I have never made. By dwelling, as I have been led to do, on their discoveries, I have become too much awakened to the glory to dream of sharing the honour. Great men must have their hewers of wood and

drawers of water; and scientific discoverers must be followed by those who will popularize their discoveries. When the woodman finds it necessary to explain that the forest is not of his planting, I may begin to particularize my obligations to Smith and Malthus, and others of their high order.[11]

Harriet Martineau and *The Wealth of Nations*

Natural law and Necessarianism

Adam Smith's ideas were clearly influential and although Martineau regarded the *Wealth of Nations* as unsuitable for teaching economics, she clearly admired the work.[12] Martineau empathised with Smith's ideas on natural laws of society (Necessarianism) and harmony of interests especially, as we shall see, in the tales on industrial conflict *The Hill and the Valley* and *A Manchester Strike*, which focus on the relationship between capital and labour with particular regard to the role of machinery.[13] However, harmony was not perfect in the *Wealth of Nations* and Harriet Martineau was aware of this and its consequent implications for laissez-faire – again as we shall see later.

Stadial theory

Adam Smith's theory of history has an important role in Martineau's first tale *Life in the Wilds*.[14] Termed *stadial theory*, Smith's concept proposed four stages in the development of society: hunting, pasturage, farming and commerce. In *Life in the Wilds* the story concerns a small British settlement in South Africa which is attacked by a group of 'savages'. Smith's four stages are not named but are implicit in the plot line which involves the family being robbed and the ways in which members seek to rebuild their world. The arms (hunting) are taken; the cattle driven off (pasturage) and the crops destroyed (agriculture). The family is left with no tools or ability to engage in commerce while their settlement lies in ruins. They recover by living in a cave and engaging first in hunting with primitive bows and other techniques, augmented by foraging. They capture antelope which they keep for milk and meat, and before long their crops have been revived. A young, fit member of the group is sent out to Cape Town to deliver the news about their situation and to bring back tools with which to build a mill, a saw-pit and a forge. The messenger arrives back safely with the necessary tools and also brings news that the authorities in Cape Town have decided to send a ship to a point nearby in order to trade with the settlement. Commerce thus begins to be re-established.

Interestingly, in the *Moral of Many Fables* section on this tale Martineau posits a fifth stage where society is 'wisely arranged':

> Is there not yet at least one other stage, when society shall be wisely arranged, so that all may become intellectual, virtuous, and happy; or, at least, so that the exceptions shall be the precise reverse of those which are the rare instances now? The belief is irresistible.[15]

This precedes J S Mill's later notion of continual social progress in his *Principles of Political Economy* (1848):

> It is scarcely necessary to remark that a stationary condition of capital and population implies no stationary state of human improvement. There would be as much scope as ever for all kinds of mental culture, and moral and social progress; as much room for improving the Art of Living, and much more likelihood of its being improved, when minds ceased to be engrossed by the art of getting on.[16]

Donald Winch has argued that James Mill had a similar notion, evident in his discussion of wages, from which the younger Mill derived his argument.[17] Martineau's fifth stage almost certainly had the same origin.

The nature of wealth

Martineau outlines the importance of other ideas of Smith in the discussion between members of the settlement and their leader Captain Adams, for instance, on mercantilism. A section in *The Wealth of Nations* is devoted to Smith's critique of mercantilism, of which a key idea is that the nation's wealth consists in the amount of 'bullion' (gold or silver) accumulated. Mercantilists argued that exports should be encouraged and imports discouraged by tariffs and other trade barriers, enabling bullion to flow into the country. The problem is that this will lead to inflation as the supply of bullion (money) increases, raise the price of the goods to be exported and thus be counterproductive. For Smith, in contrast, the wealth of a nation does not depend on gold and silver but on labour and what it can produce and thus what people can consume.

In *Life in the Wilds* the fundamental Smithian position is outlined by the Captain to his friend Mr Stone:

> I wish . . . that the people in England, who think that wealth consists of gold, silver and bank notes, would come here and see how much their money is worth in our settlement. A thousand sovereigns would not here buy a hat, nor a roll of bank notes a loaf of bread. Here, at least, money is not wealth. . . . Wealth is made up of many things – of land, of houses, of clothes, food, and of the means (whether gold or silver or anything else) by which these things may be obtained. Whatever lives, or grows, or can be produced, that is necessary, or useful, or agreeable to mankind, is wealth.[18]

The conversation continues in an optimistic mood; although they have lost much, the two men still have the power of their labour, and together with the natural resources available, they can look forward to rebuilding their community.

Productive and unproductive labour

Smith made the distinction between productive and unproductive labour, arguing that productive labour results in 'some particular subject or vendible commodity', while the services of unproductive labour 'perish in the very instant of their performance'. Smith thus drew a distinction between labour which produces 'things' – a farmer producing potatoes or a manufacturer producing shoes – and labour which produces services – of servants, lawyers and doctors, for example. A possible reaction to this is that unproductive workers are secondary to productive workers, or have less use. Smith did not say that unproductive workers were useless but that the output of productive workers – potatoes, shoes, machines – supports workers in producing future output, in ways that the services of unproductive workers cannot.

So what did Harriet Martineau make of this debate in *Life in the Wilds*? The context of the story – the small British settlement having to start again – is an excellent scenario in which to pose questions about who is of use and why, and a whole chapter, 'Hand-work and Head-work' is devoted to the topic. The Chaplain and teacher Mr Stone argue that however hard the little group of people work they are divided into productive and unproductive labourers, as in every civilised society. The debate between the characters concludes that there needs to be an appropriate mix of the two kinds of labour – servants, the clergy and lawyers are needed as much as farmers and builders. Mrs Stone asks her husband how he sees himself in this respect. He replies that he is unproductive when in the pulpit and in the schoolroom, though productive when working in his field. Martineau thus succeeded in bringing to life in the number of examples she provided, the importance of both kinds of labour.

The division of labour

To explain the idea about the division of labour, Smith used the well-known example of the pin factory, where if one man has to make pins by himself, he might manage to produce one pin per day. But, if the labour is divided into a number of separate and specialised activities such that one man draws out the wire, another straightens it, a third cuts it, a fourth points it and so on, output is increased dramatically. In total, eighteen operations are needed in the making of a pin and Smith showed that by organising a division of labour, ten workers could produce 48,000 pins a day. The increase in the quantity of work as a result of the division of labour is ascribed to three factors: increase in skill because of repeating the task, saving time at not having to switch tasks and invention of machines which 'facilitate and abridge labour'.

The pin factory example also shows how one product can benefit from various 'specialists'. Later, Smith provided a more complex example involving the different forms of labour required in the production of a woollen coat, ranging from shepherd, weaver, merchants and toolmakers to miners and bricklayers contributing to the construction of the buildings where production takes place.

Martineau's example substitutes a 'Dorsetshire' pie and a plum pudding for Smith's woollen coat but the arguments used are similar, with the various intermediate products and activities listed right down to the miners and bricklayers.[19]

It is not a surprise perhaps that *Life in the Wilds* was a huge popular success. There was the clear appeal of the little British settlement fighting back, planning its recovery and winning through after its massive setback. The illustration of Adam Smith's key ideas was skilfully managed as was Martineau's choice of how to represent Smith's stadial theory as a framework. Faced with disaster, those in the settlement pose fundamental questions – what really is wealth, who is useful, why and how can we divide up the tasks? These questions are seen to arise naturally from the narrative but in fact derive from specific theoretical ideas in *The Wealth of Nations*.

Laissez-faire and the functions of government

As Mark Blaug once put it, 'Whatever else Harriet Martineau may have preached in the *Illustration*s, the vulgar advocacy of *laissez-faire* pure and simple, is often supposed to be its hallmark.'[20] In a letter to Thomas Carlyle, John Stuart Mill mocked that 'Harriet Martineau reduces the laissez-faire system to absurdity by merely carrying it out in all its consequences.'[21] As Blaug argues, there are no grounds for this statement; indeed, her treatment is a standard treatment based on Smithian principles.[22]

Thus in *Life in the Wilds* Martineau advocated the notion that the role of government is to free society from obstacles which prevent the market working and thus for industry to find its natural reward:

> "It is not the duty of the English government," replied the captain, "to inquire who is idle in the kingdom and who is not, and to punish or encourage individuals accordingly. This would be an endless task, and an irksome one both to rulers and the ruled. But the same work may be done in a shorter way. Governments should protect the natural liberty of industry by removing all obstacles, – all bounties and prohibitions, – all devices by which one set of people tries to obtain unfair advantages over another set. If this were fairly done, industry would find its natural reward and idleness its natural punishment; and there would be neither more nor less unproductive labourers than the good of society would require."[23]

Furthermore, in *A Tale of the Tyne*, she adopted Smith's position that the duties of government do include some provision of public utilities.[24] Thus, the argument is put forward that:

> The same duty of securing the free exercise of industry requires that companies should be privileged to carry on works of public utility which are not within the reach of individual enterprize, as in the case of roads, canals, bridges, &c.[25]

Perhaps rather surprisingly she also argued that government expenditure could be used to provide entertainment for the people:

> Considering that one of the great objects of government is the security, and another the advancement, of the people, it seems as if one of the expenses of government should be providing useful and innocent amusement for the

people. All must have something to do in the intervals of their toils; and as the educated can find recreations for themselves, it behoves the guardians of the public to be especially careful in furnishing innocent amusements to those who are less fitted to choose their pleasures well. But where are the public grounds in which the poor of our large towns may take the air, and exercise themselves in games? Where are the theatres, the museums, the news-rooms, to which the poor may resort without an expense unsuited to their means?[26]

Martineau was prepared to propound government intervention despite her general stance on laissez-faire. In her tale *The Three Ages*, she set out her order of preference for government expenditure as follows: Education, Public Works, Government and Legislation, Law and Justice, Diplomacy, Defence and Dignity of the Sovereign – the reverse, she argued, of the existing state of affairs. Not only did she make a stronger case for public expenditure in certain areas than Adam Smith, but her radical credentials were evident. One area where Martineau differed from Smith was on the possibility of breakdown in harmony. Smith identified a conflict of interests between masters and workers over wages based on the difference in bargaining strength of each side. Martineau on the other hand used the wages-fund doctrine developed by Malthus and McCulloch to argue for a natural harmony between labour and capital.

Population, poverty and the preventative check

Martineau incorporated many of the ideas of Thomas Malthus in the *Illustrations*.[27] Indeed, Robert K. Webb has argued that of all classical writers, Martineau relied most on Malthus.[28] For example, the key Malthusian argument that population grows faster than food supply is outlined in *For Each and For All*. Martineau posed the questions:

> Whence, then, comes all this misery? all this tremendous inequality?
> The misery arises from a deficiency of food. . . .
> Well; whence this deficiency of food?
> From the tendency of eaters to increase faster than the supply of food.[29]

Like Malthus, Martineau understood and argued for the 'preventive check' of the delay of marriage as a way of keeping population in line with food supply, an approach consistently argued elsewhere.[30] *Weal and Woe in Garveloch* tells the story of Ronald, who is in love with Katie only to lose her to his friend Cuthbert. Cuthbert later dies, leaving Katie with four children.[31] While wishing to marry Katie, food on the remote Hebridean island is in short supply and, because he does not wish to add to the island numbers, he is content to look after the family without marriage. This is explained to the bemused Katie by the heroine Ella, brother of Ronald:

> We have not the power of increasing food as fast as our numbers may increase; but we have the power of limiting our numbers to agree with the supply of

food. This is the gentle check which is put into our own hands; and if we will not use it, we must not repine if harsher checks follow. If the passionate man will not restrain his anger, he must expect punishment at the hands of him whom he has injured; and if he imprudently indulges his love, he must *not* complain when poverty, disease, and death lay waste his family.[32]

In the Summary of *Weal and Woe in Garveloch* Martineau reinforces the point:

By bringing no more children into the world than there is a subsistence provided for, society may preserve itself from the miseries of want. In other words, the timely use of the mild preventive check may avert the horrors of any positive check.[33]

Martineau believed in moral restraint in the form of delay in marriage as a way of reducing population growth. By delaying marriage the number of children born would be lowered. In the case of Ronald and Katie, however, marriage is not delayed but voided. While her plea was for moral restraint, it gave her critics room to argue, erroneously, that she was against the institution of marriage.[34]

Harriet Martineau and the Poor Law

The background of Martineau's tale *Cousin Marshall* is the old-fashioned Poor Law, which dated back to Elizabethan legislation of 1601.[35] From that time, responsibility for support of the poor was allotted to parishes which were enabled to raise local taxes or 'poor rates'. Churchwardens and overseers, appointed by magistrates, were in charge of allocating relief and setting the poor to work. The system resulted in workhouses predominantly for the old who could not work and those unable to care for themselves. By the 1780s and 1790s in the wake of the American and French Revolutions, and with extra pressure from poor harvests, various laws were enacted to ameliorate conditions and diffuse revolutionary potential. Liberal changes included forbidding the able-bodied to be put in to the workhouse and requiring authorities instead to pay outdoor relief or allowances.[36] By the 1820s two problems emerged: first, the continuing burden of the poor rates and the resultant pauperisation of the labouring classes caused by the increase in outdoor relief to the able-bodied (including children), and second, the scale of abuse and corruption in the system.[37]

The main story of *Cousin Marshall* is of a family whose house burns down. Following the mother's death, of the four children, two lodge with a cousin – cousin Marshall – and two are sent to the workhouse. Much of the tale focuses on the children in the workhouse, the number of paupers, the size of outdoor relief and conditions of workhouse life. As with earlier tales Martineau created a particular character – here a surgeon, Mr Burke – who leads discussion on the economics and social issues involved. To his unmarried sister Louisa with whom he lives, Burke complains about the number of the indigent, and how this may be reduced. He argues that efforts must be made to increase the wages fund and the number of labourers who can draw on it. For the wages fund to expand, the usual means of increasing capital need to be actively sought. Mr Burke continues that 'the immense amount which is now consumed by the indigent should be applied to the purposes of production'. Later, Burke makes it clear that the 'usual means' implies private investment; in other words, it is not the responsibility of the state to 'increase at its will, the subsistence fund'. The reason for the increase in support is ascribed to the payment of outdoor relief; while at the same time, the fund for the payment of wages is affected by the inefficiency of those receiving such relief, who care little whether they work hard or not.[38] Later in the story, Mr Burke ventriloquises more or less word-for-word the 'abolitionist' line of Malthus:[39]

> "The best plan, in my opinion, yet proposed, is this: – to enact that no child born from any marriage taking place within a year from the date of the law, and no illegitimate child born within two years from the same date, shall ever be entitled to parish assistance."[40]

Martineau drew on Malthus for inspiration in her Summary of Principles for this story:

> What, then, must be done to lessen the number of the indigent, now so frightfully increasing? The subsistence-fund must be employed productively, and capital and labour be allowed to take their natural course; *i.e.* the pauper system must, by some means or other, be extinguished.[41]

As we shall see she was to soften her line from abolition of the Poor Laws to reform, but both positions made her unpopular.

Harriet Martineau and Poor Law reform

Martineau was asked by Lord Brougham to write four tales in *The Poor Laws and Paupers Illustrated* series in order to assist the Poor Law Commission, of which he was head. The tales[42] were published under the auspices of the Society for the Diffusion of Useful Knowledge.[43] The Society had been established by Brougham and others as part of an attempt to educate the working classes in political economy with the economist Nassau Senior, a leading voice on the Commission. Brougham and Senior were, at the time, receiving early reports from the Assistant Poor Law Commissioners, who were in the process of collecting facts and opinions throughout the country, and these were made available to Martineau. In September 1832 Senior wrote a report for Brougham based on a small sample of early findings which were but a tiny fraction of the eventual returns. This report was essentially a blueprint for the reforms introduced two years later. Senior argued for the reduction of claims for relief from the able-bodied, to be achieved by making the system harsher. Central to this was the principle of 'less eligibility', which meant that the situation of the able-bodied pauper 'on the whole shall not be made really or apparently so eligible as the situation of the independent labourer of the lowest class'.[44] This would be enforced by requiring the able-bodied and their families to go into a workhouse as a 'test' of their destitution. Conditions there would involve strict discipline, hard work, monotonous food and the separation of families.

Martineau followed Senior on the problems with the old system and the new reforms. The first Poor Law tale, *The Parish*, longer than any of the *Illustrations* tales by some 40 or 50 pages, represented Martineau's first and most comprehensive reaction to the material she was getting from Brougham and Senior. A sense of excitement and industry radiated from this piece. Martineau appeared to enjoy portraying the panoply of rogues and rascals playing their part in the abuse of the poor relief system. The second tale, *The Hamlets*, is a futuristic exposition of transition from the old Poor Law to the new. It is a highly optimistic piece of fiction – the appointment of the new overseer results in immediate change. Martineau has clearly moved a long way from the abolitionism of Malthus – for her, radical reform is now the way forward and success is guaranteed. The final two tales – *The Town* and *The Land's End* – take up various administrative aspects of Senior's proposals.

The machinery question: *The Hill and the Valley*

The prevailing view concerning machinery taken by political economists at the end of the 1820s was a positive one. It was argued that productivity and profits would increase with the introduction of machinery and that any workers who lost their jobs would soon be re-employed elsewhere. However, discussions ranged far wider than just leading political economists. It was of profound significance to ordinary working people who resisted its introduction in many ways, including machine-breaking and rioting. Major disturbances occurred in Lancashire in 1826 as a result of a financial crash with violence in the manufacturing districts directed towards machinery. This outbreak prompted numerous calls for the spread of knowledge about political economy and the benefits of machinery among the working class.[45] There were further riots against the introduction of agricultural machinery in rural areas of southern England in 1830 and for some these underlined an urgent need to educate workers in the 'truths' of political economy concerning machinery and wages. *The Hill and the Valley*, the second of Martineau's *Illustrations*, is a tale of industrial conflict and machine-breaking, set in a South Wales valley iron works, run by a man called Wallace with his partners. During a discussion about industrialization, Wallace is accused of liking to see ranks of slaves under him. Wallace replies that there is no slavery in his business because of the bond of mutual trust between the capitalist and free labourer:

> It is the interest of our men and ourselves that the productiveness of our trade should be increased to the utmost; that we should turn out as much work as possible, and that therefore we should improve our machinery, divide our labour to best advantage, and bring all our processes to the greatest possible perfection.[46]

Here we see Martineau communicating the political economy message that inherent in capitalist production is a harmony of interests between workers and capitalists. In the story, Wallace argues that both capital and labour are necessary for production. Eventually there appears a change of fortune. The price of bar-iron falls by half as a result of unstable political and economic conditions. To avoid bringing in machinery to lower costs, Wallace and his partners try to resolve this by reducing their own consumption and lowering wages. The first wage reduction is accepted quietly, the second with murmurings and the third with threats of rebellion. In the end, machinery is introduced and some men and boys dismissed. Martineau, as narrator, states that it is hoped that the sacked workers will find jobs elsewhere but they stay until they have spent all their money, encourage those still in work to resign unless wages are increased and swear at the machinery and the employers.

At this point Martineau forces up the pace and heat of the conflict. A boy is accidentally killed by the new machinery of which he is in charge. The anger at the death leads to a chain of events which results in the destruction of the factory. Soldiers are called and those responsible are led away. In addressing the workers afterwards Wallace reminds them that their jobs are gone, and that disgrace and the penalties of the law await many of them. Many of you must regret the events, he says to them, but the best course of action now is to teach the young to obey the laws and make it clear to them:

> "that, however sad undeserved poverty may be, it is easily endurable in comparison with the thought which will haunt some of you until your dying day –
> 'my own hands have brought this misery upon myself, and upon those who look up to me for bread.'"[47]

Martineau thus places the responsibility on the workers. The people sacked were the laziest and the least able so they had some part in their own misfortune. They should have tried to find jobs elsewhere but instead, they loitered and spread discontent. Their actions in setting fire to the factory were of course unacceptable and unnecessary and ultimately more detrimental to the workers than the owners. The Necessarian message was that the laws of political economy cannot be countered by human agency and that every action has its consequences. Individuals should by their actions endeavour to obey the law and avoid trouble for themselves and their families. Martineau's objective was to persuade readers of the immutable nature of the laws of political economy and the harmony of interests inherent in them. As she put it: 'The interests of the two classes of producers, Labourers and Capitalists, are therefore the same; the prosperity of both depending on the accumulation of Capital'.[48]

The wages fund at work: *A Manchester Strike*

Martineau's tale *A Manchester Strike* focused on the role of combinations (trades unions) and strike action. The main economic idea illustrated here was the wages-fund doctrine, peculiar to classical economics and abandoned in 1869, and most likely derived from the work of Ricardian economist John Ramsay McCulloch.[49] The wages-fund doctrine was based on the notion that workers' wages were part of the capital owned by employers. It originated in agricultural settings, where, by the time of harvest (the end of the production period), farmers would have accumulated a stock of 'wage goods' or 'necessaries' (food, clothing and other subsistence items) to be set aside to support workers during the next production period. With the money received as wages, workers could purchase this predetermined fixed supply of goods to maintain themselves through the period until the next harvest. Carried over into manufacturing, the sector was theorised (unrealistically) as having similar fixed periods of production. The wages-fund doctrine held that the real wage rate of a worker (the quantity of goods that can be bought by the money wage) is determined by dividing the amount of wage goods set aside by the number of workers. This concept was used at the level both of the individual farm or firm, and of the economy as a whole. An important argument for Martineau was that strike action by workers could never increase their real wages because the total amount was predetermined. Moreover, if the strike meant fewer wage goods were produced, the size of the next period's wages fund would be reduced, leading inevitably to a fall in wages.

The context of the story *A Manchester Strike* is a predicted lowering of wages by employers in Manchester. The tale begins with a not unsympathetic description of its impact on an intelligent, moderate worker William Allen, who tries to hold back his co-workers from resorting to strike action. In the end and against his better judgement, he becomes their leader in the conflict. One of the employers, Wentworth, is presented as a sympathetic, wise and kindly man. In giving advice to a deputation of union representatives, he makes use of the wages-fund doctrine in an agricultural context to explain that a strike will simply reduce the size of the wages fund for the next period. Despite Wentworth's efforts the strike goes ahead and later in the story Wentworth has the opportunity yet again to impress upon the workers the importance and relevance of wage theory. Referring to the likely situation at the end of the strike, he argues that by then the wages fund will be wasted:

> We have been consuming idly, and so have you; and there must needs have been great waste. And what is it which has thus been wasted? The fund which is to maintain you; the fund out of which your wages are paid. . . . Keep on your strike a little longer, and the question will be, how many less shall be employed, at how much less. Keep it on long enough, and the question will be entirely settled; there will be no wages for anybody.[50]

So here again Martineau explicitly uses the wages-fund doctrine to argue against strikes, a position that was in the main avoided by the major classical economists. At the back of this discussion is the argument, at times more explicit than others, that although workers are powerless in the short term, the power to improve their lot *does* lie with them in the end – by having fewer children. In the story, Wentworth argues that when things are good for workers and wages are high, they tend to respond by having larger families. The effects of this are not immediately felt, but when there is a downturn, workers often fail to associate the accompanying fall in wages with their actions a generation previously. This is a Malthusian population argument from which Wentworth draws the moral lesson, 'do what in him lies to prevent population from increasing faster than the capital which is to support it'.[51]

One flaw in the wages-fund argument (of which there are a number) is that, although the real wages fund may be predetermined and rigidly fixed, what is to stop workers striking for higher wages from employers who have money accumulated in the form of savings? In coercing higher money wages from employers, it could be argued, workers would not benefit because such increases can be spent only on the fixed quantity of wages goods. The prices of the goods would rise proportionally, leaving the workers no better off. Thus the level of wages does not matter – what counts is the quantity of stored-up wage goods. Martineau has Wentworth explaining this point:

> If a penny a week would enable a man to buy all the necessaries for himself and his family, and if a pound would do no more, would it signify to any man whether his wages were a penny or a pound?[52]

This makes the assumption that workers can spend their money only on necessities, not on other goods such as luxuries. Here Martineau deviates from Ricardo, who maintained that workers could consume luxuries in certain circumstances.

A Manchester Strike represents a powerful integration of classical theory and fictional narrative. The outcome of the story is ultimate victory for the power of popular political economy: the employers meet and agree that the firms paying the lowest wages will raise them to the average and the highest payers will likewise reduce theirs. The workers accept this equalisation and the strike ends, although not all the workers get their jobs back. Allen meets Wentworth to see if he can be re-employed but Wentworth, although sympathetic, says that he can afford now only to employ two-thirds of the previous workforce. Priority will go first to those who left their jobs unwillingly and to those who have worked for him for many years. Allen, the sensible counsellor, the wise restrainer of the men and the unwilling leader is thus punished, and condemned to a life hauling a water cart in summer and sweeping the streets in winter.

Harriet Martineau and the Corn Laws

Ricardo's major theoretical analysis arose out of the debates concerning the Corn Laws between 1814 and 1816, during the Napoleonic wars. A core economic argument then was that the growth in population led to an increase in demand for grain and that this, together with the effects of poor harvests all over Europe and a continental wartime blockade, had encouraged the landed classes to bring inferior land into cultivation. These factors had led to an increase in the price of grain and to higher rents demanded by the landlords. There was concern from the landed interests that when the war was over, cheap grain would pour into England and their profits would be undercut. Following this line of argument, two Corn Law Acts were passed in 1814 and 1815 which gave farmers an almost complete monopoly of the home market. Both manufacturers and factory workers strongly opposed the new legislation, the factory owners because the acts raised wages and reduced profits, and the workers, because rising wages failed to keep up with rising prices. Ricardo gave these concerns, which were widespread, a theoretical framework.

Martineau presented the key elements of Ricardo's distribution model in her tale, *For Each and For All.*[53] Given her agreement with Smith's identity of interests, Martineau did not take up the notion of competing interests, apparent in Ricardo's work. Additionally, she criticised Owenite ideas of self-sufficient communal societies (co-operatives) on the grounds that people would have no incentive to limit family size and that, given diminishing resources of the soil, self-sufficiency would become non-viable in the long run. She was not alone in making this argument: John Stuart Mill raised the same objection to Robert Owen's schemes at a meeting of the London Co-operative Society in 1826.[54]

One policy implication of Ricardo's work was the repeal of the Corn Laws, thus allowing grain to be imported which would in turn bring down money wages and revive manufacturing profits. It seems strange that Martineau did not put the case for repeal in *For Each and For All*, but, rather, left the discussion to a much later tale, *Sowers Not Reapers*,[55] the primary focus of which is the benefits of free international trade. However, the issues of Corn Law repeal and free trade are related. If the Corn Laws were repealed, cheap corn could be imported and resources released from agriculture could go into manufacturing. The revenue received by corn-exporting countries would allow them to buy manufactured goods from Britain. Free international trade was thus mutually beneficial.

Martineau was precise about the consequences of no repeal. In *Sowers Not Reapers*, it is explained thus:

> We pay, as a nation, 12,500,000*l.* more for corn than we should pay if our ports were open to the world. Of this, not more than one-fifth goes into the pockets of the landowners, the rest being, for the most part, buried in poor soils.[56]

Martineau staunchly supported the repeal of the Corn Laws on the grounds of the perceived positive effects on profits and free trade. She also had a firm belief in modernisation and the importance of science and technology, in developing British industry and trade. It could be argued that, as a manufacturer's daughter, Martineau was merely acting on behalf of the manufacturing interest. But as we have already suggested, Martineau had faith in the wages-fund doctrine. Increased profits would mean an increase in the wages fund, leading to either more jobs or higher wages or both; in her view, the interests of labourers and capitalists are the same.

Harriet Martineau's political economy

Harriet Martineau's achievement in producing the *Illustrations of Political Economy* was remarkable. Because she was a woman she was denied access to a university education and formal training in political economy. Despite this she read, understood and absorbed a wide range of theoretical economic ideas and was able to embody them in a series of fictional tales to immense critical and popular acclaim, all in the space of about three years.

She clearly understood the case for laissez-faire but more importantly she also brought out and extended Smith's examples of the case for government intervention under certain circumstances. Smith himself did not gather his examples together in the *Wealth of Nations* in as coherent a fashion as Martineau's bold presentations in *A Tale of the Tyne* and the *Three Ages*. At a more detailed level, she conveyed the importance of the role of money in connection with the wages-fund doctrine – not a straightforward issue and one which was still a matter of debate in the twentieth century.

Her weaknesses were mostly to do with her understanding of Ricardo. She took his ideas from James Mill and her interpretation of his distribution model was accurately conveyed although she did not take the discussion as far as James Mill did, let alone Ricardo himself. She was with Ricardo on the question of Corn Law repeal but this was a common idea as we showed previously. Where she was weaker was on the labour theory of value. She accepted in *French Wine and Politics*[57] that labour used in producing a commodity was primarily important in determining its value, and that capital was also important. There was, however, no hint that workers might have any rights to a share of the rewards of their labour; for her, their wages were determined by the wages-fund doctrine. Having said that, overall, Martineau's writings were an accurate reflection of the classical economic literature of the time. The *Illustrations* did not contain any path-breaking ideas in political economy although the tale *Demerara* on slavery was innovative in both the choice of topic and its sociological treatment.

After her series was published, Martineau became the talk of the town in London – 'lionised' as she put it. She was known, fêted and visited by many of the most important people in the capital. Much of this must be due to her realization of her original goal – to bring political economy to the attention of the public through fictional illustrations. People enjoyed the tales, especially the early ones, and sales roared. Some may have read them for the stories alone but many were captivated by the intertwining of fiction and grand ideas which were also conveniently detailed in the summaries for each tale. Others – the social reformers, the Whigs, Brougham, Senior et al. – admired her for her reforming zeal. But underneath, there was recognition of the sheer intellectual achievement, recognition which lasted in other fields as her focus on political economy faded. She was also largely ignored by the political economy profession from which she, as a woman, was excluded.

Contemporary press reactions were mixed. Praise came from her home newspaper, the *Norwich Mercury*, and from *The Spectator*.[58] William Empson admired her in the *Edinburgh Review*: 'she has already made, by a previously undreamed-of-route, a brilliant progress towards the rescue of her beloved science – the science of Adam Smith from the cloud which some persons have thought was gathering over its condition and its fate.'[59] Even John Stuart Mill had a change of heart. A year after his letter to Carlyle quoted previously, Mill reviewed Harriet Martineau's *Moral of Many Fables* for the *Monthly Repository*. Here Mill was more complimentary arguing that '. . . as an exposition of the leading principles of what now constitutes the science, it possesses considerable merit'.[60]

Critical responses focused on Martineau's advocacy of Malthus's ideas underpinned by the wages-fund doctrine, despite her clear indebtedness to other writers. Tory and Radical press and periodicals alike took exception to much of her work. The Tory *Fraser's Magazine* and *The Times* both attacked her ideas on overpopulation and Poor Law reform, based on their support for the old law and their hostility to the principle of delay of marriage which they saw as threatening to the institution of marriage. The Radical press attacked her on similar grounds. The *Voice of the West Riding* warned readers against Martineau (and also McCulloch) whom the paper regarded as 'Pseudo Political Economists'. The paper *Crisis* considered Martineau a good writer of fiction but a poor writer of political economy. The *Poor Man's Guardian* referred to her as 'the anti-propagation lady, a single sight of whom would repel all fears of surplus population, her aspect being as repulsive as her doctrines'.[61]

Scurrilous, unacceptable, sexist abuse was not confined to working-class writers. Her appearance became a target of abuse when the Tory writer William Maginn suggested that 'no one who inspects her portrait can wonder at her celibate proclivities, or is likely to attempt the seduction of the "fair philosopher" from her doctrines on the population question'; or again, 'a lady ought to be treated by reviewers, with the utmost deference, except she writes politics, which is an enormity equal to wearing breeches'.[62]

A particularly unpleasant example came from the *Quarterly Review*, which poured vitriolic criticism on the first twelve of Martineau's tales and towards the end preceded a quotation with the statement that they 'should be loth to bring a blush unnecessarily upon the cheek of any woman; but may we venture to ask the maiden sage the meaning of the following passage'.[63] The passage quoted was: 'A parent has a considerable influence over the subsistence-fund of his family, and an absolute control over the numbers to be supported by that fund.'[64]

This was clearly a deliberate hint at contraception which Martineau robustly opposed. The last thing she wanted, as a young, unmarried woman with a huge audience, was to proclaim her support for birth control. She argued alternatively for the 'mild preventive' of delay in marriage as we have seen in *Weal and Woe in Garveloch*. The writers in the *Quarterly Review* were aware of this and had written sarcastically about it earlier in the review. But the passage which they most objected to came from *Cousin Marshall*, which focused on the Poor Law. Here, pauper marriages were portrayed as a means by which parish relief could be obtained, leading to increased expenditure. Martineau was keen to argue that the state cannot increase the subsistence fund nor control the numbers which depend on it. The notion that the state can look after its citizens as a parent can look after its children was, she argued, a fallacy as indicated in the second half of the sentence quoted:

> whereas the rulers of a state, from whom a legal provision emanates, have little influence over its subsistence-fund, and no control whatever over the number of its members.[65]

Nowhere else in *Cousin Marshall* is *parental* control over numbers mentioned and it may be that this was a slip on Martineau's part, written in haste, and not revisited. Strictly speaking a decision on the numbers to be supported by a family fund does not necessarily imply birth control. For example, a family could decide to continue their support for children who have left home or adopt orphaned children of relatives. Nevertheless this half sentence, taken out of context and not properly referenced together with other remarks in the review upset Martineau as she later reported in her *Autobiography*.[66] A part of her irritation must have been with herself for having provided such an opportunity to be so grossly misrepresented.

Two other important points concern her interpretation of Malthus. First, her adherence to Malthusian basic ideas gave the appearance of being outdated even as she was writing her first tales. She seems either not to have known about or ignored key developments in political economy. Thus, for example, she showed no familiarity with Barton's argument of 1820 that it was a fall in death rate rather than an increase in the birth rate that was responsible for population increase.[67] She also seems to have ignored the fact that Nassau Senior had broken with Malthus over the question of population in 1829. In his *Two Lectures on Population*, Senior argued that the desire of man to improve his position was at least as important as sexual desire, that population tended not to outrun food supplies and that the history of many countries showed this.[68] This omission might have been understandable had she not been a collaborator with Senior on the Poor Law. Secondly, she diverged from Malthus on the question of the reform of the old Poor Law. Malthus remained an abolitionist (at least in private) while Martineau supported reform, and she also differed with Malthus over the reform of the Corn Laws. However, she remained a convinced exponent of Malthusian ideas, arguing in *The Moral of Many Fables* in 1834:

> ... owing to the inequality of soils (the ultimate capital of society), the natural tendency of capital is to Yield a perpetually diminishing return; – and that the consumers of capital increase at a perpetually accelerated rate.[69]

This continued allegiance to Malthusian ideas on the basic population principle and the criticism it thus attracted overshadowed her differences with Malthus and may at times have obscured the debt she owed to other theorists and writers.

Despite this she caught the public's imagination and her stories continued to sell well into the 1840s. The timing may have played an important role in her success. *The Spectator* pointed out ten years after the publication of the *Illustrations* that the series might not have met with the same success had it appeared a decade later.[70] The early 1830s were a turbulent time, with economic and social conflict over the impact of machinery, debates over reform and the Poor Laws, with informal education viewed as a means of informing and disseminating public awareness. In this context it may be that the older Smithian views on the immutability of economic laws and his emphasis on harmony were what most attracted and reassured Martineau's middle-class readers. Malthusian pessimism attracted criticism but Martineau was more optimistic than Malthus about the future. While he expected improved conditions if prudent restraint was exercised, he was never an enthusiastic advocate of human progress and harmony. Martineau claimed that prodigious advance had already been made, for example, in *The Moral of Many Fables* when discussing her 'fifth stage'. Martineau heralded English artisans as making the most progress:

> . . . have made a vast approach towards being employed according to their capacities, and rewarded according to their worths, – that is, towards participating in the most perfect conceivable condition of society.[71]

She argued that since we cannot predict when improvements in society will occur, we must stick to principles. Significantly, in the last sentence of the *Illustrations*, the principles fittingly and optimistically declared are of Necessarianism and Utilitarianism:

> . . . therefore shall the heaven-born spirit be trusted while revealing and announcing at once the means and the end – the employment of all powers and all materials, the natural recompense of all action, and the consequent accomplishment of the happiness of the greatest number, if not all.[72]

Notes

1 Mark Blaug, *Ricardian Economics: A Historical Study* (New Haven: Yale University Press, 1958), pp. 129–39.
2 See, for example, J. R. Shackleton, 'Jane Marcet and Harriet Martineau: Pioneers of Economics Education,' *History of Education* 19 (1990), pp. 283–97; Willie Henderson, *Economics as Literature* (London: Routledge, 1995), pp. 63–90; James P. Huzel, *The Popularization of Malthus in Early Nineteenth Century England: Martineau, Cobbett and the Pauper Press* (London: Routledge, 1995), pp. 55–104; Bette Polkinghorn and Dorothy Lampen Thomson, *Adam Smith's Daughters* (Cheltenham: Edward Elgar,1998), pp. 14–29; Claudia Oražem, *Political Economy and Fiction in the Early Works of Harriet Martineau* (Frankfurt am Main: Peter Lang, 1999); John Vint, *Capital and Wages* (Aldershot: Edward Elgar, 1994), pp. 137–42.
3 Harriet Martineau, *Illustrations of Political Economy* (9 vols., London: Charles Fox, 1832–4); *Poor Laws and Paupers Illustrated* (2vols, London: Charles Fox, 1833–4).
4 Mill, *Elements*, pp. iii–iv.
5 Martineau, *Illustrations*, 1, p. xiv.
6 David Ricardo, *Principles of Political Economy*, 1817, Vol. I of *The Works and Correspondence of David Ricardo* (Cambridge: Cambridge University Press, 1951).

7 Harriet Martineau, *Autobiography* (London: Chapman, Smith and Elder, 1877), p. 169.
8 Jane Marcet, *Conversations on Political Economy, in Which the Elements of That Science Are Familiarly Explained* (London: Longman, Hurst, Rees, Orme and Brown, 1816).
9 Martineau, *Illustrations*, No. IV, *Demerara*; No. IX, *Ireland*.
10 Martineau, *Illustrations*, No. XXV, *The Moral of Many Fables*.
11 *The Moral of Many Fables*, p. vii.
12 Adam Smith, *An Inquiry into the Nature and Causes of the Wealth of Nations*, 1776, edited by R.H. Campbell and A.S. Skinner; Vol. II of *The Glasgow Edition of the Works and Correspondence of Adam Smith* (Oxford: Oxford University Press, 1976).
13 Martineau, *Illustrations*, No. II, *The Hill and the Valley*, No. VII, *A Manchester Strike*.
14 Martineau, *Illustrations*, No. I, *Life in the Wilds*. See also Ella Dzelzainis and Cora Kaplan (eds.), *Harriet Martineau: Authorship, Society and Empire* (Manchester: Manchester University Press, 2010), pp. 121–3.
15 *The Moral of Many Sentiments*, p. 140.
16 John Stuart Mill, *Principles of Political Economy*, Volume III, of *Collected Works*, edited by J. M. Robson (Toronto: University of Toronto Press, 1965), pp. 753–7, p. 756.
17 Donald Winch, *The Intellectual History of Political Economy in Britain, 1750–1834* (Cambridge: Cambridge University Press, 1996), pp. 194–5.
18 *Life in the Wilds*, pp. 22–23.
19 Martineau, *Life in the Wilds*, pp. 80–83.
20 Blaug, *Ricardian Economics*, p. 138.
21 John Stuart Mill, *Collected Works*, volume XII, p. 152.
22 Blaug, *Ricardian Economics*, p. 138.
23 *Life in the Wilds*, pp. 92–93.
24 Martineau, *Illustrations*, No. XXI, *A Tale of the Tyne*.
25 *A Tale of the Tyne*, pp. 134–5.
26 Martineau, *Illustrations*. No XXIII, *The Three Ages*, p. 97.
27 Thomas Robert Malthus, *An Essay on the Principle of Population; or a View of Its Past and Present Effects on Human Happiness; With an Inquiry into Our Prospects Respecting the Future Removal or Mitigation of the Evils Which It Occasions*, Variorum edition of the edition published in 1803 with the variora of 1806, 1807, 1817 and 1826; edited by Patricia James, in two volumes (Cambridge: Cambridge University Press, 1989).
28 Robert K. Webb, *Harriet Martineau: A Radical Victorian* (London: Heinemann, 1960), p. 116.
29 Harriet Martineau, *Illustrations*, No. XI, *For Each and For All*, p. 38.
30 For example, she argued in *Ireland* (tale No. IX) 'the only method by which the permanent prosperity of the people could be secured was the general diffusion of such knowledge as would make them judges' (p. 116).
31 Martineau, *Illustrations*, No. VI, *Weal and Woe in Garveloch*.
32 *Weal and Woe in Garveloch*, p. 97.
33 *Weal and Woe in Garveloch*, p. 140.
34 See, for example, George Poulett Scrope, John Wilson Croker and John Gibson Lockhart, 'Miss Martineau's Monthly Novels,' *Quarterly Review*, 49 (April 1833), p. 151.
35 Martineau, *Illustrations*, No. VIII, *Cousin Marshall*.
36 An Act of 1795 allowed parishes to order outdoor relief and a further Act of 1796 excluded able-bodied labourers from all workhouses. See Anthony Brundage, *The English Poor Laws, 1700–1930* (Basingstoke: Palgrave Macmillan, 2002), pp. 21–27.
37 Samuel Finer, *The Life and Times of Sir Edwin Chadwick* (London: Methuen, 1952), p. 42. Finer argues that the poor rate had increased from £1.5 million in 1775 to £8 million in 1818 and was still £7 million in 1832 despite a fall by a third in the price of bread.

38 *Cousin Marshall*, pp. 40–46 and 82–90.
39 Malthus, 2nd edition of the *Essay on the Principle of Population*, 1803.
40 *Cousin Marshall*, p. 119. Malthus wrote: 'To this end, I should propose a regulation to be made, declaring, that no child born from any marriage, taking place after the expiration of a year from the date of the law, and no illegitimate child born two years from the same date, should ever be entitled to parish assistance' (Malthus, *Principle*, pp. 337–338).
41 *Cousin Marshall*, pp. 131–2.
42 The four tales were *The Parish, The Hamlets, The Town* and *The Land's End.*
43 See Robert K. Webb, *The British Working Class Reader 1790–1848* (London: Allen and Unwin, 1955), pp. 66–73, 85–93 and 114–27.
44 *Report from His Majesty's Commissioners for Inquiring into the Administration and Practical Operation of the Poor Laws* (London: H.M. Stationery Office, 1834), p. 228.
45 See Maxine Berg, *The Machinery Question and the Making of Political Economy 1815–1848* (Cambridge: Cambridge University Press, 1980), pp. 102–106.
46 *The Hill and the Valley*, p. 39.
47 *The Hill and the Valley*, pp. 132–3.
48 *The Hill and the Valley*, p. 140.
49 John Ramsay McCulloch, *Principles of Political Economy* (London: Ward, Lock and Co, 1825), p. 174. See also John Vint, *Capital and Wages: A Lakatosian History of the Wages Fund Doctrine* (Aldershot: Edward Elgar, 1994), pp. 82–88.
50 *A Manchester Strike*, pp. 97–98.
51 *A Manchester Strike*, p. 104.
52 *A Manchester Strike*, p. 56.
53 Martineau, *For Each and For All*, pp. 70–86.
54 Blaug, *Ricardian Economics*, pp. 143–4.
55 Martineau, *Illustrations*, No. XIX, *Sowers Not Reapers.*
56 *Sowers Not Reapers*, p. 88.
57 Martineau, *Illustrations*, No. XII, *French Wine and Politics*, p. 145.
58 See Robert K. Webb, *Harriet Martineau*, pp. 120–2.
59 William Empson, 'Mrs Marcet-Miss Martineau,' *Edinburgh Review*, 57 (April 1833), p. 2.
60 [John Stuart Mill], 'On Miss Martineau's Summary of Political Economy,' *The Monthly Repository* 8 (May 1834), p. 321.
61 See Noel W. Thompson, *The People's Science: The Popular Political Economy of Exploitation and Crisis* (Cambridge: Cambridge University Press 1984), pp. 24–25.
62 Quoted in Deborah Anna Logan, *Illustrations of Political Economy: Selected Tales Harriet Martineau* (Plymouth: Broadview Press, 2004), pp. 38–39.
63 'Miss Martineau's Monthly Novels,' p. 151.
64 Ibid. Scrope et al. fail to provide a reference for this passage.
65 *Cousin Marshall*, p. 131.
66 Martineau, *Autobiography*, ed. Linda Peterson (Peterborough, ON: Broadview Press, 2007) pp. 166–71.
67 John Barton, *An Inquiry into the Causes of the Progressive Depreciation of Agricultural Labour in Modern Times* (London: J. and A. Arch, 1820).
68 Nassau Senior, *Two Lectures on Population* (London: John Murray, 1829), pp. 26–36.
69 *The Moral of Many Fables*, p. 33.
70 Webb, *Harriet Martineau*, p. 124.
71 *The Moral of Many Fables*, pp. 142–3.
72 *The Moral of Many Fables*, p. 144.

4   Harriet Martineau

The founding and re-founding of sociology

Michael R. Hill

Harriet Martineau was not only one of the earliest and most significant founders of the discipline of sociology, but she remains today a potent source for a
much-needed conceptual and professional re-founding of the discipline. Biblio-
graphically speaking, there is little need to repeat the introductory details of Martineau's remarkable life and accomplishments as relevant outlines of Martineau's
biography are now easily available to sociologists and other social scientists.[1]
Further, Martineau's life has been (and continues to be) usefully explored, often
in considerable depth, by our colleagues in the humanities.[2] Suffice to say that
well before the appearance of university textbooks, college courses on sociology,
and the formation of professional sociological organizations, Harriet Martineau
gave 'sociology' widespread currency in English-speaking households through
her ground-breaking translation in 1853 of Auguste Comte's *Cours de philosophie positive*. Beyond this, she also produced a superb and still highly relevant
systematic treatise, *How to Observe Morals and Manners*, the first of its kind,
detailing the procedural and theoretical intricacies of sociological observation
and data collection. She conducted model sociological field studies in the United
States, the Middle East, Ireland, and England. In all, Martineau was a remarkable
interdisciplinarian who tackled – with integrity, perspicacity, and aplomb – an
astonishing range of sociological subject matter from the micro to the macro, from
the details of farming and domestic work, prisons, illness, abolition, education,
and the status of women, to manufacturing, international politics, and war. An
immediate appreciation of the exceptionally wide reach of Martineau's theoretical, methodological, and empirical grasp is provided by the several compilations
of her representative shorter writings.[3]

  Sociologists today, I shall argue, have much to gain by attending to Harriet
Martineau's life and work as we continue to wrestle with many of the same theoretical, methodological, substantive, and professional issues that exemplified her
founding contributions to the discipline of sociology. In sum, Martineau was a
thoughtful theorist, an astute methodologist, a peripatetic empiricist, and a con-
sequential social critic. Her published writings – much like those of subsequent
American sociologists Jane Addams and Charlotte Perkins Gilman[4] – were accessible to large, literate, and responsive (if not always appreciative) publics. Were
she publishing today and teaching at an elite university, Martineau would presumably be lauded as an exemplary 'public sociologist'[5] of the highest order.

Politics and translation

Comprehending the place of Harriet Martineau among the work of sociologists past, present, and future is no small or straightforward task. It is important to recognize that Martineau's intellectual development and increasing sophistication continued apace throughout her lifetime. Understanding any one of her many works depends in part on knowing where she was then located on the trajectory of her epistemological journey. Put more formally, the 'epitheoretical'[6] or 'metatheoretical'[7] connections – especially in Martineau's case – between 'theory'[8] and 'biography'[9] are dynamic, multi-faceted, and multi-valent, as we have seen in Lesa Scholl's chapter. My provisional periodization[10] is provided elsewhere.[11]

Although Martineau is most widely known in sociology as Comte's translator, that project was by no means her first or most important foundational contribution to sociology. Chronologically, Martineau's *The Positive Philosophy of Auguste Comte* (1853), a translation and condensation of Comte's *Cours de philosophie positive* (1830–42), came relatively late in her intellectual career. It was preceded by several significant sociological works, including *Illustrations of Political Economy* (1832–1834), *Poor Laws and Paupers Illustrated* (1833–34), *Illustrations of Taxation* (1833–34), *Miscellanies* (1836), *Society in America* (1837), *Retrospect of Western Travel* (1838), *How to Observe Morals and Manners* (1838), *Life in the Sick-Room* (1844), *Forest and Game-Law Tales* (1845–46), *Letters on Mesmerism* (1845), *Eastern Life, Present and Past* (1848), *Household Education* (1849), *Letters on the Laws of Man's Nature and Development* (1851), and *Letters from Ireland* (1852), as well as her two sociologically instructive major novels, *Deerbrook* (1839) and *The Hour and the Man* (1841). Her major post-*Positive Philosophy* works are *England and Her Soldiers* (1859) and *Health, Husbandry, and Handicraft* (1861). In sum, Martineau's detailed bibliographical record, including her massive correspondence and periodical work, therefore presents an enormous corpus of sociologically astute inquiry, imagination, reflection, discovery, and critique.[12] It is sobering that until very recently Martineau was perfunctorily cited by sociologists *merely* as Comte's translator.

Martineau's intellectual credentials as a translator – when evaluated by mainstream male sociologists during the twentieth century – would have been more positively valorized had she been a man. Several male sociologists have garnered wide professional acclaim by translating acknowledged foundational figures such as Émile Durkheim, Max Weber, Karl Marx, and Georg Simmel. And it is through those translations (which became assigned readings in courses taught by the translators and their myriad protégés) that Durkheim, Weber, Marx, and Simmel became championed and canonized within English-speaking sociological circles. Martineau, in contrast, was relegated to footnotes as Comte's presumably passive amanuensis. Overall, translation by men is viewed within sociology as an important scholarly endeavor and a sign of true erudition, whereas translation by women is too often deemed little more than secretarial transcription. The exclusion of pioneering women's writings from the traditional, male-dominated disciplinary canon of sociology is well documented.[13] Comte, meanwhile, has been guaranteed an essentially permanent, foundational place in sociological literature as the savant who coined the term 'sociology,'[14] despite the largely irrelevant utility of his theoretical ideas today.

Nonetheless, the scholarly translation of founding works is unquestionably a meritorious disciplinary contribution, as exemplified by the influential works of Talcott Parsons, C. Wright Mills, Hans Gerth, Tom Bottomore, Donald Levine, Kurt H. Wolff, Don Martindale, Guy Oakes, and George Simpson, among others. So too, in an equitable world, should Martineau's translation of Comte be recognized in similar terms.[15] Lesa Scholl observes that Martineau translated Comte with unmistakable authority and manipulated Comte's text in ways that emphasized topics reflecting her own interests.[16] Martineau thereby actively shaped the collective understanding of Comte's ideas among English speakers.[17] The translator is integral to all translations that move beyond autonomic transliteration *à la* Google. Martineau, as engaged translator and perspicacious condenser, became the transforming lens through which the English-speaking world was introduced to sociology as an intellectual project, and her work is still a significant English-language translation of Comte's *Cours*.

Availability of the canon and its disciplinary impact in sociology

Beyond her translation of Comte, Martineau was a prolific and astute sociological writer in her own stead. Sociologists today have no viable excuse for pointing to the relative unavailability of Martineau's works as a reason for being unacquainted with her major writings. Whereas the obscurity argument had understandable traction in the 1980s[18] it is no longer cogent. Martineau's nineteenth-century books, once found primarily in the domains of rare book collections and on the shelves of elite libraries, are now just a digital search away, with most available as PDF downloads free of charge.[19] In addition, a variety of new print editions and collections have been published recently. So, the basic Martineau canon is now easily to hand.

As a group, modern sociologists – at least in North America – have been slow in delving into the vast body of Martineau's foundational work. The first American sociologist to take Martineau seriously was Nebraska-born Edith Abbott[20] in 1906,[21] followed somewhat later by social worker Helen Bonser in 1929.[22] Seymour Martin Lipset's appreciative introduction[23] to his abridgement of *Society in America* in 1962 was an important (and for many years the only) extended statement on Martineau by a male sociologist. Alice Rossi,[24] the president of the American Sociological Association in 1983, identified Martineau as 'the first woman sociologist' in 1973.[25] British sociologist Dale Spender included Martineau in her survey of *Women of Ideas and What Men Have Done to Them* in 1981.[26] In a pedagogical journal published by the American Sociological Association, James Terry made a case in 1983 for including Martineau in classroom introductions to sociology.[27] I took considerable pride in offering the sesquicentennial edition of Martineau's methodological treatise, *How to Observe Morals and Manners*, together with a 45-page introduction, annotations to Martineau's footnotes, and an analytical index, in 1989.

From the 1990s to the present, sociological interest in Martineau has increased. Mary Jo Deegan observed in her introduction to *Women in Sociology* that:

> She [Martineau] is one of the major founders of sociology as a legitimated area of study. Her preeminence in this regard is equal to, if not greater than, that of any man in her era, including the relatively overpraised Comte and de Tocqueville. . . . Martineau is a giant in sociology.[28]

Susan Hoecker-Drysdale, a contributor to this volume, published a book-length sociological biography, *Harriet Martineau: First Woman Sociologist*, in 1992. From the early 1990s onward, Canadian sociologist Lynn McDonald included Martineau in her surveys of the origins and founding of the social sciences,[29] and as we have seen in the Introduction, the inaugural working seminar of the informally organized Harriet Martineau Sociological Society convened on Mackinac Island, Michigan, in 1997.[30] Pat Lengermann and Jill Niebrugge-Brantley made Martineau central to their widely cited 1998 text/reader on the women founders.[31]

At the turn of the twenty-first century, Joe Feagan, in his 2000 presidential address to the American Sociological Association,[32] made a strong plea for sociologists to pay attention to Martineau, Jane Addams, W.E.B. Dubois and other early sociologists, and to recognize their frequent *superiority* over many of the more commonly cited white male sociologists such as de Tocqueville. In concert with Feagan's appeal, *Harriet Martineau: Theoretical and Methodological Perspectives* appeared in 2001, based largely on papers presented during the 1997 Mackinac seminar. The subsequent activities and substantive work completed by the small group of scholars in the Harriet Martineau Sociological Society have been reported variously by myself and Deborah Logan,[33] and need not be repeated here. To summarize, a few sociologists are actively explicating Martineau's foundational ideas, but the overall impact on the discipline as a whole has been relatively superficial (as John Vint and Keiko Funaki have similarly noted in Chapter 3 in relation to Martineau's impact on economic theory, despite the popularity of her *Illustrations of Political Economy*). Beginning with the late 1990s, Martineau is increasingly cited in introductory textbooks as a foundational figure,[34] but rarely do sociologists make substantive use of her ideas and insights in the same way they routinely employ those of Tocqueville, Durkheim, or Weber. Indeed, the foundational patriarchal mechanisms[35] that obscured Martineau's sociological contributions in the first place now seem resurgent and as virulent and widespread as ever.[36] The perspectival gulf dividing privileged, status quo mainstream patriarchal visions of the discipline, on the one hand, and more inclusive, critical perspectives, on the other, is sharply illustrated by comparing the tone and content of two volumes prepared to commemorate the centennial of the American Sociological Association (ASA). Craig Calhoun's volume (published by the University of Chicago Press with a subvention from the ASA) generally represents 'business as usual' whereas Tony Blasi's work is an exemplary study in inclusive challenges to the standard, entrenched views of establishment sociology.[37] Blasi's volume was published without ASA financial assistance but with the full endorsement of the membership of the ASA Section on the History of Sociology, many of whom were then active participants in the Harriet Martineau Sociological Society. That the disciplinary history of sociology comprises a contested intellectual terrain is well illustrated by the differences in these two books, differences that include not only gender but also race, class, language, geography, and theoretical assumptions.

Methodological foundations

The most foundational – and still most relevant – of Martineau's works is her pioneering explication of sociological methods. Well before Émile Durkheim's exposition of 1895,[38] Martineau set forth the principles for systematic collection and interpretation of social facts in *How to Observe Morals and Manners* (1838). From a purely foundational perspective, Martineau was far superior. As Shulamit Reinharz puts it, Martineau's methodological treatise predates Durkheim's 'by sixty years and is nearly analogous.'[39] Moreover, Martineau's account is far more accessible for novice observers, even today. She cast her insights as straightforward advice to persons who travelled to other countries and who then wished to write about their observations.

For Martineau, facts about things, carefully recorded in journals and notebooks, form an inventory of the *manners* or patterned social relationships in a society. The discovery of manners, however, is never the primary objective of responsible observers. She wrote: 'A traveller who should report of them [manners] exclusively is not only no philosopher, but does not merit the name of an observer.'[40]

Thus, manners are merely *surface*, nothing more than manifestations of the deeper morals of a society.

Martineau directed us to identify the condition and scope of the moral underpinnings of the societies we study. This requires considerable moral preparation of our own. Only then can we properly interpret the results of our observations:

> To him, and to him only, who has studied the principles of morals, and thus possessed himself of a key to the mysteries of all social weal and wo [sic], will manners be an index answering as faithfully to the internal movements, harmonious or discordant, of society, as the human countenance to the workings of the human heart.[41]

Here, Martineau set out her version of the 'correspondence problem'[42] that plagues empirical research purporting to amplify our understanding of unobservable, theoretical entities. For Martineau, morals – the inner workings of the human heart – were her unobservable, theoretical entities. Manners – the empirical traces of institutional activity – were her observables, surface indices to interior morals.

Martineau advised researchers to concentrate on *things*, by which she meant physical artifacts, official records, and other traces of institutionalized behaviour and social organization. 'The grand secret of wise inquiry into Morals and Manners,' she wrote, 'is to begin with the study of THINGS, using the DISCOURSE OF PERSONS as a commentary upon them.'[43] Interviews, conversations, and informants have secondary importance at best: 'To arrive at the facts of the condition of a people through the discourse of individuals, is a hopeless enterprise.'[44]

Her emphasis on the importance of 'things' was keenly expressed in this key passage:

> Though the facts sought by travellers relate to Persons, they may most readily be learned from Things. The eloquence of Institutions and Records, in which the action of the nation is embodied and perpetuated, is more comprehensive and more faithful than that of any variety of individual voices. The voice of a whole people goes up in the silent workings of an institution; the condition of the masses is reflected from the surface of a record. The Institutions of a nation – political, religious or social – put evidence into the observer's hands as to its capabilities and wants, which the study of individuals could not yield in the course of a lifetime. The records of any society, be they what they may, whether architectural remains, epitaphs, civic registers, national music, or any other of the thousand manifestations of the common mind which may be found among every people, afford more information on Morals in a day than converse with individuals in a year.[45]

Conversations with the inhabitants of a society under investigation, she advised, are primarily useful for corroborating and explicating observed facts about things.

To assess the moral state of a society, each observer must attend carefully to empirical instances of manners. When observable, representative facts have been systematically collected; only then is it appropriate to make *generalizations* about morals. Martineau astutely perceived that this is no simple, mechanical process. To responsibly interpret the facts, the observer must, among other things: (1) understand the universal principles of morals (i.e., must possess a comprehensive axiological epistemology), (2) be of a sufficiently liberal mind not to be unsympathetic to societies whose superficial manners differ from one's own, and (3) be a person who seeks a moral life. How, she asked, can a scoundrel or a degenerate ever recognize the higher moral qualities potentially present in any society?

Human happiness, according to Martineau, is a universal moral good which can be achieved in a variety of ways in various societies. She posited axiomatically that it is everywhere considered desirable to give and increase happiness. Metaphysically, Martineau was no teleologist at this point, but she did view the Creator as everywhere *intending* human happiness. The fundamental principle is a universal (happiness), but the means for achieving it must be judged relative to each society. All manners are to be interpreted in context in light of the universal moral principle. She warns novice observers that the same act may be moral in one society while totally reprehensible elsewhere. One cannot use the accepted manners of one's own society as a key to the moral basis of manners in another. Ethnocentrism (a term Martineau would have used had it been coined in her day) is a dangerous peril to those who observe and would thereby understand other cultures firsthand. The observer – she reminds us – must guard continually against making hasty and unsympathetic generalizations.

Because Martineau set herself the task of assessing the moral state of societies as wholes, and because this assessment depends crucially on empirically derived facts (albeit interpreted in the light of universal principles), the quality of the observational data becomes extraordinarily important if one hopes to avoid errors of judgment.

Martineau emphasized this point repeatedly. Observations must be representative. Bias must be avoided. All institutionalized patterns must be observed in all quarters, in all classes, in all regions. Observers must not be swayed by vested interests and yet – at the same time – they must remain open to the opinions and insights of the very best minds in each society, a tricky task even for seasoned investigators.

How to Observe Morals and Manners distills Martineau's maxims, insights, and guidelines for juggling the reciprocal interrelationships between theoretical presuppositions, empirical data collection, and the process of making generalizations about unobservable social phenomena. Here are the careful instructions needed by the band of social observers that Rousseau wanted to send to all comers of the globe. Had such travellers – and there were many – who did write about their travels heeded Martineau's advice, perhaps sociologist Anthony Giddens would not have found so many of their reports untrustworthy.[46]

Martineau addressed her remarks to would-be travellers to foreign lands, but the preface to de la Beche's volume in the 'How to Observe' series states clearly that the works are intended for students and scientists as well. Martineau's use of the 'stranger in a strange land' is the first of many resorts to this imagery by sociologists, including the classic essays by Georg Simmel (1908)[47] and Alfred Schutz (1944).[48] More recent theorists also adopt the 'stranger's' perspective, including J.B. Jackson,[49] Dean MacCannel,[50] Hill and Deegan,[51] and the postmodernist Zygmunt Bauman.[52] Martineau's methodological recommendations are those of a sophisticated social theoretician who well understood two crucial principles: (1) that all observers – no matter how careful – can make mistakes, be hoodwinked, and fall prey to their own presuppositions, and (2) that as humans we are always choosing, rearranging, and giving new possibilities to the social worlds we inhabit.

The possibility of social change lies at the heart of Martineau's concept of 'progress.' She exhorted us to evaluate scientifically the potential of each society for moral advancement. Each observer, she wrote, should attend to 'whether the country he studies is advancing in wisdom and happiness, or whether it is stationary, or whether it is going back. The probabilities of its progress are wholly dependent on this'.[53]

Martineau considered environmental factors that might influence moral progress, but the greatest force for progress is deeply social: 'The need of mutual aid, the habit of co-operation caused by interest in social objects, has a good effect upon men's feelings and manners toward each other; and out of this grows the mutual regard which naturally strengthens into the fraternal spirit.'[54]

According to this view, the members of moral and progressive societies carefully tend their mutual interests, forming nations which likewise cooperate. Martineau posited no necessary teleological basis for social and international cooperation, yet she anticipated that true fraternity may one day be realized throughout the world. She was unquestionably an optimist. Progress is possible, desirable, even lawful, but not teleologically necessary. The potential for progress – as well as regression – lies within each society. Whether progress blooms or not depends in large measure on the moral character of the social institutions that its members devise and nurture.

The scientific observer examines the moral state of society, assesses its potential for moral progress, and – where possible – encourages those practices and values conducive to the social recognition of mutual interest. Clear thinking, reliable research, and universal education are fundamental to this process. Here, Martineau's purpose as an observer – and in teaching us how to observe – reveals itself. As writer, observer, and sociologist, Martineau pursued a life of scholarship, social action, and the diffusion of knowledge to persons in all social classes and every economic condition. By teaching us 'how to observe,' Martineau expanded our ability to recognize our mutual potential for cooperation and moral progress.

Field studies

Martineau applied her methodological acumen in the field to major sociological studies of the United States,[55] the Middle East,[56] Ireland,[57] and the English Lake District.[58] As historical documents, they are informative gems and might remain of interest primarily to comparative-historical sociologists were it not for the fact that a male competitor's treatise, Alexis de Tocqueville's *Democracy in America* (18355–1840), is so often and so emphatically touted as the definitive study of nineteenth-century America. As it turns out, *Martineau's Society in America* (1837) and *Retrospect of Western Travel* (1838) are more methodologically sound and are thus considerably more trustworthy.[59] For example, the contrast between Martineau's inclusive interviews and Tocqueville's elitist strategy is especially striking in their respective investigations of prison conditions in the United States.

Beaumont and Tocqueville studied prison conditions in the US. and co-authored a monograph on the topic,[60] but Tocqueville talked only to wardens and overseers, never to prisoners. Martineau also visited American prisons, but took specific steps to interview prisoners in private – in their cells without guards present.[61] Although Martineau emphasized discourse as a commentary on observable social patterns, she clearly understood – in ways that Tocqueville apparently could not imagine – the importance of talking to inmates as well as wardens if one wanted to understand the character of the fledgling U.S. prison system.

Martineau's access to women and domestic scenes stands in sharp contrast to Tocqueville's disputations with elite males. 'I am sure,' she wrote:

> I have seen much more of domestic life than could possibly have been exhibited to any gentleman travelling through the country. The nursery, the boudoir,

the kitchen, are all excellent schools in which to learn the morals and manners of a people: and, as for public and professional affairs, – those may always gain full information upon such matters, who really feel an interest in them, – be they men or women.[62]

Wherever she turned, Martineau provided insightful, foundational guidance and solid exemplars for the conduct of sociological investigations, ranging from the pure theory of *The Moral of Many Fables*,[63] to the theory-framed structural analyses of her direct observations in *Society in America*, to the phenomenologically driven perspective of *Retrospect of Western Travel*, all the way to the personal, experientially informed explorations[64] characterizing such works as *Life in the Sick-Room*[65] and *Eastern Life, Present and Past*.

Martineau and the future of sociology

The history, sophistication, and creativity of Martineau's work and ideas are dramatic, engaging, and impressive by all yardsticks used to identify and canonize disciplinary founders. Moreover, Martineau provides solid points of departure for re-founding sociological practice today. As a discipline, sociology is beset with significant institutional conundrums and intellectual contradictions. Taken full force, Martineau's engagement with the ethics, goals and methodologies of social inquiry provides a vibrant model on which to re-found contemporary sociological practice.

Disciplinary critique, from a variety of perspectives, has a venerable history in sociology, exemplified by Thorstein Veblen,[66] Alvin Gouldner,[67] Alfred McClung Lee,[68] David and Judith Willer,[69] Anthony Giddens,[70] and Joe Feagan,[71] among others. With the passage of time, the core moral and methodological problems identified by these critics have intensified, not lessened. That these issues have been neither widely addressed nor practically resolved, at least in the United States, is directly related to the structure, governance, and financing of higher education in all its guises. The hypermodern university – the institutional locale within which the bulk of organized professional sociology today resides – is, at a minimum, a complex, challenging, and ever-changing milieu within which to be a sociologist. Which brings us back to Martineau.

Harriet Martineau was not an entrenched university academic. As a model of sociological practice, Martineau created her own niche *outside* academia. She presents a decidedly different, alternative way of *doing* sociology. This was not always an easy path,[72] but it is safely said that her impact on the larger society in which she lived far outstripped the societal influence of many academic sociologists today. If we take Martineau to heart, then she challenges – in profound ways – our individual decisions to become academics. For novice sociologists-in-training, Martineau (as do Jane Addams, Charlotte Perkins Gilman, and others) provides a concrete, lived alternative to the pervasively ineffective, predominantly hamstrung intellectualism of academic sociology. If the current generation of professorial scholars (and I necessarily include myself here) has squandered the promise of sociology as a social project, then we have the obligation to acquaint our students with alternative models of how to *become* sociologists, and Martineau tops my list of proffered exemplars. Martineau – as model – exemplified solutions to several issues central to the reformation of sociological inquiry, inside or outside academia, two of which I now discuss.[73]

The first important matter is professional ethics. Martineau asserted, 'An observer, to be perfectly accurate, should be himself perfect. Every prejudice, every moral perversion, dims or distorts whatever the eye looks upon.'[74] Thus, moral rascals and 'players' who do 'whatever it takes' to secure tenure, promotion, or lucrative grants, *cannot* produce trustworthy observations.

Strict adherence to 'scientific method' is presumed by many researchers to guarantee 'objectivity' and, simultaneously, provide an effective prophylactic against the tainting of sociological inquiries by deficiencies in the personal morals of investigators. At best, this highly questionable assumption reduces investigators to unthinking automatons who presumably defer unerringly to formal rules of logic and who mechanically conduct wholly unbiased measurements and observations. This leaves open not only the morality of accepting such assumptions in the first place, but also ignores the moral aspects of framing any given research project (That is: Why this inquiry and not another? In whose real interest is the research actually conducted? What is the moral status of the premises from which the hypotheses to be tested are derived, and so on?) Further, it is all too easy in the social sciences to commit fraud, 'cook' data, disregard inconvenient findings, and otherwise camouflage multiple forms of academic dishonesty.

Complicating the ethics situation in sociology today is the bureaucratic rise of institutional review boards (IRBs), which, in the United States, must review and approve *every* research proposal before it can proceed. Similar systems exist in other countries. A key provision is that 'informed consent' must be obtained from every human subject who is to be interviewed, observed, sent questionnaires, or otherwise employed as a source of information. This makes undisclosed participant observation, long a staple of sociological investigation, nearly impossible, particularly when those to be observed are gatekeepers or members of privileged elites. The result is that academic sociologists have largely been stripped of the ability to document the 'backstage' activities of the power elite, leaving sociologists bereft of genuine, firsthand understanding of how power works. Instead, sociological investigations focus most often on the downtrodden, defenseless, and oppressed populations, to which institutional gatekeepers routinely grant access. In contrast, Martineau's societal investigations successfully drew information from all levels of society, and she adamantly protected the identities of her sources, all without restrictive IRB supervision. If the road to well-intended outcomes is sometimes paved with egregious unintended consequences, the rise of institutional review boards is a classic example. For the result – the removal of the power elite from the direct, unannounced purview of sociological investigation – is itself unethical.

The second matter noted here is the present over-reliance by sociologists on survey questionnaires as their primary data source. On this point Martineau was *very* clear and bears repeating:

> The grand secret of wise inquiry into Morals and Manners,' she wrote, 'is to begin with the study of THINGS, using the DISCOURSE OF PERSONS as a commentary upon them.'[75] Interviews, conversations, and informants have secondary importance at best: 'To arrive at the facts of the condition of a people through the discourse of individuals, is a hopeless enterprise.[76]

Yet the 'discourse of individuals,' obtained primarily through the administration of survey questionnaires, is the dominant mode of sociological research today. The methodological deficiencies of survey research are obvious and well documented,[77] but monies to conduct them keep flowing in. Further, survey research is undoubtedly one of the easiest methodologies for which to obtain IRB approval. If, however, Martineau were taken seriously, the whole methodological enterprise of sociology today would be turned on its head and systematic observation and various unobtrusive techniques would come to the fore,[78] in ways that protect the identities and legitimate interests of the people observed.

In sum, there are no bureaucratic guarantees of morality or methodological purity in sociology, but Martineau was correct to identify a high standard of personal rectitude on the part of researchers as a desirable goal to which we all should strive. She was also correct to emphasize that the 'discourse of individuals' is an insufficient source on which to build sociological understanding. The lived reality of Martineau's biography and her astonishing accomplishments also point to the very real possibility of meaningful sociological work outside the academy, as Virginia Woolf phrased it, 'in a room of one's own.'

Martineauian sociology provides a useful basis for responsible disciplinary assessment, reflection, and action. In better understanding the work of Harriet Martineau, we not only celebrate a pioneering founder but also open sociology to more rational reform, greater applied relevance, and future renewal.

Notes

1 See Linda Peterson's edition of the *Autobiography* (Peterborough, ON: Broadview Press, 2007) and Deborah Logan's *The Hour and the Woman* (De Kalb: University of Illinois Press, 2002).

2 For example, the essays in Dzelzainis and Kaplan (2010), and this collection by Lesa Scholl, Alexis Easley, Valerie Sanders, Deborah Logan, Sharon Connor, and John Warren.

3 In particular, see her *Miscellanies*, 2 vols. (Boston: Hilliard, Gray, 1836); *Health, Husbandry, and Handicraft* (London: Bradbury and Evans, 1861); *Harriet Martineau on Women*, ed. Gayle Graham Yates (New Brunswick: Rutgers University, 1985); *Harriet Martineau in the London Daily News*, ed. Elisabeth Arbuckle (New York: Garland, 1994); *Writings on Slavery and the American Civil War*, ed. Deborah Logan (DeKalb: Northern Illinois University, 2002); and *An Independent Woman's Lake District Writings*, ed. Hill Michael (Amherst: Humanity Books, 2004).

4 Mary Jo Deegan, *Jane Addams and the Men of the Chicago School, 1892–1918* (New Brunswick: Transaction, 1988); 'Gilman's Sociological Journey from *Herland* to *Ourland*,' *with Her in Ourland: Sequel to Herland*, by Charlotte Perkins Gilman, ed. Mary Jo Deegan and Michael Hill (Westport: Greenwood, 1997), pp. 1–57.

5 The widely cited definition of 'public sociology' (which lacks any reference to Martineau, Addams, or Gilman) is Michael Burawoy's, 'For Public Sociology,' *American Sociological Review*, 70 (February 2005), pp. 4–28.

6 Werner Leinfellner, 'A New Epitheoretical Analysis of Social Theories.' In: Gerald Eberlein and Werner Leinfellner (eds.), *Developments in the Methodology of Social Science* (Boston: D. Reidel, 1974), pp. 3–43.

7 Gerard Radnitzky, *Contemporary Schools of Metascience*, 3rd ed. (Chicago: Henry Regnery, 1973).

8 Michael R. Hill, 'Epistemology, axiology, and ideology in sociology,' *Mid-American Review of Sociology*, 9:2 (1984), pp. 59–77. 'Theories are content-oriented conceptual frameworks. . . . They are the organizing devices which reveal or assert that selected dimensions of social behavior or experience are related in particular ways' (p. 63).

9 On the potential relevance of biography to sociology, see C. Wright Mills, *The Sociological Imagination* (New York: Oxford, 1959); and Norman K. Denzin, *Interpretive Biography* (Newbury Park: Sage, 1989).

10 As Brian Conway points out, see Eviatar Zerubavel ('Language and Memory: "Pre-Columbian" America and the social logic of periodization,' *Social Research*, 65:2 (1998), pp. 315–30), on the 'perils and possibilities of periodization' (B. Conway, 'Foreigners, faith and fatherland: The historical origins, development and present status of Irish sociology,' *Sociological Origins*, 5:1, special supplement (2006), p. 6).

11 Michael R. Hill, 'Empiricism and Reason,' pp. xxii–lii. In: Michael R. Hill (ed.), *How to Observe Morals and Manners* (New Brunswick, New Jersey: Transaction Books, 1989).

12 See Joseph B. Rivlin, *Harriet Martineau: A Bibliography of Her Separately Printed Books* (New York: New York Public Library, 1947); the appendix in *Harriet Martineau in the London Daily News: Selected Contributions, 1852–1866*, ed. Elisabeth Arbuckle (New York: Garland, 1994); *Writings on Slavery and the American Civil War*, ed. Deborah Anna Logan (DeKalb: Northern Illinois University, 2002); the appendices in *The Collected Letters of Harriet Martineau*, ed. Deborah Anna Logan, 5 vols. (London: Pickering & Chatto, 2007); and *Harriet Martineau: Further Letters*, ed. Deborah Anna Logan (Bethlehem: Lehigh University Press, 2012).

13 See Mary Jo Deegan, 'Early women sociologists and the American sociological society: The patterns of exclusion and participation,' *The American Sociologist*, 16 (February 1981), pp. 14–24; *Jane Addams and the Men of the Chicago School* (1988); *Women in Sociology* (1991); 'Transcending a patriarchal and racist past: African American women in sociology, 1890–1920,' *Sociological Origins*, 2 (2000), pp. 37–54; and 'Textbooks, the history of sociology, and the sociological stock of knowledge,' *Sociological Theory*, 21 (September 2003), pp. 298–305, among many others.

14 Victor V. Branford, 'On the origin and use of the word sociology,' *Sociological Papers*, 1 (1905), pp. 3–24; Mary Pickering, *August Comte: An Intellectual Biography*, vol. 1 (Cambridge: Cambridge University Press, 1993).

15 For one of the first formal appreciations in modern sociological circles of Martineau's translation, see my discussion in the sesquicentennial edition of *How to Observe Morals and Manners* (New Brunswick: Transaction, 1989), pp. xliii–xlvii. For expanded explication, see Susan Hoecker-Drysdale, 'Harriet Martineau and the positivism of Auguste Comte.' In: Michael R. Hill and Susan Hoecker-Drysdale (eds.), *Harriet Martineau: Theoretical and Methodological Perspectives* (New York: Routledge, 2001), pp. 169–89.

16 Lesa Scholl, 'Provocative agendas: Martineau's translation of Comte.' In: Ella Dzelzainis and Cora Kaplan (eds.), *Harriet Martineau: Authorship, Society and*

Empire (Manchester: Manchester University, 2010), pp. 88–99. See also Lesa Scholl, *Translation, Authorship and the Victorian Professional Woman: Charlotte Brontë, Harriet Martineau and George Eliot* (Farnham: Ashgate, 2011).

17 Among French readers who rely on the translation of her abridgement back into French. See *La Philosophie positive d'Auguste Comte, condensee par Miss Harriet Martineau*, trans. Avezac-Lavigne (Bordeaux: Feret et Fils, 1871–72).

18 I was at the time an advanced graduate student enrolled in a methods seminar taught by a self-identified feminist who assigned Tocqueville as an exemplary model of comparative sociology. On hearing about the assignment, Mary Jo's reaction was: "What! Why aren't you reading Martineau?" I immediately repaired to Love Library at the University of Nebraska, found Lipset's edition of *Society in America* and – prompted by Lipset's intriguing footnotes – secured *How to Observe Morals and Manners* via interlibrary loan. This was, for me, a serendipitous, eye-opening, and life-altering chain of events.

19 See, for examples, the websites of Internet Archive (https://archive.org/index.php) and the Hathi Trust (www.hathitrust.org).

20 Mary Jo Deegan and Michael R. Hill, 'Edith Abbott (1876–1957).' In: Mary Jo Deegan (ed.), *Women in Sociology* (New York: Greenwood, 1991), pp. 29–36.

21 Edith Abbott, 'Harriet Martineau and the employment of women in 1836,' *Journal of Political Economy*, 14 (December 1906), pp. 614–26.

22 Helen Bonser, 'Illustrations of political economy: An early example of the case method,' *Social Service Review*, 3 (June 1929), pp. 243–51.

23 Seymour Martin Lipset, 'Harriet Martineau's America.' In: Seymour Martin Lipset (ed.), *Society in America* (Gloucester: Peter Smith, 1968, originally published 1962), pp. 5–42. Apparently oblivious to the disciplinary and patriarchal forces then at work, and to which he was himself party, Lipset blamed Martineau for her own obscurity in the subsequent sociological record (p. 39).

24 Mary Jo Deegan and Michael R. Hill, 'Alice S. Rossi.' In: Mary Jo Deegan (ed.), *Women in Sociology* (New York: Greenwood, 1991), pp. 342–49. Rossi was first president of the American Sociological Association in 1978.

25 Alice S. Rossi, 'The first woman sociologist: Harriet Martineau.' In: Alice S. Rossi (ed.), *The Feminist Papers: From Adams to de Beauvoir* (New York: Bantam, 1973), pp. 118–24.

26 Dale Spender, *Women of Ideas and What Men Have Done to Them* (London: Routledge & Kegan Paul, 1982), pp. 125–35.

27 James L. Terry, 'Bringing women. . . . In: A modest proposal,' *Teaching Sociology*, 10 (1983), pp. 251–61.

28 *Women in Sociology* (1991), pp. 13–14.

29 Lynn McDonald, *The Early Origins of the Social Sciences* (Montreal: McGill-Queens University, 1993); *The Women Founders of the Social Sciences* (Ottawa: Carleton University, 1994); and *Women Theorists on Society and Politics* (Waterloo: Wilfrid Laurier University, 1998).

30 Helena Znaniecka Lopata, 'Introduction.' In: Michael R. Hill and Susan Hoecker-Drysdale (eds.), *Harriet Martineau: Theoretical and Methodological Perspectives* (New York: Routledge, 2001), pp. xiii–xvii.

31 Pat Lengermann and Jill Niebrugge-Brantley, *The Women Founders: Sociology and Social Theory, 1830–1930* (New York: McGraw-Hill, 1998).

32 Joe R. Feagan, 'Social justice and sociology in the 21st century,' *American Sociological Review*, 66 (February 2001), pp. 1–20.

33 Michael R. Hill (ed.), 'Proceedings of the 2002 Harriet Martineau sociological society bicentennial seminar,' *Sociological Origins*, 3:2 (2005), pp. 66–96; Michael R. Hill and Deborah. A. Logan, 'The Harriet Martineau sociological society's fourth international working seminar: A report from the National University of Ireland – Maynooth,' *Sociological Origins*, 5 (Spring 2008), pp. 6–7; and 'The Harriet Martineau sociological

82   *Michael R. Hill*

society's fifth working seminar: A report from Boston college,' *Sociological Origins*, 6 (Spring 2010), pp. 5–7.

34 Michael R. Hill, 'Martineau in current introductory textbooks: An empirical survey,' *The Harriet Martineau Sociological Society Newsletter*, no. 4 (Spring 1998), pp. 4–5.

35 Michael R. Hill, 'Patriarchy.' In: Jodi O'Brien (ed.), *Encyclopedia of Gender and Society* (Los Angeles: Sage, 2009), II, pp. 628–33.

36 See, for example, Richard F. Hamilton, 'American sociology re-writes its history,' *Sociological Theory*, 21 (September 2003), pp. 281–97, and Mary Jo Deegan's critique, 'Textbooks, the history of sociology, and the sociological stock of knowledge,' *Sociological Theory*, 21 (September 2003), pp. 298–305.

37 Craig Calhoun (ed.), *Sociology in America: A History* (Chicago: University of Chicago, published with a subvention from the American Sociological Association (ASA), 2007); Anthony J. Blasi (ed.), *Diverse History of American Sociology* (Leiden: Brill, 2005).

38 Emil Durkheim, *The Rules of Sociological Method*, 8th ed., trans. Sarah A. Solovay and John H. Mueller, ed. Catlin (New York: Free Press, 1938).

39 Shulamit Reinharz, *Feminist Methods in Social Research* (New York: Oxford, 1989), p. 92. There are significant differences between Durkheim and Martineau. Martineau implemented a more inclusive and reflexive approach to inquiry, whereas narrow interpretations of Durkheim's *Rules* have resulted in the stream of 'scientistic' (as opposed to scientific) reports that now fill many sociology journals. An alternative, but often ignored, approach is found in Durkheim's *The Elementary Forms of Religious Life*, trans. Swain (New York: Macmillan, 1915).

40 Martineau, *How to Observe Morals and Manners*, ed. Hill, Michael (New Brunswick: Transaction, 1989), p. 222.

41 Ibid.

42 For standard introductions to problems associated with 'correspondence rules' and the structure of scientific theories, see David Harvey, *Explanation in Geography* (London: Edward Arnold, 1969), pp. 87–99; and Frederick Suppe, *The Structure of Scientific Theories* (Urbana: University of Illinois, 1977).

43 Martineau, *How to Observe*, p. 73.

44 Ibid.

45 Ibid., pp. 74–75.

46 Anthony Giddens, *Sociology: A Brief but Critical Introduction* (San Diego: Harcourt Brace Jovanovich, 1987), pp. 20–21.

47 Georg Simmel, 'The stranger,' *The Sociology of Georg Simmel*, ed. Kurt H. Wolff (New York: Free Press, 1950), pp. 402–8.

48 Alfred Schutz, 'The stranger,' *American Journal of Sociology*, 49 (1944), pp. 499–507.

49 John B. Jackson, 'The stranger's path,' *Landscape*, 7 (1957), pp. 11–15.

50 Dean MacCannell, *The Tourist: A New Theory of the Leisure Class* (New York: Schocken, 1975).

51 Michael R. Hill and Mary Jo Deegan, 'The female tourist in a male landscape,' *CELA Forum*, 1:2 (1982), pp. 25–29.

52 Zygmunt Bauman, 'From pilgrim to tourist: Or a short history of identity.' In: Stuart Hall and Paul du Gay (ed.), *Questions of Cultural Identity* (London: Sage, 1996), pp. 18–36.

53 Martineau, *How to Observe*, pp. 211–2.

54 Ibid., p. 221.

55 Martineau, *Society in America*, 3 vols. (London: Saunders and Otley, 1837); *Retrospect of Western Travel*, 2 vols. (London: Saunders and Otley, 1838). See also: *Studies of America, 1831–1868*, ed. Susan Hoecker-Drysdale (Bristol: Thoemmes Continuum, 2004).

56 Harriet Martineau, *Eastern Life, Present and Past* (Philadelphia: Lea & Blanchard, 1848). See also: Deborah A. Ruigh, 'The Sociology of Harriet Martineau in *Eastern*

Life, Present and Past: The Foundations of the Islamic Sociology of Religion,' Master's thesis (Lincoln: Department of Sociology, University of Nebraska-Lincoln, 2012).

57 Harriet Martineau, *Letters from Ireland* (London: John Chapman, 1852). See also: Brian Conway and M. R. Hill, 'Harriet Martineau and Ireland.' In: Séamas Ó Síocháin (ed.), *Social Thought on Ireland in the Nineteenth Century*(Dublin: University College Dublin, 2009), pp. 47–66.

58 Harriet Martineau, *An Independent Woman's Lake District Writings*, ed. Hill (Amherst: Humanity Books, 2004). See also: Harriet Martineau, *The English Lake District*, 5th ed. (Windermere: J. Gannett, 1876).

59 For amplification and discussion, see Michael R. Hill, 'A Methodological Comparison of Harriet Martineau's *Society in America* (1837) and Alexis de Tocqueville's *Democracy in America* (1835–1840).' In: Michael R. Hill and Susan Hoecker-Drysdale (eds.), *Harriet Martineau: Theoretical and Methodological Perspectives* (New York: Routledge, 2001), pp. 59–74.

60 Gustave de Beaumont and Alexis de Tocqueville, *On the Penitentiary System in the United States, and Its Application in France*, trans. Francis Lieber (Philadelphia: Carey, Lea & Blanchard, 1833).

61 Harriet Martineau, *How to Observe* (1838), pp. 136–9. See also, 'Sufferers,' *Society in America*, II, pp. 281–99; and 'Prisons,' *Retrospect of Western Travel*, I, pp. 199–227.

62 Martineau, *Society in America* (1837), I, p. xii.

63 Harriet Martineau, *The Moral of Many Fables* (London: Charles Fox, 1834). Vol. 25 in Martineau's *Illustrations of Political Economy*.

64 For experiential sociology, see Shulamit Reinharz, *On Becoming a Social Scientist: From Survey Research and Participant Observation to Experiential Analysis*, 2nd ed. (New Brunswick: Transaction, 1984).

65 Harriet Martineau, *Life in the Sick-Room* (Boston: Bowles and Crosby, 1844).

66 Thorsten Veblen, *The Higher Learning in America: A Memorandum on the Conduct of Universities by Business Men* (New York: Huebsch, 1918).

67 Alvin Gouldner, *The Coming Crisis of Western Sociology* (New York: Basic Books, 1970).

68 Alfred McClung Lee, *Sociology for Whom?* (New York: Oxford University Press, 1978).

69 David Willer and Judith Willer, *Systematic Empiricism: Critique of a Pseudoscience* (Englewood Cliffs: Prentice-Hall, 1973).

70 Giddens, *Sociology: A Brief but Critical Introduction*.

71 Feagan, 'Social Justice and Sociology in the 21st Century'

72 See Martineau's *Autobiography*, ed. Linda Peterson (Peterborough, ON: Broadview Press, 2007).

73 For additional points, see Michael R. Hill, 'Martineauian sociology and our disciplinary future.' In: Michael R. Hill and Susan Hoecker-Drysdale (eds.), *Harriet Martineau: Theoretical & Methodological Perspectives* (New York: Routledge, 2001), pp. 191–3.

74 *How to Observe*, p. 51.

75 Martineau, *How to Observe*, p. 73.

76 Ibid.

77 George Beam, *The Problem with Survey Research* (New Brunswick: Transaction, 2012).

78 See Eugene J. Webb et al., *Unobtrusive Measures: Nonreactive Research in the Social Sciences* (Chicago: Rand McNally, 1966); Michael R. Hill, *Archival Strategies and Techniques*, Qualitative Research Methods Series, vol. 31 (Newbury Park: Sage, 1993).

5   Harriet Martineau

Sociologist at work

Susan Hoecker-Drysdale

Sciences are only valuable in as far as they involve the interests of mankind at large, and . . . nothing can prevent their sooner or later influencing general happiness. This is true with respect to the knowledge of the stars; to that of the formation and changes of the structure of the globe; to that of chemical elements and their combinations; and, above all, to that of the social condition of man.[1]

The context of Martineau's intellectual formation

The nineteenth century, as indicated in the Introduction, was a time when modernity blossomed and where ideas, born in preceding periods in literature, science, industry, applied sciences and mechanics, philosophy and religion, economics and politics were actualized.[2] Most remarkable were the shifts within the intellectual and practical sectors or paradigms of knowledge and invention. The dynamics among literature, religion and science constituted the quintessential matrix of transformations in knowledge and invention, in the intellectual and physical contexts in which Harriet Martineau, her predecessors and contemporaries thought and wrote. These transformations appeared in the work of Adam Smith, Montesquieu, Buffon and Lavoisier, who wished to advance the sciences of economy, culture and society, as well as in the literary worlds of Goethe, Balzac, Taine and Flaubert. Interest in natural history in particular evolved into a differentiation between 'scientific modes of procedure' and 'literary modes'.[3] Wolf Lepenies describes the contestation between literature and sociology for the most efficacious understanding of modern society:

> This competing discloses a dilemma which determined not only how sociology originated but also how it then went on to develop: it has oscillated between a scientific orientation which has led it to ape the natural sciences and a hermeneutic attitude which has shifted the discipline towards the realm of literature.[4]

However, as Richard Holmes reminds us, 'the idea of a pure, "disinterested" science, independent of political ideology and even religious doctrine, only slowly began to emerge.'[5]

Sustained by the founding of the French and English academies, the natural sciences had developed at a good pace from the seventeenth century. In England the progressive Lunar Society of Birmingham (1755–1813) composed of men, and later women, of various occupations and interests, advanced knowledge of science and science education, especially for women.[6] Natural science provided for the social sciences the methodologies of investigation of the social world, in terms of prototypes of observation, logic and exact measurement. The idea of a hierarchy of sciences, built upon the foundations of mathematics, physics and chemistry, with the social sciences emergent from them, became the major paradigm for sociology in the nineteenth century, nurtured by Balzac, Zola, Condorcet and De Bonald, all of whom believed in the pre-eminence of the social sciences. Utilitarianism and political economy, as we have seen in Chapter 3, were promoted by James Mill, Thomas Malthus, Joseph Priestley, Erasmus Darwin Sr., Jeremy Bentham, David Ricardo, John Stuart Mill and Dugald Stewart, many of whom heralded the Frenchman Henri Comte de Saint-Simon's articulation of the hierarchy of the sciences and the Law of Three Stages.[7] These polymaths and scholars of society drew from existing disciplines, including literature, religion and philosophy, in developing their own terminologies, methods and means of analysis. More than any other generation, they defined the new disciplines, their subject matters and methodologies.

The emergence of social science and sociology in particular in such a context produced a rich and critical social-scientific culture. It was the protégé of Saint-Simon, Auguste Comte, who more fully explicated the theory and structure of the social sciences, particularly sociology, and captured the imaginations of contemporaries in various fields, and whose basic work[8] Martineau translated and condensed in mid-century, as we saw in Michael Hill's chapter (Chapter 4). This translation was a great achievement for Martineau, and for Comte, and a significant contribution to the establishment of the discipline of sociology.[9]

For the past six decades or more, Martineau has been recognized by those within and outside the discipline of sociology as a founder – the first woman founder – of sociology.[10] Moreover, as this volume confirms, Martineau was clearly a polymath, or 'a sage of disciplines', and a self-made intellectual. In the present exposition we focus first on the context and development of Martineau's intellectual perspective and second on her approach to understanding the world through an examination of her theory and research of the world of *work*. For Martineau, *work* is the fundamental element of human existence, much like Marx's focus on labour.[11]

At home, Martineau was early drawn to books, ideas and learning, and preferred reading to socializing in part because she was losing her hearing. She developed interests in nature, astronomy, mathematics, languages and physical sciences. Scottish natural philosophy (Adam Smith, Adam Ferguson), Malthus and British empiricism (Locke, Bentham) and German idealism (Kant, Hegel) expanded Martineau's scientific predispositions, while literature – Austen, Wollstonecraft, Shakespeare, Bunyan, Bentham, Milton, Wordsworth, Goethe – and her study of languages (Latin, Greek, Italian, German and French) inspired her imagination and curiosity. She developed a passion for translation of Tacitus and Petrarch and various writings from German and French.

As a young person, Martineau was steeped in British and European thought and used this enormous knowledge as she moved increasingly to larger philosophical, economic and social issues. Her early urge to write, to express her thoughts, led her to the *Monthly Repository* and then to other available periodicals. Throughout her life periodicals and newspapers were highly significant venues for her public voice.[12] She never changed her disciplined lifestyle of writing, reading, correspondence and socializing, all accomplished within a daily schedule, whether at home, at a friend's home or abroad.

As she entered the period of her mature writing, she knew personally key intellectuals of the time, among others, Gustav D'Eichtal, who introduced her to the work of Comte de Saint-Simon; Thomas Malthus, with whom she had many discussions on population theory, political economy and societal morals; William J. Fox, editor of the Unitarian *Monthly Repository*, who encouraged and published her writing; and Lant Carpenter, Unitarian minister in Bristol, an early influence on her. Through her reading, she became acquainted with Joseph Priestley, Charles-Louis Montesquieu, John Locke, Gotthold E. Lessing, Dugald Stewart, Anna Letitia Barbauld and William Godwin, all of whom provided the grounds for her knowledge of natural law theory, necessarianism, associationism, natural rights theory and political economy. These are reflected in her essays in the *Monthly Repository*. In the early nineteenth century, Unitarians, regarded as intellectual rationalists, contributed significantly to the culture of Britain.[13] Early on, the impact of the social environment on human beings intrigued her, as Joseph Priestley's work on Hartley provided her first scientific perspective on human behaviour. The writings of Dugald Stewart, through his influence on David Ricardo, introduced her to the basic paradigm of classical political economy. This is the period in which individuals and their writings reflected the convergences of science and literature and the interconnections between nature and human society.[14]

Women in science in the nineteenth century

The second significant development was the increasing participation of women in both science and literary genres. Early leaders of women in science included Jane Haldimand Marcet (1769–1858), scientist and educator; Mary Somerville (1780–1872), science writer, mathematician and astronomer; and Caroline Herschel (1750–1848), astronomer. Both Somerville and Herschel were made Honorary Members of the Royal Astronomical Society in 1835, yet were never granted full membership. Like the others, Jane Marcet had no formal scientific grounding but, with encouragement from her husband, studied chemistry, natural philosophy, plant physiology and political economy, and subsequently wrote *Conversations on . . .* books, *Conversations on Chemistry* (1806) in Socratic dialogue 'intended more especially for the female sex', and *Conversations on Political Economy* (1816).[15] When Martineau read Marcet's book in 1827, she realized that she had been writing political economy in her machinery and wages tales.[16] These 'pedagogical' editions by Marcet (and later by Martineau) stimulated the interests of both women and men in the sciences, and were considered by J. R. McCulloch, the Ricardian economist, to be 'the best introduction to the science that has yet appeared'.[17]

Caroline Herschel became interested in astronomy while assisting her brother William, who also tutored her in mathematics and astronomy. After he married, Caroline was free to study how she wished, and subsequently published works on astronomy, won an award from the Royal Astronomical Society and made her name in the field.[18] Mary Somerville describes the development and separation of the scientific disciplines in British universities in her 1834 book on physical astronomy, mechanics, electricity, climatology and other topics.[19] This followed her translation of Laplace's *Mechanique Celeste* in 1831, which 'remained the standard text on mathematics and astronomy for the rest of the century'.[20] Author of a number of other science books, Somerville was without doubt the most esteemed woman in science of the era.

Martineau was aware of the scientific and literary work of these and other women, many of whom she discussed later in *Biographical Sketches*.[21] This cohort of women was followed by others, who not only wrote on science and literature but also published books specifically for women and students. It is interesting that all of them, including Martineau, taught these subjects to various age levels, and especially to women and the working classes.[22]

Thus a new era of education for women by women emerged, as Martineau pursued her own self-education and life career in writing,[23] teaching and recommending practices and policies. She was joined by other women who combined science and science writing with fiction, poetry, education and practical applications of the sciences. These included Maria Edgeworth, Caroline Fox, George Eliot, Beatrice Webb and Millicent Garrett Fawcett among others,[24] literary figures producing fiction, periodical articles, poetry, children's literature and nonfiction works.

Both women and men[25] began to focus more on the lives and needs of the poor and working classes. The rise of political economy concerned in many respects how the poor would 'fit into' a growing capitalist economy. These researchers had significant roles in promoting education for children and the working classes through public lectures, mechanics institutes and professional organizations often formed originally for men only. Their widespread activities in many sectors convinced founders like Erasmus Darwin of the Royal Institution, established in 1799, that women should participate on an equal basis with men.[26] The British Association for the Advancement of Science, established in 1831, was less encouraging, and although women showed great interest in the organization's focus and activities, some like Somerville and Martineau chose not to participate. Martineau was more enthusiastic about the National Association for the Promotion of Social Science (1857–86), formed by those who were interested in political economy, education, social issues and especially social reform. Members investigated issues ignored by the more patriarchal and classist associations, but again women were excluded from the power structure.[27] Nevertheless, as Phillips shows, science education and organizational participation of women in science expanded dramatically into the nineteenth century.[28]

The sociology of work and occupations:
Martineau's theory of work

This examination of Martineau's sociology will focus on her theoretical and meth-odological projects and her own practices on the subject of *work*.[29] *Work* is both an implicit and explicit subject in all areas of knowledge in the nineteenth century. From the Enlightenment onwards, we see descriptions and analyses of 'making a living' and the meanings and contexts of *work* in all disciplines. The subject of work is thematic throughout Martineau's lifelong research, writings and practices. Her upbringing as a Dissenter, the culture of her family and reflections on her personal situation, centred on 'what to do and how to live'. Her earliest religious tales echoed a Calvinist work ethic and a resolute sense of moral duty. As a young woman who became deaf, she reflected on her own future in 'making a living' and surviving in a male-centred work world.

Two dimensions of Martineau's concerns are examined: first, her own theory of work as subject and agency; that is, work as the essence of self, as vocation, as the basis of 'being' in the world; and second, work as the object of study and analysis. In the 1820s, she addressed issues of mental, physical and scientific work in a series, 'Essays on the Art of Thinking', and on moral matters in essays including '. . . The Proper Use of the Retrospective', and '. . . the Proper Use of the Prospective Faculty'.[30] These essays concern the constructive use of memory and historical understanding to facilitate effective practical action. The respon-sibility to gain some knowledge of economic and social systems is expressed in her essay 'On the Duty of Studying Political Economy',[31] which emphasizes the duty or 'work' of the citizen and shows the centrality of *agency* in Martineau's perspective.

For Martineau, as for Karl Marx, and later for Max Weber, Emile Durkheim, Thorstein Veblen and Charlotte Gilman, work constitutes the essential lens through which to view society. Martineau's implicit position is that work and work relations express as much about the culture and politics of a nation as about economics. Like Saint-Simon, she envisioned a society of 'work for each and order for all,' – however, a society born not out of the structure and control of a central authority, but out of education, training and participation of its members. Indeed the problem of a meaningful fit between the population and the division of labour (as in Durkheim's problem of the 'forced division of labour') was to be effected, in Martineau's view, through education and training.

The best example of Martineau's understanding of societal relations through *work* is her study of domestic service, a frequent subject for her, in which are detailed the norms of reciprocity and exchange, class, gender and race relations, cultural and political power, social control and exploitation, class values and the degree of moral sympathy.[32] Decrying the paucity of research on domestic service and the prevalence of social (male) stereotypes about and ignorance of the subject, Martineau investigates the causes of the rise of the system of domestic service in an historical/comparative analysis of England, Ireland, Scotland and America, employing a typology of domestic service: (1) the slavery-patrimonial system guaranteeing maintenance; (2) employment by contract, which means freedom to work but no provision for maintenance; (3) a combination of the first two '. . . requisition of obedience and subjection to caprice of the first, and the uncertainty of maintenance of the last'.[33]

In identifying the roots of the nineteenth-century British domestic system and the class estrangement it produced, she points to three historical causes: the Norman Conquest and the resulting 'evil of arbitrary rank', that caused 'enmity between the classes of employers and employed' in England and 'imposed a foreign aristocracy on a people reluctant to serve them'.[34] Service was exacted. The second is asceticism, imposed upon workers in service, which made the lives of the disadvantaged ever more wretched as employers (or owners) forbid spontaneous gatherings and social life among the workers (slaves). Third is the growth of the commercial spirit (breeding selfishness, lack of trust, absence of traditions of service, and social struggles).

The result of all this is a decline in the value of work and an increase in class conflicts. Social relations are no longer reciprocal but instrumental. Those who do not live by manual labour cannot understand those who do. Middle-class women are excluded from labour while overworked working-class women, such as maids of all work, are overrepresented in 'lunatic asylums'. In related articles,[35] Martineau continues her analysis of society through the lens of work, looking particularly at women's work. Interested in exposing the problems, myths and conflicts related to work, and bringing remedies to them, she reminds us that the days are gone when women were supported by a father, brother or husband, when marriage and motherhood were arranged and expected, and when women worked only in family establishments.

From that time [the uprising of a middle class] to this, the need and the supply of female industry have gone on increasing, and latterly at an unparalleled rate, while our ideas, our language, and our arrangements have not altered in any corresponding degree.[36]

The study of domestic service, as Martineau shows, reveals important truths about work in society: that certain kinds of drudgery remain hidden;[37] that domestic service embodies the exploiters/exploited relationship;[38] that reciprocity and exchange are critical in social relations but not currently cultivated;[39] and that in the waning of traditions, tensions and isolation of the classes simmer toward eruption. Class reconciliation is now hindered by the reserve and anti-sociable nature of the national character [England] which is a product of these developments.[40]

Propositions regarding work and the self

Martineau argued that human work is an essential aspect of being and living in the world. Work is not only necessary for survival but also for human fulfillment. The centrality of human work has been recognized for centuries as well as in recent times, as has the importance of *meaningful* work as a basic need, seen in the writings of Marx (1844), Veblen (1898, 1914), Gilman (1898, 1903, 1915) and Weber

(1904–5).[41] Martineau recognized the significance of her own personal choice of work, to write.[42] She disparaged the enforced idleness of the privileged classes in Western society and in regimes of slavery, and of the Harem in Egypt, as violating a basic human need. Her concept of 'the nobleness of labour'[43] as opposed to 'instability of idle luxury', resonates with Karl Marx's concept of *species being*, whose humanness is defined by the desire and necessity to *labour*,[44] and predates Thorstein Veblen's *instinct of workmanship*, which operates in all spheres of life and refers quite literally to 'a proclivity for taking pains'.[45]

Work manifests and facilitates agency; it expresses the self; work is self-realization. Martineau's assumptions about work as the basis of life activity and life course derive largely from the influences of Calvinism and Necessarianism. Martineau understood that her work defined her. Providing for herself 'substantial, laborious and serious occupation', she had an extraordinarily clear view of her life and work.[46] One of Martineau's central arguments with regard to self and work pertains to the shackles of privileged women who, in their idleness, exercise 'aristocratic tyranny' over others.[47] While often accused of exaggerating the value of domestic life and work, she never assumes that they satisfy women's needs for meaningful paid work and activity in the societal sphere. She does, however, regard knowledge of home nursing, cooking, cleaning and hygiene as necessary skills for women.

Martineau experienced work as a vocation on a personal level:

> Authorship has never been with me a matter of choice. I have not done it for amusement, or for money, or for fame, or for any reason but because I could not help it. Things were pressing to be said; and there was more or less evidence that I was the person to say them. One must of course respond to one's calling . . . an author has his lot pretty much in his own hands, because it is in his power to shape his habits in accordance with the laws of nature: and an author who does not do this has no business with the lofty vocation.[48]

The discipline of vocation is manifested in a regular daily schedule with full priority given to work: 'I never pass a day without writing', claiming that even in the absence of inspiration, she would find herself 'in full train' after a quarter hour.[49] Her discussions of her own method of writing are instructive and inspiring. With increasing clarity her work is the work of social science and of policy, whose separation she rejected. Science was to be useful, and her scientific work was intended for advocacy and reform, as well as for intellectual understanding. When she wrote from a particular viewpoint or attempted to influence political decision-making, she was accused of not being objective and of 'meddling'. By contrast, when men in the sociological tradition have combined science and action, it has been seen as the convergence of intellect and praxis, as Hill also shows in the last chapter. Martineau's sense of vocation hinged upon duty, as a public educator particularly; she believed that she had a duty to impart what she could to the public and to improve the ordinary individual's understanding of society and social issues. Vocation, for Martineau, required involvement, commitment, dedication to the task, seriousness of endeavour, regular work habits and a strong belief in the significance of one's work.

Work and life are at once mental and physical. Like Saint-Simon (1825), Marx (1844), Tristan (1843), and later Veblen (1898) and Gilman (1898),[50] Martineau emphasized that work should employ both mental and physical capacities. A balance should be struck by regular mental activities outside of work for manual workers, and by physical exercise and engagement in physical work for those who work by the mind. Memorization of poetry while sewing,[51] households with reading rooms, leisure for servants, some physical work for the 'mistress' of the house and generally mental and physical activity for all classes and genders were required for productive lives. She taught at and supported mechanics' institutes and was dedicated to the idea of a literate and informed working class.

Leisure is as essential to life as work. Martineau, like Karl Marx, was committed to the idea that leisure is integral to one's life. Referring to William Godwin, whose ideas were influential on Martineau, she maintains that some degree of leisure is needed for the health of all individuals' spirits.[52]

Propositions regarding work and society

The meaning of work as socially defined, she proposed, indicates the character of a society. Martineau shows that gender inequities and the practices of slavery lead to the debasement of work. Work performed by subordinates is regarded as dirty and contaminating, to be avoided, indicative of inferior status. Therefore, work itself is demeaned and nourishes negative attitudes and practices that degrade and deteriorate social relations in society. Occupations such as teaching and needlework that involve female labour are poorly rewarded, reflecting the subordination of the sex,[53] even though women's work is often harder than men's.[54] Martineau's preferred world is one in which employer and employee work reciprocally in mutual activity and responsibility and as part of community life.[55] This is reflective of *moral sympathy*,[56] which Martineau considered critical in civilized society.[57] Martineau assumes that some level of meaning and satisfaction in work is the *right* of every individual and is worked out in social relations at work.

Total appropriation of another's work she considered to be immoral and damaging to the worker and society. The exploitation of others' work, as in slavery and sweatshop labour and the appropriation of others' physical and intellectual exertions for the singular benefit of the employer, she considered to be inhuman and destructive of individuals and society. The consequent alienation, estrangement and loss of physical control over one's work were often, though not exclusively, a function of gender. For example, pottery-making and the sewing occupations brought long hours, tedium and cruel physical consequences. Children's work was often very dangerous and unhealthy. However, Martineau was optimistic about technological developments, and perhaps as a manufacturer's daughter, tended to downplay the effects of machines on children and adults, and criticized the 'boys who put themselves in the way of the machine'[58] in her debate with Charles Dickens over the fencing of machinery for workers' protection.

Society, she held, must provide the conditions for freedom of development in work for each individual. Just as Marx crowns his future society with the idea of the 'free development of each leading to the free development of all,' Martineau emphasizes the free development of members of society by means of a free work situation.[59]

The division of labour she saw as developing according to the natural laws of political economy. Its development is not only a function of population growth and concentration, technology and increased communication and transportation, as Durkheim maintained,[60] but also reflects the realities of private ownership and control in production and markets. Martineau points out the implications of such practices as monetary speculation, which she always opposed as risky and damaging to the economic welfare of others; patriarchal practices in work, for example, in watchmaking,[61] pottery-making;[62] the practices of slavery, the most destructive, exploitative division of labour; gender inequality, pay inequities and women's lack of control over their own wages;[63] gender discrimination in all kinds of work [64] and ghettoization;[65] the exclusion of women from many venues such as the National Academy of the Arts;[66] class differentiations and even ageism. These arguments precede Durkheim's analysis by three to five decades and are missing from his writings on the division of labour.

It is axiomatic for Martineau that machine technology facilitates progress and that machines have the potential to take over arduous tasks while expanding production and opportunities for employment. She concurs with Adam Smith, rather than Montesquieu, that technology creates employment opportunities for all, including women, and that factories and manufacturers make society orderly and regulated (i.e., rationalized). She asserts that the material base of capitalism has the capacity to improve life for all, *but* that there are obstacles: gender and racial inequities in opportunities,[67] costs in product quality with industrialization and inept enforcement of government regulations. Martineau, like Smith, is often seen as an apologist for and defender of bourgeois capitalism, and if we consider its key elements as outlined by Max Weber[68] we must agree. She saw technology, a free marketplace, and a free labour force as necessary, if not sufficient, conditions for a progressive society. Nevertheless, as her American studies show, it is the morals of economic and political practices, the quality of social relations and the pervasiveness of social responsibilities in society that ultimately matter. As with Adam Smith, therefore, we find in Martineau a critique and warnings about the consequences of industrial capitalism, particularly in her articles on work and in her political economy tales.[69]

Propositions regarding work, rights and citizenship

The right to work and the right to free access to particular forms of work by all members of society are necessary (the right not to be excluded on irrelevant grounds) and central to Martineau's sociology. In the instances of slavery and the subordination of women (systems of coercion), basic rights are being violated: the right to work, to be free to choose one's work and therefore to be free to pursue other values. She objected to unionization because she believed at the time that women would be excluded, therefore negatively affected. She points to the problem of male domination at work and thereby anticipates the future suffrage cry of 'Work and Emancipation'.[70]

Moreover, the right to work is linked to citizenship. Just as society controls property and marriage rights, it controls the right to work, access to specific kinds of work and the terms of work. The subordination of women and systems of slavery, as in America in the 1830s, deny work rights resulting in an absence of excellence in work, as well as dignity, autonomy and privacy for individuals.

Work and the right to relevant education are basic tenets for her. The right to education is a corollary to citizenship and the right to work, as in Martineau's 1864 discussions on education, where she argues the case for a national educational system in England,[71] and education for intellectual and moral competency.[72] She was truly a public educator, as Ruth Watts has detailed earlier in this volume.

Martineau considered the role of the state, society and the individual as tightly interconnected in terms of human rights. The ways in which the polity and the economy work together determine the possibilities for women and men in work and occupation. She found that disparities, in the absence of education and training and the 'freedom to choose' one's work, failed to meet the imperatives of a democratic state, in the instances of America in the 1830s and Martineau's England.

Martineau's sociology of work and occupations

Empirical investigations

Industrial capitalism was approaching its zenith in the 1850s when Martineau conducted her major study of Birmingham industries. Steam power and mechanization, occurring first in the cotton industry in Birmingham, quickly spread to several sectors such as iron-making, printing and threshing. However, industries such as silk and linen production, the metal trades, leather and shoemaking, glove and hat-making required skilled labour and were changed less by mechanization than by changes in the division of labour.[73] Much work by artisans, skilled and unskilled workers continued to be carried out in traditional modes in small industries and businesses.[74] Agriculture also remained a family enterprise. The most important change was the increased participation of women in the labour force, especially in factories, although men continued to handle the machines while women performed the repetitive, labour-intensive jobs. Issues of unionization or 'combinations' arose to address health, safety and wage problems.

Objectives and methodologies

In her scientific studies of work and occupations Martineau pursues specific objectives: first, to educate the public via detailed empirical descriptions of new occupations and industries in Birmingham, in England generally and abroad, in terms of their histories, economics and technologies; second, to analyze changes in the division of labour, social structures in the workplace and the challenges to nature precipitated by industry, using census data and government documents in addition to her own investigations; third, to study various occupations in descriptive, prescriptive and relational terms; and last, to critique and advocate, as she both reveals and deplores the work conditions and social situations of slaves and women, privileged women's work deprivation, workers' rights, the exploitation of children, work and family life, safety and issues of physical well-being.

Martineau considered *work* to be a scientific object of empirical study. As early as her *Illustrations*, economic activity was a central topic, as we have seen in Chapter 3. In these fictional tales designed to educate the general reader on the principles of political economy, she explores the interrelations of labour, capital and technology; the critical importance of the changing division of labour and economic diversification; the exigencies of labour-management relations; the merits and demerits of unions, prices and wages; and money and free trade, among other themes. She positions her didactic stories within new industrial and agricultural situations to instruct the public on how to understand and deal with changing economic realities. This is precisely the location of her *praxis:* to do the research, analyze and interpret findings and instruct the public on the practical applications of this new knowledge.

Martineau innovated and used a wide range of methods and techniques of data collection that have become standard in sociology and the social sciences. These methods and techniques include direct observation, interviews, oral histories and life stories, use of official documents, census data and other sources of contemporary statistics, and historical records of all sorts. She developed typologies and a variety of classificatory systems, as in her studies of occupations, such as domestic work, teaching, business, industrial work and others to analyze and compare their characteristics in traditional, new and changing occupations.[75] She was not only a keen observer but also a participant observer in many contexts in England and abroad (America, Ireland, Egypt, Sinai, Palestine and Syria) and always became absorbed in her environment, striving to experience it as the residents did and to empathize with their life situations.

In many of her research projects, Martineau employed an individual to accompany her as a research assistant, partly for the practical reason of aiding her in hearing, but also to complement her own observations, take notes, gather documents, etc. In her studies of America and the Birmingham industries she used an organized research protocol exploring the history, context, development and current operations and production processes of these industries, and explaining them to the reader as fully as possible. She analyzed the labourers' situation, including wages, working conditions, gender and the division of labour, skill levels of the labour force, and the relation between factory employment and workers' family lives. She noted the connections of these industries with other countries in terms of raw materials and markets and included comparative and related data from other sources, in addition to her own observations.

Key concepts

Martineau's studies centred on several key concepts: the *division of labour*, especially its organization and reorganization in the work situation, conditions and technology; *the meaning of work* as a consequence of these changes; *gender and class* relations; *work and family* life; and nineteenth-century *international trade*.

Predating Durkheim's call in 1893 "to equip yourself to fulfill usefully a specific function", Martineau declares that each individual likewise must qualify her/himself to work in modern occupations.[76] As we have seen, she believed that each individual had rights and responsibilities, accruing to participation in modern society, to the means of education and training, and access to some kind of work, which is also the link between the free citizen and the state/society (major themes in the later writings of Durkheim and Max Weber). Martineau recognized that the 'honour' of work in a democratic society would be sustained and that the problems of modern employment would be addressed by, for example, clear contractual agreements between employer and employee and better employee preparation, training and education for work. Similar requirements pertain to agricultural employment as the economy of her day remained significantly agricultural. Likewise, the work settings for a major segment of the economy continued to occur in artisan shops and family workrooms. Solutions for problems related to employment should be sought through clear expectations of upgrading, defining work as honourable, establishing a court of appeal for workers and providing for health care and old age care for servants.

Martineau's studies of industrial production in Birmingham, an important industrial centre at that time, involved nine sites. Her *Household Words* articles were highly successful in informing the public of current developments in production. Numerous industrialists requested that she visit their establishments! Among the industries Martineau investigated were those making needles, guns and other weapons, glass, tin, brass and copper products, jewelry, buttons, electro-gilding, cloth, looms, spools and screws, including thorough details of their mechanized production and of those production processes that still required an enormous amount of work by hand.

Martineau's analysis of women's work began in the 1820s and expanded in her study of American society in the 1830s. She concluded that work, occupation and pay and women's status are all tightly interconnected. The underemployment of women by privilege or discrimination by class or by lack of training and education was a critical problem. The women who worked, those unmarried and of modest means, were restricted largely to seven occupations: domestic service, teaching, needlework, keeping boarders, mill work, typesetting and bookkeeping.[77] Often self-supporting and working in deplorable conditions, women suffered, often more than men, the disadvantages of industrializing societies. In her studies of the Lowell cotton mill girls[78] she saw that independent paid employment offered new opportunities both for financial rewards and self-development, on the one hand, and exploitation and vulnerability, especially for women workers, on the other. But in that exceptional case, the community of women working and living together resulted in the expansion of their skills and minds from which they profited.[79] In industrial production men were the owners and administrators; women were ill-treated and underpaid and often worked in the most unhealthy and dangerous venues of production. Nevertheless, Martineau remained optimistic about women's future prospects in industrial employment.[80]

Martineau's attention to women's industrial occupations did not obscure her analyses of women's traditional work: domestic, teaching and nursing. Domestic service she saw as a critical site of class relations. Indeed, service occupations exist on a continuum between slavery and contract labour. She contextualizes domestic work within the changing class structure and various household situations and develops a typology of domestic workers: maid of all-work, housemaid, lady's maid, dressmaker, charwoman, cook, nursemaid, gatekeeper, inn servant and so on. Twenty-five years later, in an article entitled 'Modern Domestic Service',[81] she reiterated many of her earlier concerns and analyzed the growth in domestic service, and in an 1859 article[82] she drew on census data and reports on women's work in England and the United States to explore women's participation in the major economic sectors.

She constructed typologies of women teachers, for example, including schoolmistresses, private (family) governesses, daily governesses and special teachers of music, drawing, dancing and other arts. Her analysis of each category in terms of responsibilities, prestige, control over work and personal satisfaction reveals the historical roots of contemporary prejudice.[83] Schoolmistresses enjoy greater control over their work and greater personal satisfaction and independence but suffer social stigma and low status. The daily governess is typically employed by two or three families, working long days and having no time for her own life.

Needlework and sewing was the third occupation for women in this period. Martineau worked as a seamstress for a year following her father's death and before embarking on a writing career. This is the most exploited class, she concluded: 'the grief and shame of society from the day when Hood published the "Song of the Shirt"'. It is women's most common 'profession' which suffers from a lack of training. 'In short, sewing both is and is not a professional occupation.'[84] The solution for this occupation is technology, she concluded – the sewing machine will make work endurable and the product better, cheaper and faster, with less strain on the worker. Martineau recognized that specialization and training in sewing was becoming necessary and that the increasing division of labour in a paid workforce required greater specialization. Her classification includes dressmakers and milliners, the largest category, shirt-makers and plain sewers, glovers and hosiers, hat and bonnet-makers, shoe-binders and sewers, and stay-makers, a miscellaneous category.[85]

Finally, the occupation of nursing was a major interest for both Martineau and her friend Florence Nightingale. Nursing as a profession was officially born in 1860 when Florence Nightingale opened a school of nursing at St. Thomas Hospital, London. In several articles in the 1860s Martineau campaigned for women to join the nursing profession by indicating the types and locations available: work in country parishes among the poor, the village hospitals, poor kitchens, workhouse infirmaries, family and home nursing, nursing in the colonies, maternal nursing and military nursing. In her reviews of Nightingale's 1860 *Notes on Nursing: What It Is and What It Is Not* and her own experiential *Life in the Sick-Room*, Martineau provided a critical examination of what constitutes good nursing from the point of view of the nurse, on the one hand, and the patient, on the other.[86]

In conclusion this chapter has sought to demonstrate several dimensions of Martineau's sociology: the intellectual origins of her sociological understanding of the world; the theoretical frame of her social research and analyses of work and work settings; her methodologies; and her critical understanding of how work and occupation form the nexus of the means to live, the needs of society and the fulfillment of the individual, all interdependent within the social order. From this, we can say that Harriet Martineau was indeed an innovative, self-made sociologist and a noteworthy founder of the discipline of sociology.

Notes

1 Harriet Martineau, *Illustrations of Political Economy*, vol. 1 (London: Charles Fox, 1832–1834), pp. ix–x.
2 Richard Holmes, *The Age of Wonder: How the Romantic Generation Discovered the Beauty and Terror of Science* (London: HarperCollins, 2008). The first and foundational scientific revolution in the seventeenth century is associated with Locke, Descartes and Newton. The second scientific revolution, 'the romantic revolution', emerges in the early nineteenth century, growing out of Enlightenment rationalism but inspired by a new sense of adventure, excitement of exploration and the blending of imagination and discovery in many spheres. See his Prologue.
3 Wolf Lepenies, *Between Literature and Science: The Rise of Sociology* (Cambridge: Cambridge University Press, 1985), p. 1. This is a critical work for understanding the relationships between the literary and scientific worlds of that period and the interconnections between the two spheres. For a rather opinionated treatment of the history of the science versus literature debate in nineteenth-century British sociology, see A. H. Halsey, *A History of Sociology in Britain: Science, Literature, and Society* (Oxford: Oxford University Press, 2004), pp. v–44.
4 Ibid.
5 Holmes, *The Age of Wonder*, p. xvii.
6 For a discussion on the Lunar Society's ideas and activities, see Patricia Phillips, *The Scientific Lady: A Social History of Woman's Scientific Interests 1520–1918* (London: Weidenfeld and Nicolson, 1990), pp. 162–77.
7 The Law of Three Stages refers to the idea that Western thought had transformed from the theological stage, in which the natural and social worlds were interpreted within a religious (Christian) framework with change determined by the gods or God, to the metaphysical or philosophical interpretation of the world and history reflected in rational logical explanation and theories based on general principles or abstract systems, to the third scientific stage where factual, concrete, verifiable knowledge is the outcome of direct empirical exploration of the natural and social worlds. See also Chapter 3 in this volume.
8 Auguste Comte, *Cours de Philosophie Positive*, 6 volumes, 1830–1842. See Harriet Martineau, *The Positive Philosophy of August Comte, Freely Translated and Condensed*, 2 vols. (London: John Chapman, 1853).
9 The 'Introduction' to this volume places the ultimate emergence of the 'disciplines' within the development of Western knowledge and the expansion of academia. Michael Hill's chapter 'Harriet Martineau: the founding and re-founding of sociology' provides a well-referenced account of Martineau's writings, methods and legacy.

10 Robert K. Webb (1960) Seymour M. Lipset (1962), Alice S. Rossi (1973); Michael R Hill, (1989, 1991); Susan Hoecker-Drysdale (1992), Lengermann and Niebrugge-Brantley (1998).

11 See Karl Marx, *The Economic and Philosophic Manuscripts of 1844* (Moscow: Foreign Languages Publishing House, 1961).

12 See chapter by Valerie Sanders on Martineau's journalism in this volume.

13 Raymond V. Holt, *The Unitarian Contribution to Social Progress in England* (London: Lindsay Press, 1938); Ruth E. Watts, 'The unitarian contribution to the development of female education (1790–1850)', *History of Education*, 9 (1980), pp. 273–86.

14 These convergences are seen in Martineau's work in the *Illustrations* and other tales of economy, taxation, etc.

15 Jane Haldimand Marcet, *Conversations on Chemistry, in Which the Elements of That Science Are Familiarly Explained, and Illustrated by Experiments*, 2 vols. (1806); *Conversations on Political Economy* (1816).

16 *Autobiography*, vol. I, p. 138.

17 John Ramsay McCulloch, *The Literature of Political Economy: a classified catalogue of select publications in the different departments of that science, with historical, critical, and biographical notices* (London: Brown, Green, and Longmans,1845), p. 18.

18 Holmes, op. cit., p. 180. Caroline Herschel was eventually (1787) awarded £50 per annum for life by King George III, thanks in part to her brother William's efforts. 'It . . . marked a social revolution: the first professional salary ever paid to a woman scientist'.

19 Mary Somerville, *On the Connexion of the Physical Sciences* (London: John Murray, 1834).

20 Phillips, op. cit., p. 114.

21 *Biographical Sketches* (1869).

22 See, for example, Dorothy Lampen Thomson, *Adam Smith's Daughters: Six Prominent Economists from the Eighteenth Century to the Present* (New York: Exposition Press, 1973).

23 *The Rioters, or, a Tale of Bad Times* (1827); *Principle and Practice, or the Orphan Family* 1827); *The Turn-out; or Patience the Best Policy* (1829); *Sequel to Principle and Practice; or, The Orphan Family* (1831); *The Tendency of Strikes and Sticks to Produce Low Wages, and of Union between Masters and Men to Ensure Good Wages* (1834).

24 See Patricia Phillips, op. cit., a concise and fascinating history of the emergence of women's interests and participation in science preceding and into the nineteenth century, their science writings and educational activities, and their participation in the Royal Institution and the British Association for the Advancement of Science.

25 They include Seebohm Rowntree, Charles Dickens, Charles Booth and Sidney Webb.

26 Women were welcomed into the Royal Institution and by 1800 comprised a third of the membership.

27 See Kathleen McCrone, 'The national association for the promotion of social science and the advancement of Victorian women', *Atlantis*, 8 (1982), pp. 44–66.

28 Phillips, op. cit., chapters 5, 6, 7. Another excellent work is: Eileen Janes Yeo, *The Contest for Social Science: Relations and Representations of Gender and Class* (London: Rivers Oram Press, 1996).

29 See Susan Hoecker-Drysdale, 'Words on work.' chapters 6 and 7, in Michael R. Hill and Susan Hoecker-Drysdale (eds.), *Harriet Martineau: Theoretical and Methodological Perspectives* (New York: Routledge, 2001, 2003).

30 Harriet Martineau, "Essay on the Proper Use of the Prospective Faculty," 1822, reprinted in *Miscellanies*, vol. 1 (Boston: Hilliard, Gray, 1836), pp. 224–30; "Essay on the Proper Use of the Retrospective Faculty", reprinted in *Miscellanies*, Ibid., pp. 215–24.

31 Martineau, "On the Duty of Studying Political Economy," 1831, reprinted in *Miscellanies*, vol. 1 (1836), pp. 272–88.

32 Harriet Martineau, 'Domestic service,' *London and Westminster Review*, 29 (August 1838), pp. 405–32.

33 Ibid., p. 413. See also Chapter 3 for her perspective on work.

34 Ibid., p. 414.

35 Harriet Martineau, 'Modern domestic service', *Edinburgh Review*, 115 (April 1862), pp. 409–39; Harriet Martineau, 'Female industry', *Edinburgh Review*, 109 (April 1859), pp. 151–73; Martineau, 'The Maid of All Work: Her Health,' *Health, Husbandry and Handicraft* (London: Bradbury and Evans, 1861) pp. 158–66.

36 Martineau 1859, op. cit. p. 153. This text is also discussed in Chapter 9 on Martineau's feminism.

37 Martineau, 'Domestic Service,' op. cit.

38 Ibid., pp. 409–10.

39 Ibid., p. 421.

40 Ibid., pp. 415, 419.

41 Karl Marx, *The Economic and Philosophic Manuscripts of 1844* (Moscow: Foreign Languages Publishing House, 1961); Thorstein Veblen, *The Theory of the Leisure Class: An Economic Study of Institutions* (New York: The Modern Library, 1899, 1934), and *The Instinct of Workmanship, and the State of Industrial Arts* (Macmillan, 1914) reprinted by Augustus M. Kelley (New York, 1964); Max Weber, *The Protestant Ethic and the Spirit of Capitalism* (London: George Allen and Unwin, 1904–1905); Charlotte Perkins Gilman, *Women and Economics* 1898 (New York: Harper & Row, 1966); *Human Work* (New York: McClure Phillips, 1904); and *The Forerunner*, a monthly publication (1909–1916) written and published by Charlotte Perkins in which *The Dress of Women* appeared in Vol 6, 1915.

42 Martineau, *Autobiography*, ed. Linda Peterson (Peterborough, ON: Broadview Press, 2007), p. 120.

43 Harriet Martineau, *London Daily News*, October 23, 1857, p. 4.

44 Marx, 1844, op. cit.

45 Veblen 1899,1964a, pp. 33–34; Hoecker-Drysdale, 'Words on work: Harriet Martineau's sociology of work and occupations.' In: Michael Hill and Susan Hoecker-Drysdale (eds.), *Harriet Martineau Theoretical and Methodological Perspectives* (New York: Routledge 2001), pp. 102–3; Hoecker-Drysdale, 'The nobleness of labor and the instinct of workmanship: Nature, work, gender, and politics in Harriet Martineau and Thorstein Veblen.' In: Ross E. Mitchell (ed.), *Thorstein Veblen's Contribution to Environmental Sociology: Essays in the Political Economy of Wasteful Industrialism* (Lewiston, NY: The Edwin Mellen Press, 2007), pp. 161–97.

46 Hoecker-Drysdale, op. cit., 2001, pp. 103–4.

47 Martineau, 1838, op. cit., p. 431.

48 Martineau, *Autobiography*, ed. Linda Peterson, p. 155.

49 Ibid., p. 157.

50 Saint-Simon (1825), Marx (1844), Tristan (1843), Veblen (1898), and Gilman (1898).

51 Harriet Martineau, *The Lady's Maid.* Guide to Service Series (London: Charles Knight 1838).

52 Martineau, 1837, III, pp. 43–44.

53 Martineau, 1837, III, p. 150.

54 Harriet Martineau, "Female industry", *Edinburgh Review*, 109 (April 1859), p. 154.

55 Martineau, "Domestic service," op. cit., pp. 431–43.

56 Adam Smith, *The Theory of Moral Sentiments* (London: A. Millar, and Edinburgh: A. Kincaid and J. Bell, 1759).

57 Martineau, *Miscellanies*, pp. 179–91.

58 Harriet Martineau, *The Factory Controversy: A Warning Against Meddling Legislation* (Manchester: National Association of Factory Occupiers, 1855).

59 Martineau, *Miscellanies*, op. cit., pp. 121–2, 132.
60 Emile Durkheim, *The Division of Labour in Society*, Trans. W. D. Halls (New York: The Free Press, 1893), pp. 200–25.
61 Martineau, 1859, op. cit., p. 168.
62 Ibid., p. 170.
63 Ibid., pp. 160, 170, 171.
64 Ibid., p. 155, 1859a, 1861.
65 Ibid., p. 155.
66 Ibid., p. 172.
67 Ibid., p. 166.
68 Max Weber (1904–1905). In: Talcott Parsons (ed.), *The Protestant Ethic and the Spirit of Capitalism* (London: George Allen and Unwin, 1985).
69 See Deborah A. Logan (ed.) Harriet Martineau, *Illustrations of Political Economy: Selected Tales*. 'Introduction' (Peterborough, ON: Broadview Editions, 2004).
70 For more analysis of her studies on women, see Gaby Weiner's article (Chapter 9) on feminism in this volume.
71 Harriet Martineau, 'Middle-class education in England: Boys,' *Cornhill Magazine*, 10 (October 1864), pp. 409–26; 'Middle-class education in England: Girls,' *Cornhill Magazine*, 19 (November 1864), pp. 549–68.
72 Martineau, *Society in America* III, p. 163; Martineau, *Household Education* (1849).
73 See Maxine Berg, *The Machinery Question and the Making of Political Economy, 1815–1848* (Cambridge: Cambridge University Press, 1980) for a thorough analysis.
74 Ibid., p. 29.
75 See Hoecker-Drysdale, 2001.
76 Emile Durkheim, 'Introduction,' *The Division of Labour in Society* (1893), p. 4; Martineau, 1837 II, pp. 263–369.
77 Martineau (1837), III, pp. 131–51.
78 Martineau (1844), (1859), p. 166.
79 Ibid.
80 Martineau's treatment of women, work and industrialization concurs with those of Ivy Pinchbeck and Alice Clark (Clark 1919; Pinchbeck 1930) and contemporary economic historians such as Maxine Berg.
81 Harriet Martineau, 'Modern Domestic Service', *Edinburgh Review*, 115 (April 1862), pp. 409–39.
82 'Female Industry', pp. 151–73.
83 Harriet Martineau, *Health, Husbandry and Handicraft* (London: Bradbury and Evans, 1861), pp. 188–202.
84 Ibid., pp. 26–27.
85 Ibid., pp. 222, 232, 248.
86 See Martineau's reviews in *Quarterly Review* and *Fraser's Magazine* of Nightingale's 1860 *Notes on Nursing: What It Is and What It Is Not*, p. 409.

6 Rewriting the past and present

Harriet Martineau, contemporary historian

Alexis Easley

At first glance, Harriet Martineau would seem to be a writer concerned more with the present than the past. After all, she was an outspoken commentator on the most important issues of her day, from the Crimean War to women's employment opportunities. Yet for Martineau, current events and cultural practices were best understood within a historical context. From the outset of her career, she looked to the past to gauge the progress of modern society – both in Britain and abroad. Like other Whig historians of the period, she was guided by the belief that all human societies were advancing toward a more enlightened democratic state.[1] Because Martineau's view of the past was so contingent on her conception of the present and her vision of the future, she focused primarily on contemporary history writing. Martineau was interested in illuminating recent historical events as a way of coming to terms with rapid change in political, social, and economic institutions. Part cautionary tale, part triumphant narrative, contemporary history could be used to motivate the right kind of social change. As a radical, Martineau's vision of the 'right' sort of transformation was premised on the decline of aristocratic privilege and the expansion of free markets and democratic opportunity. As we shall see in the discussion of Martineau's feminism in Chapter 9, her conception of an egalitarian state was also predicated on the expansion of women's rights. If, as she put it in *Society in America*, a crucial 'test of civilisation' was the 'condition of that half of society over which the other half has power,' then the history of women's experiences must be recounted in order to assess the progress of society toward achieving this state of advanced civility.[2]

Martineau not only situated contemporary history within a broader narrative of national progress but also celebrated the biographies of individuals who were the chief facilitators of social change. As she put it in her introduction to Reinhold Pauli's *Simon de Montfort* (1876), a mature society is interested in the 'origin of political amelioration, and the head, heart, and hands by which it was wrought.'[3] Thomas Carlyle's *On Heroes, Hero-Worship, and the Heroic in History* (1840–41) is usually credited with popularizing the 'great men' approach to history writing,[4] yet Martineau's first major contribution to the genre, *The Martyr Age of the United States* (1838–39), preceded Carlyle's and was just as instrumental in the development of historical biography. The fact that she includes profiles of notable women in *The Martyr Age* and *The History of England during the Thirty Years' Peace*

(1849–50) demonstrates her belief in their heroic potential as facilitators of positive social change. As a high-profile literary celebrity, Martineau herself modeled the kind of public activism she promoted in her contemporary history writing. She had firsthand experience associated with many of the events she described, a link that was made clear in the pages of her posthumously published *Autobiography*.[5] The depiction of activist heroes in her contemporary history writing thus echoes and reinforces her own work as a radical reformer and champion of the popular literature movement.

This chapter begins with an analysis of Martineau's 'Account of Toussaint L'Ouverture' (1838) and *The Martyr Age of the United States* (1838–39), two historical essays in support of the abolitionist cause. I will then turn to her most significant work of contemporary history, *The History of England during the Thirty Years' Peace*, which further demonstrates her democratic, proto-feminist approach to historical biography. Because Martineau's work as a historian often blends with other genres – the biographical sketch, journalistic essay, or political treatise – it is often omitted in accounts of Victorian history writing.[6] Yet for Victorians, Harriet Martineau was a pre-eminent historian. An 1878 notice in the *London Quarterly Review*, for example, called Martineau 'one of the most keen and contemplative minds of the age' whose *History* was 'deservedly popular' and 'one of the most thoroughly useful works . . . in the high class to which it belongs.'[7] Martineau was not the first Liberal thinker or the first British woman to take on the project of writing history,[8] yet her body of historical writing was significant for a number of reasons. By creating accounts of social progress, both at home and abroad, she provided a model for how seemingly 'unhistorical' individuals – women, labourers, and middle-class activists – could play a role in bringing about peaceful social change. As the *Calcutta Review* put it in 1851, Martineau's approach was groundbreaking because it departed from the 'old school' of history writing that focused on the 'cabinets of statesmen, or the camps of military commanders' and instead illuminated the 'silent labours' and 'common-place life' that shaped the 'social progress of a great people.'[9] Martineau's democratic approach anticipates the aims of social and feminist historiography by reinterpreting the notion of 'great men's history' in expansive terms.

Historical biography

Martineau's travels in America, 1834–36, most likely sparked her interest in contemporary history writing. In *Society in America* (1837) and *Retrospect of Western Travel* (1838), she depicts a nation struggling to achieve its own democratic ideals. As a young country produced from the revolutionary fervour of the late eighteenth century, the United States was an ideal test case for moral humanism and the principles of democracy. The horrors of slavery and the political non-existence of women, she argued, were barriers to social progress. In *How to Observe Morals and Manners* (1838), she extends her analysis beyond the American test case, providing guidelines for assessing the progress of nations more generally. On one hand, Martineau associates the historical past with a backwardness that threatens social advancement, arguing that the student of contemporary history must ascertain 'whether the country he studies is advancing in wisdom and happiness, or whether it is stationary, or whether it is going back.'[10] Yet she also imagines the past as a stage for heroic action which has produced the advances of the present. She writes, 'Amidst the supremacy of the worship of honour and social ease, there have always been confessors who could endure disgrace for the truth, and martyrs who could die for it.'[11]

This second approach to reading history – focusing on the heroes of the past as catalysts of reform – guides much of Martineau's work as a contemporary historian. In 'Account of Toussaint L'Ouverture' and *The Martyr Age of the United States*, she incorporates the biographies of exemplary men and women into her narrative of recent history, depicting them as martyrs in the abolitionist struggle. In doing so, she builds on a biographical tradition established within the popular literature movement – the publication of biographies of great men and women in cheap periodicals of the 1830s that were intended to provide models of self-improvement and moral activism. For example, from 1832 to 1852, *Chambers's Edinburgh Journal* published a weekly 'Biographic Sketches' series that highlighted the achievements of scientists, explorers, artists, and writers. During the same period, the *Penny Magazine*, published by the Society for the Diffusion of Useful Knowledge, incorporated profiles of 'eminent men of modern times who have given the greatest impulses to their age.'[12] In both series, portraits of female heroes such as Hannah More and Letitia Elizabeth Landon (L. E. L.) were often featured alongside profiles of notable men. Such an emphasis supported the mission of popular education magazines, which aimed to reach a mixed-gender family audience.[13] Following the approach set out in these magazines, Martineau provided portraits of notable men and women in recent history, emphasizing their exemplary actions and virtues. Her method of writing the biographies of 'great men' stood in stark contrast to the biographical approach to history employed by Thomas Carlyle in *On Heroes, Hero Worship, and the Heroic in History*. As Elisabeth Sanders Arbuckle notes, while Carlyle's 'heroes are often drawn from the distant past, beginning with Odin,' Martineau focuses primarily on 'practical' idols.[14] In doing so, she provides models of individual subjectivity that assume an active role for both men and women in the march of progress.

For Martineau, some of the most compelling heroes in recent history were leaders of the abolitionist campaigns. In one of her earliest examples of contemporary history writing, 'Account of Toussaint L'Ouverture' (1838), she recounts the life story of a Haitian leader of African descent, focusing on his exemplary actions as a popular hero. Published on the first page of an annual supplement to Charles Knight's *Penny Magazine*, the 'Account' was richly illustrated, suggesting that Knight found the article's abolitionist message worthy of special emphasis. Although Martineau's biography of L'Ouverture begins with racist references to the presumed 'inferiority of mind' among slaves in the New World, its ultimate purpose is to make an argument for 'what the negro race at large can do and become.'[15] Martineau writes, 'He had strength of body, strength of understanding, strength of belief, and consequently of purpose, strength of affection, of imagination, and of will. He was emphatically a Great Man: and what one many of his race has been, others may be.'[16] Given that Toussaint L'Ouverture (1743–1803) was born into slavery and rose through the military ranks to become the leader of the Haitian independence movement, his example reinforces the ideals of self-improvement espoused by the *Penny Magazine*.[17] Even more importantly, his story provides justification for the abolitionist cause by emphasizing the humanity and potential of Haitian people of African descent. Knight reinforces this message by commissioning illustrations that highlight L'Ouverture's European clothing and elegant handwriting (Figures 6.1 and 6.2), while still emphasizing his dark

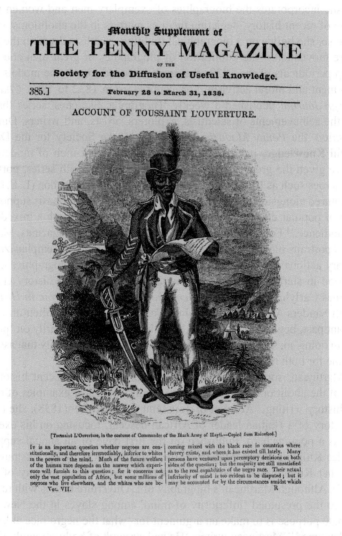

Figure 6.1 Portrait of Toussaint L'Ouverture from Harriet Martineau, 'Account of Toussaint L'Ouverture,' monthly supplement to the *Penny Magazine* 7 (28 February–31 March 1838), p. 121.

in the night he and his family were roused from sleep, hurried on board, and conveyed to the northwest coast of the island, where they were put on board the Héros, a ship of the line, in which they were conveyed to France. Two black chiefs, who attempted the great man's rescue, were shot: and about 100 of Toussaint's most devoted companions were arrested, and sent on board different ships of the squadron. No one of them was ever heard of more; and it is supposed that they were all thrown overboard.

On meeting the commander of the Héros, Toussaint observed to him, "In overthrowing me, you have overthrown only the trunk of the tree of negro liberty in St. Domingo. It will arise again from the roots, because they are many, and have struck deep." He spoke truly. Slavery has never been re-established in Hayti; and this island may be regarded as the centre from which negro liberty and civilization are destined to spread into all the countries where the dusky race is found. The outrage upon Toussaint roused the whole island. Cristóphe and Dessalines rose with their forces: the French were pressed on every side; and all the reinforcements which were sent from France seemed to do them no good. Even while Toussaint yet lived, 40,000 Frenchmen are supposed to have perished in the island. They established the torture: they introduced blood-hounds from Cuba to hunt down the blacks: but for every black whom they destroyed, two seemed to rise up; and before the invaders relinquished the struggle, they were reduced to feed on the carcases of the very dogs they had brought in to destroy their foes. On the first of January, 1804, the independence of Hayti was formally proclaimed, and its inhabitants took their place among the nations.

Toussaint was kept a close prisoner on his passage to France, not being allowed to see even his own family. On the arrival of the ship at Brest, he was allowed to meet them once, to bid them farewell for ever;—for ever in this world, he would have said; for he was a firm believer in a future life. He was escorted by a detachment of dragoons to Paris, and committed to the prison of the Temple. Napoleon repeatedly sent his aide-de-camp, Caffarelli, to him there, to question him about treasures he was reported to have buried. The only answer that could ever be got out of him was, "I have lost something very different from such treasures as you seek." When this disgraceful importunity was found to be in vain, he was conveyed to the castle of Joux, near Besançon, in Normandy, where he was deprived of the services of his only remaining attendant, Mars-Plaisir, and locked up in a dungeon, the floor of which was actually under water. It was while he, who had spent a long life in the sunshine of the tropics, and in unceasing activity of body and mind, was striving for patience under the long torture of such an imprisonment as this, that Wordsworth wrote this sonnet:—

> "Toussaint, the most unhappy Man of Men!
> Whether the whistling rustic tend his plough
> Within thy hearing, or thou liest now
> Buried in some deep dungeon's earless den;—
> O miserable Chieftain! where and when,
> Wilt thou find patience? Yet die not; do thou
> Wear rather in thy bonds a cheerful brow:
> Though fallen Thyself, never to rise again,
> Live, and take comfort. Thou hast left behind
> Powers that will work for thee—air, earth, and skies;
> There's not a breathing of the common wind
> That will forget thee: thou hast great allies;
> Thy friends are exultations, agonies,
> And love, and Man's unconquerable mind."

Of course, this captivity killed him, as his foes doubtless intended it should. He held on for ten months, during which we know nothing of his thoughts and sayings, and sank under an attack of apoplexy, on the 27th of April, 1803.

His family resided in the south of France, where his wife died, in 1816, in the arms of her sons, Placide and Isaac.

Was not this a Man—in all respects worthy of the name? He was altogether African,—a perfect negro in his organization, yet a fully endowed and well-accomplished man. In no respect does his nature appear to have been unequal; there was no feebleness in one direction as a consequence of unusual vigour in another. He had strength of body, strength of understanding, strength of belief, and consequently of purpose; strength of affection, of imagination, and of will. He was emphatically a Great Man: and what one man of his race has been, others may be.

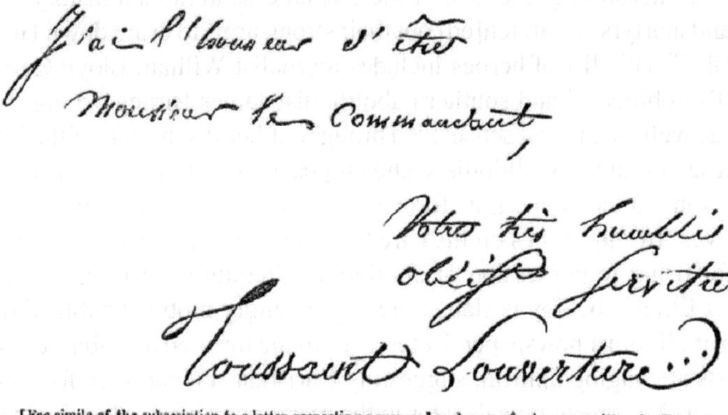

[Fac-simile of the subscription to a letter, respecting a proposed exchange of prisoners, written by Toussaint to Captain Smith, of his Britannic Majesty's ship Hannibal, dated "5th January, 7th year of the French Republic: One and Indivisible."]

⁂ The Office of the Society for the Diffusion of Useful Knowledge is at 59, Lincoln's Inn Fields
LONDON: CHARLES KNIGHT & CO., 22, LUDGATE STREET.
Printed by William Clowes and Sons, Stamford Street.

Figure 6.2 Reproduction of Toussaint L'Ouverture's handwriting and signature in the *Penny Magazine* (28 February–31 March 1838), p. 128.

skin color. Such images countered racist stereotypes and thus reinforced Martineau's abolitionist message. Indeed, in a letter to Fanny Wedgwood, Martineau indicates that her intent was 'to get at the Southern States, where they reprint the P.M. [*Penny Magazine*] fearlessly' and thereby to educate a 'few hundred people' regarding 'what a negro has been, and what other negroes therefore may be.'[18] By exposing Southerners to the heroes of contemporary history, she hoped to transform popular opinion and promote progressive social change.[19]

A few months after the 'Account of Toussaint L'Ouverture' appeared in the *Penny Magazine*, Martineau's *The Martyr Age* was published in the *Westminster Review* (December 1838). Basing *The Martyr Age* on Maria Weston Chapman's *Right and Wrong in Boston* (1835–37) as well as her own experiences in America (1834–36), Martineau celebrates the heroes of the abolitionist campaigns, 1829 to 1838. In an 1857 letter to John Chapman, Martineau claimed that the article 'did more for the character & fortunes of the review than any other article it ever published,' creating a 'ferment . . . at Cambridge, affecting for life the minds of not a few young men there; – Dr Arnold reading it to his family & guests, with the tears streaming down his face.'[20] It was subsequently re-published as a pamphlet in Britain and the United States because of 'repeated demand' for copies of the original periodical publication.[21] Proceeds from the pamphlet were used to raise £500 for Oberlin College, which enrolled African-American students during what Martineau called 'a most critical period' of the abolitionist campaigns.[22]

By focusing on contemporary history, rather than providing a broader historical perspective reaching back to the origins of slavery in America, Martineau places emphasis on recent events that have immediate relevance to the abolitionist cause, thereby attempting to spark sympathy and support among British and American readers. By defining this era of abolitionist activity as a 'martyr age,' she elevates its significance, interpreting it as one of the crucial eras in human history where 'confessors and martyrs . . . stretch[ed] out their strong arms to bring down Heaven upon our earth.'[23] This list of heroes includes journalist William Lloyd Garrison ('one of God's nobility')[24] and southern abolitionist James Birney ('a great man in a worldly as well as a moral sense').[25] Throughout her discussion of the heroic actions of these and other abolitionists, she emphasizes that personal sacrifice is necessary to bring about social transformation. In 1833, seminary student Amos Dresser receives 'twenty lashes on his bare back' in a public square in Nashville, Tennessee, for being in possession of abolitionist literature.[26] And in 1837, Illinois journalist Elijah Lovejoy is slaughtered by an angry mob for publishing the *Observer*, an abolitionist newspaper. References to the tortured and abused bodies of abolitionists are hagiographical, suggesting Christian self-sacrifice for a noble cause. Indeed, as Martineau reveals later in the essay, such martyrdom is a necessary catalyst for social progress:

> The course of events seems to be this: the abolitionists are first ridiculed, as a handful of insignificant fanatics; then the merchants begin to be alarmed for their purses, and the aristocracy for their prerogatives; the clergy and professional men act and speak for the merchant-interest, and engage the authorities

to discountenance the movement, which they do by threatening penal laws, or uttering warnings of mobs. A mob ensues, of course; the apprehensions of the magistracy furnishing the broadest hint. The business is brought home to the bosom of every citizen. All, especially the young men, look into the matter, rally in defence of the law, elect a good legislature, look carefully into their magistracy, and the right prevails.[27]

Historical progression, she suggests, takes place in a series of inevitable stages that result in positive social change. The personal and political struggles of the abolitionists influence public opinion, and by implication, the press, which brings truth 'to the bosom of every citizen.' Martineau's confidence is founded not only in her belief in democratic principles but her faith in exceptional individuals – 'the greatest people now living' who provide the initial spark of protest that ignites the process of change.[28]

What is most striking about Martineau's 'great men' approach to recounting the recent history of the abolitionist cause is that it includes so many women. Martineau begins with Prudence Crandall, the Connecticut teacher who bravely admitted black children to her school in 1833 and endured violent persecution and social exile as a result. She also includes admiring portraits of abolitionist leaders Lydia Maria Child, Lucretia Mott, and Angelina Grimké. From the outset of the campaign, she notes, women's participation 'continually increased,' but it was not until 1835, with the formation of the Female Anti-Slavery Society in Boston, that their participation became a visible force within the campaign.[29] For Martineau, the chief hero in this phase of the abolitionist movement is Maria Weston Chapman, a 'woman of genius' who not only leads the abolitionist movement but presides over a 'happy home.'[30] When a mob interrupts the first meeting of the society on 21 October 1835, Chapman stands up to them 'like an angel,' and later, when confronting a group of men that has invaded her home, she '[proceeds] with a remonstrance so powerful that, after some argument, her adversaries fairly succumbed: one wept, and another asked as a favour that she would shake hands with him.'[31] Both domestic and political, Chapman was just the kind of fearless heroine Martineau believed was needed in the modern world. The public visibility of Chapman and her followers provoked religious denunciations 'worthy of the dark ages,' which demanded female 'deference and subordination.'[32] Martineau thus associates the attitudes of these religious leaders with pre-enlightenment gender ideology that has no place in a modern, advancing society. In espousing such backward views, they inadvertently aid the cause they are attempting to defeat. While abolitionists never intended to link the 'question of the Rights of Woman with that of the Rights of Man in Slavery,' the opposition of religious leaders to women's involvement in the campaign 'compelled' the merger of the two movements.[33] The women's and abolitionist causes thus became inextricably connected as battles for justice and human rights.

Like Chapman, Martineau styled herself as a new kind of female leader – the fearless truth-teller who bravely confronts social injustice through writing and social activism. However, even though Martineau witnessed some of the agitation described in *The Martyr Age* first hand, she does not allude to her own active role in the proceedings. Readers of the *Westminster Review* who were familiar with the initials 'H.M.' affixed to the article certainly would have been aware that Martineau had returned from her American tour just two years before. Once the essay was published as a pamphlet with her name on the title page, the link between her personal travels in America and the public history of the abolitionist campaigns was even more clearly established. Thus, when she claims at the end of *The Martyr Age* that 'to appreciate them [the abolitionists] fully, one must be among them,' she indirectly alludes to her own personal recollections and experiences as source material.[34] It would not be until the publication of *Retrospect of Western Travel* (1838) and the *Autobiography* (1877) that the details of her personal involvement in the events described in *The Martyr Age* would come clearly into focus.[35] For example, in her *Autobiography*, she cross-references *The Martyr Age* when describing her participation in a meeting of the Female Anti-Slavery Society in Boston, 18 November 1835, going so far as to note the particular issue of the *Westminster Review* in which her essay had appeared.[36]

As much as Martineau downplayed her own experience as source material in *The Martyr Age*, she was nevertheless practising a method of historiography that relied upon experiential knowledge. The strategy of combining first-hand observation with conventional research was an approach she claimed to admire. In an 1862 review of the life and work of Edward Gibbon, author of *History of the Decline and Fall of the Roman Empire* (1776–88), she writes:

> He was not a man to shut himself up with books, and undertake to describe how former generations lived by taking what he pleased from books, and adding what he thought proper out of his own fancy. He grudged no time and no labour in proving the realities of things, and in ascertaining the bearings of evidence. He would go anywhere, and make any effort to obtain the smallest contribution to the materials of this history, and would put forth nothing that he had not tested by all the means at his command. It is thoroughly characteristic of him that he studied law for three years, in order to write the one chapter on Roman Law required by his history.[37]

Of course, as a woman who was deaf and suffered from ill health, Martineau could not hope to achieve the same degree of mobility and experiential engagement that Gibbon modelled; however, her travels in America provided her with the kind of first-hand experience she could use to supplement her own periods of being 'shut up' with books.

The history of the peace

Nearly a decade after publishing *The Martyr Age*, Martineau returned to writing contemporary history, this time focusing on recent events in Britain, 1816–46. When writing *The History of England during the Thirty Years' Peace*, Martineau was once again able to rely on her own experience of having lived through a recent period of national strife. However, these personal connections were omitted from the *History* when it was issued in monthly parts, 1849–50.[38] As I have noted elsewhere, Martineau's approach to history writing was premised on the notion that historians should maintain a sense of personal distance from their subject matter.[39] Consequently, in the *History*, she relies primarily on Hansard and the *Political Register*, constructing a minute account of the struggles and achievements of a nation and its vast empire. It was an ambitious project but one that ultimately highlighted Martineau's talents as contemporary historian. Her biographer R.K. Webb maintained that it was a work with 'incontestable claims to greatness.'[40] Likewise, a review of the 1864 edition published in the *National Quarterly Review* proclaimed that 'with the sole exception of [Thomas Babington] Macaulay's History, no similar work written within the last twenty years has been more extensively read in England.'[41]

The success of the *History* was particularly impressive given its rather complicated publication history. When Charles Knight (1791–1873) took on the project in 1846, he wrote the first sixteen chapters but soon became overwhelmed and turned it over to Charles MacFarlane (1799–1858) and George Craik (1798–1866), who together wrote the remainder of Book 1. Once Martineau took over the project in 1848, she wrote the remaining monthly numbers covering the years 1820 to 1846. It was a burdensome project involving intensive research and careful selection of detail, yet Martineau approached it with a sense of pride, calling it 'my great, long, glorious task.'[42] In 1846, when Knight recruited Martineau to write the *History*, he did so based on thorough knowledge of her work. He had not only printed Martineau's articles in the *Penny Magazine* but had also published a number of her book-length works, including *How to Observe Morals and Manners* (1838) and *The Peasant and the Prince* (1841). As I have shown elsewhere, Martineau's collaboration with Knight did not always run smoothly.[43] Nevertheless, in her preface to the first edition, Martineau refers to Knight's career as a publisher of popular literature as 'one of the chief national blessings of the period of the Peace.'[44] Indeed, the *History* is best understood within the context of Knight's and Martineau's involvement with the popular education movements of the 1840s.[45] As an addition to Knight's list of popular titles, the *History* was intended to be affordable and appealing to a broad audience. In an 1849 letter, Martineau underscores that the book was intended 'not for the fastidious aristocracy, but for the great middle & operative class of readers.'[46] Indeed, each monthly part of the first edition was published at the relatively affordable price of 2s., and the bound volumes, complete with steel-engraved plates, were priced at £2 2s. The *History* seems to have been a commercial success: by June 1849, Martineau reported that the sale of the monthly numbers had doubled, providing her with sufficient income to pay off the remainder of the mortgage on her Ambleside home.[47]

The success of the first edition of the *History* led to expansion of the project at either end. In 1851 Martineau published an introductory volume covering the years 1800 to 1815, and in an 1864 American edition she updated the *History* to include recent events, 1846 to 1854. In addition, from 1855 to 1858, Chambers published an illustrated edition of the *History* in monthly parts that were subsequently re-issued in volume form. Given that Martineau's work as a historian grew out of her experiences in America, it is not surprising that the expanded American edition of the *History* was a particular source of pride. In her letters, she boasts that the 'reprint was undertaken at the suggestion of leading bankers & men of business throughout the country, who hoped for good from its teachings on finance, currency, free trade &c &c.'[48] In her 1864 preface, she states her purpose as helping a young country learn from the 'errors and sufferings' of the old.[49] She does not make direct reference to the American Civil War, which had been under way since 1861, except to assert that the emancipation of the slaves was 'inevitable.'[50] Yet she implies that America, following Britain, will emerge from its own period of strife, entering into a productive period of peace yielding a 'higher character of national life.'[51]

Martineau's message about the inevitability of social progress is woven throughout the text of the *History*. For the benefit of British (and ultimately American) readers, she emphasizes that one of the chief 'blessings of the peace' after Waterloo was a nation dedicated to reform – the 'great idea' that evoked its 'best powers.'[52] This period of peace was ironically an era of intense strife on the domestic front, which produced Chartism (1838–48), the first Reform Act (1832), the Poor Law (1834), the Factory Acts (1833, 1844), and a host of other social and legislative initiatives. Like other Whig accounts of the period, Martineau's *History* is premised on the idea that the realization of democratic ideals and the expansion of economic and educational opportunity would lead to peaceful social change. She writes, 'We have what the old Tories have not, and cannot conceive of, – the deepest satisfaction in every proof that the national soul is alive and awake, that the national mind is up and stirring.'[53] Throughout the narrative, Martineau emphasizes the importance of the press in bringing about this social transformation. While in the 1820s, the 'lowest vendors of printed trash were lampooning the rulers of the country, [and] the government press was libeling the leaders of the popular party,' by 1835 a 'vast quantity of trash was immediately driven out of the market, and its place supplied by good newspapers' because of a reduction in the stamp duty.[54] She includes a detailed account of the formation of the Society for the Diffusion of Knowledge (SDUK), which provided inexpensive, improving literature for the masses and thus contributed to a 'great era in the history of popular enlightenment.'[55] She notes, however, that the society did not meet all of its lofty goals and left the people wanting a history of the 'vast change [that] was taking place.'[56] Of course, this was the very gap Martineau's book was intended to fulfil. The *History* indirectly draws attention to her own achievement: just as she had successfully written the history volumes that Knight, MacFarlane, and Craik had failed to complete, she had also achieved a goal that the SDUK had neglected to execute.

Like *The Martyr Age*, Martineau's *History* includes portraits of the heroes who brought about needed social and political change. Individuals, she notes, are best remembered for their honorable deeds and the 'immoral ideal' that they embody.[57] However, she situates this hero-worship within an expansive, detailed political history of a nation, which includes accounts of the royal family, parliamentary initiatives, working-class unrest, colonial enterprises, and economic upheavals.

The first volume edition of the *History* highlights the role of individuals in this broad historical panorama by incorporating sixteen steel-engraved portraits of noteworthy Britons – including James Watt, Jeremy Bentham, and the Duke of Wellington. The fact that there is only one portrait of a woman included in the first edition – Queen Victoria – epitomizes what a small role women play in the *History* as a whole. Given that Martineau was using the *Political Register* and parliamentary transcripts as her chief sources, this focus on male heroes is not surprising. The *History* is nevertheless remarkable for the glimpses of women's history that it *does* include. When Chambers re-issued the *History* in an illustrated edition (1855–58), he brought this content into the foreground by including portraits of Queen Victoria, Letitia Elizabeth Landon, Hannah More, Princess Charlotte, Fanny Burney, and Grace Darling. This highlighting of 'feminine' content through illustration was no doubt intended to make the *History* appealing to a broad family audience which included women. Of course, Martineau's interest in women's history went far beyond commercial concerns. As was the case with *The Martyr Age*, Martineau included models of women's moral activism – women who bravely did their part to bring about national reform. For example, she describes Elizabeth Fry as 'one of the first women of her time,' who instead of living life in 'ease and indolence' took action: 'When Mrs. Fry entered the room in Newgate where 160 guilty and ignorant wretches were shut up, and in her serene and noble countenance brought them the hope which they had believed to be forever shut out, she began that reform in the treatment of moral disease which, however vague and tentative at present, can never now stop short of completion.'[58] Fry is depicted as the instigator of a past reform effort that continues into the present; her story is thus intended to inspire others to join the cause.

One of the most intriguing segments of women's history in the volume is its portrait of Grace Darling, the twenty-two-year-old woman who helped to rescue nine people from a shipwreck in 1838. The portrait of Darling in the 1855 pictorial edition of the history further reinforces her status as a model of female heroism (Figure 6.3). Like Fry, she is depicted as a woman of action who does her duty and embodies the 'virtue which lives and acts in quietness while the turbulent elements of human life and society are making tempests on the surface.'[59] Yet after news of Darling's role in the rescue was made public, she was overwhelmed with attention and 'her health gave way'; consequently, she died a 'martyr to her own deed as if the boat had been swamped in its passage to the rock.'[60] The fact that she did her duty without thought of fame makes her a model of self-sacrifice whose story will 'rouse a spirit of heroic good-will, long after the sectarian strifes of the time shall have been forgotten.'[61] Martineau thus suggests that women of all social classes have the potential to act heroically and to embody the best values of their age. Darling's martyrdom is also transcendent, placing her above the 'sectarian strife' that characterizes her particular historical moment. Of course, as with the profiles of men incorporated into the *History*, Martineau's profiles of women are not always flattering. For example, in her profile of Hannah More, she criticizes 'all the spiritual pride and censoriousness, the narrowness of view, and the factitious interpretation of nature, life, and Scripture,

Figure 6.3 Portrait of Grace Darling from Harriet Martineau's *History of the Peace* (London: Chambers, 1855), p. 588.

which pervade her writings.'[62] Nevertheless, the fact that More is included in the history at all suggests that her life and work constitute an important chapter in the history of a nation.

Martineau also includes biographical profiles in the necrology chapters that conclude each volume of the *History*.[63] These biographical sketches of notable individuals who had died during each era reveal a great deal about Martineau's contribution to the 'great men' school of history writing. She includes misunderstood geniuses, such as Shelley and Malthus; over-rated literary celebrities, such as Byron and Fanny Burney; eminent painters, such as Benjamin West and William Turner; leading scientists such as Edward Jenner and Charles Bell; and ground-breaking journalists such as William Cobbett and James Bell. What is most remarkable about the necrology chapters is how many profiles of women are included. As noted earlier, the inclusion of women in serial biographies was standard practice in popular education magazines such as Knight's *Penny Magazine*, and this carried over into the *History* Knight commissioned from Martineau. Her incorporation of women's biography also testifies to her broader interest in women's history and sociology, as demonstrated in *The Martyr Age* and her other American writings. For example, the 1820–26 section of the *History* includes obituaries for Hester Thrale and Jane Taylor, and the 1830–34 volume incorporates profiles of writers who must have been fairly obscure even in Martineau's day, children's author Priscilla Wakefield and novelist Anna Maria Porter. She reserves her most glowing commentary for Anna Letitia Barbauld, whose works were 'small in bulk, but eminent in beauty,' and Maria Edgeworth, who was able to 'raise the character of fiction, and to gratify the popular mind.'[64] Surprisingly, at the end of the final volume of the 1864 edition of the *History*, covering the years 1846–54, Martineau does not include women on her list of living celebrities 'whose social influence was as unquestionable in 1846 as it can ever be to another generation.'[65] Dickens, Tennyson, and Carlyle are profiled, but Martineau's greatest female contemporaries, Margaret Oliphant, Charlotte Brontë, Elizabeth Barrett Browning, George Eliot, and Elizabeth Gaskell, are conspicuously absent. Perhaps Martineau believed that the literary legacy of women writers at mid-century was still unknown. As Alison Booth has noted, 'Martineau's slighting of practically everyone derives in part from an awareness that a canon of women is always in the works, always at the margins of a canon of men.'[66] Or she may have imagined that her own illustrious career, evoked by her famous name on the title page, was the most powerful embodiment of women's contribution to the spirit of the age.

Even if Martineau sometimes falls short in her accounting of women's contributions to national progress, she nevertheless incorporates powerful segments of women's history into her account of political, legislative, and social reforms during the first decades of the nineteenth century. In her overview of the early 1830s, she notes that society is in a 'transition state as regards the position of women' and makes an argument for expanded employment opportunity.[67] She writes, 'It is no longer true that every woman is supported by husband, father, or brother; a multitude of women have to support themselves; and only too many of them, their fathers and brothers too: but few departments of industry are yet opened to them, and those few are most inadequately paid.'[68] First published in 1849, this argument for women's employment opportunity anticipates the main point of focus of the Langham Place group and the women's movement during the 1850s.[69] She also lays the groundwork for her own influential essay on women's work, 'Female Industry,' which was published in the *Westminster Review* in 1859.[70] Martineau further highlights women's 'transitional' social status when recounting debates over whether a ladies' gallery should be included in the newly reconstructed House of Commons. Martineau reports that when the issue came under consideration in 1835, legislators made it into an 'ill-bred joke' rather than seriously considering the 'improvement of the women's knowledge, and the cultivation of their interest in subjects which concern every member of society.'[71] Even more worrying for Martineau was the thought of 'giddy and frivolous women, fond of novelty, and with plenty of time to lose,' who would be most likely to occupy the gallery.[72] Women who were sincerely interested in politics would meanwhile be 'reading and thinking at home,' and when it came time to reform the legal position of British women, the silly women in the gallery would unfairly serve as representatives of their sex.[73] If women are to be visible symbols of emancipation, she contends, they must assume the right kind of intelligent, earnest subjectivity. Like Martineau herself, they must first focus on reading and thinking at home and then make strategic appearances in public spaces as active participants in the battle for reform.

Yet Martineau most likely did sit in the ladies' gallery on occasion. In the section of the *History* reviewing debates over the Infant Custody Bill (1839), she notes that in the House of Lords 'two tales were told in the course of the debates on the Bill, which melted the hearts of those who heard them.'[74] Martineau does not repeat the details of these particular cases, allowing readers to imagine for themselves the agony of a 'blameless mother' being separated from her children as a result of the actions of a profligate husband.[75] She quotes extensively from Lord Brougham's passionate speech in favour of women's custody rights, arguing in response that the case reveals a broader injustice in British law: 'The party supposed, in works of political philosophy, to represent them, are precisely those against whom legislation is needed for their protection.'[76] For Martineau, women's lack of political representation was the underlying problem – a legal disability which, by implication, could only be solved through enfranchisement. Returning to her argument in *The Martyr Age*, she links abolitionism to women's rights, stating, 'When the position of mothers had once been argued, the nation which had sent out protectors of slaves, and which was striving to put an end to one-sided and tyrannical legislation in Jamaica, was not likely to neglect the suffering women at home.'[77] Martineau thus situates the expansion of women's rights within a broader narrative of social progress where positive change is not only desirable but inevitable. Indeed, she calls the passage of the Infant Custody Act in 1839 the 'first blow struck at the oppression of the English legislation in relation to women.'[78] The battle was just beginning and would eventually be won.

Martineau's confidence in asserting the inevitability of positive social change – the expansion of women's rights, the abolition of slavery, the advance of social reform, the decline of aristocratic privilege – was intended to inspire readers to work for change. Even if British society seemed mired in political and social strife, the process of reform would ultimately produce a more egalitarian society. The study of history was thus intended to give readers a broader framework in which to situate their own struggles. In the final volume of the *History*, Martineau identifies the double vision offered to those who study the past:

> Stern as is the spirit of history in rebuking presumption, and showing up
> the worthless character of transient victories, and pointing out the inevitable

recurrence of human passion and folly, in high places and in low, with all the mournful consequences of such frailty, – exactly in the same proportion is *she* genial and consoling in an adverse season, – pointing out the good that underlies all evil, shedding hope upon the most ghastly perplexities, and cheerfully teaching us how to store up all our past experience as material for a deeper knowledge and a wiser action than we were qualified for in our time of highest confidence.[79]

It is significant that Martineau personifies history using a female pronoun – 'she' who both rebukes and cheerfully instructs a nation. History, like Martineau herself, draws attention to the follies of the past and present while still 'shedding hope' for future progress.

By defining history as a woman – and interpreting women's lives and experiences as historical – Martineau laid the groundwork for the women's movements of the 1850s and for her own later contributions to the discourse on women's rights. At the same time, her historical writings fueled her lifelong battle against the slave trade – a struggle that was closely tied to the women's movement in that it provided a motivating cause for middle-class women to take an active role in confronting social injustice. As a woman who had lived through and shaped the contemporary history she recounted, Martineau herself provided a compelling model of how women could serve as catalysts of social change, even if their historic deeds were described in short segments embedded within a broader national history.

Published in the era between William Hazlitt's *Spirit of the Age* (1824–25) and Carlyle's *On Heroes, Hero-Worship, and the Heroic in History* (1840–41), Martineau's early historical writings are notable for their democratic inclusivity. While Hazlitt focused exclusively on men, Martineau, following the conventions of penny periodicals, incorporated women into her pantheon of contemporary heroes. And while Carlyle looked to the distant past to find his representative men, Martineau found them in the formative years of modern Britain after the French Revolution. This, she averred, was the period that had provided the most compelling stage for martyrdom and heroic action, the work of great men as well as the efforts of 'unhistorical' individuals to bring about needed social change. Of course, her conception of contemporary heroism was primarily focused on middle-class white activists. In Martineau's imperialist histories, *Eastern Life, Present and Past* (1848) and *British Rule in India* (1857), her emphasis on British superiority undermines her efforts at democratic inclusivity.[80] As a writer for the *Calcutta Review* said of Martineau's *History*, 'There seems to be a fatality attending all Indian episodes, introduced into the narratives of European historians.'[81] Likewise, in her 'Representative Men' series of biographical sketches for *Once a Week* (1861–62), Martineau reverts to an almost exclusively white male view of history.[82] Yet taken as a whole, Martineau's historical writings represent a large step forward in redefining the history of 'great men' in more expansive and democratic terms.

***

In the summer of 1849, just as the *History* was being issued in monthly numbers to much popular acclaim, Martineau was offered the handsome sum of £1,000 to write another 'work of historical bearing' for a 'respectable and substantial publisher.'[83] She was tempted by the project but ultimately turned it down, concerned that it would take up too much of her time. As she wrote to her sister-in-law Helen, 'I <u>was</u> sorry to let it go, – it was so honourable & pleasant in aspect. I have agreed for some light & agreeable work, occupying a few days each month of next year for £200; & some more for America. And this leaves me at liberty for any thing that may tempt me when in London.'[84] Even though Martineau declined this 'honourable' proposal, she returned to history writing throughout her career, publishing additions to the *History of the Peace*, as well as *Eastern Life, Present and Past* and *British India*. Martineau was nevertheless unwilling to tie herself down to another multi-volume history-writing project. Undertaking such an effort no doubt would have solidified her reputation as a historian rather than as a journalist, economist, or essayist. But for Martineau, it was vitally important to be 'at liberty' for exploring what issues might arise, what movements might need a champion. This resulted in Martineau's being termed a 'miscellaneous' writer for much of the twentieth century, trivializing her achievement in multiple fields of discourse, including her important work as a historian.[85] Yet it was just this miscellaneity – her sense of the interpenetration of past and present, the blurred lines between history writing and other genres, and the broad dimensions of her own intellectual interests – that made her such an astute chronicler of her age.

Notes

1 For an overview of the Whig historical tradition, see J. W. Burrow, *A Liberal Descent: Victorian Historians and the English Past* (Cambridge: Cambridge University Press, 1981); Neil McCaw, *George Eliot and Victorian Historiography: Imagining the National Past* (London: Palgrave, 2000); Bonnie Smith, "The contribution of women to modern historiography in Great Britain, France, and the United States, 1750–1940," *American Historical Review*, 89:3 (1984), pp. 709–32; Rosemary Mitchell, *Picturing the Past: English History in Text and Image, 1830–70* (Oxford: Clarendon, 2000); and Rosemary Jann, *The Art and Science of Victorian History* (Columbus: Ohio State University Press, 1985).

2 Harriet Martineau, *Society in America* (1837; repr. London: Transaction, 1981), p. 291.

3 Harriet Martineau, introduction to Reinhold Pauli, *Simon de Montfort*, translated by Una Goodwin (London: Trübner, 1876), p. iv.

4 For example, David Amigoni refers to Carlyle as a 'pivotal figure in Victorian life writing, this in part because of his idea of "heroic" biography.' David Amigoni, 'Victorian life writing: Genres, print, constituencies.' In: David Amigoni (ed.), *Life Writing and Victorian Culture* (Aldershot: Ashgate, 2006), p. 8.

5 See Alexis Easley, *Literary Celebrity, Gender, and Victorian Authorship* (Newark: University of Delaware Press, 2011), ch. 4.

6 For example, Martineau is not mentioned in Rosemary Jann's *Art and Science of Victorian History* or in Rosemary Mitchell's *Picturing the Past*. As many critics have noted, women's work as historians is best understood by working across genre. Mary Spongberg writes, "'Women's history" in the past took multiple forms, and evolved both in relation to and in reaction to masculinist conceptions of history and the prevailing

prescriptions of gender.' Mary Spongberg, *Writing Women's History since the Renaissance* (Basingstoke: Palgrave, 2002), p. 6. Such an approach is especially appropriate for investigating the work of Harriet Martineau. As Deborah Logan has pointed out, 'It is revealing to consider the intersections in her [Martineau's] writing between what we have come to regard as sharply distinct genres—biography, autobiography, journalism, sociology, history, literature, and fiction—but which are in fact quite intimately linked and ultimately resistant to the sorts of arbitrary distinctions imposed on them by individual disciplines.' Deborah Logan, introduction to *Harriet Martineau's Writing on British History and Military Reform* (London: Pickering and Chatto, 2005), vol. 1, pp. xvii–xviii.

7 Review of *History of the Thirty Years' Peace, London Quarterly Review* 50 (July 1878), pp. 527, 528. For additional contemporary critical response to the *History*, see Deborah A. Logan, *Harriet Martineau, Victorian Imperialism and the Civilizing Mission* (Aldershot: Ashgate, 2010), pp. 17–20.

8 For an overview of the variety of histories written by women during the early nineteenth century, see Spongberg, *Writing Women's History*, pp. 109–29; Mitchell, *Picturing the Past*, pp. 140–69; Rohan Maitzen, *Gender, Genre, and Victorian Historical Writing* (New York: Garland, 1998), pp. 3–26; and Rosemary Mitchell, '"The busy daughters of Clio": Women writers of history from 1820–1880,' *Women's History Review*, 7:1 (1998), pp. 107–34. See note 1 above for sources on Whig history.

9 Review of *The History of England during the Thirty Years' Peace, Calcutta Review* 16 (October 1851), p. 340.

10 Harriet Martineau, *How to Observe Morals and Manners* (1838; repr., London: Transaction, 1988), pp. 211–12.

11 Ibid., p. 112.

12 'Gallery of Portraits,' *Penny Magazine*, 1 (26 May 1832), p. 87. See also Scott Bennett, 'The Editorial Character and readership of *The Penny Magazine*: An analysis,' *Victorian Periodicals Review*, 17 (1984), p. 135.

13 *The Penny Magazine*, for example, claimed that it was for the 'sitting-room of the mechanic – for the cottage and the kitchen,' 'The Library,' *Penny Magazine* 1 (21 April 1832), p. 32. *Chambers's* included frequent articles on domestic economy, writing in 1834, 'We have more than once commended the propriety of wives attending to the various duties of their household, for nothing can be more respectable in its way, but in inculcating this principle, it is necessary to remind our female readers that it has its limitations, especially when applied to those in the higher circles of society. It ought to be remembered that the extreme of minute attention and of luxurious indulgence are equally improper, and ought to be avoided.' 'Domestic Duties,' *Chambers's Edinburgh Journal* 2 (11 January 1834), p. 399.

14 Elisabeth Sanders Arbuckle, 'Carlyle looks Askance at a hero: Harriet Martineau's Toussaint L'Ouverture,' *Carlyle Studies Annual*, 19 (1999), p. 29.

15 Harriet Martineau, 'Account of Toussaint L'Ouverture,' monthly supplement to the *Penny Magazine* 7 (28 February–31 March 1838), pp. 121, 122. See illustration 1.

16 Ibid., p. 128.

17 See Bennett, 'The Editorial Character,' p. 135.

18 Harriet Martineau to Fanny Wedgwood, in *Harriet Martineau's Letters to Fanny Wedgwood*, ed. Elisabeth Sanders Arbuckle (Stanford: Stanford University Press, 1983), p. 11.

19 Indeed, 'Account of Toussaint L'Ouverture' was a prelude to Martineau's major work of historical fiction, *The Hour and the Man* (1841), which elaborated upon her earlier biographical sketch. As Susan Belasco has argued, the novel was 'well received and widely reviewed in both England and America' and made a 'significant contribution to the American antislavery movement,' Susan Belasco, 'Harriet Martineau's Black Hero and the American antislavery movement,' *Nineteenth-Century Literature*, 55:2 (2000), pp. 176, 194. Martineau's use of fiction to establish Toussaint L'Ouverture

as an abolitionist hero built upon the success of her wildly popular *Illustrations of Political Economy* (1832–34), which similarly used fictional narrative to communicate abstract principles. Indeed, in an 1844 letter to Edward Bulwer Lytton, Martineau claims that historical fiction 'might do *more than any other means whatever* to turn political discontent into sound political knowledge and views.' Martineau's emphasis. Harriet Martineau to Edward Bulwer-Lytton, 27 April 1844, in Deborah Logan, ed., *The Collected Letters of Harriet Martineau*, 5 vols. (London: Pickering & Chatto, 2007), vol. 2, p. 290. Nevertheless, her most important work as a historian was in the form of non-fiction books and essays.

20 Harriet Martineau to John Chapman, 11 June [1857], Logan, *Collected Letters*, vol. 4, pp. 34, 35.

21 Editorial note prefacing Martineau's *The Martyr Age of the United States* (Boston: Weeks, Jordan 1839, repr. Arno Press and the New York Times, 1969). The pamphlet version of *The Martyr Age* was first printed in the United States in 1839 by Weeks, Jordan in Boston and John S. Taylor and S. W. Benedict in New York. In Britain, it was published by Blackwell in 1838 and was reissued two years later by Finlay & Charlton.

22 Harriet Martineau to John Chapman, 11 June, [1857], Logan, *Collected Letters*, vol. 4, p. 35.

23 Martineau, *The Martyr Age*, p. 81. The essay was originally published in the *Westminster Review* 32 (December 1838), pp. 1–59.

24 Martineau, *The Martyr Age*, p. 7. Martineau often invoked William Lloyd Garrison's assertion, 'I am in earnest – I will not equivocate – I will not excuse – I will not retreat a single inch – AND I WILL BE HEARD.' This was just the kind of truth-speaking bravery she most admired in contemporary heroes. She first quotes the sentence in *The Martyr Age*, p. 10, and later repeats it in *History of England from the Commencement of the Nineteenth Century to the Crimean War*, 4 vols. (Philadelphia: Porter and Coates, 1864–66), vol. 3, p. 346; 'Representative men: Social reformers,' *Once a Week*, 4 (8 June 1861), p. 657; and the *Autobiography*, ed. Linda Peterson (Peterborough, ON: Broadview Press, 2007), p. 369.

25 Martineau, *The Martyr Age*, p. 19.

26 Ibid., p. 25.

27 Ibid., p. 74.

28 Ibid., p. 82.

29 Ibid., p. 27.

30 Ibid., p. 28.

31 Ibid., p. 32.

32 Ibid., p. 53.

33 Ibid., p. 54.

34 Ibid., p. 83.

35 Even if in *The Martyr Age* and her other historical writings Martineau seems intent on generalizing her own personal experiences, she restores this context through autobiographical writings that make covert and overt cross-references to her more 'official' accounts of contemporary history. See my discussion of the link between Martineau's historical and autobiographical writing in *Literary Celebrity*, ch. 4.

36 Harriet Martineau, *Autobiography*, p. 349. For an overview of Martineau's engagement in the abolitionist campaigns, see Deborah A. Logan's introduction to Martineau's *Writings on Slavery and the American Civil War* (DeKalb: Northern Illinois University Press, 2002). Logan perceptively interprets Martineau's speech before the Female Anti-Slavery Society in Boston as 'one of the most pivotal decisions of her life' because 'she chose to act on her principles rather than simply write about them' (xxi). This is supported by the fact that she highlights the incident and makes reference to *The Martyr Age* so prominently in her *Autobiography*.

37 Harriet Martineau, 'Representative men: Men of letters,' *Once a Week*, 6 (18 January 1862), p. 109.

38 In the final volume of the *History*, covering 1846–54, which was published in 1864, Martineau does allude to 'personal reasons' that require her to write with 'less fulness than the plan of the previous history required.' She is no doubt referring to her failing health during this period. Martineau, *History*, vol. 4, p. 547.

39 See Easley, *Literary Celebrity*, pp. 106–7.

40 R. K. Webb, *Harriet Martineau: A Radical Victorian* (New York: Columbia University Press, 1960), p. 277.

41 'Miss Martineau's *The History of the Peace*,' *National Quarterly Review* 9 (September 1864), p. 387.

42 Harriet Martineau to Helen Martineau, 5 July 1848, in Deborah A. Logan, *The Collected Letters of Harriet Martineau* (London: Pickering & Chatto, 2007), vol. 3, p. 119.

43 Easley, *Literary Celebrity*, p. 98.

44 Harriet Martineau, preface to *History of the Peace* (London: Knight, 1849), vol. 1, p. iii.

45 *The History of England during the Thirty Years' Peace* was one of a series of works of popular history published by Knight. His other publications in this vein include George Porter's *The Progress of the Nation, in Its Various Social and Economical Relations, from the Beginning of the Nineteenth Century to the Present Time* (London: Knight, 1836–43); *The Penny Cyclopaedia of the Society for the Diffusion of Useful Knowledge* (London: Knight, 1833–43); and George Craik's *The Pictorial History of England: Being a History of the People, as well as a History of the Kingdom* (London: Knight, 1849). See R. K. Webb for a discussion of Martineau's early development as a national instructor. Webb, *Harriet Martineau*, pp. 99–133.

46 Harriet Martineau to Richard Monckton Milnes, 4 June 1849, in Deborah Logan, ed., *The Collected Letters of Harriet Martineau*, 5 vols. (London: Pickering & Chatto, 2007), vol. 3, p. 144.

47 Harriet Martineau to Helen Martineau, 13 June 1849, in Logan, *Collected Letters*, vol. 3, p. 145.

48 Harriet Martineau to Henry Reeve, 6 May 1864, in Logan, *Collected Letters*, vol. 5, p. 63.

49 Martineau, *History*, vol. 1, p. 10.

50 Ibid., vol. 1, p. 9.

51 Ibid., vol. 1, p. 7.

52 Martineau, *History*, vol. 2, p. 297.

53 Ibid., vol. 3, p. 164.

54 Ibid., vol. 2, p. 303, vol. 4, p. 63.

55 Ibid., vol. 3, p. 196.

56 Ibid., vol. 3, p. 195.

57 Ibid., vol. 3, p. 220.

58 Ibid., vol. 3, p. 165; vol. 4, p. 543.

59 Ibid., vol. 4, p. 214.

60 Ibid., vol. 4, p. 215.

61 Ibid.

62 Ibid., vol. 3, p. 385.

63 Later, Martineau continued her 'necrology' by publishing *Biographical Sketches* (1869), a collection of obituaries originally published in the *Daily News*.

64 Martineau, *History*, vol. 2, p. 496; vol. 4, p. 605.

65 Ibid., vol. 4, p. 606.

66 Alison Booth, *How to Make It as a Woman: Collective Biographical History from Victoria to the Present* (Chicago: University of Chicago Press, 2004), p. 185.

67 Martineau, *History*, vol. 3, p. 181.

68 Ibid.

69 For background on the Langham Place group and efforts to expand women's employment opportunity during the 1850s, see Candida Lacey, ed., *Barbara Leigh Smith Bodichon*

and the Langham Place Group (1986; repr., London: Routledge, 2001); Solveig Robinson, '"Amazed at our success": The Langham place editors and the emergence of a feminist critical tradition,' *Victorian Periodicals Review*, 29:2 (1996), pp. 159–72; Sheila Herstein, '"*The English Woman's Journal* and the Langham place circle: A feminist forum and its women editors.' In: Joel Weiner (ed.), *Innovators and Preachers: The Role of the Editor in Victorian England* (Westport, CT: Greenwood, 1985), pp. 61–76. See also Gaby Weiner's chapter in this volume.

70 [Harriet Martineau], 'Female industry,' *Edinburgh Review*, 109 (April 1859), pp. 293–336.
71 Ibid., vol. 4, p. 75.
72 Ibid.
73 Ibid.
74 Ibid, vol. 4, p. 186.
75 Ibid.
76 Ibid.
77 Ibid., vol. 4, p. 187.
78 Ibid., vol. 4, p. 188.
79 Martineau, *History*, vol. 4, pp. 1–2. My emphasis.
80 For post-colonial readings of Martineau's *Eastern Life* and *British India*, see, for example, Sahar Sobhi Abdel-Hakim, 'Gender politics in a colonial context: Victorian women's accounts of Egypt.' In: Paul and Janet Starkey (eds,), *Interpreting the Orient: Travellers in Egypt and the Near East* (Reading: Garnet, 2001), pp. 111–22; Sangeeta Ray, *En-Gendering India: Woman and Nation in Colonial and Postcolonial Narratives* (Durham, Duke University Press, 2000), pp. 53–67. For a thorough discussion of Martineau's writings on empire, see Deborah A. Logan, *Harriet Martineau, Victorian Imperialism and the Civilizing Mission* (Farnham: Ashgate, 2010). Logan interprets Martineau as both a 'cautious advocate and severe critic of British Imperialism' (9).
81 Review of *History of England*, p. 341.
82 Of the thirty-five 'representative men' profiled in the series, only one woman is included: Elizabeth Fry. Harriet Martineau, 'Representative Men,' *Once a Week* 4 (20 April 1861), pp. 455–59; (18 May 1861), pp. 575–80; (8 June 1861), pp. 652–58; 5 (6 July 1861), pp. 35–40; (17 August 1861), pp. 203–9; (7 September 1861), pp. 289–94; (5 October 1861), pp. 401–6; (9 November 1861), pp. 539–46; (14 December 1861), pp. 693–700; 6 (18 January 1862), pp. 103–10.
83 Harriet Martineau to Helen Martineau, 13 June 1849, in Logan, *Collected Letters*, vol. 3, p. 146. The topic of the projected history and the identity of the publisher are unknown.
84 Ibid.
85 The characterization of Martineau as a 'miscellaneous writer' in *The Dictionary of National Biography* defined the terms by which she would be understood throughout much of the twentieth century. 'Harriet Martineau,' in *The Dictionary of National Biography*, vol. 36, ed. Sidney Lee (London: Smith, Elder, 1893), p. 309.

7 'The liberty of fiction' in Harriet Martineau's novels

Sharon Connor

Harriet Martineau was at the forefront of two significant shifts in the writing of fiction during the 1830s. Her first innovation was through her series of short stories *Illustrations of Political Economy* (1832–4), which used fictional tales to educate the reading public on social and economic matters, as well as brought in greater class inclusiveness to the characters she portrayed. Martineau's second pioneering move was her groundbreaking 1839 novel *Deerbrook*, in which she pre-empted many of the issues that became popular topics for female authors who followed her. These include the condition of governesses, local community and the danger of gossip, the medical profession, and the subjects of politics and public health. The term of novelist is pertinent for Martineau, appropriating Samuel Johnson's dictionary definition of 'Novelist' as 'Innovator of novelty' [newness].[1] Yet Martineau's significant contribution and skills as an author were overshadowed at the time of writing by critics who mocked her unmarried status and her attempts to engage with the 'masculine' topics of politics and economics, despite her adoption of the acceptably 'feminine' vehicle of fiction. The resurgence of interest in Martineau's work by the second wave of feminists in the 1980s and '90s understandably tended to focus more on her feminist journalism and politics than her works of fiction. It is significant that Ali Smith chose as her subject for the Inaugural Harriet Martineau lecture in 2013 Martineau's role as a social reformer, admitting that she had not read *Deerbrook*.[2] Instead Smith focused on Martineau's 1840 historical novel *The Hour and the Man*, a choice reinforcing Martineau's reputation as political commentator rather than novelist.

This chapter examines Martineau's emerging voice as a novelist. Beginning with her first short tales, *Illustrations of Political Economy*, which combined factual information within the frame of fiction, it reassesses *Deerbrook* as an outspoken response to the plight of single women in the late 1830s. Martineau had been recognised as stridently single from the time of her controversial political economy tales, especially *Weal and Woe in Garveloch* (1832), an image reinforced by the publication of her *Autobiography* in 1877. My reading of *Deerbrook* unpicks a far more complex attitude to marital status displayed by Martineau, as she works out her personal understanding of a woman's place in society, a topic which remained at the forefront of mid-nineteenth century social culture.

The collapse of the Martineau family business, the death of her father and the end of her short betrothal to John Hugh Worthington in the late 1820s left Harriet, her mother and her sisters almost destitute. This might be viewed as a catastrophically humiliating position for the Martineau women. Instead, as Martineau recollected in her *Autobiography*, the immediate need to avoid a life of poverty provided the opportunity for Harriet and her sisters to expand their horizons and actively seek paid employment outside the home. The financial misfortunes that befell her family thus liberated Martineau to commit herself to writing as a career:

> I call it a misfortune, because in common parlance it would be so treated: but I believe my mother and all her other daughters would have joined heartily, if asked, in my conviction that it was one of the best things that ever happened to us. [. . .] In a very short time, my two sisters at home and I began to feel the blessing of a wholly new freedom. I, who had been obliged to write before breakfast, or in some private way, had henceforth liberty to do my own work in my own way; for we had lost our gentility. Many and many a time since have we said that, but for that loss of money, we might have lived on in the ordinary provincial method of ladies with small means, sewing, and economising, and growing narrower every year: whereas, by being thrown, while it was yet time, on our own resources, [. . .] have truly lived instead of vegetated.[3]

Her writing previously had been something akin to a hobby; now it became a means of survival to which she could fully and publicly commit herself. Having already published a number of articles in the Unitarian journal *The Monthly Repository* during the 1820s, as noted in other chapters in this volume, she embarked on a scheme to write a series of fictional tales to illustrate the workings of political economy. The tales, published in monthly instalments between 1832 and 1834, have been viewed as a hybrid form of fiction, rooted in the desire to educate the reading public on factual matters of economics, politics and social reforms. In an article for *Tait's Edinburgh Magazine* entitled 'The Achievements of the Genius of Scott,' Martineau argued for recognition of 'the power of fiction as an agent of morals and philosophy'[4] and made clear her belief that a different form of fiction was needed. She continued:

> The bulk of the reading public, whether or not on the scent of utility, cannot be interested without a larger share of philosophy, or a graver purpose in fiction, than formerly; and the writer who would effect most for himself and others in this department must take his heroes and heroines from a different class than any which has yet been adequately represented.

Martineau embraced the challenge of producing fiction with a 'graver purpose', featuring heroines and heroes from a 'different class'. Her series proved immensely popular and a commercial success. Her informative yet entertaining tales appeared to meet the needs that Martineau felt had long been lacking in fiction. Critics however, took a less enthusiastic view. One reviewer described *Ella of Garveloch* as 'improbable, but amusing [. . .] if we skip the political economy in it, which consists of sundry long and doleful dialogues on the nature of *rent*.'[5] Indeed, the review – which covered the first twelve tales of her series – acknowledged the noble intent of Martineau's work, but ultimately lambasted the tales:

> It is equally impossible not to laugh at the absurd trash which is seriously propounded by some of her characters, in dull didactic dialogues, introduced here and there in the most clumsy manner; and worst of all, it is quite impossible not to be shocked, nay disgusted, with many of the unfeminine and mischievous doctrines on the principles of social welfare, of which these tales are made the vehicle (p.136).

Much of the criticism aimed at Martineau can be attributed to the misogynistic attitudes of the predominantly male critics of the period. Martineau had publicly and controversially moved beyond the socially acceptable boundaries of ideal womanhood. Not only was she earning her living as a writer and journalist – at a time when respectable middle-class women were not expected to work – but also she was writing on topics which had hitherto been viewed as exclusively male. The 'disgust' the reviewer felt no doubt refers to Martineau's tale *Weal and Woe in Garveloch* (1832), in which Martineau argued the need for population control: 'By bringing no more children into the world than there is subsistence for, society may preserve itself from the misery of want.'[6] Martineau's argument was viewed as a shockingly unseemly topic for a young unmarried woman to be publicly promoting.

The *Quarterly Review* categorised Martineau's tales as a 'series of novels'[7] and we can see how their interpretation could be justified by recourse to Johnson's definition of the novel as 'a small tale'.[8] The harsh dismissal of her writing as 'absurd trash' overlooks the more intimate voice of the novelist which emerges in Martineau's tales. For example, in *Ella of Garveloch* (1832), the vivid description of Ella's three brothers provides imaginative relief from Martineau's more pragmatic prose:

> They were three boys, the elder two of whom were strong, ruddy, well-grown youths, apparently of the ages of sixteen and fourteen. The third was either some years younger, or was made to look so by his smallness of size and delicacy of appearance. He fixed the attention of the laird at once by the signs of peculiarity about him. His restlessness of eye and of manner was unlike that which arises in children from animal spirits, and contrasted strangely with the lost and melancholy expression of his countenance.[9]

Here Martineau's portrayal of Ella's twelve-year-old brother, Archie, provides more than the matter-of-fact description expected in a tale aimed at educating the public. Glimpses of such vulnerable and complex human beings allow Martineau's novelistic voice to break through. That aside, one cannot dispute that her series had at its heart the aim of educating her readers, which she happened to couch in the form of fiction. In writing the tales, Martineau recognised the power of fiction as an agent of influence and education, and in creating characters who came from classes other than the aristocracy, she sought to introduce a form of realism that had hitherto been lacking.

For example, in a parody of the fashion of the day for aristocratic heroes and heroines, Martineau's tale *For Each and For All* (1832) tells the story of Letitia, a former stage actress who marries into the aristocracy, and then uses her position of privilege to educate the general public on the characteristics of the labour market. Martineau explicitly showcases what she saw as the equally important stories to be told about other classes. The revolutionary Lord (Henry) and Lady (Letitia) F__ of the tale, discuss here the reasons why artists fail to portray different areas and classes of life:

> 'Because our painters of life do not take into the account, – in fact know little of, – some of the most important circumstances which constitute life, in the best sense of the word. [. . .] They take Love: and think it more becoming to describe a Letitia going to the altar with a lord F__, than a weaver and his thoughtful bride taking possession of their two rooms, after long waiting and anxiety'.[10]

Letitia is in a position to provide such advice and insight because (paralleling Martineau's experience) she has been plunged into poverty and has had to seek financial independence, following the collapse of her father's business. The tale displays something of an autobiographical impulse which Martineau was able to explore more fully in *Deerbrook*, especially the issues of whether all women were suited to marriage, and how single women might live active, purposeful lives. Importantly, Letitia's enthusiasm and eloquence on matters that she feels strongly about, are admired by friends and her husband's family alike, with one praising her outpourings as felt 'in her heart, as well as [spoken] by heart' (p.12). The implication is that Letitia is not simply repeating social and political ideals that she had learned by rote ('<u>by</u> heart'), but advocating them because she believes them '<u>in her</u> heart'. It could be argued that Martineau's passion was doing something similar in *Deerbrook*.

After completing the *Illustrations of Political Economy* in 1834, Martineau continued to enjoy success as a journalist and social commentator, but by 1837 she felt the need to return to fiction, and so wrote her major novel, *Deerbrook*. In her *Autobiography*, she described her decision to tackle writing a novel:

> For many years now my writing had been almost entirely about fact:- facts of society and of individuals: and the constraint of the effort to always be correct, and to bear without solicitude the questioning of my correctness, had become burdensome. [. . .] I longed inexpressibly for the liberty of fiction.[11]

Not only did this work differ from Martineau's other works, fiction or otherwise, in respect of its tone of emotional vulnerability but it was also innovative as a form of literature. Gaby Weiner has argued that the 'purple prose' passages in *Deerbrook* sound 'inauthentic as they are so unlike anything else written by Martineau.'[12] The fact that it was written with no particular political, historical or social motive does indeed make *Deerbrook* stand out from her other work. However, far from being 'inauthentic', I want to argue that Martineau's writing in *Deerbrook* is her most emotionally authentic piece of work. By this I mean that the novel is rooted in what she described in her *Autobiography* as her 'true [. . .] state of thought and feeling'.[13] It thus shows a depth of vulnerability not apparent in the more secure structure of her factual writing. The poet Dora Greenwell celebrated this form of fiction as pioneered by Martineau, more than a decade later, in an article for *North British Review.* Although not mentioning *Deerbrook* specifically, Greenwell considered novels to be providing the most authentic and knowledgeable insight into the female experiences of life:

> Yet it is not from books *about* women, useful and suggestive as many of these are, that our deepest lessons have been won. [. . .] above all, in the novel – that epic, as it has been truly called, of our modern day, – a living soul, a living voice, should seem to greet us; a voice so sad, so truthful, so earnest, that we have felt as if some intimate secret were at once communicated and withheld, an Open Secret, free to all who could find its key – the secret of a woman's heart, with all its needs, its struggles and its aspirations.[14]

The novelist and journalist Margaret Oliphant proclaimed the decade of the 1850s the 'age of the female novelists',[15] identifying as a key factor the realism expressed by writers such as Charlotte Brontë, whose female protagonists defied the patriarchal ideals of womanhood and offered unconventional role models for female readers. Often considered a conservative and anti-feminist writer, Oliphant nevertheless revelled in the new, real heroine that showed women as flawed human beings:

> She is not an angel. In her secret heart she longs to rush upon you, and try and grapple with you, to prove her strength and equality. She has no patience with your flowery emblems. Why should *she* be like a rose or lily anymore than yourself? Are these beautiful weaklings the only type you can find of *her*? (p. 558)

Yet Harriet Martineau had already produced unconventional heroines more than a decade earlier. Indeed, Charlotte Brontë acknowledged the influence of *Deerbrook* on her own literary imagination.[16] Martineau's *Deerbrook* may therefore be viewed as a literary bridge between the templates set by Jane Austen and Walter Scott, and realist novelists such as Charlotte Brontë and George Eliot.

Published in 1839, *Deerbrook* was groundbreaking as the prototype of the middle-class, domestic novel.[17] It centres on the arrival of sisters Margaret and Hester Ibbotson at the home of their distant relatives, the Greys, in the village of Deerbrook, following the death of their father. The reluctance with which *Deerbrook* was taken up by the publishing industry demonstrated their failure to anticipate the shift towards domestic realism by women writers. The male-dominated world of publishing assumed that the reading public would not have any appetite for fiction which was not of the 'silver-fork novels set in aristocratic circles, or "Newgate" novels set in the underworld'[18] or the helpless heroines of Dickens. Contemporary reviewers of *Deerbrook* expressed a reluctant admiration for the novel. The lingering bias against Martineau was primarily rooted in her reputation as a controversial political commentator, as the review in *Blackwood's Magazine* indicates:

> We believe that the authoress would in a short time have outlived the partial dislike which they [her *Illustrations of Political Economy*] occasioned against her literary character. Her next work of importance had far graver faults and peculiarities, which made it more obnoxious to the higher classes of English society. She went to America with an evident determination to find good results, [. . .] unfortunately, there ran through all her eulogies of America, a meaning bitterness which shows that she delights in preferring it to England.[19]

The reviewer here clearly questions Martineau's professional objectivity in her previous work in suggesting that she had an 'evident determination to find' the results she wanted, at the same time expressing doubt about Martineau's loyalty to her own country. The phrase 'meaning bitterness' resonates with the derogatory terminology of the time used to describe spinsters, and can be read as an indirect criticism of her unmarried status and her gender. Yet though reviewers began their articles stating their disapproval of Martineau, they appeared grudgingly to be impressed by the novel:

> The novelists of contemporaneous social life may also enlarge our experience, by teaching us to think and feel with characters dissimilar to our own, and incidentally, by the practical truths which those are most likely to discover who have made human nature most their study. [. . .] In this, Miss Martineau shows true genius (p.188).

One of Martineau's aims in writing *Deerbrook* may have been to 'teach' – as she had sought to do with her short stories – yet more convincingly *Deerbrook* functions as a vehicle for Martineau to express her most intimate thoughts and feelings, and to explore her individual experience. The ideal medium for this, it could be argued, was the realist novel. Both *Blackwood's* and *The Athenaeum*[20] compared *Deerbrook* with the novels of Jane Austen. Certainly Martineau was a great admirer of Austen's work, and made use of the technique of free indirect discourse pioneered by Austen.[21] Margaret Oliphant described Austen's writing as imbued with 'the fine vein of feminine cynicism . . . [she] tells the story with . . . fine stinging yet soft-voiced contempt for the actors in it,'[22] a trait that Oliphant recognised as a tendency of her own. Yet Austen was often sympathetic to her characters' emotional dilemmas, whereas Martineau engaged more closely and empathetically with their moral decisions. This may be illustrated by comparing Austen's Captain Wentworth from her 1818 novel *Persuasion*, with *Deerbrook's* Edward Hope. Both men find themselves under social pressure to propose marriage to women they do not love. Austen ultimately allows her hero to escape such a fate, with his short commentary – seemingly rather glib – on a situation which has now safely passed:

> 'I found,' said he, 'that I was considered by Harville an engaged man! [. . .] I was startled and shocked. To a degree, I could contradict this instantly; but, when I began to reflect that others might have felt the same – her own family, nay, perhaps herself – I was no longer at my own disposal. I was hers in honour if she wished it.'[23]

Austen has a sympathetic but brief engagement with the concerns of men as victims of social propriety. In *Deerbrook* Martineau, more bravely perhaps, explores the destructive emotional impact on the parties involved, when such a state of affairs cannot be evaded and a betrothal is inevitable. Edward Hope has an initial admiration for both Ibbotson sisters, but writes to his brother Frank of his warmer feelings for Margaret. To his misfortune, the interference and gossip that abound in the small community of Deerbrook result in a general belief that he has encouraged Hester, Margaret's sister, to expect a proposal of marriage. His distress and internal conflict are palpable:

> But what was his duty now? Amidst the contradictions of honour and conscience in the present case, where should he find his accustomed refuge? At one moment he saw clearly the obligation to devote himself to her whose affections he had gained – thoughtlessly and carelessly, it is true, but to other eyes purposely. At the next moment, the sin of marrying without love, if not while loving another, – rose vividly before him, and made him shrink from what, an instant before, seemed clear duty.[24]

Conventionally, Edward falls back on the dutiful social imperatives by which he is bound. His 'obligation' and 'duty' offer him no alternative but to propose to Hester. Martineau thrusts the reader into the anguish Edward suffers, not only in facing marriage to a woman he does not love – but now forbidden to marry the woman he does. No convenient resolution is offered such as that by Austen (who gives Wentworth a second chance with Anne Elliot instead of a dutiful union with Louisa Musgrove). Moreover, as Edward faces the prospect of a loveless marriage, Martineau gives an anguished description of his situation, 'the sin of marrying without love [. . .] rose vividly before him and made him shrink.' And in ensuring that Edward is doing his duty by marrying Hester, Martineau engages with yet further innovative topics. On the evening that Edward and Hester return home from their honeymoon, Edward is shaken by the lived reality of his new life:

> He was amazed at the return of his feelings about Margaret, and filled with horror when he thought of the days, and months, and years of close domestic

companionship with her, from which there was no escape. There was no
escape. [. . .] It was a mistake. He could scarcely endure the thought; but it
was so.[25]

Two controversial issues are raised here: Edward's claustrophobic sense of entrap-
ment in his marriage and his emotive response not normally associated with men.
That a new husband is shown to have such intense feelings of bitter regret about
his choice of bride flies in the face of the dominant ideology of the period surrounding the sanctity of marriage. More shocking is Edward's dread of the future,
based not only on his unsatisfactory marriage but on having to share his home
with the woman he wanted as his wife. Until 1835, there had been legal ambigu-
ity surrounding brother and sister-in-law relationships, which were perceived by
some as incestuous: based on the notion that if husband and wife are one flesh,
then a wife's sister, or brother's wife, should also be regarded as a sister. A legal
judgement on such relationships was sought and clarified in 1835 by Lord Lyndhurst, in order to aid his friend the seventh Duke of Beaufort. Beaufort had a son
by his second wife (who was his first wife's half-sister) and to ensure the son's
legitimacy, Lyndhurst put forward a bill which granted retrospective legal recognition of marriages up until 31st August 1835. Any marriages after this date were
designated legally invalid. The bill was enacted and it was another 70 years before
the legislation was overturned, with the passage of The Deceased Wife's Sister's
Marriage Act of 1907.[26] The legality and morality of such relationships were the
cause of much public debate from the 1830s onwards, and Martineau was thus
brave but also aware of the public interest, in exploring the personal complexities
of such a situation.

Both *The Athenaeum* and *The Morning Chronicle* recognised the strength of
Martineau's method of 'tracing thoughts',[27] and nowhere, they said, was this
better displayed than in the character of Hester Hope (formerly Ibbotson), the
undesired wife. *The Morning Chronicle* reviewer found Martineau's depiction of
unamiability exemplary:

> The moral to be derived from it is excellent; for it is impossible for any one
> afflicted with the infirmities of bad temper, or who has been led away by an
> indulgence in petty envy, in miserable jealousies, or unworthy suspicions,
> and have thus made themselves the curse, the torment, and the affliction of
> their families – it is impossible for any such to read "Deerbrook," and not rise
> from its perusal with the determination to correct propensities which render
> themselves and others miserable.[28]

Martineau was, by her own admission, predisposed to bad temper. In her depiction
of Hester's (and to some extent Margaret's) suffering in *Deerbrook*, she does not
excuse such behaviour nor encourage pity. Rather, she exposes and explores the
psychological flaws of a minority of people, for the greater insight of the majority –
while those who tend towards ill-temper will learn that they are not alone in the
hurt they feel. The personal account that Martineau gives through Hester – which

engages with the 'secret[s] of a woman's heart', makes *Deerbrook* more than just a didactic tale of moral instruction. As Hester again overreacts to a perceived slight, causing tension and hostility within her home, the narrator seeks to explain:

> Of all mortals, none perhaps are so awfully self-deluded as the unamiable. They do not, any more than others, sin for the sake of sinning; but the amount of woe caused by their selfish unconsciousness is such as may well make their weakness an equivalent of other men's gravest crimes. [. . .] They, per- haps, are the only order of evil ones who suffer hell without seeing and know- ing that it is hell. But they are under a heavier curse even than this; they inflict torments, second only to their own, with an unconsciousness almost worthy of spirits of light.[29]

Martineau makes clear that the misery caused by the 'unamiable' is not deliberate, but rather rooted in a 'weakness' of character. However, she does not advocate a stance of passive victimhood: in fact she points to the need for individual responsi- bility, so that sufferers do not see themselves as exceptional. What makes Hester's behaviour difficult is that her family suffers in what should be a safe domestic ref- uge, which renders her the antithesis of the Victorian womanly ideal of the 'Angel of the House'. Martineau offers in Hester a new type of heroine, not perfect or subservient, but a woman who is flawed, and increasingly admirable in her struggle to overcome those flaws. Moreover, her strength comes from rising to challenges of hardship rather than from the conventional roles of wife and mother. As Edward's medical practice begins to fail, and the Hope household is ostracised by neighbours because of Edward's political views, Hester is called upon to support her husband. Hester has failed to make Edward happy as his wife, but in his need for 'a friend made for adversity' (p.341) their roles are reversed and Hester becomes the 'pro- vider.' Her small inheritance is used to keep the family going and she acts as guide to Edward, morally and socially. In redefining herself in the role of friend, Hester is not simply fulfilling a social duty but acknowledging that she now has dependants. So while *The Athenaeum* may have been critical of Martineau's portrayal of the Hope household 'welcom[ing] such heavy trials,'[30] without the challenges facing Hester, her life might indeed have been viewed as an unredeemed failure.

In *Deerbrook* Martineau departed from the straightforward, novelistic conven- tion of happy endings and marriage for the hero and heroine. Instead, by the close of the novel, though apparently happier, Hester warns her husband that their pre- sent harmonious state might be only temporary:

> 'I have caused you much misery, I know, – misery which I partly foresaw I should cause you: but that is over, I trust. It is over at least for the time that we are poor and persecuted, I dare not and do not wish for anything otherwise than as we have it now.'[31]

Hester places her current marital contentment very much in the moment, the result of challenging circumstances faced together 'now'. Using a forceful tone of warning, a perhaps wiser Hester conveys to Edward her belief that this harmonious state could deteriorate, should their current social and financial conditions improve. Hester's belief that her potential for causing misery for her husband is over, is tempered by the tentative 'I trust.' The remission from her previous unamiable self may be limited to the present period, the 'now' of poverty and persecution. In Hester's 'dare not' and 'do not' there is a sense of foreboding and of returning to the conventional middle-class marriage that they had before this crisis. The conscious anxiety of returning to a life of 'peace and comfort' (p.497) thus holds the prospect of causing the return of Hester's 'propensity to self-torment' (p.497). Martineau suggests here that the culturally accepted ideal of women as married with children is not completely fulfilling for all women.

If Martineau refused to create a comfortable future for her married heroine, neither did she offer a conventional romantic happy ending for her sister, the newly betrothed and previous object of Edward's affections, Margaret. The reader is in a more privileged position than Margaret, in knowing that her fiancé Philip Enderby has had feelings in the past for Maria Young, until her potential for perfect wifehood is suddenly destroyed. A riding accident has left Maria lame, coinciding with the unhappy discovery that her father (who died in the accident) has left her unprovided for. Although Enderby is away when the accident takes place, his demeanour on his return makes it clear that he now views her only as a neighbour and acquaintance. Margaret also suffers from Enderby's unreliable nature during their own courtship and as they prepare to depart Deerbrook for London, the reader is left doubting whether married life will run smoothly for the future Mr and Mrs Enderby. Yet their married future is not without hope for a contented life together, Margaret has overcome her own emotional issues, and has the determination to help and reassure her future husband during his own moments of emotional weakness. Like Hester, Margaret has the potential to be a dependable and supportive 'friend made for adversity' (p. 341). Martineau thus crushes the myth that marriage automatically provides a happy-ever-after ending at the altar. Instead, perhaps more realistically, she suggests that a happy married life is something that has to be hard fought for.

Martineau recollected in her *Autobiography* written nearly two decades after *Deerbrook* was published, that the novel provided her with 'A relief to many pent-up sufferings, feelings, and convictions: and I can truly say that it was uttered from the heart.'[32] Her portrayal of Maria Young as a lone woman adapting to her never-to-be married status, framed in positive terms, was reflective of Martineau's own journey towards considering herself 'the happiest single woman in England'.[33] Maria attempts to draw out a constructive place for herself in society, while not denying the many social and practical obstacles she may face, and ultimately challenges the prevalent culturally held understanding of the limitations imposed on unmarried women. In her early internal monologue we find Maria searching for a useful and active way to live, whilst recognising at the same time that she will not experience the normative path of marriage and motherhood:

> 'I am out of the game, and why should not I look upon its chances? I am quite alone, and why should I not watch for others? Every situation has its

privileges; and its obligations. – What is it to be alone, and to be let alone as I am? It is to be put into a post of observation on others: but the knowledge so gained is anything but a good if it stops at mere knowledge, if it does not make me feel and act. Women who are to have what I am not to have, – a home, an intimate, a perpetual call out of themselves, may go on more safely perhaps without any thought for themselves than I with all my best consideration: but I, with the blessing of my peremptory vocation, which is to stand me in stead of sympathy, ties and spontaneous action, – I may find that it is my proper business to keep an intent eye upon the possible events of other people's lives, that I may use slight occasions of actions which might otherwise pass me by. If one were thoroughly wise and good, this would be a sort of divine lot.'[34]

Maria is here beginning to come to terms with being 'out of the game' – that is, she no longer considers herself eligible in the marriage market. However, her disability and poverty do not signal the end of the possibility of a fulfilled life; rather, there is hope for an emotional, if not romantic, future. Maria's 'why should not I' places a heavy emphasis on the 'I'. The use of 'should not' is at odds with the conventional expectation of female obedience, the 'I' asserting boldly the opportunity of alternative 'chances', compared with those offered by the 'game' of romance. As with the first section of the first sentence, the beginning of the second sentence – 'I am quite alone' – is self-affirmatory, and the next phrase proposes a purpose for a future single self. The repositioning of the subject pronoun from 'why should not I?' to 'why should I not watch for others?', seems to move to a more personal level of introspection, thus making sense of Maria's individual role in the world, and allowing her to gain confidence to challenge cultural expectations of what a single woman *should* or should not be allowed to do. There is a sense of liberation in Maria's final question: 'What is it to be alone, and to be let alone as I am?' The first 'alone' in the sentence questions its place in a generalised way – 'alone' is at first a static concept which shifts into individual freedom in the formulation 'let alone as I am' – while the second 'alone' is offered as one of the personal 'privileges' of Maria's social situation. She is attempting to find the potential good in aloneness, without avoiding confronting the difficulties of the future. For example, Maria compares herself with married women. She asserts that they enjoy benefits which will play no part in Maria's future – 'Women who have what I am not to have' – with the absolutist 'not' closing off any belief that her future could offer the same benefits. Unlike married women who have a future role as wives, Maria has consciously to find another fulfilling station in life. Her 'peremptory' vocation is set against the supposedly 'natural' vocation of wifedom, and is conceived of as a 'blessing', which could offer something besides just 'ordinary happiness'. Yet it will be a 'blessing' only so long as she exercises the privileges it confers (of observing others) in the 'proper' way. Mere observation serves only to highlight Maria's isolation from society. She needs to be involved for the benefit of those others. By the close of the passage, Maria has transformed a second-best life situation not merely into a neighbourhood duty, but potentially into the true purpose of her life – 'my proper business.' If there is a danger of Maria's mission taking on a tone of zealous religiosity, the final two sentences reinforce the human ordinariness of her expectations for the future. It is a 'business', not a calling, and thus Maria extricates herself from any charge of making herself a moral guardian angel by denying such a possibility. 'If one were thoroughly wise and good, this would be a sort of divine lot.' The wryly self-deprecating 'if' separates what Maria is from what she is not. Maria is aware that she is not 'thoroughly wise and good'. The opportunity she has appropriated because of her emerging optimistic rather than resigned acceptance of her single status allows her to consider a positive future that combines both emotional investment and practical demands; the imperative to 'feel' and 'act' is a crucial element in her conception of her role. Through her development of Maria's character, Martineau sought to challenge the stereotypical image of 'aloneness' equating to 'lonely', by producing in her fiction an unmarried woman who is not prepared to accept the future as an impotent victim of societal expectations.

In considering the importance of Martineau's achievement in exploring the marital status of women in *Deerbrook*, and the literary legacy she provided for female writers, it is ironic that her friendship with Charlotte Brontë was irretrievably damaged by Martineau's critical review of *Villette*. In that review for the *Daily News* Martineau argued that there was 'unconsciously too much' (1853) love and passion in *Villette*. Such a claim could also be made about *Deerbrook*. Both novels deal with wider interests beyond simply romantic love, but for both, love and specifically romantic love and its consequences, are key themes and central to the plotlines. Martineau's comments on *Villette*, however, were made fifteen years after the appearance of *Deerbrook*, and by this stage in her life and career, she was clearly somewhat embarrassed by her earlier novel, and its portrayal of female emotional vulnerability. It is possible that Martineau may have wished to advise Brontë against falling into a similar trap, having written to her privately in similar vein prior to her review. Surprisingly, perhaps, she overlooks a final resemblance between Maria and Brontë's Lucy Snowe, who discovers a version of acceptance not unlike Maria's – as someone who has known love, but, 'out of the game', has lived her life observing the romantic relationships of others, albeit less benignly than Maria.

Martineau was at pains in her *Autobiography* to distance her older 1855 self (and her identity as a serious political journalist) from her younger who had produced a text driven by personal feeling:

> My own judgment of 'Deerbrook' was for some years more favourable than it is now. [. . .] I should now require more of myself, if I were to attempt a novel, – which I should not do, [. . .] I should require more simplicity, and a far more objective character, [. . .] The laborious portions of meditation, obtruded at intervals, are wholly objectionable in my eyes.[35]

Interestingly, four years before writing the *Autobiography*, Martineau had drafted a novel which she attempted to publish under a pseudonym with Charlotte Brontë's publisher Smith, Elder & Co. *Oliver Weld* was rejected as a 'badly written political and religious polemic',[36] and Martineau destroyed the manuscript without ever publishing it. After Martineau's death and the publication of the *Autobiography*, Margaret Oliphant scathingly dismissed Martineau as 'not very much of a woman at all',[37] basing the main thrust of her disapproval on the very aspect of her life that Martineau had wanted to retain in her *Autobiography*: her public image as a serious political journalist. Later, Vineta Colby noted the heartfelt personal experiences that could be found within its pages and described the *Autobiography* as 'potentially a first-rate Victorian novel'.[38] Martineau was never to replicate the style of writing of *Deerbrook*, but in intermittent moments in her *Autobiography*, which Valerie Sanders describes as 'the frank sharing of confidences',[39] Martineau's novelist voice continues to resonate.

Notes

1 Samuel Johnson, *Dictionary of the English Language* (London: Strachan, 1775), p. 373.
2 Ali Smith, 'It's All About The Money,' 14 May 2013. Inaugural Harriet Martineau Lecture for Norwich UNESCO City of Literature.
3 Harriet Martineau, *Autobiography* (1877), ed. Linda Peterson (Peterborough, ON: Broadview Press, 2007), p. 126.
4 Harriet Martineau, 'The Achievements of the Genius of Scott' *Tait's Edinburgh Magazine* (October 1833), p. 459.
5 'Illustrations of Political Economy,' also titled 'Miss Martineau's Monthly Novels,' *Quarterly Review* 49 (April 1833), p. 140. The online *Wellesley Index to Victorian Periodicals 1824–1900* attributes the article conjointly to J. G. Lockhart, G. Poulett Scrope, and J. W. Croker.
6 Harriet Martineau, *Weal and Woe in Garveloch* (London: Charles Fox, 1832), p. 140. See also Vint and Funaki's discussion of this controversy in Chapter 3 of this volume.
7 'Miss Martineau's Monthly Novels,' p. 136.
8 Johnson, *Dictionary of the English Language*, p. 373.
9 Harriet Martineau, *Ella of Garveloch* (London: Charles Fox: 1832), p. 6.
10 Harriet Martineau, *For Each and For All* (London: Charles Fox, 1832), p. 128.
11 *Autobiography*, p. 403.
12 Gaby Weiner, unpublished conference paper: '*Deerbrook*. True Love and Purple Prose,' The Martineau Society Conference, Bristol, July 2012.
13 *Autobiography*, p. 409.
14 Dora Greenwell, 'Our single women,' *North British Review*, 36 (1862), p. 63.
15 Margaret Oliphant, 'Modern Novelists great and small,' *Blackwood's Magazine*, 77 (May 1855), p. 555.
16 Under the guise of Currer Bell, Brontë wrote, 'When C.B first read "Deerbrook" he[sic] tasted a new and keen pleasure, and experienced a genuine benefit in his mind. "Deerbrook" ranks with the writings that have really done him good, added to his stock of ideas, and rectified his views of life.' Margaret Smith (ed.), *The Letters of Charlotte Brontë* (Oxford: Clarendon Press, 3 vols., 1995), p. 288.
17 Vineta Colby, *Yesterday's Woman: Domestic Realism in the English Novel* (Princeton: Princeton University Press, 1974), p. 244.
18 *Autobiography*, p. 408.
19 [G.S.Venables], 'Harriet Martineau – *Deerbrook*,' *Blackwood's Edinburgh Magazine* 47 (Feb 1840), p. 178.
20 A review in *The Athenaeum* described *Deerbrook* as 'a village tale, as simple in its structures [. . .] as one of Miss Austen's,' but recognised that Martineau's characters

were 'of a higher order of mental force and spiritual attainment than Miss Austen ever drew.' Anon, '*Deerbrook: a Novel*,' *The Athenaeum* (1 April 1839), p. 254.

21 John Mullan, *How Novels Work* (Oxford: Oxford University Press, 2006), p. 76.

22 Margaret Oliphant, 'Miss Austen and Miss Mitford,' *Blackwood's Magazine* 107 (March 1870), p. 294.

23 Jane Austen, *Northanger Abbey* and *Persuasion* (1818) (London: Collins, 1953). p. 370.

24 Harriet Martineau, *Deerbrook* (1839) ed. Valerie Sanders (London: Penguin Classics, 2004), p. 318.

25 *Deerbrook*, p. 205.

26 Adam Kuper, *Incest & Influence: The Private Life of Bourgeois England* (Harvard: Harvard University Press, 2009), p. 77.

27 '*Deerbrook* – A Novel,' *The Athenaeum* (April 1839), p. 255.

28 'Literature,' *The Morning Chronicle* (17 April 1839), p. 17.

29 *Deerbrook*, pp. 244–5.

30 '*Deerbrook – A Novel*' p. 255.

31 *Deerbrook*, p. 533.

32 *Autobiography*, p. 407.

33 *Autobiography*, p. 120.

34 *Deerbrook*, pp. 46–7.

35 *Autobiography*, p. 408.

36 Juliet Barker, *The Brontës* (London: Abacus, 2010), p. 817.

37 Margaret Oliphant, 'Harriet Martineau' *Blackwood's Magazine* 121 (April 1877), p. 472.

38 Vineta Colby, *Yesterday's Woman*, p. 230.

39 V. Sanders, 'Sibling Performances: HM and JM as Autobiographers' in *A Harriet Martineau Miscellany* (Oxford: Harris Manchester College, 2002), p. 63.

8 Harriet Martineau, Victorian sciences of mind and the birth of psychology

Beth Torgerson

It might seem strange at first to link Harriet Martineau to the birth of psychology as a discipline since her death in 1876 preceded the establishment of experimental psychological laboratories in the 1880s and 1890s as well as Freud's formulation of psychoanalysis in 1896. However, thanks to cultural historians such as Alison Winter and Roger Cooter, studying Victorians' interest in mesmerism and phrenology, and scholars such as Adam Crabtree, Graham Richards, Rick Rylance, Jenny Bourne Taylor, and Sally Shuttleworth, studying what has been called the 'long history of psychology,' we can better see Martineau's position in this long history and the ways in which she participated in and contributed to it.[1] Martineau's gender automatically excluded her from a university education, a fact that ruled out her becoming either a physician or a scientist; yet she was born at a time when intellectual discussions about the new sciences of the mind were conducted by everyone, generalists and specialists alike. Indeed, the term 'scientist,' coined in 1834, was not yet widely in use. Originally a non-believer in phrenology, Martineau followed the phrenological experiments of the 1820s and 1830s, especially the work of her friend George Combe.[2] In the 1830s and 1840s, Martineau remained interested in the mesmeric experiments after the second arrival of mesmerism from France.[3] Already intrigued by Charles Bell's physiological work distinguishing sensory and motor nerves, Martineau carefully attended to the research of mental physiologists as they published more specialized work from the 1850s onwards. Victorian experiments in three areas – phrenology, mesmerism, and mental physiology – contributed to the cultural milieu in which all levels of Victorian society actively discussed the mind's capabilities and what they might mean for individuals and society at large. Before psychology solidified into a scientific discipline, Victorians saw how the mind worked as an excitingly new and important area for investigation and debate. Martineau's interest in the new sciences of mind resulted in her publishing on mesmerism in 1844; on phrenology, specifically phreno-mesmerism, in 1845; on all three areas – mesmerism, phrenology, and mental physiology – in 1851; and on mental physiology alone in 1868.

Today mental physiology has morphed into neuroscience. And while today mesmerism and phrenology are dismissed as 'pseudo-sciences,' this phrasing indicates twenty-first century awareness of the historical rejection (in the case of phrenology) or revision (in the case of mesmerism) of the 'science' of these two

Victorian sciences of mind. Yet, historically, because mesmerism and phrenology created new ways to think about the mind, they generated the need for increasingly sophisticated scientific investigations to test the theories they raised, thereby contributing to the emergence of scientific disciplines of the brain and mind, including psychology. Reassessing the historic significance of mesmerism and phrenology, Graham Richards asserts, 'Both sought to present themselves as scientific, both involved refashioning the psychological to reflect changes in the external world, and both discovered – or created for themselves – a social role akin to that of modern Psychology. [. . . And] they were both engaged in some degree in the construction of that discipline.'[4]

Harriet Martineau and mesmerism

Martineau first promoted scientific investigations of the mind in *Letters on Mesmerism*. Originally published as a series of six letters in *The Athenæum* in November and December of 1844, *Letters on Mesmerism* appeared as a book in January 1845.[5] Martineau's decision to publish on mesmerism followed her unexpected recovery following a five-year illness. In her first letter, Martineau gave

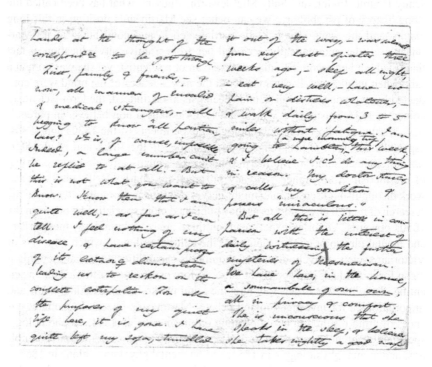

Figure 8.1 Harriet Martineau's letter of October 27 [1844] to Richard Monckton Milnes written the month before *Letters on Mesmerism* first appeared in *The Athenæum*. Houghton Paper 16/78, Courtesy The Master and Fellows of Trinity College Cambridge.

extensive details about her own case, declaring, 'My recovery now, by means of mesmeric treatment alone, has given me the most thorough knowledge possible that Mesmerism is true.'[6] And, in the second, Martineau reported on the case of Jane Arrowsmith, the young orphan niece of her landlady, whom Martineau simply refers to as 'J.' Because Martineau believed that both her case and Jane's resulted in recovery, she consequently endorsed mesmerism as a therapeutic agent for healing. The second letter also included Martineau's observations on Jane's abilities with what became known as the 'higher phenomena' of mesmerism, such as Jane's clairvoyance, including her ability to foresee the details of a particular shipwreck and her ability to diagnose and prescribe remedies for herself and others.

In the remaining letters, Martineau repeatedly encouraged her educated readers to study all aspects of mesmerism: clairvoyance as well as medical anesthesia and healing. Proclaiming that 'the claims of Mesmerism to a calm and philosophical investigation are imperative,'[7] Martineau endorsed scientific investigations to be conducted by those working with 'the human frame,'[8] and she named specific occupations to undertake this important work: 'medical men,' 'physiologists,' and 'mental philosophers.'[9] The latter two occupational titles in this list indicate inter-related historical shifts. Physiology was historically in the process of expanding to include mental physiology and, as a result of such work, in an even bigger cultural shift, mental philosophy was being challenged by more scientifically based understandings of the mind. Martineau's plea for more knowledge – 'Let the *savans* really inquire, and combine to do so. Experiment is here, of course, the only means of knowledge' – led to her call for 'a sound set of experiments' and a 'systematic investigation.'[10] Martineau admitted her concern that '[a]t present, the knowledge of Mesmerism, superficial and scanty as it is, is out of the professional pale' rather than 'within.'[11] This concern motivated her selection of *The Athenaeum* in which to publish since, as Martineau noted, it reached 'large numbers of educated and professional men; and I trust some of them may possibly be aroused to consideration of the part it behoves [*sic.*] them to take.'[12]

After the first edition sold out within only four days in January of 1845, a second edition with a new appendix was immediately published, appearing that same month. Robin Waterfield notes that *Letters on Mesmerism* 'boosted the fortunes not only of the magazine, but also of mesmerism in general, which became the most talked-about subject of the day.'[13] If the journal articles generated a heated discussion among *The Athenæum*'s educated male readers, the book *Letters on Mesmerism* created a cultural sensation throughout England, since it reached a much broader readership. In April of 1845, the *Zoist* reported, 'The subject which the critic a few months since would not condescend to notice, has been elevated to a commanding position, – it is the topic with which the daily papers and the weekly periodicals are filled; [. . .] The immediate cause of all this activity is the publication of the case of Miss Martineau.'[14] Alison Winter considers that 'Martineau's was the most significant claim to a mesmeric cure so far' because she had what other mesmeric subjects did not have: 'credibility as witnesses despite their status as experimental subjects.'[15] Martineau's fame and reputation as a moralist gave credibility to her reports.

As Winter reports, 'From December 1844 onward, a high-profile public debate took shape.'[16] The details of this debate indicate that, as medicine struggled to become a profession, the majority of British physicians stridently opposed mesmerism. Yet some physicians either started or continued experiments with it. Among them was James Braid (1795–1860) (Figure 8.2), who became the most

Figure 8.2 Portrait of James Braid. Wellcome Library, London.

historically significant since his work transformed mesmerism into hypnotism. In addition to Braid, others published their experimental results in the *Zoist*, the journal founded by John Elliotson (1791–1868) in 1843, and in *The Medical Times*, the medical journal with the most pronounced pro-mesmeric stance. Intriguingly, in the preface to *Letters on Mesmerism*, Martineau announced her creation of a register of physicians who had contacted her after *The Athenæum* series had started about their own mesmeric experiments and their hesitation to publish their cases because of professional backlash.[17] The location of this register is unknown, possibly indicating that the document may no longer exist; however, were it to be found, it too would provide additional historical information concerning the medical men experimenting with mesmerism in the early 1840s.

Because scholarship has focused on Martineau's promotion of mesmerism as a challenge to the young medical profession, it has been overlooked that, in *Letters on Mesmerism*, Martineau was herself critical of the theories being offered in 1844. To place Martineau's text within the larger historical shift that moved mesmerism to hypnotism, her reticence in blindly endorsing these early theories and her awareness of the problematic nature of the term 'mesmerism' are both important. Martineau emphasized that mesmerism was an unknown phenomenon in need of research and that this research would develop its full significance. For example, she repeatedly stressed that it was dangerous to theorize 'prematurely' about the active agent behind mesmeric manifestations, which many speculated was a magnetic fluid, an ether, or electricity.[18] Similarly, she pointed out the inadequacy of existing theories to explain all of the known facts, writing, 'no one of them will hold good with all the facts that are established.'[19] She speculated that 'it seems to me most improbable that we can yet be near the true theory.'[20] In her analytical review of the field, Martineau even offered examples and questions to challenge the early theories.[21]

Martineau declared that 'a better name is sadly wanted' for mesmerism.[22] She consistently maintained, 'The truth in question is safe, whether it be called Mesmerism, or by another and better name.'[23] And she foresaw a future when there would be 'no more wrangling about the old or new names by which the influence is to be called.'[24] We can safely assume Martineau was referring to the ongoing debate over the two most common terms 'animal magnetism' and 'mesmerism'; however, other terms would already have been in use, including Braid's new term 'neuro-hypnotism,' which eventually became the term 'hypnosis.'[25]

In scholarship concerning the historical conversion of mesmerism into hypnosis, Alan Gauld, Adam Crabtree, and Waterfield each include Martineau's experiences with mesmerism.[26] Although none of these scholars directly links Martineau's promotion of mesmerism to Braid's promotion of hypnotism, connections existed both in terms of how Martineau and Braid's lives intersected with other Victorians writing about mesmerism and their beliefs about mesmerism/hypnotism. For example, both Martineau and Braid knew Spencer T. Hall (1812–85) and John Elliotson. Hall was the 'first significant non-medical practitioner of mesmerism'[27] while Elliotson was the most famous medical promoter of mesmerism in England. In *Neurypnology* (1843), Braid recorded the progress he made with his own experiments after he read Hall's work, attended Hall's public lectures, and even worked together with Hall.[28] Because of their early collaboration, Hall followed Braid's work, even referring to Braid's theory of hypnosis – which Hall also termed 'self-mesmerism' – in *Mesmeric Experiences* (1845).[29] In this same book, Hall dedicated a chapter to Martineau's recovery since it was his initial mesmerizing of Martineau in June of 1844 that led to her reported cure.[30] If Martineau read Hall's book, she would have known Braid's work as early as 1845. Or, since Martineau read and contributed to the *Zoist*, she might have become familiar with Braid's theory there, although Elliotson's comments on Braid were not always positive.[31]

Significantly, Martineau and Braid shared a belief that something 'real' happened during mesmeric trances. In this, they both followed Marquis de Puységur's understanding of artificial somnambulism, a discovery that had already revised Franz Anton Mesmer's (1733–1815) early theory and is credited by Waterfield with 'lead[ing] directly to the development of modern psychiatry and psychology.'[32] The 'truth in question' that Martineau was concerned with in *Letters on Mesmerism* had two layers: first, mesmerism's ability to induce a trance state (i.e., artificial somnambulism), and second, the realization that a new realm of the psyche existed, which could best be explored through this artificially induced somnambulism. Braid's work showed that the mesmerists' inducing methods, the so-called mesmeric passes, were dispensable; nevertheless, he documented that such methods could successfully induce trance states, but for a different reason from that given by the mesmerists. Whatever the inducing method, the opening into this new world of the psyche, what we now call the unconscious, was the deeper 'truth' behind mesmerism. Call it mesmerism or hypnotism, both Martineau and Braid believed artificial somnambulism offered something real and beyond dispute to a scientific understanding of human nature. So, as Martineau concluded, 'the truth in question is safe.'

Martineau and Braid's shared belief drove both of them forward in their respective promotions of mesmerism and hypnotism, even when both were working against the currents of the larger medical community. Although Braid's work is accepted today, at the time, he struggled to be published and taken seriously. Crabtree notes that William Benjamin Carpenter (1813–85) (Figure 8.3) was 'one of the few prominent medical men in Britain to appreciate' and write about Braid's early work.[33] Before Braid's theories were taken seriously by other British scientists in the late 1880s, they were earlier refined and expanded by French scientists from the 1860s to the 1880s.[34]

While Martineau and Braid believed in the reality of the trances, they differed in their explanations of that phenomenon, including its induction. Although she declined to theorize about the cause of mesmeric manifestations in 1844, just two years later – perhaps in reaction to criticism of *Letters on Mesmerism* – Martineau's writings show that she was confident that a material force produced mesmeric phenomena. In 1846, after Baron Karl von Reichenbach's (1788–1869) discovery of 'odyle' (a hypothetical force responsible for a variety of phenomena), which many mesmerists felt proved the existence of a material power at

Figure 8.3 Portrait of William Benjamin Carpenter. Courtesy US National Library of Medicine.

work, Martineau promoted the German's research by writing widely to her various correspondents, including Elizabeth Barrett, Thomas Carlyle (who was to pass the information on to Erasmus Darwin), Lord Morpeth, Lord Grey, and others.[35] Her letter of March 5, 1846, to Carlyle is especially interesting because it provides a rare instance when Martineau broke from her carefully chosen neutral phrase 'the mesmeric influence.'[36] Instead, Martineau referred to 'that branch of electricity vulgarly called Mesmerism,' an indication that, at least in 1846, she understood the force at work to be electricity.[37] Five years later, she more formally promoted Reichenbach's theory, which he had expanded in 1850, in *Letters on the Laws of Man's Nature and Development* (1851).[38] Whereas Martineau's promotion of Reichenbach indicates her belief that some type of material force was at work, Braid critiqued Reichenbach, arguing against the existence of any external material force.[39] Nevertheless, throughout his writings, Braid continued to use the term 'mesmerism' in conjunction with his preferred term 'hypnotism' so that he could stress their connections while simultaneously emphasizing that his theory of hypnotism explained most phenomena experienced under mesmerism.[40]

Martineau's *Letters on Mesmerism* was her first contribution to Victorian psychology. It documented her mesmeric experiences and those of Jane Arrowsmith, pointed out logical flaws in existing theories on mesmerism, and called for additional scientific experimentation and for open communication of what was known. In her role as a popularizer of this new science of the mind, Martineau advocated both mesmerism and scientific inquiry. In her final letter, after articulating a commonly held mesmeric belief, she commented, 'If this view is mistaken, if it is founded on too small a collection of facts, let it be brought to the test and corrected. Let the truth be ascertained and established; for it cannot be extinguished, and it is too important to be neglected.'[41] Throughout *Letters on Mesmerism*, Martineau simultaneously promoted mesmerism and scientific inquiry, yet, ultimately for her, given the problems she saw with how mesmerism was then understood, promotion of scientific inquiry was the higher goal.

Martineau, phrenology, and phreno-mesmerism

In the appendix to the second edition of *Letters on Mesmerism*, Martineau gave her first endorsement of phrenology: 'Since these Letters were written, phenomena have presented themselves which leave no more possible doubt in the minds of witnesses of the truth of Phrenology than of that of Mesmerism.'[42] Before this point, as her letter of September 24, 1841, to George Combe (1788–1858) indicates, although Martineau followed his writings on phrenology, she considered herself 'a thorough unbeliever.'[43] Phrenology, or 'Craniology,' emerged in Franz Joseph Gall's (1758–1828) work on brain anatomy and physiology; however, it was Johann Spurzheim (1776–1832) who brought phrenology to Britain and popularized it. Spurzheim's ideas about how to apply Gall's findings to everyday life proved particularly influential. Because Combe was a lawyer, not a scientist, his own popularizing of phrenology followed and extended Spurzheim's work rather than Gall's.

Six years after this appendix appeared, Martineau again explored aspects of the mind in *Letters on the Laws*, including phenology, mesmerism, and the nature of the senses. Martineau largely depended on her co-author's greater knowledge of phrenology since Henry George Atkinson (1812–84) had already published multiple articles on it in the *Zoist* and elsewhere.[44] Other phrenologists hailed Atkinson for his discoveries of new mental faculties[45] and for a 'new means' to study the mind that became known as 'phreno-mesmerism.'[46] Martineau contributed her insights about mesmerism, her own experiences with sensory impairments (both hearing and smell), and her sense of the significance of their project in documenting current knowledge and promoting future scientific inquiries into the mind. Rather than recount her own recovery by mesmerism, she focused on what she had learned since becoming a practicing mesmerist herself. Indeed, she revisited her own use of mesmerism only to emphasize the almost incommunicable nature of being in the trance state.

Reviewers such as J. Stevenson Bushnan (1807–84) found it odd that *Letters on the Laws* had no reference to Combe in the text as it was ostensibly focused on phrenology.[47] However, this omission makes sense on two levels. First, the co-authors wanted to include more recent phrenological findings, including those made by Atkinson, as well as scientific discoveries, such as Faraday's work on electricity, that they thought had significance for ongoing studies of the mind. Secondly, Martineau knew of Combe's limitations as a scientist. In her obituary of Combe, Martineau criticized his lack of scientific aptitude, writing, 'To George's "practical" eye, the human brain and mind appeared as in a map of a completely surveyed country.'[48] Martineau lamented that Combe accepted the science of phrenology where he found it without advancing new scientific knowledge.[49] Martineau also criticized Combe and his followers for 'organizing a sect.'[50] Martineau's awareness of how such a situation can undermine scientific advancement still seems pertinent in light of phrenology being so derided today.[51] In 'Neurology's Debt to F. J. Gall,' MacDonald Critchley lists Gall's historical contributions to neurology while simultaneously explaining why the historical significance of Gall's work has been dismissed. Critchley posits that Gall differed from other earlier medical pioneers in that 'these others never aspired to a scientific philosophy and never became willy-nilly the founders of a cult.'[52]

Although now considered a pseudo-science, phrenology played an important role in the birth of psychology. As Jenny Bourne Taylor and Sally Shuttleworth indicate, phrenology marked an advance from Johann Casper Lavater's physiognomy.[53] Phrenology, with its focus on multiple faculties, offered an important step forward in explaining the mind's complexity. Gall pointed out that it could explain the 'double man within' for, unlike the static nature of the mind endorsed by physiognomy, phrenology understood the mind as dynamic, allowing for a person's conflicting desires or competing dispositions.[54] Moreover, in its emphasis on the possibility of a person's development, phrenology emphasized the plasticity of the mind, a concept that had social ramifications for various Victorian reforms, including education and penal reforms.[55] Even Rick Rylance, who belittles phrenology as 'a nonsense science,' admits its historical scientific importance, including its 'influence on genuine research into the localized faculties, not least by providing a theoretical model that invited a programme of investigation.'[56] He notes that 'this model provided a specified account of how actual behavior might be correlated with anatomical and physiological features.'[57] In addition, Rylance positions phrenology's contributions to the founding of psychology via Auguste Comte's (1798–1857) espousal of it, since Comte's ideas about phrenology influenced George Henry Lewes, John Stuart Mill, Frederic Harrison, and others. In particular, Rylance argues that the chapter 'Psychology: A New Cerebral Theory' in Lewes's *Comte's Philosophy of the Sciences* (1853) marked a historical shift in its having 'carved out a space for psychology from Comte's theories that the master himself did not allow.'[58] In tangible ways, phrenology laid important groundwork for the beginning of the modern science of psychology.

Martineau and Atkinson shared three primary goals for publishing their correspondence in *Letters on the Laws*, each connected with psychology as Victorians understood it. First, Martineau and Atkinson wished to share what was currently known about the human mind with their chosen audience of popular readers. In an early letter, Martineau made this explicit request of Atkinson: 'I should like to be aware *where, exactly, you think our knowledge stops.*'[59] In context, the term 'knowledge' specifically refers to existing scientific knowledge about the human mind. Martineau wanted this knowledge to be available to all, not only to professional men of science.

Secondly, Martineau and Atkinson wanted to emphasize that scientific methods of inquiry were the only way forward to greater knowledge of the mind, and, thus, of human nature, and that such knowledge was accessible to all since it was based on universal natural law. Towards their second goal of promoting scientific methods of inquiry, Martineau questioned why 'Natural Philosophy and Mental Philosophy are arbitrarily separated' and 'why Mental Philosophy is not yet included among the sciences.'[60] From there, she pondered, 'My wonder is, – not that there are few so-called Mental philosophers who use or even advocate any experimental method of inquiry into the science of mind; but that there seem to me to be none.'[61] Throughout *Letters on the Laws*, Martineau explored the contentions between mental philosophy and mental physiology, making her readers aware that it was the 'fear of impiety' that impeded scientific knowledge of the mind.[62]

Martineau scholars have shown how *Letters on the Laws* contributes to our understanding of her personal shift towards a scientific belief system.[63] The significance of Martineau's paradigm shift for the birth of psychology becomes clearer once we look at the larger cultural context. Nineteenth-century natural theology emphasized man's God-given place in the universe, viewed the mind as the location of the soul or spirit, and rejected the mind's material connection with the body as de-sanctifying the concept of the soul or spirit.[64] To move their readers beyond the traditionally accepted theological reading of the mind as immaterial or as 'soul,' Martineau and Atkinson continually stressed the mind as dependent upon material conditions of the body. Atkinson revisited this point in the final letter, writing, 'The body cannot be understood when studied as a matter separate from its phenomenon Mind; nor Mind irrespective of physical conditions, causes and laws.'[65] Viewed in this light, *Letters on the Laws* demonstrates the authors' belief that Martineau's personal paradigm shift needed to be mirrored by a larger cultural shift not only for the direct benefit of science but also, via science, for the benefit of society. Consequently, Martineau's sharing of her own paradigm shift should be understood as her offering readers a psychological path to follow, towards a scientific understanding of the mind.[66]

Two levels are evident within the goal of promoting scientific inquiry into the mind. In the first, Martineau and Atkinson argued for applying the scientific method to the mind in general. In the second, they promoted mesmerism, particularly phreno-mesmerism, as the best way to learn more about the function and structure of the mind. Later readers would find signs of Braid's idea of 'suggestibility' at work in Atkinson's descriptions of his so-called scientific inquiries employing phreno-mesmerism. Thus, while *Letters on the Laws* promoted scientific inquiry in general, the one specific method of inquiry – that is, phreno-mesmerism – being offered ultimately proved to be unscientific.

Martineau and Atkinson's third goal, emphasized within their title, was that their general readers be made aware of the value of scientific knowledge of human nature because, once known, 'the laws of human nature' would provide readers with the capability of 'development.' The co-authors emphasized the mind's potential for development and related it to a person's sense of identity. This third goal is historically important for two reasons. First, ideas of development and identity remain ongoing psychological concerns. Secondly, Atkinson and Martineau's efforts at psychologically understanding a person's continued identity within a materialist model of the brain anticipated early studies of human identity within the emerging field of mental physiology.

Letters on the Laws received much attention and was considered by some as scandalous. Its materialist attack on religion earned Martineau and Atkinson the label of atheists.[67] Although their objective was to help move readers forward to embrace science as the better way of understanding the mind and, by extension, the world, their critique of religion distracted many readers. Even for scientific reviewers such as Braid and Lewes, the shock of Martineau's break with Christianity had to be addressed before they could attend to the scientific dimension.

Braid's critique of *Letters on the Laws* appeared in the appendix to *Electro-Biological Phenomena Considered Physiologically and Psychologically*.[68] After commenting on 'their full-fledged, daring, unblushing atheism,' Braid raises his primary scientific concern.[69] Braid feared that their promotion of mesmerism as 'the only infallible means whereby to interpret nature' within a larger materialist argument that rejects Christianity could foster a prejudice among its readers against mesmerism – and, by extension, hypnotism.[70] Despite his reservations, Braid ended with this praise: 'still I quite concur with the author of the review in the "North British," that, "so extensive, orderly, and authentic a narrative of sensuous illusions, is an invaluable contribution to the science of medical psychology."'[71] Lewes's initial unsigned review in *The Leader* focused exclusively on Martineau's religious crisis such that he noted that a fuller review was forthcoming.[72] Lewes's reservations primarily concerned their ideas on clairvoyance, yet, like Braid, Lewes ended his review by commenting that Atkinson's phrenological work would prove significant.[73] With reservations, Braid and Lewes emphasized that aspects of *Letters on the Laws* contributed to existing scientific inquiries on the mind.

Martineau and mental physiology

In its material basis for the mind, phrenology contributed to the new field of mental physiology. However, as the nineteenth century progressed and mental physiology advanced, the earlier theory was eclipsed. Thanks both to Martineau's letters to Henry Reeve, editor of *The Edinburgh Review*, about a possible review of Charles Upham's *Salem Witchcraft*, and to the review itself, we know that as late as 1868, Martineau still kept abreast of the latest developments in mental physiology.

In a letter to Reeve of February 23, 1868, Martineau argued that a review of Upham's *Salem Witchcraft* that included recent work in mental physiology was a good fit for *The Edinburgh Review*. She asserted that the subject of 'Body & Mind' had already been 'introduced in the very complete way in the review of Sir H. Holland, Brodie & Laycock in 1856.' She posited that this earlier article 'might, in fact, serve as a sort of introduction to the physiological portion of the review.'[74] In this letter, Martineau simultaneously established her awareness of recent discussions on mental physiology and herself as the best possible reviewer for the envisioned scientific reading of the Salem witch trials.

In the unsigned review, published in July of 1868, Martineau insisted that mental phenomena be seriously studied by physicians and scientists, returning to themes from *Letters on Mesmerism* and *Letters on the Laws*. However, a new focus is also evident. Whereas the two earlier works addressed the significance of Bell's physiological studies,[75] in the 1868 text, Martineau went beyond Bell to reference the newest discoveries by the three most important mental physiologists of the day – Henry Holland (1788–1873), William Benjamin Carpenter, and Henry Maudsley (1835–1918). In her review, Martineau included specific physiological findings on the mind reported by these three mental physiologists; she praised physiologists in general; and, after a gibe at Spiritualism, she concluded that 'the scientific physiologists are proceeding, by observation and experiment, to penetrate more and more secrets of our intellectual and moral life.'[76]

In referring to Maudsley's *The Physiology and Pathology of the Mind*, published the year before, Martineau intimated that her knowledge of mental physiology was up to date.[77] Four months earlier, in a letter to Reeve of March 11, 1868, she had compared Holland, Carpenter, and Maudsley, which shows her understanding of their work and of how the science of mental physiology was changing. First, she acknowledged, 'Sir H. Holland's book is old now,' and commented on its shortcomings, 'more than half his writings are limitations & modifications & mollifications. And his rather elegant, but dim & doubtful suggestions & proposals do not look well now, by the side of recent works, – of Dr. Carpenter on unconscious cerebral action etc.'[78] She continued, 'I did think of putting Maudsley's book at the head of the article, with Upham's; but I can say very little about it, – can do little more than hold it up for what it is.'[79] Martineau's comments on Holland's writing style and on her own limitations in reading Maudsley emphasize her awareness of the era's progression towards an increasingly scientific style in writings about the mind. As a generalist interested in what she calls 'these brain books,'[80] Martineau found she could continue to promote science even when it appeared that she could no longer actively participate in the increasingly specialized scientific discussions.

Nevertheless, the fact that Martineau had already participated in these early discussions meant her influence continued – not only through reviews and responses to *Letters on Mesmerism* or *Letters on the Laws*, but also through specific works on mental physiology written by Carpenter himself. For, while Martineau referenced Carpenter in her 'Salem Witchcraft' review, Carpenter had already referenced Martineau in his earlier work and he continued to do so. Starting with the fifth edition of *Principles of Human Physiology* (1855), Carpenter included Martineau's references to 'her cases of idiocy' in *Household Words* as well as discussing Martineau and Atkinson's 'Materialist doctrine' developed in *Letters on the Laws*.[81] Then, when Carpenter took material on mental physiology from the fourth and fifth editions of his *Principles of Human Physiology* to expand upon in his *Principles of Mental Physiology* (1874), he kept the earlier Martineau references but also added several paragraphs on her reports concerning the language abilities of 'J,' (i.e., Jane Arrowsmith), while mesmerized.[82] In 1877, the year after Martineau's death, Carpenter returned to Jane's language abilities in a final point of connection between Martineau and Braid. In his lectures of that year, published in *Fraser's Magazine*, Carpenter compared Braid's phreno-mesmeric experiments on a young working girl with the phreno-mesmeric experiments on Jane Arrowsmith witnessed by Martineau.[83] Considering that Thomas Henry Huxley credited Carpenter with contributing 'in no small degree to the foundation of a rational, that is to say, a physiological psychology,'[84] it is significant that Carpenter built upon Martineau's experiences and observations.

Conclusion

If Martineau, like other early mesmerists, erred in believing that mesmeric phenomena were caused by a material force, then she was proven correct in several of her other assessments about the mind. First, she realized that scientific experiments were needed to advance our understanding. Throughout *Letters on Mesmerism*, *Letters on the Laws of Man's Nature and Development*, and her unsigned review of *Salem Witchcraft*, Martineau advocated additional scientific inquiry, in the hope that her advocacy would result in new scientific research on the mind.

Secondly, in positing that mesmeric phenomena belonged to a new natural law that affected everyone, she asserted the idea that everyone can be mesmerized because, even though she did not yet have this term, everyone has an unconscious. The idea that everyone – or, at least those willing to consent[85] – can be mesmerized/hypnotized was still under debate as late as the 1880s when Charcot connected hypnosis with hysteria and avowed that only hysterics could be hypnotized, a position that Hippolyte Bernheim eventually disproved.[86] Although mesmerism had been potentially connected with hysteria from its beginnings,[87] Charcot's clinical work with the hysterics at the Salpêtrière took this idea to an entirely different level, not least in turning hypnosis into, as Waterfield asserts, 'a viable subject for scientific research. Psychology became an academic discipline in its own right, distinct for the first time from philosophy.'[88]

Lastly, Martineau's awareness of the larger paradigm shift imbedded in her promotion of the new sciences of mind marks an important historical turning point, which goes beyond her personal rejection of religion. In her three texts on the sciences of the mind, Martineau repeatedly visited the shift from religion to science in terms of understanding the mind's functions. She understood correctly the significance of the new science's ability to reconfigure explanations about religious visions, possession, and witchcraft. Events that were once explained externally as spiritual or demonic possession could now be understood as internal processes of the mind.

Martineau's promotion of these three Victorian sciences of the mind was underpinned by her interrelated beliefs in the importance of scientific inquiry and of science to society. Together, Martineau's early interest in David Hartley's associationist psychology, her early work as a sociologist, and her understanding of her own mesmeric cure enabled her to identify the importance of promoting experiments in psychology. Her increasing commitment to science led to her final big project of translating and abridging *The Positive Philosophy of Auguste Comte* in 1853. Because of Comte's important role in the birth of the scientific disciplines, Martineau's translation of Comte is yet another aspect of her contributions to the birth of psychology as a discipline.

Notes

1 Scholarship linking Martineau with mesmerism is more extensive than that linking Martineau with phrenology. For mesmerism: Alison Winter, *Mesmerized: Powers of Mind in Victorian Britain* (Chicago: U of Chicago P, 1998), pp. 213–30; Roger Cooter, 'Dichotomy and Denial: Mesmerism, Medicine and Harriet Martineau,' *Science and Sensibility: Gender and Scientific Enquiry, 1780–1945*. Ed. Marina Benjamin (Oxford: Blackwell, 1991), pp. 144–73; and Anka Ryall, 'Medical Body and Lived Experience: The Case of Harriet Martineau,' *Mosaic* 33/4 (2000), pp. 35–53. For Martineau, mesmerism, and phrenology: Caroline Roberts, *The Woman and the Hour: Harriet Martineau and Victorian Ideologies* (Toronto: U of Toronto P, 2002), pp. 122–38 and pp. 169–92; and Diana Postlethwaite, *Making It Whole: A Victorian Circle and the Shape of Their World* (Columbus: Ohio State UP, 1984), pp. 58–109 and pp. 136–55. For the history of phrenology: Roger Cooter, *The Cultural Meaning of Popular Science: Phrenology and the Organization of Consent in Nineteenth-Century Britain* (Cambridge: Cambridge UP, 1984). For the history of psychology: Adam Crabtree, *From Mesmer to Freud: Magnetic Sleep and the Roots of Psychological Healing* (New Haven: Yale UP, 1993); Graham Richards, *Mental Machinery: The Origins and Consequences of Psychological Ideas, 1600–1850* (Baltimore: Johns Hopkins UP, 1992); Rick Rylance, *Victorian Psychology and British Culture, 1850–1880* (Oxford: Oxford

UP, 2000); and Jenny Bourne Taylor and Sally Shuttleworth (eds.), *Embodied Selves: An Anthology of Psychological Texts, 1830–1890* (Oxford: Oxford UP, 1998).

2 George Combe, *Essays on Phrenology* (Edinburgh: Bell & Bradfute, 1819) and *The Constitution of Man* (Edinburgh: John Anderson, 1828). Martineau addressed the cultural significance of *The Constitution of Man* in Combe's obituary she wrote for the August 18, 1858 issue of *The Daily News*, reprinted in *Biographical Sketches* (London: Macmillan, 1869), pp. 266–77.

3 Mesmerism had first been brought to England from France in the 1780s, but interest was limited.

4 Richards, p. 285.

5 Harriet Martineau, *Letters on Mesmerism* (London: Edward Moxon, 1845).

6 Ibid., 3.

7 Ibid., 44.

8 Ibid., 62.

9 Ibid., 60–61.

10 Ibid., 45 (emphasis in original), 45, x.

11 Ibid., 62.

12 Ibid., 62.

13 Robin Waterfield, *Hidden Depths: The Story of Hypnosis* (New York: Brunner-Routledge, 2003), p. 194.

14 L.U.G.E., 'Miss Martineau and her Traducers,' *Zoist* 3/9 (April 1845): 86–96; pp. 86–87.

15 Winter, p. 224.

16 Ibid., 225. See Winter, Cooter ('Dichotomy'), Ryall, and Roberts for discussions of the ensuing medical debates.

17 Preface, *Letters on Mesmerism*, p. viii.

18 *Letters on Mesmerism*, p. 50.

19 Ibid., 50.

20 Ibid., 50.

21 Ibid., 24, 50–51.

22 Ibid., 59.

23 Ibid., 46.

24 Ibid., 44–45.

25 Robertson notes that Braid's first use in a medical text of the term 'neuro-hypnotism' occurred in Braid's letter to *The Medical Times* 6/146 (1842) although it had already appeared in Braid's popular pamphlet *Satanic Agency and Mesmerism Reviewed*, self-published earlier that same year. Donald Robertson (ed.), *The Discovery of Hypnosis: The Complete Writings of James Braid* (London: National Council for Hypnotherapy, 2008), pp. 372–81, p. 372.

26 Alan Gauld, *A History of Hypnotism* (Cambridge: Cambridge UP, 1992), p. 205; Crabtree, p. 151; Waterfield, pp. 193–95.

27 Crabtree, p. 151.

28 James Braid, *Neurypnology, or the Rationale of Nervous Sleep Considered in Relation with Animal Magnetism* (London: John Churchill, 1843). Rpt. in *The Discovery of Hypnosis*, pp. 314–18.

29 Spencer T. Hall, *Mesmeric Experiences* (London: H. Baillière, 1845), p. 10.

30 Ibid., 63–75; Martineau, *Letters on Mesmerism*, p. 7.

31 Braid commented on Elliotson's representation of him in an appendix entitled 'Excerpts from *The Zoist*' following *The Critics Criticised* (1855). Rpt. in *The Discovery of Hypnosis*, pp. 89–90.

32 Waterfield, p. 107.

33 Crabtree, p. 162.

34 Braid sent a paper in 1860 to be read at the French *Académie des sciences*.

35 Karl von Reichenbach's *Abstract of 'Researches on Magnetism and on Certain Allied Subjects.'* Trans. William Gregory (London: Taylor and Walton, 1846); HM to Elizabeth Barrett, Deborah Logan, *Further Letters* p. 155; HM to Thomas Carlyle, Deborah Logan, *Collected Letters*. 3: 49–50; HM to Lord Morpeth, *Collected Letters* 3: 50–51; HM to Mrs. Ogden, *Collected Letters* 3:51; HM to Lord Grey, *Collected Letters* 3: 54.

36 Martineau refers to the 'mesmeric influence' six times and to 'the influence' eight times in *Letters on Mesmerism*. She discusses her cautious use of language on page 50.

37 HM to Thomas Carlyle, *Collected Letters* 3: 50.

38 Karl von Reichenbach, *Researches on Magnetism, Electricity, Heat, Light, Crystallization, and Chemical Attraction, in Their Relations to the Vital Force.* Trans. William Gregory. (London: Taylor, Walton, and Maberly, 1850); Henry George Atkinson and Harriet Martineau, *Letters on the Laws of Man's Nature and Development* (London: John Chapman, 1851), pp. 114, 167, 268–69. Hereafter, cited as *Letters on the Laws*.

39 Braid, *The Power of the Mind over the Body* (1846). Rpt. in *The Discovery of Hypnosis*, pp. 238–50. Braid continues to critique Reichenbach in later writings.

40 For an excellent example, see Braid's 'Hypnotic Therapeutics,' *Monthly Journal of Medical Science* (July, 1853). Rpt. in *The Discovery of Hypnosis*, p. 92.

41 *Letters on Mesmerism*, p. 64.

42 Appendix, *Letters on Mesmerism*, p. 67.

43 HM to George Combe, *Collected Letters* 2: 97.

44 Cooter documents 15 articles written by Atkinson, eight published in the *Zoist*. Roger Cooter, *Phrenology in the British Isles: An Annotated, Historical Bibliography and Index* (Metuchen, NJ: Scarecrow P, 1989), p. 15. Postlethwaite discusses Atkinson's influence on Charles Bray. Postlethwaite, pp. 143–4.

45 *Letters on the Laws*, pp. 75–76, 124.

46 *Letters on the Laws*, pp. 30, 34. Gauld notes how a Mr. Mansfield in Britain and a Mr. Collyer in America vied with Atkinson for the distinction of introducing the phrenomagnetic phenomena to England. Gauld, p. 205.

47 J[ohn] Stevenson Bushnan, *Miss Martineau and Her Master* (London: John Churchill, 1851), p. 119.

48 Martineau, "George Combe," *Biographical Sketches*, p. 271.

49 Ibid., 270–71.

50 Ibid., 275.

51 Ibid., 275–76.

52 In his list of medical pioneers, Critchley includes such notaries as Boerhaave, Haller, Laennec, and Bichat. MacDonald Critchley, "Neurology's Debt to F.J. Gall," *British Medical Journal* 2/5465 (2 October, 1965): 775–81; p. 780.

53 Taylor and Shuttleworth, pp. 3–5. See also Sally Shuttleworth, *Charlotte Brontë and Victorian Psychology* (Cambridge: Cambridge UP, 1996), pp. 59–61.

54 Franz Joseph Gall, *On the Functions of the Brain* (1822–1825). Rpt. in Taylor and Shuttleworth, p. 26.

55 Taylor and Shuttleworth, p. 5.

56 Rylance, *Victorian Psychology and British Culture* (2000), p. 97.

57 Ibid., 97.

58 Ibid., 98.

59 *Letters on the Laws*, p. 164, emphasis in original.

60 Ibid., 2.

61 Ibid., 3.

62 Ibid., 11, 250.

63 R. K Webb, *Harriet Martineau: A Radical Victorian* (London: Heinemann, 1960); Valerie Kossew Pichanick, *Harriet Martineau: The Woman and Her Work, 1802–1876* (Ann Arbor: U of Michigan P, 1980); Shelagh Hunter, *Harriet Martineau: The Poetics of Moralism* (Aldershot, England: Scolar P, 1995); Shalyn Claggitt, "Harriet Martineau's Material Rebirth," *Victorian Literature and Culture*, 38/1 (2010): 53–73.

64 Rylance, pp. 24–27.
65 *Letters on the Laws*, p. 287.
66 Offering herself as a model for shifting from religious to scientific thinking also guides much of Martineau's self-representation in her *Autobiography*. Harriet Martineau, *Autobiography*, ed. Peterson (2007), pp. 521–32 and pp. 567–86.
67 The more appropriate term 'agnostic' was not yet common; however, Thomas Huxley introduced this term in 1869.
68 In his appendix, Braid reviewed recent works, including *Letters on the Laws*. James Braid, *Electro-Biological Phenomena Considered Physiologically and Psychologically* (London: John Churchill, 1851), pp. 23–33. The next year, Braid contrasted himself with Atkinson and Martineau in defence against representations of him as a materialist. Braid, *Observations on J.C. Colquhoun's History of Magic, etc.* (1852). Rpt. in *The Discovery of Hypnosis*, p. 134.
69 Braid, 'Appendix,' *Electro-Biological Phenomena*, p. 30.
70 Ibid., 31.
71 Ibid., 33.
72 [George Henry Lewes], 'Literature,' *The Leader* 49 (22 February 1851), p. 178.
73 [Lewes], '*Letters on Man's Nature and Development*,' *The Leader* 50 (1 March 1851), pp. 201–203; and 51 (8 March 1851), pp. 227–28; p. 227.
74 HM to Henry Reeve, *Collected Letters* 5: 207.
75 *Letters on Mesmerism*, p. 2; *Letters on the Laws*, pp. 22, 32, 33, 43, 49, 61, 129, 135 and 337.
76 [Martineau], 'Salem Witchcraft,' *Edinburgh Review* (July 1868), pp. 1–25; p. 25.
77 Henry Maudsley, *The Physiology and Pathology of the Mind* (London: Macmillan, 1867).
78 HM to Reeve. *Collected Letters, 5:* 213, emphasis in original.
79 Ibid., 213.
80 HM to Reeve. *Collected Letters*, 5: 212.
81 William Benjamin Carpenter, *Principles of Human Physiology* 5th ed. (London: John Churchill, 1855), pp. 601, 630, 548.
82 William Benjamin Carpenter, *Principles of Mental Physiology* 4th ed. (New York: D. Appleton and Co., 1883), pp. 4, 349–50, 431, 457–58.
83 William Benjamin Carpenter, "Mesmerism, Odylism, Table-Turning and Spiritualism, Considered Historically and Scientifically" *Fraser's Magazine* 95 (February 1877): 135–57; pp. 143–44.
84 Huxley's praise of Carpenter's scientific work is quoted by J. Estlin Carpenter. Roger Smith, 'Carpenter, William Benjamin (1813–1885),' *Oxford Dictionary of National Biography* (2004; online 2006): par. 2.
85 Waterfield, p. xxvii.
86 Waterfield, p. 222.
87 Roberts, pp. 131–33.
88 Waterfield, p. 220.

Part III

Contribution to fields of knowledge

9 Harriet Martineau and feminism

Gaby Weiner

Nobody can be further than I am from being satisfied with the condition of my own sex; under the law and custom of my own country . . . Often as I am appealed to, to speak, or otherwise assist in the promotion of the cause of Woman, my answer is always the same: – that women, like men, can obtain whatever they show themselves fit for. Let them be educated, – let their powers be cultivated to the extent for which the means are already provided, and all that is wanted or ought to be desired will follow of course. Whatever a woman proves able to do, society will be thankful to see her do, – just as if she were a man. If she is scientific, science will welcome her, as it has welcomed every woman so qualified.[1]

Harriet Martineau's brand of feminism is typically associated with nineteenth-century liberal political thought and the conception of rationality as the defining characteristic of human nature. For classic liberals, the ideal state is limited to protecting a range of civil liberties, for example, property rights, voting rights and freedoms of religion, speech and association, so that individuals have equal chances to determine their own future.[2] The best known, early advocate of liberal feminism is Mary Wollstonecraft (1759–1797), who argued some decades before Martineau that (middle-class) women were prevented from developing rational thought because of the limitations, especially of marriage, placed on their autonomy, education and physicality. Like Martineau, Wollstonecraft celebrated reason over emotion though she herself was criticised by Martineau for being overly influenced by passion.

Martineau showed interest in what was later to be called the 'Woman Question' in her earliest articles in the Unitarian journal *The Monthly Repository* entitled 'Female Writers on Practical Divinity' (1821) and 'On Female Education' (1823),[3] and in her major work *Society in America* published in 1837. In the 1850s, she made clear her continued commitment to women's equality, stating that if women received equal treatment to men, then the 'Woman Question' would be resolved. Yet, as Yates notes, while the statement at the beginning of this chapter incorporates her most consistently held views – dissatisfaction with the position of nineteenth-century women, importance of female education, respect for women's potential achievements and belief in the primacy of individual action – it is less representative of the more 'radical' aspects of Martineau's thinking on women, such as her bold challenges to nineteenth-century conventions of women's writing.[4] It is this aspect of Martineau's work that I also want to emphasise. For example, particularly in the 1830s when she was making her name with the *Illustrations*, Martineau was less concerned with propriety and more with youthfulness, radical politics and excitement. Her frame of mind is reflected in a letter to a friend Eliza Flower in 1832 at the start of her period of fame. Martineau writes how happy she is 'that I have my darling series' and that in an article celebrating the life of Walter Scott, she has 'pleaded for Woman till my heart turned sick'. She is full of the joys of life and is clearly delighted at the success of the *Illustrations:* 'I am perfect as to ease & sanity & ready to jump for glee at the thought of the business to come – to say nothing of pleasure'.[5] This is not the 'respectable' Martineau of later years but a young radical thinker who counted as her intellectual equals, Charles and Erasmus Darwin and Thomas and Jane Carlyle. It is therefore important to consider this self-positioning, as well as the actual content of her writing in any analysis of Martineau's feminism.

This chapter seeks to update the literature on Harriet Martineau's relationship to feminism, to discuss the extent to which her views on women's status changed over her lifetime, and to re-evaluate her standing among feminist scholars. The chapter draws on four sets of texts to show the range of her scholarship, her self-positioning in the present-ness of her time and her theoretical and political ideas on women. The first is a section entitled 'the Political Non-Existence of Women' in her book *Society in America* published in 1837 when she was thirty-five and a rising star in London's intellectual firmament. The second comprises several leaders written nearly twenty years later in 1853 and 1854 for the *Daily News* in support of divorce legislation. The third is an article entitled 'Female Industry' for the *Edinburgh Review* in 1859 about the dismal conditions of women workers in Britain (also referred to in Chapter 5). The final text is the four letters written later in her life for the *Daily News* in 1863 in support of the repeal of the Contagious Diseases Acts which had legalised medical inspections of women in military towns. I argue that these four pieces show not only the breadth of Martineau's scholarship on women but also her attention to the key issues facing women in the nineteenth century: political under/representation; marital legal in/justice; women's right to, and conditions of, work; and male and female sexuality.

A key issue in the debates and scholarship about the extent and quality of Martineau's feminism focuses on the manner of her textual positioning. Both Deirdre David and Linda Peterson focus on Martineau's relationship to male-dominated culture, particularly her use of 'masculine' discourse and her attention to masculine subject matter.[6] Caroline Roberts challenges these concerns with the 'masculine' which she says ignore and misrepresent Martineau's demystification of 'boring and obscure' upper-class, masculine language, and her introduction of so-called feminine language as in the *Illustrations*.[7] Indeed, Roberts observes that Martineau's entry into literary life was enabled 'by her imposition of 'feminine' discourse on 'masculine' preserves and modes'.[8] Deborah Logan is, however, somewhat critical of polarised and dichotomous paradigms such as male/female and masculine/feminine, suggesting that feminist scholarship requires a more fluid interdisciplinary approach. Logan argues that it is more productive to offer alternative interpretations of Martineau's work by contrasting her public (political) and private (personal) writing and language, and considering how they overlap and to what end.[9] Martineau's private writing to her friends is particularly revealing, as we have already seen, about her state of mind and perception of what is happening to her in the public sphere.

Roberts situates Martineau's controversial texts within prevailing 'Victorian ideology'. I aim to do the same with selected Martineau feminist texts but within contemporary ideologies of gender. She was adroit at establishing herself as a prominent voice at the centre of her society's most vexatious issues, and the 'noisy reception'[10] that her work received suggests that she was interested in addressing the immediate interests of her society rather than in advancing her intellectual standing or guaranteeing her historical legacy. In so doing, however, she has been marginalised by historians for being of value only as an interpreter of an age long gone. Recent literary and feminist work has restored Martineau's intellectual reputation, it is true, but as Roberts argues, there has been less sustained interest in, and analysis of, her lesser known texts.

Martineau's positioning within feminist activism has also been a factor in her marginalisation. Until the 1860s there was no recognisable British women's movement in Britain, so her voice was 'one of the very few raised in lonely and mainly futile protest against the accumulated prejudice of generations.'[11] Later in life she stood apart from other, younger, feminists representing what is known as the first feminist wave, such as Barbara Bodichon and Jessie Boucherett, possibly because of her seniority as an older writer with considerably more experience both of writing and activism, or perhaps because she was seen as representing the outdated views of a previous generation or even because of her celibate risk-averse lifestyle. Yet, articles written by Martineau were instrumental in establishing two of the most influential feminist pressure groups of the nineteenth century; the *Society for Promoting the Employment of Women* (Langham Place Group) and the *Ladies' National Association for the Repeal of the Contagious Diseases Acts*. The Langham Place Group took inspiration from her 'Female Industry' article written in 1859, and the movement led by Josephine Butler against the notorious Contagious Diseases Acts commissioned from her a series of letters for the *Daily News* in 1863.

To summarise, Martineau was an early lone feminist voice, of considerable relevance later to first-wave feminism and, I shall argue, of continuing importance today. Her writing on women was influential not only because of her social positioning and her sensitivity as an observer and commentator but also because of her accessible writing style which enabled her mainly progressive ideas to be disseminated to a wide and varied audience. As noted earlier, the focus in the next sections is on Martineau's writing on four key areas of policy regarding women in mid nineteenth-century Britain.

Women's political rights

Martineau was a consistent proponent of women's political rights, arguing that, if only women could achieve domestic and economic self-reliance, their political advancement would follow as a matter of course. She took different stances at different times of her life: sometimes she was cautious about advocating women's suffrage – prepared to ruffle feathers, as Pichanick says, but not to risk a 'violent conservative retroaction'.[12] So, for example, in 1857 when she advocated the extension of the male franchise, there was no hint of the possible inclusion of women because such a suggestion, she assumed, would inhibit rather than advance the changes she wanted.

Her most confident and comprehensive statement on women's political rights came much earlier, in her book *Society in America* written in 1837, when she was glowing and buoyant in the aftermath of her huge success with the *Illustrations*. *Society in America* is recognised as an important early effort to describe and explain American society, as we have already seen from Michael Hill and Susan Hoecker-Drysdale. A source of considerable controversy on both sides of the Atlantic when it was published, it played a major role in forming the liberal and progressive opinion of her contemporaries. A visit to the new democracy in 1834–6 had coincided with Martineau's increased intellectual curiosity about the nature of the political process. Her approach was deliberately analytic. She argued that being a woman was an advantage as a traveller and commentator because, as well as seeing the great institutions, she was able, unlike her male equivalents, to observe the routines of domestic life. She sought to identify key factors in social and political life, for example, government, politics, economy, morals, religion – and women. Central to her argument in the book was, first, the assumption that the moral values of a country are a major factor in determining social structure and, second, that as a young democracy with invigorated morals, the United States could/should work to eradicate traditional injustices such as 'fixed class lines' and 'aristocratic norms'.[13] In her chapter on women entitled significantly 'Political Non-existence of Women', she questioned how, if the fundamental principle of the Declaration of Independence was that government derives power from consent of the governed, this could be reconciled to the existing non-emancipated condition of women:

> Governments in the United States have power to tax women who hold property; to divorce them from their husbands; to fine, imprison, and execute them for certain offences. Whence do these governments derive their powers? They are not "just", as they are not derived from the consent of the women thus governed.[14]

She opposed the position taken by James Mill, Thomas Jefferson and others that women had no need of emancipation because their interests were identical with those of their fathers and husbands. She claimed no obligation, she wrote, to respect the laws to which she as a woman had not assented. For Martineau 'real' freedom meant that individuals should be able to exercise control over their own lives and destinies. So, eventual achievement by women of power and status within society would rest on the removal of restrictions placed on them. Equal political rights for women, she predicted, were inevitable in a democracy:

> The principle of the equal rights of both halves of the human race is all we have to do with here. It is the true democratic principle which can never be seriously controverted, and only for a short time evaded. Governments can derive their just powers only from the consent of the governed.[15]

Martineau frequently drew parallels between the plight of slaves and the condition of women. In other parts of the book, she was explicit about rape and the sexual abuse of slaves and offered details about the murder and mutilation of young girls, and of men who used their debauchery to increase, by the number of slave children then sold on the market, their property and wealth.[16] She returned to this critique of the essentialisation of male sexuality in her writing on the Contagious Diseases Acts as we shall see later, and the abolition of slavery was to become a major campaigning issue for Martineau for the rest of her life.

Before travelling to America, she had expressed optimism about the position of women in the young democracy. On arrival, she was quick to identify the most pertinent argument for women's rights in the United States: the inconsistency between the principles inherent in the American Constitution and the political status of women and also slaves. Later in life, she was more guarded and tactical about how greater rights for women could be achieved. A cool rational head was preferred to passion, she implied, in her autobiography written in the mid-1850s:

> I have no vote at elections, though I am a tax-paying housekeeper and respon-sible citizen; and I regard the disability as an absurdity, seeing that I have for a long course of years influenced public affairs to an extent not professed or attempted by many men. But I do not see that I could do much good by personal complaints, which always have some suspicion or reality of passion in them.[17]

Always clear about the need for political equality for women, her older self dwelt more on the need for respectability and strategizing on the part of women activ-ists. Respect, she said, had to be earned if women were to gain acceptance in pro-fessional and business communities and secure for themselves an active place in society. So whilst she gave her support to the first petition for women's suffrage, delivered to Parliament by John Stuart Mill in 1866, its decisive rejection was a disappointment to her rather than a surprise.

Marriage and divorce

Martineau was betrothed in her early twenties to a friend of her brother James, and at that time was clearly positive about her own involvement in the institution of marriage. According to letters to her sister-in-law Helen Martineau written in 1827, she bore her fiancé, John Worthington's long illness and early death with sadness and stoicism, drawing on her faith to carry her through:

> Yet I shall feel nothing but peace when I reflect hereafter that my friend's struggle is over, that the seal is set on a character more fit for heaven than earth; and surely I can never sink into apathy or despondence when I remember what a task I have in front of me, in preparing for a reunion.[18]

But she was not to be tempted by matrimony again and indeed, thirty years later, expressed much relief at her enduring spinsterhood:

> It was happiest for both of us that our union was prevented by any means. I am, in truth, very thankful for not having married at all. I have never since been tempted, nor have suffered anything at all in relation to that matter which is held to be all important to women, love and marriage'.[19]

Her first comments on marriage as an institution were made after her visit to America, in the mid-1830s. She positioned herself somewhat distanced from conventional married women. She had been struck when in America by what she saw as the decline in American women's status after marriage and therefore was interested in calibrating the state of the institution of marriage against the moral health of society:

> The traveller everywhere finds women treated as the inferior party in a compact in which both parties have an equal interest. Any agreement thus formed is imperfect, and is liable to disturbance; and the danger is great in proportion to the degradation of the supposed weaker party. The degree of degradation of woman is as good a test as the moralist can adopt for ascertaining the state of domestic morals in any country.[20]

Martineau's chief contribution to contemporary debates concerning marriage and divorce, however, was made after 1852, when she began writing leaders for the *Daily News*. Then, established as a journalist and writer and well into her middle years, she felt able to withstand challenges to her femininity and unmarried status which might result from forthright criticisms of the state of marriage. Her leaders were also unsigned. As Alexis Easley has shown, women writers like Martineau capitalized on publishing conventions associated with anonymity in order to create their own spaces and agency within a predominantly male publishing industry.[21]

Long overdue divorce reforms were being considered by Parliament, and in particular a report had been issued following a Commissioner enquiry into the state of divorce. Previous attempts at legislating for changes in the institution of marriage had been long drawn out, for example, changes in custody legislation which had been supported overwhelmingly in the House of Commons but had been 'thrown out' by the Lords in 1838. The Infants' Custody Bill was eventually passed a year later.[22] The recent report showed, however, that there was much to do. How, she asked her readers in 1853, could they tolerate a marriage compact in which the wife was regarded as the inferior party? How could they continue to ignore the gross injustice of a law which gave a wife no protection, by which her property and earnings could be appropriated by her husband, by which she could be divorced but could not petition for divorce herself, and under which she had no right of appeal or redress? How could they condone the bias against women and the Victorian double standard?

> It is assumed as a matter of course in our Legislature that the sin of conjugal infidelity is immeasurably greater in the wife than the husband; and a murmur of applause follows when a legislator asks whether any father would not infinitely rather see his son fall into vice than his daughter.[23]

She drew on the case of Caroline Norton[24] though not by name, to report on a 'not uncommon' circumstance of 'the case of a lady maintaining by her ability and industry an adulterous husband, who claims all her earnings and threatens the seizure of her whole property'.[25] The solution, she argued, was to change the law so that women could take responsibility for their own debts and obligations: it was only then that 'the women of England are sure of being put in possession, like the women of other countries, of their personal fortunes, and of their earnings of their talents and their toil.'[26]

Martineau took the material view of Victorian marriage – that it was an economic pact – challenging the widely held notion of its permanent and sacramental nature. She had witnessed incompatibility and unhappiness in the marriage of others, she said, – she was later to take Charles Dickens to task for his poor treatment of his wife – so divorce should be more readily available. She judged existing divorce proceedings to be too expensive and unwieldy, discriminating not only against women but against the poor. It was the poor working-class wife who was most likely to fall victim to the existing system, compelled thus to remain in a brutalised marriage. Martineau was more favourable to the divorce laws in Scotland which, unlike England, allowed wives to petition for divorce, and cost less:

> In Scotland, there were ninety-five cases in the five years from 1836 to 1841, while in England there have been 110 from the first day of this century until now. Of the ninety-five Scotch divorces, one third were at the suit of the wife; whereas in England the wife cannot seek a divorce at all, except in cases of unnatural atrocity; so that only four successful suits are on record. In Scotland, the parties in the ninety-five cases were almost all from the labouring classes, the expense being from £15 to £30, whereas in England, divorce is wholly out of the reach of all but the rich – the expense rising from £500 to many thousands.[27]

Divorce, she argued, should be granted according to need, not financial status or sex. Mistresses, she said, were more advantaged than wives as a mistress could walk away but a wife could not. 'The husbands are the lawmakers; and the wife is dumb before the law, and Parliament, and the Commission which is to decide on her interests'.[28]

When the laws were finally changed in 1857, Martineau noted with some satisfaction that women could now request a judicial separation and could keep hold of their own earnings as 'bread-winners'.[29] She focused on the economic rather than the political as the way forward for women. For her, the problem was that legislation had not reflected changes in employment patterns, particularly of women:

> By the changes in our marriage law much more happiness is caused than belongs to the mere relief of a certain number of sufferers, hitherto hopeless . . . We shall hear no more of the absolutely unendurable cases; and for all the hardest there is more or less remedy now provided.
>
> The benefit . . . under the reform of our marriage law is the full, practical recognition of women as "breadwinners" . . . But the fact is, and has been, that a vast proportion – some say nineteen-twentieths – of the women of the kingdom work for their bread, although our laws remain applicable to a very different state of society, to a social state in which nearly every woman was maintained by husband, father, mother or kinsman.[30]

Here, as with women's work as we shall see later, Martineau drew on evidence in the form of census and statistics as well as police reports to show that society was changing, that women were participating more in the public as well as the private sphere, that many were terribly abused by their husbands rather than supported by them, and that laws should be changed to recognise these factors.

Martineau employed an authoritative journalist discourse to argue her case – perhaps this is what Martineau scholars have referred to as 'masculine'. However her role as un-named leader writer was presumably to offer straightforward accounts of contemporary events of the day. It was her choice of topic and the position she took – abuse of women and protecting them through granting them rights on the same basis as men – that marks her out as a feminist, and an effective one at that.

Employment conditions and opportunities for women

In 1859, Harriet Martineau could write that there is a 'jealousy of men in regard to the industrial independence of women'.[31] Drawing on the greater availability of statistical and government reports and writing on girls and women as already mentioned in earlier chapters, her article on women's employment for the *Edinburgh Review* was remarkable both for its scholarship and its direct and accurate consideration of the problems of women's work. She drew predominantly on the 1851 census returns and on various erudite articles[32] to argue against the 'artificial depreciation' of women's work based on the assumption that women were primarily the financial responsibility of fathers and husbands. The census had shown that there were at least half a million more women than men, so arithmetic dictated that marriage was not an option for a substantial number of women. Neither could such women rely on economic help from brothers or fathers: 'So far from our country-women being all maintained as a matter of course by us, the breadwinners, 3 million out of 6 [million] adult women work for subsistence; and two out of three for independence'.[33]

She argued that in pre-modern times, men and women had worked side by side to sustain themselves and their families. It was only with the growth of the middle class and its practical dependency on other people that women's work had become an issue of concern. Census figures showed that women were increasingly working outside the home in essential occupations, for both themselves and their families but also for the economy of the country as a whole. In the article, Martineau divided female labour according to the industries in which women were visible, namely agriculture, mining, 'waters' (fishing etc.), domestic service, shop-keeping, printing and bookbinding, textiles, needlework, education (as governesses) and so on. She noted important new areas of work opening up to women such as nursing (following the reforms of Florence Nightingale) and in emerging technologies such as 'manipulation of type' (typesetting) and telegraphing.

She railed against the lowly pay of domestic servants, in particular, the lowest of the low maid-of-all-work and general servant as well as the needlewoman and governess, and the hardship that befell many of them as they reached old age and infirmity. One outcome was their disproportional presence in almshouses and asylums. She displayed an acute sense of hierarchy within and across occupational areas as well as knowledge of the different categories of employment overall. For instance, she included the following occupations connected to domestic service: maid of all work, general servant, charwoman, housekeeper, cook, housemaid, lady's maid, nursemaid and inn-servant. She also noted other forms of 'service' such as sick nurse, matron, asylum nurse and hospital nurse. She referred to quaintly named occupations such as bee-mistress and butcheress. She reported that women occupied in textile work were often home-based, such as lace-makers, weavers, clear starchers and menders, straw-platters [sic], artificial flower makers, embroiderers and dress-makers.[34]

Women working in 'water' industries included shrimp and lobster catchers, fish curers, workers in pilchard production and fish sellers at Billingsgate market in London and elsewhere. Also included in the 'waters' industries were women making and repairing the nets and spreading seaweed and fish remains on the fields as compost. Very little it seems escaped her attention.

She was sharply critical of areas of potential employment, such as watch-making, from which women were excluded by the guild system. She argued that watches were expensive for the working classes generally because most were imported from Switzerland. But, she observed, many of the imported watches were made by women. Why did this not happen in this country? Why could prices not be held down? 'Simply', she said, 'because the caste or guild of watchmakers will not permit it.'[35]

Martineau was firmly against monopolies and anything that prevented fair and unfettered competition for women's labour in the market place. Like other feminists in the 1850s, she argued that the answer to the increasing incidence of female labour was better education for women, as already noted by Ruth Watts, and new and better-paid forms of occupation[36]:

> In other words, we must improve and extend education to the utmost; and then open a fair field to the powers and energies we have educed. This will secure our welfare, nationally and in our homes, to which few elements can contribute more vitally and more richly than the independent industry of our countrywomen.[37]

Once again, as in her *Daily News* journalism, there was no authorial acknowledgement for the article, so Martineau was able to invert her gender identity and assume the male authoritative voice, for instance, by inserting herself in the category 'us, the breadwinners' more usually associated with males – although she had asserted, as we have seen, that women could be breadwinners too. And as already noted, the 'Female Industry' article was taken up by younger mid nineteenth-century feminists and became an important informational text for first-wave feminism and beyond.

Sexual politics

Martineau was not afraid of tackling controversial issues as we have seen, and none were so controversial in mid nineteenth-century England as issues around sexuality. Early on in her writing career in 1833, she had been castigated for broaching the issue of birth control in her tale *Weal and Woe in Garveloch* for the *Illustrations.*[38] The opportunity to reassert her position came towards the end of her writing career when she was approached by Florence Nightingale on behalf of Josephine Butler to support the campaign to repeal the Contagious Diseases Acts. In four letters to the *Daily News* in 1863, eventually published as a pamphlet in 1870, she questioned whether legalising control of prostitution was the best way to go about preventing the spread of venereal disease in the military and if 'the sin and disease in question can be dealt with only by a system of police regulation; that is, by the establishment of a systematic registration of prostitutes, and inspection for the purposes of preventing the spread of disease.'[39]

The first Contagious Diseases Act, passed in 1864, dictated that any woman in a garrison town could be stopped in the streets, summarily arrested as a prostitute, imprisoned, forcibly examined and if found to be infected, confined to a designated, secured hospital. The second Contagious Diseases Act, passed two years later, eradicated anomalies and extended the geographical area of imposition of the Acts. Why did the need to legislate against venereal disease become such a concern in Britain in the 1860s? Judith Walkowitz suggests that this was a reflection both of a concern for the high incidence of venereal disease in the British army (in 1864, one out of three cases of sickness was diagnosed as venereal in origin) and enthusiasm for intervention into the lives of the poor on medical and sanitary grounds.[40] The rhetoric underpinning the legislation revealed the sexual double standards of mid-Victorian culture as noted earlier, as is evident in the following extract from a Royal Commission report:

> We may at once dispose of any recommendations founded on the principle of putting both parties to the sin of fornication on the same footing by the obvious but not less conclusive reply that there is no comparison to be made between prostitutes and the men who consort with them. With the one sex the offence is committed as a matter of gain; with the other it is an irregular indulgence of a natural impulse.[41]

Despite Florence Nightingale's opposition to the Acts, there was little public antagonism until Josephine Butler embarked upon her campaign in the 1870s and 1880s. The Contagious Diseases Acts were finally repealed in 1886.

As already stated, Martineau's four letters, published in *the Daily News* in September 1863 (4, 15, 20, 25) were the first shots fired in one of the main British feminist campaigns of the nineteenth century, as acknowledged later by Josephine Butler in her autobiography.[42] In the letters, doubtless written as letters rather than editorials (as Deborah Logan indicates elsewhere in this volume) because of their 'delicate' nature, Martineau advanced four arguments against the suggested legislation. First, she said, the remedy for venereal disease lay in moral rather than in preventive measures and therefore the best way of tackling the problem was to remove temptation from soldiers by keeping them busy, active and occupied, and also healthy and well fed. Second, if the Acts were passed, there was no guarantee or evidence that they would prevent disease. Third, the legislation would imply state support and approval of immorality; and fourth, the legislation would sanction intervention of civilians in military affairs.

Martineau was particularly critical of the Victorian conviction of the unremitting nature of male sexuality: in the case of the military, she argued, the perception was of the need to gratify the soldier's sexual appetites [his 'animalism'] 'provided for like his need of food and clothing':

> This admission of the necessity of the vice is the point on which the whole argument turns, and on which irretrievable consequences depend. Once admitted, the necessity of a long series of fearful evils follows of course. There can be no resistance to seduction, procuration, brothels, disease and methods of regulation, *when once the original necessity is granted.* Further, the admission involves civil as well as military society, and starts them together on the road which leads down to what the moralists of all ages and nations have called the lowest hell. [Original emphasis][43]

Nearly a year later, in July 1864, she felt able to reintroduce the issue to the *Daily News* readership once more. She apologised for the awkwardness of the subject but pronounced it her duty as a journalist to warn against legislation which endangered the rights of innocent women. She trusted that her representatives in Parliament would not back the proposed legislation and that they would:

> surely not forget that to pass such a measure as this is to enter on a new and fearful province of legislation, from which we can never withdraw to the previous moral position; and that it is proposed to us to do this while existing laws against brothels and violations of decency in our streets remain unenforced, and while there is evidence in existence of the operation in other countries of laws for the protection of men from the consequences of their own passions which would make it a less evil to any conscientious member to quit public life than to have the smallest share in bringing down such a curse on his nation and on the moral repute and prospects of his country.[44]

She also put her signature to a letter, along with Florence Nightingale, Josephine Butler and twenty-eight prominent women, from the 'Ladies' National Association for the Repeal of the Contagious Diseases Act' printed in the *Daily News* in 1869.[45]

Despite poor health, Martineau continued to support Josephine Butler's campaign by writing posters and contributing 'fancy work'. Also, in collaboration with John Stuart Mill and other feminist activists, she helped mount a challenge against Sir Henry Storks, a supporter of the Acts, when he ran against a 'repealer' in an 1870 Colchester by-election. Colchester was a garrison town which came under the jurisdiction of the Acts. Martineau's *Daily News* letters of 1863 were reprinted in pamphlet form,[46] and a poster in the form of a letter from Martineau, Ursula Bright and Josephine Butler was addressed to the women of Colchester.[47] Though without voting power, the women of Colchester were urged to 'lift up your voices within your homes and neighbourhoods, against being ruled by lawmakers like the authors of these Acts; in other words, against Henry Storks as candidate for Colchester'.[48]

Storks, the official Liberal Party candidate, failed to be elected and the loss of the seat caused Prime Minister William Gladstone to reconsider the Acts. A parliamentary commission was constituted for this purpose and following its decision to repeal the Acts and propose new legislation, the campaigners were jubilant. Sir John Richard Robinson, *Daily News* editor, wrote to congratulate Martineau. 'You have done more than anyone, I really believe, to defeat the plans of the military.'[49] With typical scrupulousness, she pencilled the margin of his letter with the private comment, 'No, Mrs Butler'. In the event, the congratulations were premature, because the new bill was introduced too late in the parliamentary session to complete its passage. The Acts were not finally repealed until 1886, a decade and a half later.

In re-reading the letters some century and half after they were written, there is a visceral power in Martineau's challenge to the assumption of the unrelenting nature of male sexuality and her defence of what we now call sex workers, the prostitutes who 'serviced' the forces in garrison towns throughout the country. This was all the more impressive because she could only allude to the subject matter. For example, she referred to venereal disease as 'vice and disease under discussion' and 'this disease'.[50] Martineau's preferred course of action was to treat soldiers and 'all other men' as moral agents rather than animals. 'It is a national disgrace', she said, 'that our people should even have been asked to regard and treat their soldiers and sailors as predestined fornicators'.[51] The letters were unsigned although presumably their authorship was known to more than a few; but no doubt she felt that her age and intellectual seniority would protect her from the kinds of outrage against women writing about such topics that she had experienced when younger. Also, this time she was not alone but was part of a movement which shared her views and analysis. Nevertheless her decision to target male sexuality and to relate its perceived unremitting nature to the oppressive treatment of women was as brave as it was insightful.

Harriet Martineau and feminism

To summarise what the texts have shown us, Martineau's strategy in the earliest chosen for this chapter, *Society in America* written in 1837, was to disrupt the original American colonists' demand for no taxation without representation by applying the same principle in relation to 'the political non-existence of women'. If the argument was relevant to the status of the male colonists, then it also applied to women in the new democracy. The demand for the equal treatment of men and women was also used in her appeal, in *Daily News* leaders in 1853 and 1854 in support of divorce reform which allowed women to petition for divorce on the same basis as men. She argued for divorce to be made easier and cheaper primarily so that working-class women could extract themselves from abusive marriages. Martineau's article entitled 'Female Industry' in 1859 was a tour de force, drawing on a number of authoritative reports to show the extent and breadth of women's work in mid-Victorian England and the ubiquity of low pay, respect and status assigned to women workers. Her response to what she considered a dire situation for women was to demand better education for girls and women generally, and the removal of restrictions in the workplace which placed limitations on their skills and earning power. The final text, a series of four letters written to the *Daily News* in 1863, could be seen as amongst the most radical of her writing – as a powerful rejection of the essentialisation of male sexuality in preference to a moral argument about the need for male self-control, self-respect and restraint.

Harriet Martineau's analysis of the condition of women whether in terms of politics, rights, employment or sexuality as just discussed confirms her position as a feminist theorist. She is well known as a forerunner in acknowledging the importance of political representation for women (and for slaves in the United States) and as a proponent of the importance of material improvements in the condition of women, both in the labour market and within the home. But her contribution to feminism is much more than that. As we have seen, her earliest writing for the Unitarian *Monthly Repository* overtly addressed the unfairness of women's condition, and in her breakthrough series *Illustrations of Political Economy* she sought to erase the distinction between domestic and political economy and between private and public spheres.[52] Later work focused on every aspect of women's life and employment, whether autobiographical, concerning travel, or in relation to social and political life.

To categorise her feminism within a modern framework, Martineau was a liberal feminist concerned, albeit passionately at times, to change the social position of women by means of reform and self-help.[53] This is how, for example, Dzelzainis and Kaplan portray her: 'As a liberal feminist and radical Unitarian, she was early in assessing women's equal entitlement to full civic participation', which was an intrinsic part of her commitment to liberal ideas and laissez-faire economics.[54] Her rejection of the 'woman on a pedestal' notion of gender relations and her will to replace it with the rational recognition of the actual and potential abilities and realities of 'half the human race' were underpinned by a social scientist mentality. She increasingly relied on facts and evidence as a means of persuasion – as seen in the texts analysed for this chapter. She was also aware that changes could be reversed and that improvements in the condition of women could be lost. In her 1863 letters on the Contagious Diseases Acts, she warned that decades of reforms were being compromised by the proposed legislation which allowed the arrest, incarceration and enforced treatment and examination of *any* woman suspected of prostitution. Theoretically, no woman was exempt. This was no writing of an even-handed liberal: it was more akin to the radical feminist polemic of a century into the future.

Much of Martineau's work involved popularising views which were gaining currency in her society and as Roberts says, though she was very much of her time, she was also often ahead of it.[55] Her ideas, shared with other feminists, liberals and radicals, became mainstream and normalised through her writing which reached an ever wider audience through her journalism and fiction. As a consequence, her early so-called radical insights into women's inequality had become almost unfashionably consensual among liberals and progressives by the time of the appearance, late in her life, of the letters against the Contagious Diseases Acts. The sharpness, vigour and passion of her analysis in the letters restored her reputation once more to her younger contemporaries, as a feminist theorist and courageous proponent of women's cause. That is also her legacy and her gift to us today.

Notes

1 Harriet Martineau, *Harriet Martineau's Autobiography*, ed. Peterson (2007), pp. 303–4. The autobiography was published in 1877 shortly after Martineau's death but was written in 1855 when she thought she had not long to live.
2 Rosemarie Tong, *Feminist Thought: A Comprehensive Introduction* (Sydney, Australia: Allen & Unwin, 1989).
3 Harriet Martineau, 'Female Writers on Practical Divinity', *Monthly Repository*, vol. 17 (November, 1822), pp. 593–96; Harriet Martineau, 'On Female Education', *Monthly Repository*, vol. 17 (December, 1822), pp. 746–50.
4 Gayle Graham Yates, *Harriet Martineau on Women* (New Brunswick, NJ: Rutgers University Press, 1985)
5 Deborah Logan (ed.), *The Collected Letters of Harriet Martineau* (5 vols., London: Pickering & Chatto, 2007), vol. 1, p. 161.
6 Deirdre David, *Intellectual Women and Victorian Patriarchy: Harriet Martineau, Elizabeth Barrett Browning, George Eliot* (Ithaca, NY, Cornell University Press, 1993) *passim*. including pp. 31, 48, 58, 92-3; Linda H. Peterson, 'Harriet Martineau: Masculine discourse,

female sage.' In: Thaïs Morgan (ed.), *Victorian Sages and Cultural Discourse: Renegotiating Gender and Power* (New Brunswick: Rutgers University Press, 1990), pp. 171–86.

7   Caroline Roberts, *The Woman and the Hour: Harriet Martineau and Victorian Ideologies* (Toronto, ON: University of Toronto Press, 2002), p. 14.

8   Ibid., p. 16.

9   Deborah Logan, *The Hour and the Woman: Harriet Martineau's 'Somewhat Remarkable Life'* (Dekalb, IL: Northern Illinois University Press, 2002), p. 224.

10   Roberts, *The Woman and the Hour*, p. 4.

11   Valerie Kossew Pichanick, 'An abominable submission: Harriet Martineau's views on the role and place of women,' *Women's Studies*, 5:1 (1977), p. 14.

12   Ibid., p. 20.

13   Seymour Martin Lipset, 'Harriet Martineau's America: Introductory essay', Harriet Martineau, *Society in America* [edited, abridged and with introductory essay] (Gloucester, MA: Peter Smith, 1968), pp. 5–42, p. 13.

14   Harriet Martineau, *Society in America* (London: Saunders and Otley, 1837), vol. 1, p. 148.

15   Ibid., p. 206.

16   Roberts, *The Hour and the Man*, p. 47.

17   Martineau, *Autobiography*, p. 305.

18   Logan, *Collected Letters*, vol. 1, p. 44.

19   Martineau, *Autobiography*, p. 119.

20   Harriet Martineau, *How to Observe* (London: Charles Knight, 1838), pp. 168–9.

21   Alexis Easley, *First-Person Anonymous: Women Writers and Victorian Print Media, 1830–1870* (Farnham, Surrey: Ashgate, 2004)

22   Harriet Martineau, untitled leader, *Daily News*, Thursday 25 March 1853, p. 4.

23   Ibid.

24   Caroline Norton (1808–77) was a writer and campaigner for the improvement of women's legal position which stemmed from personal marital experiences and concentrated on the rights of mothers to their children, and of wives to keep their own property. After the passage of the Infant Custody Bill (1839), she was reunited with her own children. She was also involved in campaigns which helped bring about the Matrimonial Causes Act (1857) and the first Married Women's Property Bill (1882).

25   Martineau, *Daily News*, 25 March 1853, p. 4.

26   Ibid.

27   Ibid.

28   Martineau, *Daily News*, 8 September 1853, p. 4.

29   These views were reiterated by Martineau in untitled leaders for the *Daily News*, Thursday 8 September 1853, p. 4 and Wednesday 28 June 1854, p. 4.

30   Harriet Martineau, untitled leader, *Daily News*, Friday 28 May 1858, p. 4.

31   Harriet Martineau, 'Female Industry', *The Edinburgh Review*, vol. 109 (April 1859), pp. 293–336, p. 329.

32   Martineau's sources for her 1859 article were: Edward Cheshire, *The Results of the Census of Great Britain in 1851*, London (1853); *Report of the Assistant Poor-law Commissioners on the Employment of Women and Children in Agriculture*, London (1843); *Minutes of the Committee of Council of Education; Reports of the Governesses' Benevolent Institution* (1855–6); *The Industrial and Social Position of Women in the Middle and Lower Ranks*, London (1857); Barbara L. Smith (Mrs Bodichon), *Women and Work*, London (1857); Mrs Austin, *Two Letters on Girls' Schools and on the Training of Working Women* (1857); M. M., *Experience of Factory Life*; *The Lowell Offering*. Lowell, Massachusetts, United States (1857); Elizabeth Blackwell, *The Laws of Life, with Special Reference to the Physical Education of Girls*, New York (1858).

33   Martineau, 'Female Industry', p. 336.

34   Ibid., p. 321.

35   Martineau, 'Female Industry', p. 326.

36   Jane Rendall, *The Origins of Modern Feminism: Women in Britain, France and the United States 1780–1860* (Houndmills, Basingstoke: Macmillan, 1985), p. 184.

37 Martineau, 'Female Industry', p. 336.
38 Martineau was roundly criticised by John Wilson Croker for declaiming against child-bearing and marriage. See John Wilson Croker, 'Miss Martineau's Monthly Novels', *Quarterly Review* vol. 49 (April 1833), p. 136. See also the chapter by John Vint and Keiko Funaki in this volume.
39 Harriet Martineau, *Daily News*, 20 September, letter, republished in pamphlet form with the title *Contagious Diseases Acts as Applied to Garrison Towns and Naval Stations* (Liverpool: T. Brakewell, 1870), pp. 17–22.
40 Judith Walkowitz, *Prostitution and Victorian Society* (Cambridge: Cambridge University Press, 1980), pp. 69–89.
41 Report in Royal Commission on the Administration and Operation of the Contagious Diseases Acts 1866–69 quoted in Walkowitz, *Prostitution and Victorian Society*, p. 71.
42 Josephine Butler, *Personal Reminiscences of the Great Crusade* (London: Horace, Marshall & Son, 1896), pp. 7–8.
43 Martineau, *Daily News*, 20 September 1863.
44 Martineau, *Daily News*. 2 July 1864.
45 Reproduced in Maria Weston Chapman, *Memorials* (London: Smith, Elder & Co, 1877)
46 Martineau, *Contagious Diseases Acts*.
47 Chapman, p. 430.
48 Ibid., pp. 433–5.
49 Unpublished letter from John Richard Robinson to Harriet Martineau, 22 May 1871. Harriet Martineau Papers (MS 758), University of Birmingham Library.
50 Martineau, *Daily News*, 4 September 1863.
51 Martineau, *Daily News*, 20 September 1863.
52 Ella Dzelzainis, 'Feminism, speculation and agency in Harriet Martineau's *Illustrations of Political Economy.*' In: Ella Dzelzainis and Cora Kaplan (eds.), *Harriet Martineau: Authorship, Society and Empire* (Manchester: Manchester University Press, 2010), pp. 118–37.
53 Yates, *Harriet Martineau on Women.*
54 Ella Dzelzainis and Cora Kaplan, 'Introduction'. In: Ella Dzelzainis and Cora Kaplan (eds.), *Harriet Martineau: Authorship, Society and Empire* (Manchester: Manchester University Press, 2010), pp. 1–8, p. 3.
55 Roberts, *The Woman and the Hour*, pp. 195–6.

10 Harriet Martineau
Travel and the writer

Iain Crawford

In *Penelope Voyages*, her foundational study of women's travel writing, Karen Lawrence argues that the genre was especially appealing to female authors because it offered 'a set of alternative myths or models for women's place in society' and 'a particularly broad spectrum of generic possibilities.'[1] That is, travel itself allowed the woman author to experience and describe models of women's lives that interrogated those paradigms prevailing in her home culture, while the fluidity of travel writing as a genre provided an opportunity to experiment both by taking on different writerly selves and by presenting subjects through a range of formal lenses. As Lawrence and others have shown, it was this range of experience and opportunity that made travel writing such an appealing genre to women writers throughout the nineteenth century. In particular, it led to a proliferation of women's travel narratives during the early Victorian years, when visiting the American experiment in democracy allowed British travelers to examine processes of social change in the new world that were becoming increasingly relevant to issues at home. Harriet Martineau, even more than such contemporaries as Frances Trollope and Anna Jameson, embraced the possibilities that travel made available, combining an exceptional range of subject matter with an ongoing use of the genre to explore fundamental elements of her social philosophy and so assert her own potential as a contributor to the intellectual life of the period.

Interrupted by her extended illness during the early 1840s and brought to an end by the emergence of the health issues that reshaped her life in 1855, Martineau's extended travel into other cultures and writing about them falls into three main episodes. The first of these was her two-year stay in America (1834–36), out of which came three books: *Society in America* (1837), *Retrospect of Western Travel* (1838), and *How to Observe Morals and Manners* (1838). Second, following her recovery from the illness that had kept her housebound for some five years, she traveled to Egypt, Palestine, and Syria over the winter of 1846–7 and published her account of the experience in *Eastern Life, Present and Past* (1848). Finally, in August 1852 and as part of her new engagement to write leaders for the *Daily News*, she began a two-month visit to Ireland, out of which she published two very different sets of articles: a series of twenty-seven Letters from Ireland, which launched her into a career with the paper that would comprise more than 1500 pieces over the next dozen years; and eight pieces on Irish subjects for Dickens's popular weekly, *Household Words*, which turned out to be almost the last of her forty-eight contributions to the magazine. The focus of this chapter is upon the first and last of these phases of her travel writing and, by comparing her writing about America with her accounts of Ireland, I show both how she interrogated the form itself as part of her ongoing evaluation of social development and how she evolved away from it as a professional author to claim a role for herself at the heart of mid nineteenth-century journalism.

America

The contrasting forms and identities of Martineau's three American books embody the disciplinary diversity that Lawrence has identified as fundamental to travel writing. Drafted first but published last, *How to Observe Morals and Manners* describes her analytical method, lays the foundation of the new discipline of sociology, as we say in the chapters by Michael Hill and Susan Hoecker-Drysdale in this book, and, in the words of two modern critics, comprises 'the classic statement of fundamental ideas about methodology in the history of [the field].'[2] Written next but published first, *Society in America* operationalizes the methodology laid out in *How to Observe* and includes material ranging from the constitutional system to the workings of the economy, to religious life, and to cultural morality, especially in relation to slavery and the position of women. Placed between these two texts is *Retrospect of Western Travel*, a book that appears to follow the traditional manners and customs emphasis of women's travel writing. But even here, however, Martineau will challenge readerly expectations both of herself and of the genre and thus, despite the fact that she is apparently working within a conventional form, readily asserts her authority to render assessments that are unconventional both for the genre and for a woman author.

The complexity of stance Martineau develops in her writing about America originates in two elements that were foundational to her intellectual and ideological formation. On the one hand, her fundamentally optimistic vision of the New World and her belief 'that America was meant to be everything'[3] has its origins in eighteenth-century classical political economy, specifically Adam Smith's stadial model of history. For Smith, as we have already seen in Chapter 3, history was to be understood as a progressive evolution based upon economic development through a four-stage series of phases or stades: the Age of Hunters; the Age of Shepherds; the Age of Agriculture; and, finally, the Age of Commerce.[4] In all her travel writing, Martineau worked within Smith's paradigm as she analyzed where a particular society lay along this timeline and used her analysis to examine the paradigm itself. On the other, while she clearly merged this intellectual legacy with more contemporary Utilitarian values and a belief in laissez-faire capitalism as a primary agent of social change, Martineau was also a product of early nineteenth-century Unitarianism. Even though she would move away from and eventually abandon the foundation of her faith tradition, its commitments to the ameliorative workings of human agency and, above all, to advancing opportunities for women were core values throughout her life. Throughout her travel writing we thus find her testing the validity of the stadial model as she measures it against the actual substance of what she observes and analyzes.

In her travels through America, Martineau both reveled in discovering a society that was enjoying rapid evolution through its blend of immense natural resources and dynamic entrepreneurship and yet was also deeply troubled by what she saw as the nation's reactionary cultural mores around the issues of slavery and the role of women. As she writes about this new world, she not only describes its various regions but also examines where the different parts of the country are situated in terms of historical progress. In the process, and most disturbing to her of all, she recognizes that the supposedly advanced regions are not always as distinct from the more regressive parts as she, or her readers, might have anticipated, particularly around the issues of slavery and the role of women. Although her fundamental optimism about America remains intact despite this discovery, her realization of its regressive tendencies produces a more nuanced representation of the young nation than has always been appreciated.

Just as important as the conclusions that she reaches are the means by which she comes to them. For the methodologies of Martineau's investigation of America reveal how she took full advantage of what Lawrence has called the 'hybrid forms' of travel writing[5] both to represent the New World itself and to position her as an author comfortable in a variety of writing modes and not limited to forms of discourse traditionally regarded as feminine. Thus, for example, the American books include far less material dealing with her own subjective experience of traveling than was the case, say, in Trollope's *Domestic Manners of the Americans* or Jameson's *Winter Studies in Canada*. Moreover, when she does include such material, Martineau typically does so to differentiate herself from conventional feminine conduct. Perhaps the most notable instance of this occurs early in *Retrospect of Western Travel* during the voyage across the Atlantic. There, leaving the other ladies sheltering below, she describes how she fastened herself 'to the post of the binnacle' during a hurricane in order that she might observe the storm. Struck by the immensity of the ocean's power and how 'the scene was perfectly unlike what I had imagined,' she concludes that 'the delight of the hour I shall not forget' and thus celebrates what she has gained from her willingness to move outside cultural norms of feminine behaviour.[6]

Once she actually reaches the United States, Martineau's investigative methodology continues to resist feminine norms, even as she repeatedly positioned herself in the role of domestic guest in the communities she visited. Perhaps the most striking illustration of this is the way in which she represents the natural environments of North America and focuses the reader on understanding the part the very physical substance of the continent plays in the stadial formation of a new society.

Nowhere is this more evident than in Martineau's accounts of America's great river systems, in particular the Mississippi and the phenomenon of Niagara Falls, to both of which she responds in ways that are intense and complex and that point to the interaction between the continent itself and the forces of human progress.

As she takes a nine-day voyage up the Mississippi from New Orleans, for instance, she notes that the river has 'grandeur,' 'beauty,' and 'vastness,'[7] and yet that it could also become oppressive in its monotony:

> The scenery by this time was very wild. These hundreds of miles of level woods, and turbid, rushing waters, and desert islands, are oppressive to the imagination. Very few dwellings were visible. We went ashore in the afternoon, just for the sake of having been in Arkansas. We could penetrate only a little way through the young cotton-wood and the tangled forest, and we saw nothing.[8]

Yet, even while she records this sense of oppression and is careful to mark the isolation of those carving out tenuous lives on the remote banks of the river, she is also well aware of the 'busy world' to which the steamboat on which she is traveling connects each of these remote settlements.[9] Moreover, if she cannot yet see much actual progress in the scenes she describes, her text repeatedly draws the reader's attention to the fact that she is traveling on the 'Henry Clay,' the one riverboat that she names in all her travels. Dubbed for the Kentucky legislator whom she had seen and admired during her stay in Washington and who was responsible for many of the nation's early initiatives to improve its infrastructure, the name also anticipates Martineau's discussion in the following chapter of the Missouri Compromise and her recognition of Clay's decisive role in its privileging 'temporary expediency in preference to everlasting principle.'[10] Similarly, in the epigraph selected for this chapter she combines a sense of faith in social amelioration with an awareness of the ambivalent steps often intrinsic to that progress:

> Hic vir purpureum: varios hic flumina circum
> Fundit humus flores: hic candiate populus antro
> Imminet, et lentae texunt umbracula vites.[11]

Taking her text from Virgil's ninth *Eclogue*, a poem that focuses upon the transformation of the natural world through human endeavour and the conflicts often attendant upon that process, Martineau quotes in Latin to establish her own intellectual authority and, alluding back to Clay's work for social progress, simultaneously suggests that, however difficult life along the river may still be, the forces of change are at work and will, in the course of time, bring civilization even to the remotest parts of the continent.

A different perception of these forces of change is apparent in her response to Niagara Falls, which she visited twice during her stay in North America. In writing about the Falls, Martineau begins from a conventional touristic emphasis upon their 'beauty' and the way in which she derived a feeling of 'enjoyment' in going behind the fall that 'was intense.'[12] Rather like her delight in braving danger during the Atlantic hurricane, however, she then goes on to recount how she learned 'the secrets of the cataract' by daring to stand precariously on a bridge 'projected out over the precipice' suspended above the 'dizzying whirl' of the water.[13] While she is again positioning herself as the unconventional woman, willing to embrace the thrill of physical danger, even more striking and significant, however, is the way in which she brings together her experience of the two rivers to make a larger statement about the fundamental nature of America. For in *Society in America*'s chapter on the economy she unites the Mississippi and Niagara into a single vision of progressive change. Discussing the process of 'world-making,' she reflects upon the two rivers as complementary representations of natural evolution. On the one hand, standing behind the Falls and seeing in the crumbling rock face tangible evidence of geological change, she understands that 'Niagara itself is but one of the shifting scenes of life, like all of the outward that we hold most permanent' and that 'the spot on which I stood shall be the centre of a wide sea, a new region of life.'[14] On the other, that process of change is an essential part of the work of world-making that underlies the stadial evolution of history:

> So it was on the Mississippi, when a sort of scum on the waters betokened the place of new land. All things help, in this creation. The cliffs of the upper Missouri detach their soil and send it thousands of miles down the stream. The river brings it, and deposits it, in continual increase, till a barrier is raised against the rushing waters themselves. The air brings seeds, and drops them where they sprout and strike downwards, so that their roots bind the soft soil, and enable it to bear the weight of new accretions.[15]

For Martineau, then, the natural world she explored during her travels in America thus offered compelling evidence of forces of natural change that aligned with her vision of the restless dynamism of the American economy and its driving forward the evolution of a society that, while still profoundly flawed, was intrinsically progressive and contained unlimited potential.

If that potential is to be fulfilled, however, she argues, American society will have to address the major obstacles it has created to its own progress. For her these lie in the interconnected issues of slavery, the cultural position of women, and the nature of public discourse, especially as manifested in the press. While making connections between the positions of slaves and of women was a standard trope in progressive rhetoric of the time, Martineau's distinctive contribution was, on the one hand, the extent to which she used her travel writing to situate these issues within a comprehensive analysis of the condition of American society and, on the other, the thoroughness with which she explored the role of the press in sustaining the status quo and, indeed, in forestalling the kinds of public debate that could lead to change. For my argument here, I will focus upon her innovative representation of the American press, a subject about which she wrote more extensively than did any of her contemporary travelers from Britain.

One of the most striking paradoxes that emerged in her experience of the new democracy was the realization that the power of public opinion constituted the single greatest barrier to social progress in America and, in particular, to the movement against slavery. She wrote that a 'cautious subservience to public opinion – their deficiency of moral independence' was 'a prevalent fault in the United States,'[16] and she suggested that it characterized the entire nation. Moreover, while she suggested that this 'self-imposed bondage' was most fully developed in the southern states, where the fear of destabilizing the slavery-based order was most intense,[17] she also noted that even the avowedly more progressive north was marred by it as she criticized Boston for being 'the headquarters of Cant' in its failure 'to redeem society from false morals, and empty religious profession.'[18] In a young society that had still to develop a national literature and where public opinion had enormous power to extinguish discussion of – let alone dissent from – prevailing norms, newspapers assumed an essential role in shaping the public sphere, and Martineau, like all the other British travelers, was fascinated by the phenomenon of an American press as unfettered in its workings as the country's laissez-faire economy.

In this fascination, she, at one level, participated in a larger British reaction to American newspapers. Writers from Captain Marryat to J.S. Buckingham wondered how, with such a press, it was possible that 'the community should not have their taste corrupted, their moral perceptions deadened, and their horror of crime frittered away to indifference.'[19] At a time when the debate over 'the taxes on knowledge' was intensifying at home, these British observers of the New World were given pause by the experience of an entirely free press operating without restraint in a fluid cultural context and supported by both the fear of public opinion and the potential retributive workings of the masculine honor code. And yet, although Martineau herself shared these concerns and noted that 'of all newspaper presses, I never heard anyone deny that the American is the worst,'[20] she also differentiated herself from the other British observers. In the more nuanced detail of her recording the range of the American press as well as in her faith in its potential to play a role in the spiritual awakening and onward progress of society as a whole, she followed the pattern that consistently characterizes her writing about American society.

For each of Martineau's American books explores the role of the press in aiding, or inhibiting, social progress and, although she did not dispute the verdict her fellow travel writers came to on the quality of the American press overall, she also showed much greater confidence in its importance as an institution and its function in representing underlying dispositions in the culture she had already identified as foundational to democracy. For, she suggests, 'the very existence of the newspapers . . . testifies to the prevalence of a habit of reading, and consequently of education – to the wide diffusion of political power – and to the probable safety and permanence of a government which is founded on so broad a basis, and can afford to indulge so large a licence.'[21] Although she certainly echoes the horror many expressed over the 'slough of rancour, folly, and falsehood' that she sees as the special feature of American newspapers,[22] she is, then, encouraged by the connection she is able to make between the nation's foundational ideals and constitutional nature and that commitment to intellectual engagement she finds pervasive in its culture.

Indeed, her greatest concern is not with what American papers print but with what they refuse to cover, and much of her discussion of the press deals with the extent to which, despite their ostensible freedom, American newspapers play into the culture's larger deference to prevailing opinion through their exercise of self-censorship. Most notably, she finds, this occurs in matters related to slavery, and she emphasizes in particular the failure of the press to report lynchings, even in the most notorious cases and especially in the South, where state constitutional guarantees of free speech have given way to the practices of a citizenry that has 'fettered their own presses.'[23] She thus cites an incident in Mobile, Alabama, where two men 'were burned alive there, in a slow fire, in the open air, in the presence of the gentlemen of the city generally' and follows the deliberate rhythms of her sentence with a brisk commentary on the reaction of the local press: 'No word was breathed of the transaction in the newspapers: and this is the special reason why I cite it as a sign of the times; of the suppression of fact and repression of opinion which, from the possibility of their being long maintained, are found immediately to precede the changes they were meant to obviate.'[24] Suggesting the economic value of acts of violence committed to maintain the status quo, her use of 'transaction' here connects this representation of the press to the larger themes of her narrative, and that connection is extended further as she immediately proceeds to describe how a 'lady of Mobile' had confided to her 'the trouble caused by the licentiousness of the whites, among the negro women.'[25] Bringing together the economic and sexual exploitation of African-Americans and demonstrating the complicity of the local papers in suppressing exposure of the various kinds of violence inflicted upon the slaves, Martineau's account makes an inverted argument for the vital role of the press in forwarding social progress, since it is the 'miserable quality of the southern newspapers, and the omission from them of the subjects on which the people most require information' that goes 'far to account for the people's delusions on their own affairs.'[26]

The pervasiveness of this suppression of free discourse is evident from Martineau's repeated accounts of another lynching where a slave was again burned alive. In this incident, which occurred in St. Louis in 1836, an abolitionist newspaper editor who did not follow the code of silence was assaulted and ultimately murdered. For Martineau this incident becomes the single most important example both of the extent to which public discussion is suppressed in America and of the importance of martyrs willing to sacrifice themselves in the name of a social progress. After touching upon the event in *Society in America*, where she represents it as one more instance of press self-censorship – 'The gentlemen of the press dared not reprobate the outrage, for fear of consequences from the murderers. They merely announced the deed, as a thing to be regretted, and recommended that a veil of oblivion should be drawn over the affair'[27] – she returns to it at length in her 1838 *London and Westminster Review* article, 'Right and Wrong in Boston,' when she describes E.P. Lovejoy, the editor of the *St Louis Observer*, heroically resisting the mob that destroyed his printing press and types four times before it launched an assault upon his office and shot him to death.[28] As horrifyingly as she describes the episode, however, she also consistently positions it as an instance of the progress to which such sacrifice can lead, as she notes the response it stimulated among the abolitionist movement in Boston and points to the emergence of other voices of protest in the nation's press. When mob violence is resisted, that is, she is able to conclude that things can change and, as a result, both public opinion and the press are beginning to advance, as 'the influence of the awakening people is already seen in the improved vigour in the tone of the newspapers against outrage.'[29]

Indeed despite, and even because of, this terrible incident, Martineau was, then, ultimately optimistic about the potential of the American press. Seeing the press within the larger context of her progressive vision of American culture, she also records incidental examples of excellent newspapers that she comes across during her travels and recognizes that American society does possess leaders who will resist the prevailing patterns of public discourse. As is often the case in her representation of America, it is in the western states that she finds models of practice that belie the larger trend as she praises the unnamed local paper in Ann Arbor, Michigan, and then in Ohio comes across 'the very best newspaper' that she saw in America, a copy of the *Cleveland Whig*: 'The whole of this particular number was valuable for the excellence of its spirit, and for its good sense. It had very important, and some very painful subject matter, – instances of overbearing the law, – to treat of. It was so done as nearly to beguile me, hungry traveller as I was, of my dinner, and of all thought of my journey.'[30] With instances like these, she is able to report local examples of that spirit of intellectual engagement in the business of democracy that she prizes as one of America's best characteristics and that encourages her faith in that 'influence of the will of the awakening people.'[31] Connecting that awakening to the advancement of the national literature, she is thus able to claim that, however dreadful its current state may be, the American press is, along with the larger society of which it is but one expression, progressing towards a higher state, albeit slowly: 'There will be no improvement in the literary quality of American newspapers till the literature of the country has improved. Their moral character depends upon the moral taste of the people.'[32]

Finally and going back to her consistent representation of the role of Unitarians in shaping American society, she identifies a group that has the capacity to produce leaders who will take on the task of guiding public opinion towards such progress. For, and again in keeping with her representation of Unitarian Abolitionists as the guardians of the nation's future, she identifies three of its principal figures as key shapers of public opinion: Channing, Garrison, and Follen, singling out the latter, her closest male friend in Boston, as a potential exemplar of editorial leadership:

> An editor worthy of the work would decline the responsibility of suppressing any views, coming within the range of subjects embraced. He would merely weed out personalities; cherish the spirit of justice and charity; and for the sake of these, strengthen the weaker side, where he saw that it was inadequately defended. It may be said that editors who would thus discharge their function are rare. They are so: but there is Dr. Follen; a living reply to the objection.[33]

Follen never did take on the kind of editorial role for which Martineau deemed him so well suited, but her praise of him and the other Unitarian leaders points to her ultimately optimistic hopes for the press in America. Although she thus starts from a point similar to that of the other British travel writers of the period, roundly denouncing the worst features of American newspapers, her extended and pervasive exploration of the press in the new society makes a far more complex and affirming case for its potential to play a role in realizing the promise of democracy advancing by addressing what she had defined as the key obstacles to social progress. That she should so idealize her closest Boston male friend into such a paragon of magisterial editing speaks also, however, to a pattern in her own editorial relationships, one that had begun with William Johnson Fox, and would reach its height with Frederick Knight Hunt at the *Daily News* as his mentoring advice helped transform her into the great leader writer that she became in the early 1850s.

Ireland

In April 1852, sixteen years after she had returned from America, Martineau unexpectedly received an invitation letter from Frederick Knight Hunt to contribute leaders to the *Daily News*. This offer proved to be one of the most important turning points in her career and as she made the transition into daily journalism, what turned out to be her final major journey and the writing that resulted from it played an essential role. Martineau herself quickly recognized that, even though she already had a substantial record of contributing to the press, Knight's offer held a new level of opportunity. As she would write in her *Autobiography* just three years later, she 'saw that this might be an opening to greater usefulness than was likely to be equaled by anything else that I could undertake.'[34] She moved quickly to wrap up some of her outstanding commitments for Dickens and his weekly magazine *Household Words* and turned to writing for Hunt, relishing the chance to appear in the authoritative role of leader writer for the most progressive national daily.

Almost immediately, however, there was a hitch: the leader was a genre in which she had no prior experience, with demands that were entirely different from the largely descriptive vignettes she had learned to master for Dickens. Clearly things did not go smoothly, and just six weeks after her first piece had appeared, she wrote in concern to Hunt: 'We are not getting on very well, – are we? My papers are not what you want: & yet, we both *know* that they might be, if I could have a lesson from you, & learn something of what your paper was before I saw it.'[35] These early difficulties, however, became an opportunity for their relationship to develop, as Hunt responded actively to his new writer's appeal. Late that July, he traveled to visit her in Scotland and, as Martineau later wrote in the *Autobiography*, 'for two half days he poured out so rich a stream of conversation that my niece could not stand the excitement.'[36] Evidently, treating her as an intellectual equal and making this exceptional effort to tutor her in the requirements of the new genre, Hunt won her loyalty and initiated a close friendship that was broken only by his untimely death just two years later.

The immediate effect of Hunt's mentoring was apparent when, a month later, Martineau left for a two-month tour of Ireland with a commitment to produce three leaders a week from her travel experiences. She duly delivered the first of her twenty-seven Letters for publication on August 13; the series would continue through mid-October, and Martineau followed it with three further leaders on Irish topics before the end of the year. In parallel, meanwhile, she mined her travels for material that produced half a dozen articles on miscellaneous Irish topics that came out in *Household Words* between September 11 and November 13, as well as a final piece on butter that drew in part on the Irish trip and that appeared on Christmas Day. By contrast with the American books she had written some fifteen years earlier, her accounts of this journey to Ireland barely mention her own role as a traveler and do not show her challenging the conventions of travel writing itself. Instead, as she relinquishes the forms of travel writing, she transforms its materials into a rhetoric of public discourse in which she could express herself authoritatively and assumes a new role for herself as a daily journalist.

As Deborah Logan has noted in her selection of Martineau's pieces of Irish writing, Ireland was a subject that engaged her throughout her career.[37] Although the specifics of her focus inevitably evolved, she was remarkably consistent in her core belief as an unabashed unionist, seeing the nation's best hope for the future lying within the United Kingdom. If her themes remained consistent, however, the ways in which she was able to write for *Household Words* and the *Daily News*, respectively, were bound to be different. By looking at, first, the structure of her contributions to each publication, and, second, the way she varies her authorial voice and her appeal to the implied reader, we can see how different were the opportunities at each venue, how much more substantial a role became available to her at the *Daily News*, and how this role allowed her to use her travel to develop a new authorial position.

Although they include numerous verbal echoes of each other and often overlap in their subject matter, the two sets of articles took on very different roles in their respective publications. Ranging in subject from butter to peat bogs, Irish workhouses to the life cycle of salmon, appearing at irregular intervals, and placed at a variety of positions within the issues, the articles for *Household Words* were inevitably a disconnected lot. That 'The Irish Union' should have been the lead article on November 6 with its trenchant discussion of the operations of the Poor Law in Ireland at the end of the famine made perfect sense, for example; but that a much lighter piece on the carriage construction business in Dublin should have been given the same prominence two weeks earlier was a far less compelling call.

By contrast, the twenty-seven Letters from Ireland in the *Daily News* derive much of their force from their placement and internal structuring. First, by appearing three times a week, placed almost invariably in the same position on page 4 and typically coming immediately before the Court News, for example, they claim authority through their very regularity. In several instances, the stark contrast between their accounts of life in Ireland at the end of the famine and the quotidian details of royal life that follow adds to their gravitas while also implicitly commenting on the misplaced foci of British leadership. Second, in the way she structures the Letters as a group, Martineau repeats a narrative and argumentative pattern she had employed fifteen years earlier in writing *Society in America*: beginning by writing from the most familiar region for her English readers – in this case, Ulster – she gradually moves farther and farther away, coming finally to the far 'wild west' and thereby carrying her readers on her own journey of exploration of Ireland and its Otherness. And, following the precepts she had defined for cultural analysis in *How to Observe Manners and Morals*, she explicitly resists drawing larger conclusions in the early articles, holding off until she has gathered, sifted, and measured a far larger set of data. Only then, as she brings the series to its conclusion, does she allow herself the kind of broad conclusions in measured language that we find in Letter XXVII:

> The miseries of Ireland, it has been often and long agreed, proceed from economical and religious causes. The worst economic maladies are in course of extirpation by a method of awful severity, but one that discloses unbounded promise. The old barriers are thrown down day by day; the country is opened to occupation and industry . . .[38]

Deferred in this way, built towards by an accumulation of evidence, anticipated for the reader by a series of prior accounts, the conclusions she offers acquire the appearance of inevitability and her role in articulating them assumes the power of entirely reasonable logic. Although such a diagnosis of the Famine as ultimately working for Ireland's benefit may well be chilling to our eyes, Martineau's reading was by no means unusual even among the progressive Whigs with whom she aligned herself and who were in office during Ireland's most difficult years. Moreover, where in her earlier travel-derived texts such writing had been folded into texts that included a variety of discourse forms, now she evidently feels able to concentrate exclusively on expressing herself in this magisterial voice and makes no concessions to conventional expectations of the woman author.

The shift that she is making in her positionality is especially evident in the ways in which she differentiates her representation of both her own voice and the definition of her implied readers between her writing for the *Daily News* and *Household Words*. This contrast is strikingly visible at one of the few points of direct overlap in subject matter: two very different accounts of the Island of Valentia off the southwest coast of County Kerry. Valentia was the remotest location to which she traveled, the farthest point of remove from Britain, and, most important of all, it was immediately adjacent to the home of Daniel O'Connell, 'the Liberator.' Although he had died in 1847, O'Connell, and the antagonistic radical nationalism for which he stood, were still very much a presence in Irish political life. Just as important, he was someone whom Martineau rejected both because in his separatist views he was so antipathetic to her core beliefs about Ireland and for his characteristic inflammatory rhetorical style that differed so strikingly from her own preferred logocentric mode of public address.

'Hope With a Slate Anchor,' which appeared in *Household Words* on October 30, is a largely upbeat descriptive account of the island, its population, and its economic progress. Although Martineau touches on some details of agricultural poverty and makes a passing reference to the Cholera Hospital, her emphasis focuses upon the area's rugged natural beauty, colorful stories of smuggling, and the rambunctious behavior of the local young men recklessly sailing across from the mainland for an evening of drunken partying. She refers briefly to O'Connell's nearby and now-ruined home and then shifts to the topic anticipated in the article's title: the local slate quarry. After describing the production process in some detail and referring to the jobs the quarry has created, she closes with an extensive description of the domestic uses to which slate has been put:

> No insect can penetrate it; and this indicates the value of slate furniture in India, and in our tropical Colonies, where ants hollow out everything wooden, from the foundation of a house to its roof-tree. Hearth-stones of slate were a matter of course in this house; and we wished they had been so in some others, where there has been repeated danger of fire from sparks or hot ashes falling between the joins of the stones composing the hearth. Then, there were a music-stand, a what-not, a sofa-table . . .[39]

This conclusion literally domesticates the scene, normalizing it, collapsing the differences between the remote wilds of Ireland and the English homes in which *Household Words* was read, and appealing in particular to the guardians of those homes – the magazine's female readership.

In the *Daily News* just three weeks earlier, by contrast, Martineau's twenty-fourth Letter from Ireland had offered a far more trenchant reading of Valentia, exemplifying the directive she had given herself and her readers in an earlier Letter: 'Our business,' she wrote in Letter XVI, 'is to tell of things as they are, and not to sentimentalize about how they might be expected to be.'[40] After opening with an account of the island's name, its connections to Spain, and its colorful past – an account that matches the beginning of her piece for Dickens – she shifts tone and direction dramatically, referencing O'Connell's importance to the region before moving into a powerful account of the state in which much of the population lives:

> The cabins of the rural population are wretched. The thatched roofs are rounded, and have no eaves; and the dwellings are usually set down one before another; so that a hamlet has the appearance of a cluster of Hottentot kraals. In our eyes, they are less respectable than Indian wigwams, because of their darkness, and the infamous filth surrounding them, and the hollows in which they are sunk.[41]

Focusing not on the alignment with English domestic values she emphasizes for *Household Words* but, instead, on the savage Otherness into which a nominally civilized society has descended, she is almost Swiftian in her excoriation. Where she provides Dickens's readers with an extended and enthusiastic account of the production of slate and its domestic uses, here she condenses her treatment of the slate quarry into a single paragraph. What does remain intact in both pieces, however, is her insistence upon the importance of English investment and management both in the quarry and in the fine local inn. In the *Daily News*, however, rather than becoming an end in itself, this detail is connected back to her initial references to the remoteness of the island and what she considers the pernicious role played by O'Connell as she powerfully closes by emphasizing the value to this location, and, by implication, to Ireland as a whole, of its place within the United Kingdom:

> There is no need to explain how earnest is the desire . . . for more and more English to come and settle. Valentia is called the next parish to America. We do wish that the Americans who are sympathizing with repealers, and acting and speaking on the supposition that all Irishmen are praying day and night for release from English oppression, could step into this 'next parish' . . . and hear for themselves how much the Irish are thinking about repeal, and what is their actual feeling towards the English, on the one hand, and on the other, towards their own landlords, who would have composed their 'Parliament in college-green' long ere this, if the Liberator had had his way.[42]

Writing in a voice that has none of the feminine characteristics allowed for and even required in *Household Words* and making her case through rational logic and carefully crafted composition, Martineau thus concludes her series of Letters firmly established as a writer of assured public authority, appealing, as it were, as one man of reason to a like-minded audience.

Linda Peterson's 'Harriet Martineau: Masculine Discourse, Female Sage,' offers a helpful contextual framework for exploring and understanding the transformation that took place between Martineau's writing about her travel in America and the ways in which she positions herself in these accounts of Ireland. Peterson argues that, in her effort 'to gain access to traditional male domains, and to prove that women can master those domains, in both style and content,' Martineau consciously eschewed the role of the Victorian sage. That role, one typified by such male authors as Carlyle and Ruskin, was characterized by visionary insight and the use of highly emotive oratory. Instead, she sought to cast herself as a wisdom writer, focusing upon rational analysis and argument and using logos-driven language to persuade a readership primarily understood to be male.[43] Through her transition from working as a contributing author for Dickens at *Household Words* into a very different position as leader writer for Frederick Knight Hunt and the *Daily News*, Martineau repositioned herself within Victorian public discourse as she moved away from a role in which gendered constraints shaped both her subjects and her authorial voice and took on instead the mantle of the wisdom writer – adopting a dispassionate, reason-based voice that claimed a public authority and that had heretofore been the preserve of male authors.

Back in May 1837, *The Times* had greeted the appearance of *Society in America* with disdain:

> Had Miss Martineau estimated the tether of her talents a little more accurately, had she confined herself to a simple and vivid description of what she witnessed in the new world, and interspersed her far from ordinary powers of

picture with those just and shrewd remarks which occasionally figure in her pages, she might have produced a very pleasant and popular work, instead of a very absurd and a somewhat dull one.[44]

Martineau, however, had no interest in remaining within the conventional boundaries of expectation. Instead, she showed that she was determined to use the experience of travel for two distinct, if connected, purposes. First, she was intent upon assaying what she found, examining what she regarded as foundational elements of a successful society and diagnosing the impediments to progress. Second, through the process of writing about that examination she also explored how various forms of discourse contributed to a society's advance and what role she herself might best take on. Both purposes, as we have seen, come together in the ways in which her travel writing moves towards analyzing the function of the press and enacts her own evolution as a contributor to the fourth estate. Through her travel to both America and Ireland, then, Martineau did indeed discover that 'set of alternative . . . models for women's place in society' Karen Lawrence has argued is central to women's travel writing,[45] and she used that discovery to shape her own position at the heart of mid nineteenth-century journalism. Although *The Times* clearly had no inkling, Martineau's own awareness of the direction in which she was moving was evident within a few months after the paper's dismissive review. As she wrote to Lydia Maria Child on 10 January 1838,

> The design for the newspaper on behalf of Woman rather flags, owing to our not having perfect confidence in the proposer of the plan. When I have any further light, you will be sure to know. The scheme is too important to be perilled by being put into any but the best hands.[46]

Although nothing came of this specific project, that Martineau was thinking about a 'newspaper on behalf of Woman' and that she was writing about it to one of her closest American friends evidences both the importance of her travel to the United States and the ways in which she was projecting her own future role as a writer. It would be more than a decade before she would fulfil these ambitions but the long career that she began in 1852 as one of the most important leader writers for the *Daily News* can surely be traced back to her travel to America in the mid-1830s and to what she learned and wrote about the power of the press there. And, as she made that transition into the journalistic role that would be at the heart of her writing throughout the 1850s, it was perhaps only fitting that she should have used her final extended experience of travel to write in new ways and to confirm the authoritative voice of the opinion-shaper she had become.

Notes

1 Karen R. Lawrence, *Penelope Voyages: Women and Travel in the British Literary Tradition* (Ithaca and London: Cornell University Press, 1994), p. xi.
2 Patricia Madoo Lengermann and Jill Niebrugge, 'The meaning of "things": Theory and method in Harriet Martineau's *How to Observe Morals and Manners* (1838) and

Émile Durkheim's *The Rules of Sociological Method* (1895).' In: Michael R. Hill and Susan Hoecker-Drysdale (eds.), *Harriet Martineau: Theoretical and Methodological Perspectives* (New York and London: Routledge, 2001), p. 76.

3 Harriet Martineau, *Society in America* (London: Saunders and Otley, 1837), vol. 2, p. 222.

4 For a discussion of this theory, see *The Oxford Handbook of Adam Smith*, ed. Christopher J. Berry, Maria Pia Pagnelli and Craig Smith (Oxford: Oxford University Press, 2014), pp. 121–2.

5 Lawrence, *Penelope Voyages*, p. 21.

6 Harriet Martineau, *Retrospect of Western Travel* (London: Saunders and Otley, 1838), vol. 1, pp. 28–9.

7 Martineau, *Retrospect*, vol. 2, pp. 11, 15.

8 Martineau, *Retrospect*, vol. 2, p. 20.

9 Martineau, *Retrospect*, vol. 2, p. 23.

10 Martineau, *Retrospect*, vol. 2, p. 27.

11 Martineau, *Retrospect*, vol. 2, p. 5. Translation: 'The spring is here . . . / Earth scatters her many varied flowers here . . ., / And here the poplar leans above the grotto . . .' *The Eclogues of Virgil*, trans. David Ferry (New York: Farrar, Strauss, and Giroux: 1999), p. 75.

12 Martineau, *Retrospect*, vol. 1, pp. 97, 104.

13 Martineau, *Retrospect*, vol. 1, p. 108.

14 Martineau, *Society*, vol. 1, pp. 210–11.

15 Martineau, *Society*, vol. 1, p. 211.

16 Harriet Martineau, *How to Observe Morals and Manners* (London: Charles Knight and Co, 1838), pp. 37, 27.

17 Martineau, *Society*, vol. 2, p. 144.

18 Martineau, *Society*, vol. 3, p. 31.

19 J. S. Buckingham, *America: Historical, Statistic, and Descriptive* (London: Fisher, Son, & Co. n.d. [1841]), vol. 1, p. 155.

20 Martineau, *Society*, vol. 1, p. 147.

21 Martineau, *How to Observe*, p. 198.

22 Martineau, *Retrospect*, vol. 1, p. 40.

23 Martineau, *Society*, vol. 2, p. 352.

24 Martineau, *Society*, vol. 2, p. 141.

25 Martineau, *Society*, vol. 2, p. 142. See also Weiner's chapter in this volume.

26 Martineau, *Society*, vol. 2, p. 345.

27 Martineau, *Society*, vol. 1, p. 151.

28 Harriet Martineau, 'Art. 1.-1. Right and Wrong in Boston in 1835.' *London and Westminster Review* 32:1 (December 1838), pp. 41–6.

29 Martineau, *Society*, vol. 1, p. 152.

30 Martineau, *Society*, vol. 1, p. 153.

31 Martineau, *Society*, vol. 1, p. 152.

32 Martineau, *Society*, vol. 1, pp. 149–50.

33 Martineau, *Society*, vol. 3, p. 222.

34 Harriet Martineau, *Autobiography*, ed. Linda H. Peterson (Peterborough, ON: Broadview Press, 2007), p. 610.

35 *The Collected Letters of Harriet Martineau*, ed. Deborah Anna Logan, 5 vols. (London: Pickering and Chatto, 2007), vol. 3, p. 235.

36 Martineau, *Autobiography*, p. 611.

37 Deborah A. Logan (ed.), *Harriet Martineau and the Irish Question* (Bethlehem: Lehigh University Press, 2012), p. ix.

38 'Letters from Ireland, XXVII,' *Daily News*, 14 October 1852, p. 4.

39 'Hope with a Slate Anchor,' *Household Words*, 30 October 1852, p. 161.

40 'Letters from Ireland, XVI,' *Daily News*, 17 September 1852, p. 4.

41 'Letters from Ireland, XXIV,' *Daily News*, 4 October 1852, p. 4.

42 'Letters from Ireland, XXIV,' *Daily News*, 4 October 1852, p. 4.
43 Linda H. Peterson, 'Harriet Martineau: Masculine Discourse, Female Sage.' In: Thaïs E. Morgan (ed.), *Victorian Sages and Cultural Discourse: Renegotiating Gender and Power* (New Brunswick and London: Rutgers University Press, 1990), p. 178.
44 'Society in America, By Harriet Martineau,' *The Times*, 30 May 1837, p. 5.
45 Lawrence, *Penelope Voyages*, p. xi.
46 Martineau, *Letters*, vol. 2, p. 14.

11 'I have an all important review to write'

Harriet Martineau's journalism

Valerie Sanders

'It is just a year now since you made me a "gentleman of the press," – or Maid-of-all-work to D. News,' Harriet Martineau reminded her editor, Frederick Knight Hunt, in 1853. The ironic second thought, or redefinition of her role, seems telling in view of her lifelong concern for the fair treatment of servants, but she was also prompted by her consciousness of 'being so entirely alone, – so far off, – that I can never be sure of being right, & doing what is best.'[1] She was referring to her now permanent residence in the Lake District, away from the hurly-burly of London. Although she did go to London, Birmingham, and other places both for business and pleasure, in the early 1850s, Martineau was clearly conscious of her unusual position as a newspaper leader-writer living in relative obscurity. She also, like many other nineteenth-century women journalists, exploited the practice of author anonymity for much of her career, varying this with the use of pseudonyms ('Discipulus' at the start, 'From the Mountain' towards the end), and as anonymity declined in the 1860s, with the occasional use of her own name or initials.[2] As Alexis Easley has indicated, Martineau's presence in a wide range of periodicals and newspapers allowed her to adapt and disguise her voice to suit her multifarious purposes, 'alternately revealing and concealing her gendered identity as a means of gaining cultural power.'[3] For Linda Peterson she also functions as a 'wisdom writer', adapting the traditional prophetic and elevated style of the Carlylean or Arnoldian 'sage' to suit her more down-to-earth engagement with the practical realities of modern life.[4] For both Peterson and George P. Landow, the distinction between the Victorian 'sage' and the 'wisdom' writer derives not only from the differences in their rhetorical style but also their position vis-à-vis society. Whereas the sage is a prophet who speaks from the margins, the 'wisdom' writer voices the society's 'essential beliefs and assumptions'.[5] Martineau's position – both inside society, as the voice of shared experience and common sense, and on the margins, so often vilified as an 'unfeminine' eccentric – complicates our attempts to categorise her as definitely one thing or the other: a problem further exacer-bated by the characteristics of her prose style and stance as a journalist.

Like many of her contemporaries who wrote non-fictional prose, Martineau is a distinctive stylist. Compared with the key 'sage' writers of her day – Ruskin and Carlyle – she may sound understated. As a journalist who felt strongly about the issues she discussed she needed to express herself clearly, and would always eschew the elaborate metaphors or biblical prognostications of her loftier rivals. Nevertheless her prose is rarely purely functional, and over her career of half a century she develops a recognisable 'voice', foregrounding the practical and commonplace over the extraordinary, and the homely over the exotic, while never quite losing sight of the romantic possibilities of the everyday. Either way her prolific periodical writing makes her integral to any history of nineteenth-century journalism, and key to our understanding both of its openness to newcomers and its initial distrust of those outside 'the club'.

Unlike some of the other aspects of her career discussed in this volume, journalism is not exactly a 'discipline', defined as a branch of learning, though it can be viewed as something akin to that, a 'field of expertise'(OED). Martineau's impact on such a vast field, it goes without saying, is difficult to summarise either succinctly or definitively, and her significance so far has mainly been discussed – by Alexis Easley, Barbara Caine and Linda Peterson, among others[6] – in terms of her gendered role, and pioneering career as a source of authority in a male-dominated profession. The ephemerality of journalism is another obstacle to judging the impact of any one practitioner, especially in Martineau's case, given that practically everything she wrote was in response to a topical issue of the time. That said, her lifelong habit of expressing opinions on a wide range of topics makes her 'ephemeral' articles a barometer of contemporary debate, and thus a valuable resource for social and literary historians. The aim of this chapter is therefore to reassess Martineau as a major figure in the evolution of the nineteenth-century periodical press, to identify her distinctive voice and to evaluate her lasting importance as an outspoken and versatile contributor to national debate on the concerns of her day.

Harriet Martineau and the periodical press

Harriet Martineau began and ended her miscellaneous career primarily as a writer of periodical articles, with intense periods of activity between 1822–34 and 1852–66. Her work as a journalist spanned five decades and at least eighteen periodicals (excluding the *Daily News*, to which she was a regular contributor from 1852 to 1866). Her career in fact developed through and alongside the rise of the mainstream nineteenth-century periodical, her earliest pieces appearing in *The Monthly Repository* (1806–38), and her latest in Dickens's journals, *Household Words* (1850–9) and *Once a Week* (1859–80). When she first started publishing, the great 'heavyweight' journals of the day were the *Edinburgh Review* (1802–1900) and the *Quarterly Review* (1809–1967), and *Blackwood's Edinburgh Magazine* (1817–1980), all more or less dominated by male cliques. Although she published in the *Edinburgh* (then edited by her distant relative, Henry Reeve) and once in the *Quarterly* (a review of Florence Nightingale's *Notes on Nursing* in 1860), Martineau's relationship with these grandees of the periodical world had begun on a wrong footing with their hostile reviews of her *Illustrations of Political Economy* (1832–4). While the *Edinburgh* was friendly, the *Quarterly's* virulence, directed at her personally as a woman, served to reinforce the sense of a male hegemony which Martineau never extensively breached, while quietly maintaining her right to express herself freely elsewhere.

Instead she allied herself with the more radical, experimental periodicals, such as the *Westminster Review* (1824–1914), managed in the early 1850s by John Chapman and his assistant editor, the young Mary Ann Evans (not yet 'George Eliot'). Eliot's respect for Martineau's achievements as a journalist was readily offered: her piece on 'Christian Missions: their principle and practice' (1856), for example, Eliot praised as 'at once solid and interesting as most of her articles are,' and 'a very valuable article, especially for the excellent spirit in which it is written and I think it quite turned the scale in favour of the Westminster against the "National" this quarter.'[7] As Deborah Logan has shown, Martineau belonged for a while to 'the intellectually-cutting-edge, socially bohemian Chapman circle', even investing £500 in its crumbling fortunes while loftily passing comment in the *Daily News* on the *Review*'s qualities compared with its competitors, including the 'dull imbecility of the grandmotherly Edinburgh.'[8] As Logan indicates, Martineau seemingly had no qualms about hopping back to the grandmother when it suited her (or about asking the editors of the *Daily News* and *Household Words* to invest in her Ambleside Building Society).[9] As it was, she worked for some of the century's most celebrated editors, including William Johnson Fox, Charles Dickens and Henry Reeve, and by her own account was constantly in demand. Her letters, alternately amused by her own popularity, and then guilelessly self-satisfied, register a stream of editorial invitations through the 1850s and early '60s. 'I am always refusing work; and everything prospers that I send out,' she assured Erasmus Darwin (Charles's elder brother) in 1861. In the same letter she told him her earnings for 1859 were £620, rising to £700 the following year: a comfortable supplement to her independent income of £300.[10] Among the offers she declined in this heady period were Thackeray's *Cornhill Magazine* ('I don't fancy Thackeray as an editor')[11] and *Fraser's Magazine* ('Having refused the "Cornhill" and others, I did not incline to write for Fraser').[12] Her *Autobiography* similarly teems with references to editors soliciting her contributions – whether 'Mr Barnes' of *The Times* (p. 178), Robertson of the *Westminster Review* (p. 314), John Sterling (p. 181), or the editor of *The People's Journal* (p. 296), culminating in Hunt's overtures for the *Daily News*, when 'a bright new career was indeed open to me' (p. 611).When not cherry-picking offers, she gossiped about the shortcomings of other contributors' work, changes of editor, and badly run enterprises, from the perspective of a true 'gentleman of the press.' If the *Edinburgh* had become 'grandmotherly', this was due in no small measure to the editorship (before Reeve) of Sir George Cornewall Lewis, whom she dismissed as 'that old woman', while what she liked about the *Westminster* was its 'manly, sensible, and more truly philosophical treatment of topics which immediately concern the living and moving men, and not the mere dreamers of the time.'[13] When she first began writing for the *Daily News* in 1852 she was entertained by her readers' assumption that 'leaders' on emigration and 'Manly Sports' must have been written by a man.[14] Momentarily anxious about a switch of *Daily News* editors, from William Weir to Thomas Walker, in 1858, she worried 'as to our probably *suiting* or not'. Her apprehension was needless: 'He frankly said he could not get on without me.'[15]

It is hard to know how seriously to take this self-estimate, especially given the exaggerated modesty of the obituary she prepared for posthumous publication by the *Daily News*, which downplayed her ability to do anything other than 'popularize'.[16] From the beginning, however, there were some peculiarities about Martineau's experience as a periodical writer. Alexis Easley suggests that her career was 'unusual for a woman of letters of her time', not least because she operated 'both within and against patriarchy . . . constructing her radical viewpoints from multiple narrative and ideological positions.'[17] While this opens her to charges of inconsistency, or, as Easley indicates (p. 39), internalizing or reinforcing patriarchal values that obliged her to employ a masculine rhetoric, Martineau remained an independent voice, continuously refashioning herself to keep abreast of changing times as well as her own new interests, and spreading her periodical contributions widely. If we take a representative year – 1859, for example – apart from her regular *Daily News* 'leaders', she published articles in the *Edinburgh Review* ('Female Industry' in April), *Chambers's Journal* ('Flood and its Lessons' and 'Drought and Its Lessons' in July and August, respectively), and *Once a Week* (twelve articles on miscellaneous subjects between July and the end of the year). A few years earlier, before she began working for the *Daily News* (a representative year would be 1851) her main outlets were *Household Words* (twelve articles) and *The Leader* (nine articles). Promiscuous as they seem, her simultaneous and successive relationships with various periodicals were less unusual than they might appear.

As this essay collection argues, the 'disciplines' as we understand them, were in Martineau's lifetime, still in the making, as were the key middle-class professions, and the 'gentlemen's club' atmosphere of the first major journals – the *Edinburgh, Quarterly* and *Blackwood's* – had conceded by the 1850s to a much more varied print culture. Comparison with some of Martineau's better-known contemporaries shows that, while some journalists were chiefly associated with one publication (e.g., Margaret Oliphant, with *Blackwood's*, despite forays into the *St James's Gazette* and *Spectator*), many were just as eclectic as Martineau herself. One such case is Abraham Hayward (1801–84), who, though mainly an *Edinburgh* and *Quarterly* reviewer, also wrote for the *Fortnightly, Fraser's Magazine, New Monthly Magazine*, the *Foreign Quarterly* and *North British Review*. He was also chief leader-writer for the *Morning Chronicle*. Nor was Martineau significantly different in this respect from the leading female journalists. Lady Eastlake (1809–93) wrote for the *Edinburgh, Quarterly, Foreign Quarterly, Longman's* and *Fraser's*, while in the next generation, Eliza Lynn Linton, credited in the *Dictionary of National Biography* with being the first woman journalist to draw a fixed salary, and subsequently a regular contributor to *The Saturday Review*, also wrote for *Ainsworth's, Macmillan's, New Quarterly Magazine, Nineteenth Century, Temple Bar, North British Review, Dark Blue, Fraser's* and *St. Paul's Magazine*.[18]

What becomes clear from reading both Martineau's *Autobiography* and her letters is that she was frequently solicited to write articles on a specific theme for a particular periodical. As these themes were often 'of the moment', arising from topical circumstances, she had to act quickly, and when the 'moment' had passed, might have little further to do with either the topic or the periodical. A short run in the *London and Westminster Review*, for example, was triggered by an invitation to write about Catharine Maria Sedgwick, followed by a vague remembrance of supplying 'about half-a-dozen articles in the course of the next two years' (*Autobiography*, p. 402). On other occasions, she proposed the articles herself, as with her 'Birmingham industrial series' in *Household Words*. While she was staying in Birmingham for five weeks with her brother Robert's family in 1851, it 'struck' her, as she put it, 'that a clear picturesque account of manufactures might suit "Household Words." Mr Dickens jumped at the offer; and before I left Birm^m, I did three (which have appeared) and since my return, I have done Kendal carpets, and Ambleside Bobbins.'[19] Martineau's career as a journalist therefore has something of an ad hoc feel to it, which in many ways gave her a market advantage. Despite long bouts of ill health, a call to arms from an editor usually had a rousing effect, and her letters convey a level of excitement, even glee, which sounds naïve for an experienced writer in her fifties. Without a doubt she loved her work as a periodical writer, and of all her authorial activities this is the one that was most compatible with her infirmities. The title phrase of this chapter – 'I have an all important review to write' – captures the sense of purpose and self-importance her journalism gave her.[20] It should also be remembered that Martineau was writing at a time when, although some journalists did confine themselves to specialist areas, such as politics, history or literature, the majority of regular contributors had a much wider range than most of today's review writers. She was very far from being the only journalist who handled topics as varied as politics, history, industrial conditions, travel, slavery and dress.

Martineau's 'voice' of the 1850s and '60s

The next section of this essay considers representative examples of Martineau's journalism from what might be regarded as her 'heyday' – the 1850s and early '60s – when she was at her most versatile. The aim is to identify what might be called her distinctive 'voice' as a journalist, citing mature articles expressive of her key interests: work, industrial processes, education and self-improvement, and employers and servants. These are themes that resonate through all Martineau's writing, not just her journalism: several of her books – for example *Household Education* (1849) and *Sketches from Life* (1856) – beginning life as article series. According to Alison Winter, Martineau became known and admired as 'a model of observational precision and reliable reporting': 'Martineau's journalism,' she claims, 'gained a reputation for a kind of rational and scientific ideal. Her admirers considered her to be the epitome of observational purity tutored by sound morals.'[21] While allowance must be made for Winter's focus on a slightly earlier period of Martineau's career (the later 1830s to '40s), I would contend that she was not consistently as 'scientific' as this description implies, given that wry remarks on individuals, or high-flown romanticism (as in the Birmingham articles discussed later in this chapter) frequently offset her recourse to economic theory.

She may have been an attentive observer, but her style as a journalist, at least by the 1850s, had become much more individual, even quirky and unpredictable, than these designations imply. The terms she uses to describe the tone of her Birmingham manufactures pieces are 'picturesque' and intended 'both for instruction and entertainment'.[22] It was indeed the unexpected 'picturesqueness' of the Birmingham manufactories that most intrigued and attracted Martineau, who, despite her subsequent falling-out with Dickens over issues of factory safety, shared his taste for the language of romance and wonder as announced in his 'Preliminary Word' to the opening of *Household Words*. When Dickens declared, 'No mere utilitarian spirit, no iron binding of the mind to grim realities, will give a harsh tone to our Household Words,' he might have expected Martineau to be the last person to enlist under his banner, but in fact she pitched into the spirit of Dickens's new venture with exactly the requisite willingness to celebrate the brave new world taking shape around her.[23]

Martineau's Birmingham industries series are a good place to begin an evaluation of her distinctive contribution to the Victorian periodical. Beginning with 'Flower Shows in a Birmingham Hot-House' (18 October 1851), these stretched to 'more than thirty additional articles on manufacturing, specialised vocations, and educational methods for *Household Words* before 13 January 1855.'[24] 'I am printing fast (i.e., being printed),' she told her Lake District friend, Frances Ogden, in the autumn of 1851, as she prepared a dash to Coventry in pursuit of the ribbon industry.[25] Her choice of phrase – 'printing fast' – which for a moment conflates her materially with a periodical print run, captures the breathless excitement of the challenge, while the article on ribbon manufacture, romantically titled 'Rainbow Making', mounts to a crescendo of 'wonder' and 'astonishment' as she walks her readers around the stages of 'dipping, wringing, splashing, stirring, boiling, drying' needed to transform unpromising bundles of silk into the sunlit rainbows of these common personal accessories.[26] The article is full of such declarations of wonderment, beginning with an imaginary global tour from Lombardy to Lebanon, the Indian Peninsula and China, which takes the reader back to the silkworm as the source of the rainbow ribbons. If this were not sufficient to broaden the reader's sense of perspective, the next paragraph is an even swifter historical overview, from Henry VIII sporting 'the first pair of silk stockings brought to England from Spain' (p. 485), to the series of laws and regulations governing the production and wearing of silk. A similar rhapsodic passage opens an earlier article, 'The Wonders of Nails and Screws' (1 November 1851) where Martineau speculates on the fate of each humble nail, destined for the banks of the Danube, or Russia, India or Australia: even washed up 'to the feet of some Robinson Crusoe, who will start at this trace of a man's hand, and seem to hear once more the pant of the steam-engine . . .'[27] Manufacturer's daughter as she was, Martineau ratchets up her own and the reader's excitement as she passes from one stage of the production process to the next. 'From trough to trough we go,' she enthuses, 'breathing steam, and stepping into puddles, or reeking rivulets rippling over the stones of the pavement; but we are tempted on, like children, by the charm of the brilliant colours that flash upon the sight whichever way we turn' (p. 486).

For much of the article, Martineau's approach remains conversational, directly addressing her readers as if they were touring the factory with her, and questioning the workers about their role in the production process. 'This is a brilliant blue,' she observes; ' – indigo, of course? Yes, sulphate of indigo, with tartaric acid. – Here are two yellows: how is that?' (p. 487). Her curiosity about the yellows builds to the keeping of a secret: 'The inferior one is the old-fashioned turmeric, with the tartaric acid. And the improved yellow? – O! we perceive. It is a secret of the establishment, and we are not to ask questions about it.' She evidently tries, but 'the men cannot be tempted' (p. 487). Martineau thus provides a dialogue in which the readers' questions and the workers' responses are acknowledged, but subsumed into her own commentary as she gathers information and explains the technical terms ('The name of this novelty is the Clouding Box', p. 487). Gradually, how-ever, she introduces a more unsettling element of social and political commentary: women are not allowed to work in the dye-house; Coventry has a long history of resistance to steam power, but there are now 'thirty steam power-loom factories in Coventry, producing about seven thousand pieces of ribbons in the week, and employing about three thousand persons' (p. 488). The statistics all come at once in a rush towards the end of the article, as if Martineau has suddenly reminded herself not to be so entranced by the beauty of ribbon manufacture that she over-looks the economic consequences of a city's, and by extension, individual fami-lies', over-dependence on one precarious industry. The earlier light-heartedness disappears under a dire warning, that 'This cannot go on', and care must be taken that 'the men of Coventry shall be fit for something else than weaving ribbons' (p. 490). Martineau's gloomy prognostications may sound melodramatic, but rib-bon manufacture in the city did in fact begin to decline in the very next decade.[28] Martineau had viewed the business in the last years of its heyday.

As Tamara Ketabgian has argued, Martineau also noticed the factory work-ers' taste for luxury goods, such as coral necklaces and Indian shawls, estab-lishing 'a powerful associative link between suffering, luxury and improvident risk-taking'.[29] Unable to resist a pun, for example, in 'The Wonders of Nails and Screws,' Martineau ventures a hope that the women 'respectably earning their bread . . . would look to it that there was no screw loose in their household ways'.[30] Repeatedly, in this series of articles she comments on the 'picturesque' or 'pretty' nature of the industrial process before transferring her attention to the people who perform it; she notices how machine-like they have become, then imagines their lives, both within and beyond the factory, praising those who establish reading or cricket clubs, rather than squandering their wages. Finally, she extrapolates from what she sees to warn of a grim future. 'If we all spent, day by day, whatever we have, we should be fighting in the gutters for existence,' she concludes her survey of Lucy's bread mill in Birmingham.[31]

The example of the industrial articles illustrates the conflicting tendencies in Martineau's development as a periodical writer at this high point of her career. Entranced by the mysteries of the industrial process, she focuses first on these and then on the human subjects operating them, and their tendency to treat themselves when flush with funds. As if pulled up short by the reminder of their improvidence,

Figure 11.1 The Egyptian Court at the Crystal Palace, Sydenham (c. 1854) by Philip Henry
         Delamotte.

she resumes the kind of argument she is noted for, the purely economic, which
is where she ends. A recurrent focus on the human, in place of a more abstract or
impersonal recourse to theory, which displaces the topic she purports to be writing about, similarly affects her more substantial articles, such as her review of the
Crystal Palace at Sydenham (Figure 11.1).

The Crystal Palace

Martineau found time, in between her various commissions, to visit the Great
Exhibition, first in its original location in Hyde Park, and then in its rebuilt con-
figuration in Sydenham in 1854. The Sydenham visit was already arranged when
she received 'a curious sort of intimation,' she told Frederick Knight Hunt, 'that
some of the artists in the Sydenham palace are inquiring about me, as if with a
view to my describing what they are about.'[32] Lodging with the Superintendent of
the Crystal Palace Gardens in a house previously occupied by Sir Joseph Paxton,
designer of the Hyde Park exhibition building, she was joined on one of several forays by Erasmus Darwin and her friends Fanny and Hensleigh Wedgwood.
Martineau was clearly treated as a celebrity visitor and afforded all necessary

advantages for the gathering of impressions subsequently published in the *West-minster Review* of October 1854, yet there was nothing new about her subject. The *Wellesley Index to Victorian Periodicals* lists fourteen articles containing the words 'Crystal Palace' published between 1851 and 1856, and Martineau's contribution was one of the later responses. The list of eleven handbooks at the head of her article implies that it will be a serious review of the Exhibition's narrative of aesthetic history from the ancient civilizations of the Egyptians and Assyrians through to the portrait gallery, but instead, Martineau is from the outset distracted by the people milling around the exhibits, and making ignorant remarks. Stationing herself in a corner near the band, she amuses herself counting 'the babies that are being danced over the heads of the crowd below' and watching 'the wagging heads, the thumping sticks, the kicking infants, [and] the proud mothers' uninhibitedly beating time to the polka.[33] This time, rather than walk her readers through the exhibition rooms (as Andrew Wynter does in his report for *Fraser's*),[34] Martineau is more interested in the children standing in the Natural History area 'with their thumbs in their mouths', and the incongruous figure of the country labourer contemplating the models of savages (p. 537).

Nor does her deafness preclude her from eavesdropping on the most shocking examples of ignorance in those who should know better, as when she overhears 'a party of well-dressed tradespeople' greeting a named statue of Diana, the goddess of hunting, with a cry of ' "And there's Dinah" ' (p. 545). Nor can she forgive an ill-informed parent for confidently telling a child that the bronze casts of 'the three Printers – Gutenberg, Faust, and Schoeffer' – now aged with verdigris – 'are Robin Hood and Little John, dressed all in green' (p. 545). While Martineau can smile at the innocent wonderment of country labourers, she now views the Crystal Palace, not as a celebration of human achievement, but as 'the place in which to see how high the fogs ascend from the swamp of ignorance in which the multitude have been lying' (p. 545). Largely ignoring both the Sydenham artists, who wanted her to write about them, and the bevy of handbooks she is supposed to be reviewing (and which no one appears to be reading), she instead deplores the widespread evidence of failed education, turning her sights on the random nature of the exhibits, the prominence of 'provision counters', incongruously overlooked by busts of kings and queens (pp. 548–9), and the missed opportunity to provide systematic information about the history of the human family. The Crystal Palace becomes for her yet another example of educational mismanagement in a phase of modern civilization where the nation should be demonstrating its advanced response to popular entertainment. 'Let it not be a phenomenon only,' she warns, 'but an institution' (p. 550).

Domestic service

Although by this time Martineau had abandoned her earlier, tentative career as a novelist, she retained a lifelong interest in telling stories as a means of engaging audiences with human problems. This had been her technique in the *Illustrations of Political Economy*, and it remains her favourite approach to exposing tracts of ignorance and misunderstanding in common human experience. By the early

1860s, the enlightened employer of loyal Ambleside servants, whose education and welfare were always important to her, she turned to another problem she felt was widely misunderstood, 'Modern Domestic Service,' for a major article in the *Edinburgh Review*. Already the author of a set of 'Guides to Service' (including volumes on 'The Housemaid' and 'The Lady's Maid', 1838–9), 'Domestic Service' in the *London and Westminster Review* (1838), 'The Maid Servant' (1850) for *The Leader*, and more recently 'The Maid of All Work: Her Health' (1860) and 'The Domestic Service Question' (1861) for *Once a Week*, Martineau was returning to a subject on which she held strong opinions. Because her 1838 article, 'Domestic Service' had previously warned of a serious crisis in the employment of servants – a crisis which for Martineau remained unresolved in 1861–2 – this last section of the chapter compares the two articles, both as a means of measuring her development as a journalist, and of identifying her enduring characteristics, her distinctive 'voice' as an author who repeatedly claimed not just the moral high ground, but also the perspective of common sense. While some of the same anecdotes appear in both articles, and both appeal to the middle-class mistresses of households to provide moral and practical leadership, the later article marks just how far Martineau has advanced in her skills as a journalist.[35]

In 1838, Martineau's memories of her American visit (1834–6) were still vivid, recalling the extreme domestic examples of slavery in the southern states, mitigated by her conviction that 'the Americans have got nearer to the right principle of domestic service than any of our European societies.'[36] She was also at that time still using religious language in her writing, having not yet fully abandoned her Unitarian standpoint on social and ethical issues. While her theme in both articles is the age-old great gulf of understanding between employers and servants, the 1838 piece confidently attributes this to two apparently unrelated causes: 'original sin' (p. 407) and 'the Norman Conquest' (p. 414). If original sin, in turn, spawns 'ill-temper' (p. 407), the word 'temper' reverberating throughout the article, the Norman Conquest has established a habit of 'feudalism' (p. 415): hence the rarity of frank and mutually trustful relationships between servants and their mistresses. Martineau's concern is indeed largely for the female half of the servant population and their employers, where the problem seems to be more pervasive and deep-rooted. In neither article, however, does she place any faith in religious tracts, looking, as always, to sociological and practical solutions, despite a few reverent allusions in 1838 to 'One who declared that those who would be chief must be servants' (p. 430). Ending with her customary warning of trouble, in the shape of 'retribution' increasing 'the evil', she exhorts those who can do so, to tear open the 'black cloud-canopy' (p. 432) and let in the sunshine.

By 1861, masquerading as a hermit under the pseudonym 'From the Mountain', Martineau still sounds like a woman who has extensive experience of employing and training domestic servants. Instead of expecting perfection from servants who have never been taught to do anything, runs her argument, employers have a stark choice between two models: 'One order of service is a domestic relation: the other is a selling and purchase of a particular type of labour.'[37] Reverting to the language of her political economy tales from thirty years ago, only to eschew it, Martineau again particularises the experience of village girls leaving home to work in much larger and more complex households, but needs the scope of her 1862 article to develop her theories to the full. By this point she believed the problems employers were experiencing in finding servants to suit was indicative of a major shift in social attitudes, based on the servant class's preference for the freedom of working in factories as opposed to the more restricted lifestyle of the live-in domestic. She also deplored the lack of training for servant girls who had only their mothers' (generally poor) domestic skills to learn from. Gone are all allusions to original sin and the Norman Conquest: in their place are employers' complaints rendered by Martineau through a collection of colloquialisms:

> The morning rolls are bitter; the potatoes have 'a bone,' in them; the soup is sour; – something is wrong at every dinner. Upstairs there is 'slut's wool' under the beds; and if the housemaid is reproved, she says the mistress may sweep the chambers herself, for there is no other way of pleasing her.[38]

The voices of disgruntled maids and mistresses reverberating through the first half of the article, with phrases such as 'the girl requires more teaching than she is worth' (p. 410), and 'these youthful servants are very trying' (p. 411), offset by occasional recognition for a 'treasure of a servant' (p. 411), give Martineau's opening survey of the problem both vitality and a feeling of authenticity. Briskly dismissing the relevance of Hannah More and the old eighteenth-century pieties about servants, she deploys an early form of investigative journalism which builds an irrefutable argument through believable examples and trenchant summaries. There are few of the employed class, she reminds her readers 'who would not prefer a herring and potatoes in a room of their own to the choicest meals in the servants' hall' (p. 414). In short aphoristic statements – characteristic of the 'wisdom' writer, as Peterson and Landow argue – she summarises: 'In one word it is *independence* against *dependence*' [Martineau's italics: p. 415]; 'Service is becoming a mere contract for wages' (p. 415); 'while one class is growing too high for service, the next class remains too low for it' (p. 416), building to a climactic: 'What have we ever done, let each one ask, to entitle us to be skilfully as well as honestly served?' (p. 417), 'Can any human being, anywhere, "live by bread alone"?' (p. 431), before a final, oracular: 'What, then, is to be done?' (p. 434). The rest of the article shows how trust, training, privacy and sufficient pay are essential to improved relations between employers and servants, as is time out for rational pursuits: 'Why not good music and good literature,' she asks, 'wherever the domestics can be led to prefer them to ruinous cardplaying or frivolous gossip?' (p. 429). Above all, she reminds her readers of their own responsibility for change, especially in the provision of training schools for servants, drawn from workhouse children and paupers. Only through mutual understanding of the work, between employers and servants, will these skills ever be imparted and appreciated. Like any other form of employment, domestic service needs to be professionalised, and both 'the housewives of England' and social reformers who can establish training schools, must take responsibility.

Ultimately, Martineau's 'voice' in her long career as a journalist mutates by the 1850s into something recognisable and distinctive, but also sufficiently flexible to serve multiple purposes and readerships. Although she cannot be designated the first professional woman journalist in Britain (Eliza Lynn Linton is usually awarded this accolade),[39] Martineau's opinions were both sought and respected by a wide range of prominent editors. There is no doubt that she was highly regarded as a journalist, and in constant demand. Moreover, she was free in this field to express her own opinions instead of popularizing others', as she did in her political economy tales. Apart from her specialised assignments for periodicals, she was contributing several 'leaders' a week for the *Daily News* for fourteen years, long after she had otherwise withdrawn from the public scene, her work as a journalist outlasting all the other phases of her career. George Eliot remained an admirer, famously declaring: 'she is a *trump* – the only English woman that possesses thoroughly the art of writing'.[40] She is still difficult to categorise, however, or associate with a group. For Alexis Easley elsewhere in this collection Martineau is a 'miscellaneous' writer, while for Iain Crawford she is a 'wisdom' writer, characterised by rational analysis, and also a believer in the power of the press to aid or inhibit social progress. This sense of power undoubtedly drove the campaigning tone of much of her journalism as she tried to stir her readers into action. At the very least she maintains a trenchant, energetic but 'homely' style, in the sense of applying practical ideas and filling her articles with examples drawn from familiar household life. Her voice sounds honest and trustworthy, motivated by the sense of justice that drives the childhood sections of her *Autobiography*, with frequent appeals to the empathy of her implied reader: assumed to be an equally reasonable person of middling rank and responsible social convictions. When she asks in her 1838 'Domestic Service' article: 'What was the Maid-servant once, and what has her rearing been?' (p. 425), she is inviting her reader, as do many journalists today, to personalise a social issue and imagine what it feels like to be a victim of injustice, or of callous and unreasonable expectations. Over twenty-five years later, in her *Once a Week* article on the same subject, she reiterates how hard it is to be sure of servants' views, and urges her readers to consider 'for a moment who they are, and where they come from' (p. 430). For all her insistence on respecting the immutable 'Laws' (economic and otherwise) by which she believed human life was governed, Martineau never lost sight of the value of individual personal experience, and evidently relished any opportunity to capture the voice and accent of the people she observed: a position hard to reconcile with her distant persona as a mountain hermit in the *Once a Week* series.[41] Her decision to adopt the guise of an old man towards the end of her career may be explained by her wish for enhanced objective authority, but she sounds much the same as she does in her other mature articles. As a journalist she seems both close up and at an omniscient remove, recalling the telescope she installed in her Tynemouth sitting room during her long period of invalidism in the 1840s.[42] While it may be impossible to claim for her as specific an impact on Victorian journalism as she made (for example) on the evolution of sociology, or proto-feminism, Martineau was a significant pioneer and role model for women in this profession, as George Eliot acknowledged. She proved that women could write about anything, need not be based in London, and might remain professionally engaged into their sixties. Martineau's homely wisdom, versatility, outspokenness and lifelong concern for the plight of individual persons, classes and communities, make her both representative of her times and a key precursor of the modern journalist.

Notes

1 HM to Frederick Knight Hunt, 28 April [1853], *The Collected Letters of Harriet Martineau*, ed. Deborah Anna Logan, Vol. 3 (London: Pickering and Chatto, 2007), p. 276.
2 Martineau used 'Discipulus' and 'V' in *The Monthly Repository* and 'From the Mountain' in *Once a Week*, though she was signing herself 'H.M.' as early as the 1830s (for example) in 'Domestic Service,' *London and Westminster Review* (August 1838).
3 Alexis Easley, 'Victorian women writers and the periodical press: The case of Harriet Martineau,' *Nineteenth-Century Prose*, 24:1 (1997), pp. 39–50. See also Chapter 9 of this volume. www.thefreelibrary.com/Victorian%20women%20writers%20and%20the%20periodical%20press:%20the%20case%20of%20Harriet . . . . -a0188966768 [accessed 5 April 2014].
4 See Linda Peterson, 'Harriet Martineau: Masculine Discourse, Female Sage,' in *Victorian Sages and Cultural Discourse: Renegotiating Gender*, ed. Thaïs E. Morgan (New Brunswick and London: Rutgers University Press, 1990), pp. 171–86 and 'Sage Writing' in *A Companion to Victorian Literature & Culture*, ed. Herbert F. Tucker (Blackwell Publishers: Malden and Oxford, 1999), pp. 373–87. See too Iain Crawford's chapter in this Martineau essay collection.
5 George P. Landow, 'Elegant Jeremiahs: The Sage from Carlyle to Mailer. A Victorian Web Book', www.victorianweb.org/genre/ej/intro1.html [accessed 15 February 2015].
6 Barbara Caine, 'Feminism, Journalism and Public Debate,' in *Women and Literature in Britain 1800–1900*, ed. Joanne Shattock (Cambridge: Cambridge University Press, 2001), pp. 99–118; Linda H. Peterson, *Becoming a Woman of Letters: Myths of Authorship and Facts of the Victorian Marketplace* (Princeton: Princeton University Press, 2009).
7 *The George Eliot Letters*, ed. Gordon S. Haight, 9 vols. (New Haven: Yale University Press, 1854–78), II, p. 257.
8 Deborah A. Logan, '"I am, My Dear Slanderer, Your Faithful Malignant Demon": Harriet Martineau and the *Westminster Review's* Comtist Coterie,' *Victorian Periodicals Review* 42:2 (Summer 2009), pp. 171, 182.
9 HM to Miss Holt, 13 January [1854] *Collected Letters* 3, p. 305.
10 HM to Erasmus Darwin, 20 May 1861, *Harriet Martineau's Letters to Fanny Wedgwood*, ed. Elisabeth Sanders Arbuckle (Stanford: Stanford University Press, 1983), p. 208.
11 HM to Fanny Wedgwood, 18 November 1859, *Letters* ed. Arbuckle, p. 182.
12 HM to Fanny Wedgwood, 13 March 1860, *Letters* ed. Arbuckle, p. 190.
13 HM to John Chapman 22 October [1854], *Collected Letters* 3, p. 332; *Daily News*, January 1855.
14 HM to Mrs Ogden, 5 June [1852], *Collected Letters*, ed. Logan, vol. 3, p. 231.
15 HM to Fanny Wedgwood, 25 October 1858, *Letters* ed. Arbuckle, p. 169.
16 'An Autobiographic Memoir,' *Harriet Martineau's Autobiography*, with Memorials by Maria Weston Chapman, 3 vols. (Boston: James R. Osgood, 1877), III, p. 469.
17 Alexis Easley, *First Person Anonymous: Women Writers and Victorian Print Media, 1830–70* (Aldershot: Ashgate, 2004), pp. 58, 60.
18 Nancy Fix Anderson, 'Linton, Elizabeth Lynn (1822–1898)', *Oxford Dictionary of National Biography* (Oxford: Oxford University Press, 2004), www.oxforddnb.com/view/article/16742 [accessed 7 April 2014]
19 HM to Fanny Wedgwood, 13 November [1851], *Letters*, ed. Arbuckle, p. 121.

20 HM to Mrs Ogden, 19 July [1854], *Collected Letters* 3 (2007), p. 325.
21 Alison Winter, 'Harriet Martineau and the reform of the invalid in Victorian England,' *The Historical Journal*, 38:3 (1995), pp. 601–2.
22 *Autobiography*, p. 596.
23 Charles Dickens, 'A Preliminary Word,' *Household Words*, 30 March 1850, p. 1. In 1855 he and Martineau came to blows over the 'Factory Controversy' in which she challenged the allegations of a series of articles in *Household Words* about the danger posed to factory workers by unfenced machinery.
24 Arbuckle, *Letters*, p. 123.
25 HM to Mrs Ogden [Autumn 1851], *Collected Letters* 3, p. 209.
26 'Rainbow Making,' *Household Words*, 14 February 1852, pp. 485–90.
27 'The Wonders of Nails and Screws,' *Household Words*, 1 November 1851, p. 140.
28 'The city of Coventry: Crafts and industries: modern industry and trade.' In: *A History of the County of Warwick: Volume 8: The City of Coventry and Borough of Warwick* (1969), www.british-istory.ac.uk/report.aspx?compid=16026#s7 [accessed 12 April 2014].
29 Tamara Ketabgian, 'Spending Sprees and Machine Accidents: Martineau and the Mystery of Improvidence.' In *Harriet Martineau: Authorship and Empire*, ed. Ella Dzelzainis and Cora Kaplan (Manchester: Manchester University Press, 2010), p. 155.
30 'Nails and Screws,' p. 141.
31 'The Miller and His Men,' *Household Words* 24 January 1852, p. 420.
32 HM to Frederick Knight Hunt [early May 1854], *Collected Letters* 3, pp. 318–319.
33 [Harriet Martineau], 'The Crystal Palace,' *The Westminster Review* 62:6 (October 1854), p. 538.
34 [Andrew Wynter], 'The New Crystal Palace at Sydenham,' *Fraser's Magazine* 48 (December 1853), 609–622.
35 For example, both articles cite Dublin employers who lock up their supplies after distributing the exact rations for the day (LWR, p. 417), ER (p. 422). She also comments on locking up food in her *Once a Week* article.
36 [H.M.], 'Domestic Service,' *London and Westminster Review* 7:29 (August 1838), p. 428.
37 'The Domestic Service Question' [signed 'From the Mountain'], *Once a Week* (12 October 1861), p. 432.
38 'Modern Domestic Service,' *The Edinburgh Review* 115 (April 1862), 409–39; p. 410.
39 For example by Andrea Broomfield and Sally Mitchell in their *Prose by Victorian Women: An Anthology* (New York and Oxford: Routledge, 1996), p. 352, or Susan Hamilton who describes her as 'the first salaried woman journalist in Britain', in 'Women's Voices and Public Debate.' In: *The Cambridge Companion to English Literature 1830–1914*, ed. Joanne Shattock (Cambridge: Cambridge University Press, 2010), p. 104.
40 *George Eliot Letters*, II, p. 32.
41 She frequently cited panoramic mountain-summit surveys in *Eastern Life, Present and Past* (1848).
42 *Life in the Sick-Room: Essays by an Invalid* (London: Edward Moxon, 2nd edn, 1844), pp. 36–7, and *passim*.

12 Harriet Martineau and childhood

John Warren

In 1855, Martineau wrote her autobiography under the mistaken assumption that she was dying. It was consigned to the care of her American friend and fellow-abolitionist Maria Weston Chapman, and following Martineau's death in 1876 was published to considerable critical outcry. Contemporary commentators on the *Autobiography* hastened to criticise Martineau's unwomanly lack of reticence, but failed to note that her rhetorical strategies were multifaceted and included extraordinary, lengthy passages where the sights, sounds, textures and impressions of childhood were given emotive power with all the resources of fiction.

Modern scholarship has noted Martineau's frequent references to her own childhood, but has shown little interest in accounting for her interest in childhood itself, beyond reducing it to her supposed predilection for essentially determinist ideologies. In this way, her children in fiction were allegedly used to demonstrate the cruder lessons of political economy and to service bourgeois respectability.[1] However, this chapter argues that it is not possible to recapture Martineau's perception of the nature of childhood without appreciating how far it was shaped by what might be termed her 'heartland concepts': the core values both intellectual and emotional which were the product of her understanding of her own upbringing in the Martineau family in Norwich and the relationships within and beyond that household, allied to the cultural, religious and intellectual context which owed much to her Unitarianism and its engagement with contemporary ideologies. It is thus argued that Martineau's teachings on childhood, although heavily influenced by the Associationism of David Hartley, represented no slavish adherence to a single ideological viewpoint. She was not, for instance, a crude Associationist who therefore posited the child's mind as a *tabula rasa*, shaped purely by interactions with the environment and the manipulation of sensory stimuli to link feelings with actions. Instead, her teachings were a complex melange of influences as refracted through her heartland concepts – that is, a preoccupation with justice in household relationships, the clarion call of duty, and the salutary teachings of vicissitude. These heartland concepts provide emphasis and shape to Martineau's presentation of childhood in key writings: namely, the manual *Household Education* of 1849 and her fiction. After all, fiction was for Martineau the most potent of moral educators.[2] Our new reading of Martineau's fictional children also acts as a corrective to those who see her fiction as a whole in terms of artistically impoverished peddling of economic doctrine (the *Illustrations of Political Economy* of 1832–4),[3] or her children's tales (*The Playfellow* of 1841) as potboilers full of fisticuffs, derring-do and embedded patriarchy.[4]

Furthermore, Martineau's presentation of childhood is more complicated than that of her immediate predecessors and contemporaries. Her decision to teach by means of fiction owed much to the personal influence of the Unitarian minister, theologian and teacher Lant Carpenter, who called for a successor to Maria Edgeworth, Anna Laetitia Barbauld and Hannah More as a moral educator: 'in the scale of utility she will probably stand unrivalled'.[5] The middle-class children in Barbauld and Aikin's *Evenings at Home* (1794–8) are associationist vessels into which information and precept are poured: neither they, their families, nor tutors are more than abstractions. Maria Edgeworth's juveniles in her *Moral Tales for Young People* (1801) and *The Parent's Assistant* (1796–1800) are written to illustrate a largely associationist credo which emphasises that learning must not be associated with pain or the expectation of reward. An environment in which good habits are consistently inculcated would triumph over corrupt later influences – as in Franklin's routing of malevolent servants in *The False Key*.[6] The tales 'Forester' and 'Angelina; or, l'amie inconnu' tilt respectively at the Rousseau principles of free learning through experience and romantic sensibility; her impossibly upright young heroes and heroines stand for probity, sociability and due deference, and their moral standing is often defined by their attitude towards squashing caterpillars. Hannah More, on the other hand, rejected such determinist concepts of childhood: nurture did not account for the spiritual state which defined a child. Her evangelical approach rested upon a conviction that children were tainted by Original Sin:

> Is it not a fundamental error to consider children as innocent beings . . . rather than as beings who bring into the world a corrupt nature and evil dispositions, which it should be the great end of education to rectify?[7]

In her *Cheap Repository Tracts*, More placed her emphasis on individual sin, piety and repentance. There is no environmental reason, for example, why one of the sons of the appalling Black Giles the poacher should be good at heart whilst the others share their father's venal criminality. Similarly, Betty Brown, brought up in ignorance and squalor, nevertheless preserves her innocence, and is rewarded with retail success: 'by industry and piety, [she] rose in the world, till at length she came to keep that handsome sausage shop near the Seven Dials.'[8] Others undergo a conversion experience. Despite unpropitious beginnings Hester Wilmot blossoms at Sunday School and converts her unwholesome family.

Martineau's *Monthly Repository* article 'Female Writers on Practical Divinity' attested to her intimate acquaintance with Barbauld and More in particular. The *Autobiography* shows that Barbauld was very much a part of the Norwich family's wider Unitarian networking;[9] moreover, her letters offer evidence of an intimate acquaintance with *Evenings at Home*.[10] The *Illustrations of Political Economy*, which established her fame, owe something to *Evenings at Home* in the way in which dialogue is made to serve a didactic purpose. Even so, this is merely occasional in the *Illustrations of Political Economy* and endemic to Barbauld's work: indeed, Martineau eschewed the adult/child dialogue which largely shapes *Evenings at Home*. The format of the *Illustrations* bears striking similarity to the *Tracts*: both were published monthly and offered plots which focused on life of the working and lower middle classes. Indeed, there are instances where the specific content of an *Illustrations* tale is so close to that of a *Cheap Repository Tract* that one can posit, at the very least, a lasting impression made on Martineau. For instance, Martineau's tale 'The Parish' (1833) describes how the venal and improvident Bloggs family sends its children to beg from well-to-do passengers at a crossroads; and, in More's tale 'Black Giles The Poacher' (1796), the venal, improvident *and* criminal Giles sets his 'ragged brats . . . to lie all day upon a sand bank . . . At the sound of a carriage, a whole covey of these little scare-crows start up . . . and all at once thrust out their hats and aprons'.[11]

A longer-term echo of More appears in Martineau's collection of her earlier short stories, *Sketches from Life* (1856): in particular, her tale 'The Factory Boy' (pp.130–8) presents a lachrymose account of a nine year-old boy who vows at his widowed mother's deathbed to keep himself and his even younger siblings out of the workhouse. Through a mixture of hard work and piety he succeeds, and is rewarded by the applause of the community and an early but didactically satisfying death in a factory accident. This tale sits uneasily with the majority of Martineau's portraits of children, which are often lively, realistic and at times hard-hitting. One thinks in particular of Roger Redfurn in *The Playfellow* tale *The Settlers at Home* (1841): his selfishness, his cruelty and ultimately his tears of loneliness. The atypical emphasis on the factory boy's docility is a particular echo of More's good children, such as James Stock in 'The Two Shoemakers' (1795) who 'had begun to learn of Him *who was meek and lowly of heart*'.[12] If Martineau's tale was indeed a sketch from life, it may account for the suspension of her habitual interest in the impact of environment and circumstance on character and the otherwise complete absence of the evangelical childhood from her tales.

Indeed, it is an associationist approach which, it would seem, most frequently shapes her child characters. In *The Rioters, or a Tale of Bad Times* (1827), the Brett family of weavers is destitute and desperate, and Martineau stops well short of blaming them for their children's role in machine-breaking; they are guilty of error, but their criminality is the product of extreme want and circumstances outside their control. She cites neighbours as independent witnesses of how respectable and hard-working the family originally was and so corroborates the mother's cry of anguish:

> 'Fine boys they were, Sir, six months ago: but they are so changed! I thought they had been too old for mischief; but the times have crazed them, I think: and that's my worst trouble.'[13]

Biddy Brand, the mentally and physically handicapped child in *The Parish* (1833), is degraded by the noxious environment of her mother's new alehouse;

her limited intellect is compromised and her tractable behaviour sabotaged by the habits encouraged by the drinkers and her mother's preoccupied ignoring of her needs. The *Illustrations* are replete with binary opposite households: the 'bad' households resound with examples of what happened to children when their upbringing was soured by a poor environment. Thus, the Peeks children in *The Farrers of Budge-Row* (1834) are utterly ill-disciplined and a torment to neighbours: the uncontrollable product of a household with no sense of purpose, responsibility or duty. The Murdoch household in *Ella of Garveloch* (1832) is compromised by the father's improvidence and frequent physical and intellectual indolence. His boys are correspondingly lumpen, painfully incapable of answering the questions of the Laird's English visitors. Murdoch sells up his farm and purchases a cottage in the hope of 'ease and domestic peace'.[14] This is a significant conjuncture of terms: it is Murdoch's laziness that in large part results in his fractured household, where his riotous daughters interfere with the work of the very men who are building their new home. Martineau's irony may be heavy-handed, but the point is made.

The 'good' households are characterised by the instilling of good habits in the accepted associationist manner, but, as with the 'bad' households, the quality of the relationships is more vividly portrayed than the habit-forming process itself. Thus, the good household seeks to stimulate and empower children, underpinned by a sense of justice and duty. Ella's younger brothers, under her care following her mother's death and her father's decline, are intelligent and informed, and the laird is driven to ask her 'what had made her brothers so unlike the boys within, [the Murdochs] and most of the other lads belonging to the islands?'[15] Ella does not reply, but one key reason is mutual respect. As the boys mature, Ella is prepared to relinquish her authority bit by bit 'before the change was demanded or even wished for' (p.117). This vital aspect of household relationships is honoured in its breach in the Le Brocq household in the *Illustrations of Taxation* tale *The Jerseymen Meeting* (1834); the father is dictatorial, and treats his adult son Aaron as a child. The result is that Aaron is sullen, stubborn and addicted to the aggressive and counterproductive phrase ' "What is it to you?" ' as an attempt to assert himself in the community.[16]

Martineau's fiction is permeated with the issue of just and unjust treatment of children. Mrs Rowland in the novel *Deerbrook* (1839) uses her children as weapons in her power struggle with her neighbours the Greys. Her ammunition is the language of parental love and empowerment, whereas its reality is very different. Her children are encouraged to walk in the garden following a loudly voiced expression of parental concern and respect for their liberty, but, once its apparent aim has been achieved (to criticise the Greys in the hearing of their guests), then her daughter Matilda is curtly ordered inside. Small wonder that the governess Maria Young, isolated without her own household, should lament over how little she could do to repair the damage done by the poor upbringing of children, so often subject to bad parental example and ill-temper. ' "If I had them in a house by myself, to spend their whole time with me, so that I could educate, instead of merely teaching them." '[17]

Justice to the child also required a willingness to answer their questions, since the ability to frame a question was to be taken as betokening an ability to understand the answer. In this way, Anna in *The Tenth Haycock* (1834) asks whether it was not better for her clergyman father to be given honey as a well-meaning gift rather than attempting to extract it by tithe in the name of the rights of the church. But she is brushed aside with the comment that she is too young to understand.[18] The 'good' household, however, involves children in its most important decisions. Cousin Marshall in the eponymous tale consults her children on which of her cousin's orphans she should succour by taking them into their home.[19] In the novella *Mary Campbell, or, the Affectionate Granddaughter*, Martineau presents the young Mary and her grandfather as intellectual companions. They share the *Life and Correspondence of Dr. Franklin* as their afternoon reading, and Mary is startled by Franklin's frank avowal of his sins in earlier life. She understands that a sense of duty might lead him to make them public, but that ' "a proper awe of the holiness of that Being against whom he has offended, would lead him to express his sorrow in a different manner." '[20] These are the grandfather's words as he interprets Mary's own objection, and he concurs – having known Franklin personally, he felt that his religion was vague and his wisdom too worldly. This is precisely the kind of intellectual dialogue that Martineau found so compelling. Mary's grandfather provides the necessary guidance and framework, but listens with discrimination and encourages her, through conversation, to develop and express her viewpoint. Campbell is worried that she will see Franklin as a good man who did not need religion to be good, and so would overrate mere reason as a pathway to morality. In the manner of Barbauld, he objects to Franklin's supposed tendency to see Christianity as primarily a moral system, thus depriving himself of illumination and warmth for mind and heart. But he does not allow this genuine concern to lead him to an authoritative pronouncement, even though Mary would accept it out of love. Instead, grandfather and granddaughter come to an agreement. In a further echo of Barbauld, they award the prison reformer Howard ' "a deeper sanctuary in our affections than that of FRANKLIN" ' (p. 57).

Arguably, in outlining the perfect companionship of old and young within a family, Martineau was incorporating her interpretation of a troubled relationship with her mother into her message. In this way, autobiography informed her understanding of childhood. Martineau's *Autobiography* indicted her mother's conduct of the household and upbringing of her children through a lengthy and bitter catalogue of sufferings. That condemnation was echoed in Chapman's *Memorials* and summed up vigorously in a published lecture by Florence Fenwick Miller, in which the mother was accused of being 'deficient in the gentler qualities, and wanting in the wisdom of the heart.'[21] Martineau's *Autobiography* hit equally hard: 'I really think, if I had once conceived that any body cared for me, nearly all the sins and sorrows of my anxious childhood would have been spared me.'[22] She believed that her childhood was marred by a failure on her parents' part to recognize a child's emotional needs, and that her physical ailments, which included digestive problems and encroaching deafness, were in large part the consequence. She supposedly exacerbated physical symptoms by a tendency to indulge in reveries of endurance, martyrdom and sainthood: a sympathetic maternal understanding and guidance would, she argued, have curbed such excesses. Her account of that childhood was peppered with terms such as 'severity', and she linked the severity of her treatment with that of the equally disempowered servants: 'Justice was precisely what was least understood in our house, in regard to servants and children' (p.45). Chapman, having accepted this account as veracious, pounced gleefully upon every opportunity to criticise Elizabeth Martineau's harsh treatment of her daughter, which was allegedly the result of a 'setting-down' system which oppressed in the name of salutary discipline. Chapman quoted extensively from an unnamed friend of Harriet's youth who confessed herself apprehensive to the point of sickness when faced with the imminent arrival of the formidable mother: ' "It was the *setting-down way* she had, which was so terrible to sensitive young people . . . I remember *no* tenderness towards her, but the same severity and sharpness of manner, cleverness of management." '[23] James Martineau's 'Biographical Memoranda' strove to combat such negative portraits, but was at best equivocal and concluded with an indictment as severe as that of his sister, albeit without her force of expression and exemplification. He described his mother thus:

> Of great energy and quickness of resource; and married to a man of more tenderness and moral refinement than forces of self assertion, she naturally played the chief part in the governance of the household . . . Her children were trained in wholesome habits & clever arts, and stimulated by her sparkling talk: and though my childhood was not happy, I attribute this, not to any sharp or repressive discipline on her part or my father's, but to well-meant but persecuting sport on the part of my older brothers, and to the rough treatment at the hands of a great public school; and still more, to the simple absence of any apprehensive sympathy with the growing inner life of the boy.[24]

The last sentence cannot be interpreted as other than condemnatory. Significantly, the manuscript has the word 'discipline' crossed out and replaced by 'governance'; the change is more likely to be an attempt at cool-headed balance than a stylistic embellishment.

Harriet Martineau's interpretation of the dynamic between her mother and herself as child had a formative impact on her writings and life. This is why, in the appropriately titled *Household Education*, she offered her own experience as at once self-exposure and truth: 'The early life of that child was to me a long course of intense emotions which, I am certain, have constituted the most important part of my education.'[25] The metaphor of the bursting heart resonates through the childhood sections of the *Autobiography*, and this is why the *Autobiography* so powerfully communicates the memories of childhood – the sight, sound and touch – and why both her fiction and non-fiction offered up those experiences in a way which appears surprisingly unmediated. The *Autobiography* described her very first memory:

> I remember standing on the threshold of a cottage, holding fast by the doorpost, and putting my foot down, in repeated attempts to reach the ground. Having accomplished the step, I toddled . . . to a tree before the door, and

tried to clasp and get round it; but the rough bark hurt my hands. At night of the same day, in bed, I was disconcerted by the coarse feel of the sheets . . . and I was alarmed by the creaking of the bedstead when I moved.[26]

The very same episode reappeared in *Five Years of Youth* in Mary's conversation with her former nurse:

'You had a wooden step at the door then; and I used to take fast hold of the door-post, and put down first one foot and then the other . . . the bed creaked, and frightened me; and the feel of the coarse sheets was not like what I had been accustomed to. And that old elm too, how its rough bark hurt my little hands when I used to try to get round it.'

(pp. 5–6)

The relationship between Martineau's heartland concepts, autobiography and her interpretation of childhood is strikingly evident in the ways in which adversity is presented as a stimulus to personal improvement and, indeed, a litmus test of the quality of an adult's relationship to children. In so doing, she was building upon her own experiences: in particular, the advancing deafness which was not sympathetically handled by her family (*Autobiography*, pp. 81–4), and her guilt at temporarily abandoning in play her friend 'E', whose leg had been amputated by her surgeon uncle Philip Meadows Martineau (*Autobiography*, p. 63). In *Briery Creek* (1833), Temmy Temple, a boy cowed into intellectual and moral torpor by his status-obsessed father, finds his faculties stimulated as, despite his fears and self-doubt, he is forced to invent a long story about a lamb to prevent his feverish and mortally ill uncle from leaving his sickbed.[27] And, in *The Playfellow* tale *The Settlers at Home*, Martineau provided a seventeenth-century setting in the Isle of Axholme where the hard-working, trusting and mutually supportive household of Huguenot settlers, the Linacres, are seen as agents of the King and attacked as a result. Their mill is cut off by flooding as Parliamentarians open the sluices; the miller is swept out to sea, the fate of the mother unknown and the children are left in a collapsing mill with a well-meaning but ignorant and ineffectual servant. The impact of the flood is presented in unswerving detail. The baby falls desperately ill, and the children are forced to abandon the mill. But affliction has, as ever, its very real positives. Eleven-year-old Oliver, struggling to act as head of the household, is turned from a rather vapid boy into a resourceful and brave young man:

He was no taller, and no stronger;- indeed he seemed to-day to be growing weaker with fatigue: but he was not the timid boy he had always appeared before. He spoke like a man; and there was the spirit of a man in his eyes. It was not a singular instance. There have been other cases in which a timid boy has been made a man of, on a sudden, by having to protect, from danger or in sorrow, some weaker than himself.[28]

Another *Playfellow* tale, *The Crofton Boys* (1841) (Figure 12.1), has been criticised for an endorsement of patriarchy and labelled as a fiscally prudent potboiler, but

END OF "THE CROFTON BOYS."

Figure 12.1 'End of "The Crofton Boys"', illustrated by A. W. Cooper (Routledge 1895).

this is to fail to recognize its key theme: the way in which vicissitude stimulates its young hero, Hugh Proctor, to overcome the flaws in his character. His foot is amputated as a result of a playground accident (and another boy's foolhardiness), but his response awakens a new mental and emotional resilience which brings an end to the moral weakness which his mother identifies as his key failing: 'you sadly want courage of a better kind – courage to mend the weakness of your mind.'[29] Indeed, rather than endorsing patriarchy, *The Crofton Boys* offers an indictment of the father's role in the household, where his unthinking and insensitive behaviour is a barrier to the improvement which Mrs Proctor demands from her son.

The needs of the afflicted child are used by Martineau as a litmus test of the way in which a household responds to its duty towards children. In *Ella of Garveloch*, Ella's young brother Archie, in nineteenth-century terminology an idiot, is presented without sentimentality. His odd appearance, lack of responsiveness to strangers and restlessness are catalogued, and his ill-treatment by the Laird's agent, Callum, is described without attempts to arouse sympathy in the reader. His presence in the tale is accounted for by the insights it provides into the moral standing of those with whom he comes into contact. Callum is thereby condemned for unjust behaviour and an obsession with his own authority, which, for him, implies the enjoyable use of power without responsibility to community. Similarly, the considerable moral standing of Cousin Marshall is in part defined by her willingness to serve individual and community by taking into her relatively poor household a near-blind niece, rather than see her consigned to the workhouse. And, in *Messrs. Vanderput and Snoek* (1833), the afflicted child resurfaces as the moral litmus test in the form of Christian – unable to walk, and suffering from a recurrent and dreaded agony. The selfish Fransje will only sit with him if her assiduity is applauded by a spectator, whereas the infinitely more worthy Gertrude, who 'said nothing about the pleasure, had frequently held the boy in her arms for hours during his agony.'[30]

So far, it has been argued that Martineau's fictional teachings on childhood were fundamentally associationist, but that her underpinning heartland concepts led to a departure from crude associationist tenets. In *Five Years of Youth* (1831), for example, the Byerley household is well-meaning but imperfect, since the father, distracted by valetudinarianism, political causes and prejudice, fails to provide his daughters with the correct instruction in their household tasks. Habits linked to duty are not developed. The result in the case of Anna is particularly unfortunate, since she falls victim to the vacuous emotionalism of sensibility and is sedated by reverie and lassitude. But her sister Mary, subject to an identical environment, nevertheless transcends it by linking feeling to duty. Indeed, the relationship between heartland concept and the didactic message on childhood is particularly clear in *Five Years of Youth*: Anna's luxuriating in emotion compromised both intellectual and emotional progress and jeopardised the safety of her transition to the presence of God. I have argued elsewhere that this failure to follow the religious call of duty – termed by Lant Carpenter 'social piety' – was particularly potent for the young Martineau, since her Norwich household was beset by the perceived failings of her sister-in-law Helen Bourn Martineau, whose emotionalism supposedly tainted the memory of her late husband, Tom Martineau: the brother idolized by Martineau herself.[31]

Martineau's Associationism and the *Monthly Repository*

Martineau's early essays on Hartleian Associationism for the *Monthly Repository* (and her later manual *Household Education*) echoed the explicit and implicit teachings of her fiction. Thus, the emphasis placed by Martineau on the strength of a child's feelings and need for justice implies a concept of childhood which does not reject the possibility of the mind having a structure more complex than the connections made between experiences imposed upon a *tabula rasa*. The *Monthly Repository* essays often follow a pattern: namely, a deviation from a line of argument, or, at times, an inconsistency, which often reflected the interpolation of personal experience. Her introduction to the essays 'On the Art of Thinking' (1829), for instance, suddenly veers into a discussion of families where the parents had 'more taste for power than for right reason. Their children are intelligent and conscientious. They are strongly recommended to do something which they do not altogether approve, but they think it will occasion less harm to comply than to resist, or even object.'[32] To interpose what is most probably a comment on her mother's alleged misuse of discipline and her child's view of what was just meant that Martineau was perhaps positing an innate sense of justice in children, and in this way compromised that associationist credo. The *Autobiography* is replete with examples of the youthful Harriet following her mother's orders (or apparently so) whilst objecting to their unfairness or irrationality: 'One of my chief miseries was being sent with insulting messages to the maids, – e.g., to "bid them not to be so like cart-horses overhead"' (p. 49). The household was the court where Martineau chose to present her case for children based on principle and practice.

A sense of right duty, it seems, was the *sine qua non* for the integration of principle, morality, action and intellect, not only for adults in the household but also for the growing child. In essay VI on the 'Art of Thinking', she considers how an invigorated intellect might advance one's moral sense, and its first service to morality was the power to distinguish between the 'essentials and the non-essentials of duty'. This link between the act of thinking, the search for the truth and duty may not be an obvious one, but is a further example of the interaction between heartland concept, interpretation of childhood experience, intellectual speculation and parallel teachings on adult/child relations in fiction such as *Five Years of Youth*.

Household Education (1849)

Such interaction duly shaped her views on household education: a theme which Martineau claimed should concern readers 'as seriously as any in the world'.[33] Concealed autobiography is apparent whenever Martineau prefaces a comment with 'I knew a girl.' We can be tolerably certain that the girl was Martineau herself and that the same passage will appear in the *Autobiography* with the addition of the personal pronoun. She claimed in *Household Education* that:

> I knew a girl of eleven, thoughtful and timid . . . [who] opened a theme of perplexity, to get a solution from a grown-up brother . . . Her brother answered her with kindness in his tone, but injudiciously. He told her that that was a very serious question which she was too young to consider yet . . . She felt that if she could ask the question, – thus put it in a definite form, – she must be capable of understanding the answer.
>
> (pp. 233–4)

The incestuous relationship between her fiction, her autobiography and *Household Education* could scarcely be clearer. The axiom in the last sentence of the *Household Education* paragraph appeared – as mentioned previously – both in Alice's thoughts in *The Tenth Haycock*[34] and in the *Autobiography*, which, in offering a more concise and vigorous version, emphasised the feeling rather than the intellectual disappointment: 'I felt that if I could feel the difficulty, I had a right to the solution' (p. 44).

As for the overt autobiography, perhaps the most heartfelt reminiscence was of her sister Ellen: 'I well remember that the strongest feelings I ever entertained towards any human being were towards a sister born when I was nine years old.'[35] The reader might well question the relevance of such reminiscences in a book of advice on household education and, perhaps, wonder whether the claim to authenticity was any more than a rhetorical device. Martineau clearly felt the need to account for what might appear to be self-indulgence, and did so by claiming that her experiences validated her arguments. Then came part one of the familiar *cri de coeur*: 'I tell it the more readily because I am certain that my parents had scarcely any idea of the passions and emotions that were working within me' (p.59) – to be followed by the equally familiar part two: the child's thirst for justice. 'Too many little hearts are made to swell in silence because they cannot get justice, or to burn under the suspicion that their aspirations are despised' (p.82).

Under the heading 'Care of the Powers', Martineau discusses nine powers, but three predominate in length of treatment – fear, patience/infirmity and truth. The chapter on fear is replete with her own childhood terrors, and she then makes a series of rather oblique connections which were meaningful to her as they fed on personal experience and on the Hope household in *Deerbrook*, where adversity rescued it from potential disasters of jealous temperament and thwarted love. She links the overcoming of fear with the enduring of adversity, and then attaches a sense of duty which she claims was dependent on a feeling of awe in the face of some power or principle greater than oneself. The most effective method of overcoming fear through adversity, duty and awe is where the household itself focuses on one fear: 'And if the one dreaded thing be sin, it is well' (p.95). Here we might remind ourselves of the importance of the influence on Martineau of the Unitarian minister Lant Carpenter.[36] Carpenter offered a seductive blending of enthusiasm for Hartley, advocacy of the importance of harnessing the imagination in moral teaching and a clarion call to duty which he defined variously but in ways to which Martineau could readily relate. Carpenter's *Principles of Education, Intellectual, Moral and Physical* (1820) emphasised the duty of the household to stimulate the affections towards individual and societal progress and, in his *Sermons on Practical Subjects*, he argued that duty included parents accustoming children to view them as friends to whom they could open their minds and that, in this and other ways, justice was a 'department of duty'.[37]

The links with *Deerbrook* are reflected by a startling mimesis at the level of rhetorical flourishes. In a paean to the faculty of imagination in *Household Education*, Martineau sees the imaginative child as one who could visualise 'by his mind, far far beyond the bounds of human measurement and the human sight;- sees the universe full of rolling suns; worlds for ever moving in their circles, and never clashing' (p.249). This recalls the line from *Deerbrook*: 'On it rolls, – not only the great globe itself.'[38]

Household Education, then, complicates Martineau's Associationism with its injection of heartland concepts and personal experience: references to specific 'powers', 'imagination' and thirst for justice come close to positing innate ideas or potentialities and structures in a child's mind. Moreover, Martineau's emphasis on the intensity of childhood feelings distances her from standard association-ist thinking which, as Sally Shuttleworth argues, 'held that children, due to lack of accumulated experience, could not suffer as intensely as adults.'[39] Martineau insisted that the proud and timid child (herself, of course) suffered through 'the agonies of its little heart, the spasms of its nerves, the soul-sickness of its days, the horrors of its nights.'[40] Oddly enough, Shuttleworth then appears reluctant to accept that Martineau's account of her own childhood terrors was in conflict with Associationism, as Martineau was supposedly following the middle-class practice of making scapegoats out of servants who, as ignorant and disruptive agents, frightened children with tales of horror: 'The associative logic is made quite plain – the fears are not caused by the mysterious play of light . . . but rather entirely by lower-class foolishness' (p.52). This is to misunderstand the responsi-bility Martineau placed squarely on employers to ensure that servants were truly seen as full members of the household whose own educational needs were to be met. It also ignores the daughter's indictment of Elizabeth Martineau.[41]

Scholars who have habitually labelled Martineau as a thorough-going Associa-tionist have attempted to support their arguments with references to comments in the *Autobiography*. Rick Rylance, for instance, argues that Martineau, having found herself floundering in the seductive metaphysics of the 'Scotch proposition of Common Sense', eagerly grasped the doctrines of Associationism as a way of attaching a 'secular doctrine to anchor belief'.[42] In fact, the *Autobiography*, despite its tendency to telescope Martineau's intellectual shifts, is rather more nuanced than Rylance suggests. Writing of the 1820s, Martineau commented that:

> I was moreover entirely wrong in not perceiving that the Scotch philosophers had got hold of a fragment of sound truth which the other [Hartleian] school had missed, – in their postulate of a fundamental complete faculty, which could serve as the basis for the mind's operations, – whereas Hartley lays down simply the principle of association, and a capacity for pleasure and pain.[43]

The so-called Common Sense school of Hamilton and Reid argued that the faculties of the child's mind were innate: they developed through experience, but were not the product of it. Such Faculty Psychology combined readily with Kant-inspired metaphysics to emphasise the importance of imagination and intuition in revealing God through the wholeness of nature. Wordsworth, of course, pos-ited a response to nature – particularly on the part of the child – which was far more profound than any arising from repeated experience of physical stimuli, and Coleridge, a radical Associationist in his youth, claimed that Associationism could not explain the generation of the imagination, which lies at the heart of 'the mind's self-experience in the act of thinking'.[44] Martineau's thinking was ever remote from Cartesian dualism, but her paean to the child's imagination was far less remote from Coleridge and Wordsworth than might be anticipated. The *Autobiography* testifies to Martineau's early discipleship – 'There had been a period for a few years, in my youth, when I worshipped Wordsworth' – and, despite the debunking style of the *Autobiography*, the mature Martineau praised him for rescuing poetry from the 'fashion of pedantry, antithesis and bombast, in which thought was sacrificed to sound, and common sense was degraded'. Her use of the phrase 'common sense' in this context is not without significance, and neither is the ultimate praise – Wordsworth was 'A benefactor, to poetry and to society'.[45]

This is not to argue that Martineau subscribed to a fundamentally Romantic concept of childhood which evoked what Hugh Cunningham has termed a 'reverence for, and a sanctification of childhood'.[46] Such Romantic reverence identified childhood's essential qualities as imagination, proximity to nature and natural law and an ability to see truth which transcended the concrete. In short, as Judith Plotz argues, most male Romantic writers saw children 'not as integrated into the social realm but as a race apart'.[47] Martineau's children are neither innocent nor guilty; nor are they a race apart, since they have the need and capacity to understand adult principles and are largely the product of the social, moral and intellectual environment of the household. But they are more than products, in part because they are endowed with particular faculties and, as we have seen, a capacity for intense feeling, sense of justice and imagination.

Household Education itself rests upon the instilling of habits through the manipulation of that environment, but it has been noted that, in common with her fiction, it transcends a narrow Associationism in refracting such ideas through the prism of the heartland concepts. Martineau's children are vulnerable, largely because Martineau was herself vulnerable as a child. Affliction was presented as a great teacher because Martineau learned from it – at length, and with pain. Her fictional children, excoriated by intense feelings, dream of martyrdom; so did the young Martineau.[48] Justice to children was a household duty in part because Martineau was deprived of it. After all, Martineau saw the way in which individuals and households treated children as the ultimate moral indicator of the household itself. And her focus on household meant that her children were realistically conceived as the product of that environment.

Laura Berry comments that 'Victorian representations of childhood are more likely to focus on childhood distress rather than transcendence, and to position their discourse in relation to social reform projects and debates,'[49] and one might add that orphans such as Oliver Twist added potency to distress when used to illustrate social evils. Much of Martineau's fiction addressed controversial social questions such as poor law and indirect taxation, but, given that her children are more often members of households rather than isolated as orphans, they do not follow the Bunyanesque routes of Oliver Twist's Parish Boy's Progress. Nor do they follow the *Bildungsroman* in the manner of Jane Eyre, where, as Barry Qualls has suggested, Jane's tortured path represents a precarious balance between 'religious and Romantic heritages . . . knowing their innocence and yet constantly reminded of – and often feeling – their guilt.'[50] Nor are Martineau's children redemptive symbols such as Eppie in George Eliot's *Silas Marner, The Weaver of Raveloe* (1861). In any event, we have seen that Martineau's portrayal of childhood in fiction and non-fiction was nuanced and the result of a potent admixture of cultural context, personal experience and self-fashioning. It serves as a warning that reductive attempts by scholars to label Martineau as a combination of propagandist and tyro are wide of the mark, and that to recapture her views on childhood demands an understanding of the reciprocity between her life and writings.

Notes

1 See Lauren Goodlad's characterising of Martineau's tale 'The Hamlets' as an object-lesson in bourgeois Individualism in *Victorian Literature and the Victorian State: Character and Governance in a Liberal Society* (Baltimore: Johns Hopkins Press, 2003), pp. 57–60.
2 Harriet Martineau, *Miscellanies*, 2 vols. (Boston: Hillard, Gray & Co., 1836), I, pp. 27, 56.
3 See in particular Freedgood's ' "Banishing Panic": Harriet Martineau's Political Economy of Everyday Life,' *Victorian Studies* 39 (Autumn 1995), pp. 33–53. Freedgood claims that the *Illustrations of Political Economy* represented a mendacious salve applied to bourgeois consciences. Their artistic failings supposedly compromised their long-term effectiveness. For a critique of such views, see John Warren, ' "Now try and recollect if you have done any good today". Household, Individual and Community in the Early Fiction of Harriet Martineau, c. 1825–41.' University of Oxford D.Phil. thesis, 2014, p. 214.
4 Pichanick claims that *The Playfellow* tales were penned out of financial necessity and correspondingly conventional: 'Her small heroes and heroines . . . were made to mouth proper and pious cant' (Pichanick, p. 127).
5 Lant Carpenter, *Principles of Education, Intellectual, Moral, and Physical* (London: Longman, Hurst, Rees, Orme, and Brown, 1820), p. 42.
6 Edgeworth's works are full of warnings to parents to beware the baleful influence of servants over the young. By way of contrast, Martineau saw servants as an intrinsic part of a household; as with children, justice dictated that their emotional and intellectual needs were met.
7 Hannah More, *Strictures on the Modern System of Female Education.* 2 vols. (London: Cadell and Davies, 1799), I, p. 57.
8 Hannah More, *The Shepherd of Salisbury Plain, and Other Tales: Tales for the Common People* (Philadelphia: Lippincott & Co., 1866), p. 203.
9 'It was a remarkable day for us when the comely elderly lady in her black silk cloak and bonnet came and settled herself for a long morning chat.' Martineau, *Autobiography*, ed. Peterson, p. 234.
10 Martineau identified which pieces were written by Barbauld herself and which by her brother Dr Aikin: 'Mrs B & the Aikins have always anxiously explained this'. Logan (ed.), *Letters* v, 180.
11 More, *Salisbury Plain*, p. 205.
12 More, 'The Two Shoemakers.' In: *The Shepherd*, p. 48.
13 Harriet Martineau, *The Rioters, or a Tale of Bad Times* (Wellington: Houlston, 1827), p. 9.
14 Harriet Martineau, *Ella of Garveloch* (London: Charles Fox, 1832), p. 123.
15 Ibid., p. 24.

16 Harriet Martineau, *The Jerseymen Meeting* (London: Charles Fox, 1834), p. 88.
17 Harriet Martineau, *Deerbrook* (1839); rpt. ed Valerie Sanders (London: Penguin, 2004), p. 30.
18 Harriet Martineau, *The Tenth Haycock* (London: Charles Fox, 1834), pp. 62–3.
19 Harriet Martineau, *Cousin Marshall* (London: Charles Fox, 1832), p. 14.
20 Harriet Martineau, *Mary Campbell; or, the Affectionate Granddaughter* (Wellington: Houlston, 1828), p. 23.
21 Florence Fenwick Miller, *The Lessons of a Life: Harriet Martineau: A Lecture Delivered Before the Sunday Lecture Society St George's Hall, Langham Place on Sunday Afternoon, 11 March, 1877* (London: Sunday Lecture Society, 1877), p. 10.
22 Martineau, *Autobiography*, ed. Peterson, p. 52.
23 *Harriet Martineau's Autobiography, with Memorials by Maria Weston Chapman*, 3 vols. (London: Smith, Elder, 1877), III, p. 11.
24 James Martineau, 'Biographical Memoranda,' HMC, MS. J. Martineau 13 (Oxford: Harris Manchester College), p. 11/117.
25 Harriet Martineau, *Household Education* (London: Edward Moxon, 1849), p. 58.
26 Martineau, *Autobiography*, ed. Peterson, p. 39.
27 Harriet Martineau, *Briery Creek* (London: Charles Fox, 1833), pp. 125–6.
28 Harriet Martineau, *The Settlers at Home* (London: Charles Knight, 1841), p. 248.
29 Harriet Martineau, *The Crofton Boys* (London: Charles Knight, 1841), p. 30.
30 Harriet Martineau, *Messrs: Vanderput and Snoek* (London: Charles Fox, 1833), p. 68.
31 See Warren, 'Now Try and Recollect,' pp. 65–84.
32 Harriet Martineau, *Miscellanies*, 2 vols. (Boston: Hillard, Gray & Co., 1836), I, 117.
33 *Household Education*, p. 1.
34 *The Tenth Haycock*, p. 63.
35 *Household Education*, p. 56.
36 Ibid., p. 16.
37 Carpenter, *Principles*, p. 77.
38 *Deerbrook*, p. 416.
39 Sally Shuttleworth, *The Mind of the Child: Child Development in Literature, Science, and Medicine, 1840–1900* (Oxford: OUP, 2010), p. 16.
40 *Household Education*, p. 90.
41 For a discussion of how Martineau's sense of responsibility for the well-being of servants was translated from fiction into her own practice, see John Warren, 'Harriet Martineau and the Concept of Community', pp. 228–34 in particular.
42 Rick Rylance, *Victorian Psychology and British Culture, 1850–1880* (Oxford: OUP, 2000), p. 62.
43 Martineau, *Autobiography*, ed. Peterson, p. 103.
44 Samuel Taylor Coleridge, *Biographia Literaria; or, Biographical Sketches of My Literary Life and Opinions* (New York: Leavitt, Lord & Co, 1834), p. 78.
45 Martineau, *Autobiography*, ed. Peterson, p. 493.
46 Hugh Cunningham, *Children and Childhood in Western Society Since 1500*. 2nd ed. (Harlow: Longman, 2005), p. 72.
47 Judith Plotz, *Romanticism and the Vocation of Childhood* (Basingstoke: Palgrave, 2001), p. xv.
48 See Warren, 'Now Try and Recollect' for a Discussion of Martineau's Martyrdom Discourse,' pp. 287–8.
49 Laura Berry, *The Child, the State and the Victorian Novel* (Charlottesville: University Press of Virginia, 1999), p. 17.
50 Barry Qualls, *The Secular Pilgrims of Victorian Fiction* (Cambridge: CUP, 1982), p. 5.

13 Harriet Martineau's correspondence

Rhetorical practice and epistolary writing

Deborah A. Logan

I cannot really think without pen or pencil or book in hand.

Harriet Martineau[1]

During a career spanning half a century, Harriet Martineau wrote dozens of books: fiction ranging from political economy to historical romance and children's tales; and non-fiction, including travel memoirs, self-help, biography, and autobiography, as well as thousands of periodical articles (for dailies, weeklies, monthlies, quarterlies, and annuals) – an extraordinarily prolific literary output, even by Victorian standards. Distinct from those consciously literary productions – a category in which I include what is now termed 'self-writing' – my work collecting HM's letters is based on the premise that her intellectual and literary legacies are best known through her correspondence, public and private, personal and professional. An exceptionally copious letter writer, she wrote thousands of letters to friends, family, and business associates. My claim that her letters are 'her most significant literary production'[2] reiterates the view of many of HM's contemporaries and subsequent commentators who found her edict against publication regrettably inconvenient and ill-judged. Central to the controversy generated by her aim to control the public fate of correspondence designed for private consumption is the role played by the *Autobiography* in shaping her posthumous reputation. Horrified by the notion that some authors – under the plea of exerting agency over one's private words – prepared their letters for posthumous publication, she was adamant that her *uncollected* letters not serve as a haphazard substitute for a carefully crafted autobiography: hence, her request to correspondents that they destroy her extant letters and hence, the determination to shape her legacy through a formal autobiography.

While I am privileging Martineau's epistolary writing over other genres, my broader interest here concerns the ways her correspondence – even the most ostensibly private and personal – resonates with her writing intended for publication. There are two primary points in this exploration: first, her insistence that she did not draft or revise her published material, claiming that the most honest and direct expression was that which came first – a thoroughly Wordsworthian value (spontaneity) complicated by another thoroughly Wordsworthian value: revision, revision, and more revision, as her extant letters eloquently attest. The second, related factor – that Martineau did indeed employ a process of continual revision – requires more specific examination of the ways her correspondence served as the drafting now widely considered crucial to good writing, to the point of employing near-exact phrasing in material both intended and not intended for publication. Such a focus highlights the idea that correspondence *as* authorial practice was, for her, the most spontaneous, authentic expression, its clarity being essential to the quality of her most polished, published works.

Epistolary utterance, public and private

Martineau's affinity for the epistolary format, and for the tone of familiarity and immediacy it enables, is everywhere evident throughout her *oeuvres* – from the wealth of extant letters that survived her instructions to return or destroy them (an estimated 3,000 pieces) to writing intended for publication. In some instances, her letters served as an introduction to others' work, such as John Collins' *Right and Wrong among the Abolitionists* (1841) and *Mind Amongst the Spindles* (*Lowell Offering* 1845), while "Letter to the Deaf" (*Tait's* 1834) was addressed to 'My Dear Companions' and signed 'with deep respect, Your affectionate sister, Harriet Martineau.' Although such examples are designed to evoke her known associations with literary, intellectual, and experiential authority, the reverse is true of *Life in the Sickroom* (1844); predicated on her desire for anonymity, the epistolary introduction is addressed 'To ____' and signed 'Yours, ____.' Articles structured as letters include those published in Maria Weston Chapman's abolitionist annual *The Liberty Bell* (e.g., 'To Elizabeth Pease' [1845]) and *Two Letters on Cow-Keeping* (1850), the latter offering her experiments with small farming for public – particularly workhouse – use.[3]

A consummate journalist, Martineau wrote leading articles regularly yet still found time to write letters to the editor for publication, some signed – as with her two 1837 letters to the *Spectator* objecting to its levity regarding the American slavery issue – and some employing a pseudonym, as in *Daily News*, the latter permitting her to broaden journalistic objectivity by employing a distinctly opinionated, because unremunerated, platform; her most notable use of this resource was her letters condemning the Contagious Diseases Acts (1869). Some letters to editors were serial, as in 'Letters on Mesmerism' (*Athenaeum* 1844): categorized as self-writing, these too were unremunerated by design. Alternatively, 'Letters from Ireland' (*Daily News* 1852) marks Martineau's singular foray as a travelling correspondent assigned to report on socio-economic reconstruction in post-famine Ireland. Between 1858 and 1862, she wrote a fortnightly column as 'Our European Correspondent' for the American *National Anti-Slavery Standard* addressed to the editor; by turns friendly and critical, she was quite comfortable with lecturing (some claimed *hectoring*) the Americans as they stumbled awkwardly toward resolving the slavery issue. In this instance, the question of remuneration took an interesting turn: challenged by fiscal difficulties, the *Standard*'s editor accepted Martineau's offer to continue writing the column *gratis*; whether she acted on this enhanced opportunity for subjective commentary consciously or subliminally, irate readers demanded her resignation, objecting to her candor even when offered free of charge.

The sole instance of publishing private correspondence was, interestingly, at Martineau's instigation; this was *Letters on the Laws of Man's Nature and Development* (1851), the notorious 'Atkinson book' that earned her charges of vulgarity and resulted in her permanent break with brother James. Although condemned as an atheist (more accurately, agnostic) and patronizingly pitied for investigations that precluded Christianity's compensatory afterlife, Martineau maintained that philosophical exploration was essential to her spiritual well-being. Although her fascination with mesmerism eventually died a quiet death, her commitment to philosophical inquiry persisted, requiring open-minded investigation and affording her great intellectual satisfaction. Writing to Mary Estlin about Maria Weston Chapman's role in compiling the *Memorials*, Martineau notes that 'Mr. Atkinson will do the one part that she is not competent to, – the philosophical training & results.'[4] Indeed, much of period four in volume two of the *Autobiography* addresses her philosophical investigations, while an entire chapter of *Memorials* is devoted to 'Philosophy' (based on Atkinson's contribution), signifying that what was to many an unaccountable embarrassment was in her view central to her intellectual and literary life.[5] Martineau's pursuit of what Atkinson termed 'the religion of philosophy'[6] was evident in her earliest *Monthly Repository* writings (from 1822), leading inevitably to her work translating and condensing Auguste Comte's *Positive Philosophy* (1853).[7]

A related idea involving letters is Martineau's singular scheme, conceived during the economic upheavals of the 1820s, to offer an education course for young ladies through correspondence, her deafness precluding traditional modes of teaching.[8] Although the idea foundered because of an apparent lack of interest, it bore fruit in another iteration: her association with W. J. Fox, editor of *Monthly Repository* and literary mentor who quickly filled the gap resulting from James Martineau's removal to college. In the *Autobiography*, she asserts that Fox's 'editorial correspondence with me was unquestionably the occasion, and in great measure the cause, of the greatest intellectual progress I ever made before age thirty.'[9] These letters, for decades believed lost or destroyed, ultimately surfaced during the twentieth century, bearing eloquent testimony to what must have been for her a most gratifying period of professional development.[10] Throughout her life, visitors and guests marveled at the amount of writing she produced – typically under physical duress, much of her professional life having been played out against a backdrop of illness; after writing a good part of the day, she was often awake past midnight, writing letters; if too ill to write, she dictated to an amanuensis. It was *despite* chronic illness that she produced such quantities of writing, and it was *because* of chronic illness that she was determined to control her correspondence and thus, shape her literary legacy.[11]

The letter doctrine

The year 1843 represents Martineau's most aggressive pursuit of such control – again evidenced, ironically, through extant correspondence that was supposed to have been destroyed. We have the recalcitrant Henry Crabb Robinson to thank for a record of the protracted wrangling resulting from her sickroom-induced concerns about letters – indeed, he was impervious to her insistence that he conform with the edict. Theirs was a comparatively new correspondence, dating from the Tynemouth era (1841 through 1850) and characterized by mutual literary interests. In February 1843, Martineau wrote:

> I do hope you don't keep my letters. . . . my correspondents generally, knowing my feeling about letters, – that they are talk, & shd be treated as such, – are kind enough to give me perfect freedom in writing by destroying my letters. . . . I have no fear of the posthumous publication of my letters, for I have guarded against it, in my testamentary dispositions of my affairs. I think it of more importance to make my own arrangements of my papers, than of my few hundreds. . . . there is no possible Ex[ecuto]r whom I wish to admit to a sight of my private letters, – my letters of affection, & I write no others. My letters are all talk; & I cd not write them if they were not to be sacred to the friend to whom they are addressed. . . . for the sake of my own freedom of epistolary speech. . . . I may possibly be found to have sufficiently provided for society knowing what it likes of me, without having prostituted my private correspondence to that end.[12]

The striking term 'prostituted' speaks more profoundly for the intensity of her views than many pages of narrative eloquence on the topic, although such pages are available as well.

The same month, she wrote to George Combe more forcefully, wielding decidedly muscular legal rhetoric:

> Permit me to give notice to you . . . that I have made testamentary provision against any private letters of mine being ever printed. . . . My Exr has directions to see the law observed in my case; & I give notice of this to my correspondents. . . . in regard to my future letters, – wh depend on this condition being observed. . . . it arises from no care in regard to my own reputation, – wh I never tried to gain or to keep, & shall not begin to trouble myself about now.[13]

While in this instance the matter seems settled, what was presented to Robinson as non-negotiable continues to require negotiating: 'I see I have not made myself understood by you,' she wrote again, explaining 'I discovered that my most private letters were kept labelled & prepared for publication after my death: & also that those who were corresponding with me on an agreement that letters shd not be kept had not kept the agreement on their side' (pp.155–56). Her points heavily underlined, she defends her personal 'freedom of epistolary speech' as well as the general 'principle of the inviolability of private correspondence' and concludes: 'If I must take your letter as a refusal, – as a declaration that you will continue to keep my letters, I must take it as declining my correspondence. My letters are (not "like talk" but) talk, – a flowing out of the moment to you.'[14] One more such exchange provoked ill-disguised frustration: 'Now I must say that I am more & more puzzled by your thorough misunderstanding of my ideas about letters. . . . Once more, (& I hope for the last time) my sole aim is to avoid all possible risk of my letters being published. . . . What can be simpler?' (p. 206). As it turned out, Robinson overtly conceded the point while covertly preserving her letters, thus continuing the (deceptive) relationship; if there was any further discussion, somebody, somewhere, destroyed the evidence – perhaps.[15]

Martineau's frustration was only partially due to Robinson's persistence. Her allusion to the hoarding of letters for publication could refer to her brother James; to Fox, she wrote: 'I am glad you are of my mind about the Letter doctrine. Many are, – but so many are not (James for one)'.[16] James rejected her 1843 request to destroy or return her letters, and summarized and paraphrased 192 of them (dating from 1819 to 1845) into a shorthand code; decades later, the material was translated and, later still, transcribed and published. That material evidences, in 1843, a sharp decline in what had long been regular communications with James, indicating his willingness to forego the epistolary relationship rather than comply with her wishes. Interestingly, Martineau continued to write to his wife Helen through 1854, knowing full well those letters would be shared with her estranged brother. In light of the public family feuding over 'that Atkinson book' and James's review of it ('Mesmeric Atheism,' 1851) and, in 1854, the attempted absorption by *Prospective Review* (with which James was affiliated) of the *Westminster Review* (with which Harriet was affiliated), the siblings' relationship clearly underwent a long, acrimonious process of deterioration.[17]

In an alternative context, business correspondence with Richard Monckton Milnes during this period addressed pending education reform legislation. Although Martineau's May 1843 communication reads more like a formal tract than a letter (*CL* 2:158–62), she subsequently informs Milnes, 'I decide not to print the Education letter' (207). Despite the professional context, the occasion affords her another opportunity to convey the 'Letter doctrine': 'I have never spoken to you, I think, about my course in regard to letters, – ours having been, more or less, on business. Let me commend that matter to your remembrance, assuring you that it is an affair of conviction & conscience with me. Scarcely a letter of mine is in existence, – except those on business, or questions of public concern' (209) – despite her confidence, as is now known, she was quite deceived on that point. Milnes too, apparently, requested further clarification: 'As for "where I draw the line," (about publishing & letters) why – at the intentions of the writer, to be sure. . . . private letters are understood to be between four eyes. . . . you have no right to give up any one's right of privacy but your own' (215).

Whether we understand or agree with Martineau's 'Letter doctrine,' it is worth bearing in mind the rhetorical vigour of the foregoing 'conversations' in view of the *Autobiography*'s opening passage, subtitled 'Publication of Letters.' The placement alone of this discussion indicates that, to her, the intersecting issues posed by private correspondence and a carefully crafted autobiography are of paramount concern: 'When my life became evidently a somewhat remarkable one, the obligation presented itself more strongly to my conscience: and when I made up my mind to interdict the publication of my private letters, the duty became unquestionable.'[18] Epistolary conversations are predicated on trust and thus susceptible to betrayal, prompting her to invoke the term 'traitor' (p. 36) – an aggressiveness she here partially minimizes:

> It is rather a piece of self-denial in me to interdict the publication of my let-ters. I have no solicitude about fame, and no fear of my reputation of any sort being injured by the publication of anything I have ever put upon paper. . . . it would be rather an advantage to me than the contrary to be known by my private letters.
>
> (p. 35)

That said, her conclusion reiterates the prohibition: 'I am therefore precisely the person to bear emphatic practical testimony on behalf of the principle of the pri-vacy of epistolary intercourse.' Her language so emphatically resonates with those 1843 letters to Robinson, Combe, and Milnes as to cast them as a rehearsal for this striking introduction to the definitive account of her life: 'Epistolary corre-spondence is written speech; and the *onus* rests with those who publish it to show why the laws of honour which are uncontested in regard to conversation may be violated when the conversation is written instead of spoken' (p. 35).[19]

After 1843, Martineau's inner circle of trusted correspondents shrank consid-erably; in terms of arranging for the *Memorials* volume, there were only two on whom she felt she could rely: Maria Weston Chapman and Henry Atkinson. To Chapman, she wrote:

> You desire my permission to publish, after my death, certain letters of mine to yourself. Mr. Atkinson desires permission to give you some of my letters to him for publication. I give you my sanction with entire willingness, and I hope you will employ it as freely as you like in regard to these two sets of letters. Such use of them is perfectly consistent with the principle on which I have forbidden, in my will, the unauthorized publication of my private correspondence.[20]

No betrayal of trust occurs 'when writer and receiver agree to make known what they have said to each other.' Martineau was convinced of three related points: the consummate value to literary and intellectual history of preserving her letters; the necessity of destroying them, according to her idea of trust; and the proposi-tion that the *Autobiography* alone adequately speaks for her life and legacy. Mar-tineau scholars are compelled to negotiate the intersection of those three disparate points, with some letters preserved, some forever lost, and an official account of 'a disposition naturally open and communicative'[21] that is notoriously partial and selective.

Method of work

Maria Weston Chapman writes about the impressions Martineau made on Ameri-cans during her tour, despite her deafness and their concerns about the social awkwardness posed by her ear trumpet: 'Her one great gift seemed then to be utterance; not rhetoric, not elocution, not eloquence, not wit . . . but the faculty of rapidly communicating thought and feeling. Her fulness of sympathy made it natural to her to meet every mind in private society just as she unfailingly did the public mind in her writings, – exactly where it laboured'.[22] Echoing those terms in 'An Autobiographic Memoir' (1855), Martineau wrote: 'Her stimulus in all she wrote, from first to last, was simply the need of utterance' (p. 662).[23] That same year, she wrote in the *Autobiography*: 'my authorship was the fulfilment of a natural function, – conducive to health of body and mind. . . . Authorship has never been with me a matter of choice. . . . I could not help it. Things were pressing to be said; and there was more or less evidence that I was the person to say them.'[24] Just as the facility with which Martineau wielded her ear trumpet assuaged social awkwardness, so too was her pen a natural extension of her intellect.

In 'Times of Working,' she rejects waiting for inspiration or negotiating writer's block, the 'waiting for congenial moods, favourable circumstances' rather than 'summoning' them at will; for her, the act of sitting down with pen and paper quickly resulted in 'finding myself in full train. . . . I could work when I chose'.[25] The vigour of her 'stimulus' and compulsion for utterance, combined with clarity of vision, is at the centre of her authorship: 'it has always been my practice to devote my best strength to my work; and the morning hours have therefore been sacred to it' (p.157). The discipline underpinning those 'sacred' hours (7am – 2pm) foregrounds unimpeded concentration as essential to productivity: 'it is an indispensable condition that there shall be no interruptions. The dissipation of mind caused by interruption is a worse fatigue than that of continuous attention' (p. 328).

While protecting her time and energy from distractions, Martineau was also economical with it, having early decided 'it would not do to copy what I wrote; . . . I discontinued the practice . . . thus saving an immense amount of time. . . . The prevalent doctrine about revision and copying . . . made me suppose copying and alteration to be indispensable'; instead, she concludes, 'I, once for all, committed myself to a single copy' (p. 113). Not surprisingly, her views on copying out manuscripts anticipate those on revision:

> There was no use in copying if I did not alter . . . distinctness and precision must be lost if alterations were made in a different state of mind from that which suggested the first utterance. . . . know first what you want to say, and then say it in the first words that occur to you. . . . I have always made sure of what I meant to say, and then written it down without care or anxiety. . . . I perceive that great mischief arises from the notion that botching in the second place will compensate for carelessness in the first.
>
> (pp. 113–14)

Most writers, those who are bound by such limitations as stifled inspiration and sluggish mental processes necessitating drafting and revision, may well marvel at the self-confidence evidenced by such statements. Charlotte Brontë 'was as much surprised to find that I never copy at all as I was at her imposing on herself so much toil which seems to me unnecessary' (p. 325). The primary key to comprehending such clarity returns to the concept of epistolary writing, as in this assertion regarding her 'method of work': 'I paged my paper; and then the story went off like a letter. . . . As to the actual writing, – I did it as I write letters, and as I am writing this Memoir, – never altering the expression as it came fresh from my brain' (p. 159). Authorship is no mystical process requiring muses or inspiration: what, she implies, could be simpler? Just sit down and write!

It is characteristic of Martineau to minimize what is to most authors an extraordinary facility for synthesizing thought with writing quickly and efficiently. In the words of her 'Self-estimate,' she notes: 'With small imaginative and suggestive powers, and therefore nothing approaching to genius, she could see clearly what she did see, and give a clear expression to what she had to say' (p. 670). Such insight is worth repeated scrutiny: the foundation of her authorial success rests on clarity of vision and expression; simply put, such enviable qualities precluded drafting, revising, and copying – or would seem to. As Chapman notes, the *Illustrations* 'was printed at a cheaper rate than it would have otherwise been, on account of the clearness of the writing; a thing worthy to be put on record in vindication of the rights of printers'.[26] Commenting on her 'Methods of Composition,' Henry Hallam expressed 'surprise at my venturing to press before the whole was finished and tied up', indicating an intellectual comprehension capable of linking individual increments (small pictures) with broader organizational vision (the big picture) that exceeds the capacities of most authors.[27]

Journalising

The most valuable materials offered in Chapman's *Memorials of Harriet Martineau* are the extracts from Martineau's personal journals, including those recording her American and Eastern travels and the 'Tynemouth journal.' Of the prodigious publications produced during the period between 1836 and 1848 – sixteen titles, many of which were multi-volume, as well as periodical articles – Chapman asserts that:

> a parallel record exists, to which one may have recourse, that tells of much besides, – not only what she saw and thought, but what she heard, resolved, and felt. . . . a series of small, unlettered volumes, thick and closely written, – the diary of the years between 1836 and her retirement to Tynemouth and afterwards; in which the most interesting entries are of things she provides no place for elsewhere.
>
> (p. 187)

In the *Memorials*, the travel journal excerpts are enhanced by what Chapman calls 'long journalising letters' written to her family, a hybrid format for recording daily experiences collectively, and ostensibly aimed at sharing with a select circle of readers upon returning home.[28] By supplementing her regular letters to her family in England, such 'journalising' subverted the inconvenience and long delays of international mailing while also serving as early versions of the American and Eastern travel books – in other words, *drafts* of material subsequently *revised* for publication. Her preface to *Eastern Life, Present and Past* alludes to the book's earlier version, noting that she had read the Egyptian journal to her travel companions, 'that I might have the satisfaction of knowing whether they agreed in my impressions.'[29] True also of the Martineau letters Chapman employed in *Memorials*, whether the original journals still exist or have been destroyed or lost is uncertain, making this book the sole known resource of primary materials for some of her most significant writing. Martineau herself clearly recognized that significance: when threatened with lynching in America for her views on abolition, arranging for the safety of her journals and papers superseded her physical well-being. She famously, and defiantly, concluded that the murder of an English traveler might accelerate the slavery question to a quicker resolution: were she to be physically silenced, those written accounts would continue to bear witness on her behalf.

Aside from the practical value of keeping travel journals, and given the prodigious amount of writing she daily produced (professional and correspondence), Martineau hesitated to add yet another literary chore: 'I have dreaded beginning to keep a diary, for fear of increasing my great fault, – bondage to rules and habits.' But, she reasoned, the creative impulse is ephemeral and requires perpetual nurturance: 'I have long been uneasy at the thought of how many valuable things I suffer to go out of my mind for want of energy to record them'; and she determines to 'try whether I can reconcile journalising with ease and freedom of mind.'[30] Distinct in style and content from both travel journals, Martineau's private journals (the 1836–39 writing journal and the 'Tynemouth' journal) evidence 'the fullest proof that it was kept for her own use and behoof exclusively; and she would then have been startled at the thought of its being seen by other eyes or after times; and, excepting only as given by the friend [Chapman] to whose judgment she entrusted it.'[31] Following the whirlwind of early fame, the intensity of American travel, and publishers' clamouring over her travel books on her return to England, she now revels in uneventful 'Quiet days' that facilitate self-reflection:

> On these days, when there is nothing to set down, how full is the life of the mind!. . . . An alternation of work and society is, I think, best for me. . . . How I love life in my study, – all alone with my books and thoughts! Books are not sufficient companions if one only reads. If one adds writing, one does not want the world. . . . What a blessing is this authorship! . . . it helps me over indisposition and failure of spirits better than any holiday. . . . There is no education like authorship, for ascertaining one's knowledge and one's ignorance. What light is thrown into my dark places. . . . What entirely new ideas are opened to me!. . . . I do hope to grow wise by mistakes, – one way of being made perfect by sufferings.[32]

This period was occupied with studying authors she admired – Shakespeare, in preparation for her on-site topographical research for Knight's *Pictorial Shakespeare* (Scotland and Italy); and the novels of Walter Scott and the 'glorious'

Jane Austen, in preparation for writing *Deerbrook* (1839): 'I *think* I could write a novel, though I see a thousand things in Scott and her which I could never do. My way of interesting must be a different one.'[33] Although at this stage in her career Martineau had fully established her authorial voice, she continued to explore alternative 'way[s] of interesting,' all the while fending off an array of 'anxious meddlers.'

Interference

Martineau early recognized the need to maintain her idiosyncratic 'way of interesting' against the aggressive 'interference' of critics both amateur and professional.[34] Responding to her brother Tom's commentary on *Devotional Exercises* (1824), she defended her still-developing authorial voice: 'I must thank you with all my heart, dear Tom, for the attention and thought which you have given to my little book. Your criticism is just what I wanted, for before, I had heard nothing but indefinite praise, except indeed some little blame from [brother] Robert, of which I could not admit the justice, though not I hope from conceit, of which he complains, as being shewn in the Preface. I did not intend it certainly.'[35] The 'conceit' of asserting narrative authority – here, 'the young are best fitted to write for the young . . . where the feelings and affections are concerned' (Preface) – is a charge she confronted throughout her career.

With characteristic candour, she addresses this issue in the *Autobiography*: 'my method has been to ask advice very rarely, – always to follow it when asked, – and rarely to follow unasked advice. . . . I have always declined assistance . . . from persons who could not possibly be competent to advise, for want of knowing my point of view, my principle, and my materials'.[36] An illustration of intellectual interference concerns the machinations of an 'anxious meddler' who presumed to advise this internationally established author on her American books (specifically, urging that she avoid the topic of women altogether), even implicating *Edinburgh Review* editor William Empson in the endeavour. To Empson, Martineau complained of:

> the clear impertinence . . . of questioning an author as to what is to be in his book. . . . how earnestly I have been besought by various persons to say nothing about Democracy, nothing about Slavery, Commerce, Religion. . . . it is one of the most sacred acts of conscience to settle with one's own intellect what is really and solemnly believed, and is therefore to be simply and courageously spoken. . . . I analyse society in America, – of which women constitute the half. I test all by their own avowed democratic principles. The result, you see, is inevitable.[37]

The author's responsibility is to offer 'a steady, uncompromising, dispassionate declaration of his convictions. . . . The encroachment of mind upon mind should be checked in its smallest beginning, for the sake of the young and timid who shrink from asserting their own liberty' (p.166). Having early asserted that liberty among her brothers, she well understood how constructive criticism might shift into aggressive manipulation; her fidelity is to her own voice and conscience, and that is not to be tampered with by others' personal agendas or biases. Given her prohibition against publishing letters, her closing remark is particularly notable: 'May I ask you not to destroy this letter: but to keep it as a check upon any future solicitudes?'

The *Autobiography* records another episode of 'interference,' this time by her long-time associate, Charles Knight – unnamed but identifiable as the publisher of *How to Observe Morals and Manners* and *The Playfellow*. Knight – whose suggestions Martineau generally valued – read part of *Retrospect of Western Travel*, returning the manuscript to her 'covered with pencil marks' that 'altered about half the words'.[38] On this occasion, she restored the original by erasing the marks, prompting him to term her 'conceited and obstinate' but without, she claims, lasting 'detriment on either side' (p.168). Such was not the case on a subsequent occasion, when 'all the author's care in guarding her sole responsibility proved . . . insufficient to contend with the terrors of the publisher lest his pecuniary interests should suffer'.[39] Knight deemed part of *History of the Peace* controversial and feared losing government printing business by publishing the material; although reassured by Martineau of its validity, he censored it anyway: 'Long after, he told me he had taken the responsibility of ordering that page to be cancelled. I then told him he should never more publish for me. Had he submitted the matter to me, I would have consented to all reasonable change, but he did not.' She elsewhere concludes, 'I hardly needed further evidence that one mind cannot (in literature) work well upon the materials suggested by another: but if I had needed such evidence, I found it here'.[40] Authorial integrity as Martineau defined it results in writers being termed 'self-willed and obstinate . . . for not writing their books in some other way than their own' (p. 161). Her insights as a young writer in 1824 remained central to her mature vision in 1855: the young author 'need feel no remorse, no misgiving about conceit or obstinacy, if he finds it impossible to work so well upon the suggestions of another mind as upon those of his own. . . . when convictions have to be uttered, – advice cannot, by the very nature of things, be taken, because no conscience can prescribe or act for another' (p.442).

Yet Martineau was not inflexible on this point, and there were occasions when she invited editorial advice. Regarding *Life in the Sickroom* (1843), she wrote to publisher Edward Moxon: 'If you should see any line that you think could hurt any body's feelings, just have the kindness to tell me of it'.[41] Emphasizing the unique 'need of utterance' underpinning this book, she informs Milnes: 'I wrote it off almost without pause . . . The matter was not only ready, but pressing hard for utterance. Here is the MS – written as fast as pen would go, without a word changed. I asked Moxon to tell me if he saw a line which could hurt any one's feelings. . . . He saw nothing, & there was no word changed.'[42] This assertion is most interesting, considering the commentary by her friend, Elizabeth Bellenden-Ker, regarding the 'Letter doctrine':

> I regret infinitely that she desired all her letters to be destroyed. I had so large a boxful that it took some time to read and burn them. They would have been worth much to you, as you may guess when I tell you that on reading that

most charming of all her publications, 'Life in the Sick-Room' about which there is but one opinion, I said, 'Oh, but I have read it all before! – this is only my burnt letters!'[43]

Clearly, what was 'pressing hard for utterance' had already been thoroughly rehearsed in her letters; insofar as it was 'written as fast as pen would go, without a word changed,' some credit clearly belongs to earlier iterations of her thoughts, making the book less an original product than an example of manuscript copying that she elsewhere rejects.

In the spirit of being amenable to 'all reasonable change'[44] Martineau also collaborated with certain editors – Henry Reeve (*Edinburgh Review*), for example. Notable for sparking an international uproar, one of her most significant review articles – 'The Slave Trade in 1858'[45] – necessitated editorial 'compression,' an unprecedented experience for her:

> I never before reduced anything I had written. I have always had my things printed as they were written, in a single copy. I fully see the necessity in this case . . . but I feel confused as to the clearness of the story: E.g, doubtful whether the original fatal compromise is left apparent. . . . If I have not met your wishes, you must just do what you think necessary . . . But I hope my obliterations will serve. . . . I have no doubt of your agreeing in these little alterations: & now I hope the thing is compact & clear.[46]

Distinct from the 'meddlers,' Reeve was apologetic – prompting Martineau's gentle teasing: 'You are too kind by half about my excisions. You would not make a good schoolmaster if you pay compliments to truants instead of whipping them.'

Private to public

An important example of the interlacing of Martineau's correspondence with her published texts involves her collaboration with Florence Nightingale on sanitary reform in the military. Nightingale initiated the exchange, expressing concern that her 'Subsidiary Reports' – based on statistics gathered by her during the Crimean War – had evoked a rather sluggish response from the War Office. She solicits Martineau's help to 'popularize' those findings through her various periodical platforms, with a view toward pressuring Parliament to enact meaningful reform legislation. Determined to shield her source, Martineau assures Nightingale that she will protect her privacy, 'without citing you or the Report, or imputing blame to individuals'.[47] After consulting with *Daily News* editor Thomas Walker, she relays 'his desire that I will use, at my own discretion, the facts in these Reports, & his promise to use what I shall send. . . . If there is any particular direction in which you would wish to see 'D. News' at work. . . . just let me know, & I will see what can be done.'[48] Her objective is to stimulate public pressure: 'That multitude once convinced that our national security depends on a well-preserved army . . . the thing would be virtually affected.'[49]

During this period, Martineau applied Nightingale's findings in articles on 'Army Hygiene' (*Daily News* 14, 18, & 26 Jan. and 11 & 16 Feb. 1859); 'Army Medical Reform' (*Daily News* 1 Feb. 1859); and 'Military Health Reform' (*Daily News* 5 Mar. 1859). At the same time, she proposed to Nightingale a 'cheap volume consisting of chapters, in which your . . . experience would exemplify your doctrine, point by point.'[50] This project she offered to publisher George Smith of Smith, Elder, again emphasizing the Report's urgency – 'We want it utilized' – and its collaborative underpinnings: a 'popular statement should be published, by my hand, & in my name. . . . from the facts of the secret report. . . . My idea is of a cheap volume. . . . it is to be my work, & your treaty is with me'; Nightingale's 'share' (as silent or invisible partner) will be to revise and 'secure us against mistakes.'[51] Responding to Smith's queries, Martineau states her object is 'to get Military Hygiene systematically applied in practice, at home & in peace, in readiness for war' and refers him to her *Daily News* leaders, which model – indeed, they draft and rehearse – 'the character of what I propose to do in this book.'[52]

Published in April 1859, *England and her Soldiers* provides an historical overview of the disastrous rates of non-combat–related mortality in the military which, as established by Nightingale, are largely preventable. The Preface parallels confidentiality and collaboration with authenticity and urgency: 'This book is not a work of invention. . . . The materials are . . . contained in the Reports of various Commissions . . . supplied by the latest authorities.'[53] But although 'the [Crimean] war has been over nearly three years. . . . the thing is not done,' a point reiterated in her conclusion: "The thing has to be done. There is no time to lose. . . . Why is it not done?' (p. 269). Nor do the book's composition and production slow the steady stream of related periodical articles published from 1859 through 1861: in *Daily News*, 'Recruiting and Health' (14 Apr. 1859); 'Sidney Herbert and Army Administration' (27 June 1859); 'Recruiting and Army Reorganization' (15 July 1859); 'Indian army medical service' (26 Aug. 1859); 'Nightingale fund' (25 June & 21 Aug., 1860); 'Military Organization' (21 & 25 Aug. 1860); 'Sidney Herbert' (9 Jan. & 2 Dec. 1861); 'Soldiers' Recreation' (8 July 1861 & 3 May 1862); and 'Morals in the Army' (24 & 26 Apr. & 2 May 1862). For the American *Atlantic Monthly*, she wrote 'Health in the Camp' and 'Health in the Hospital' (Nov. & Dec. 1861); for *Macmillan's*, 'Death or Life in India' (1863); a series on occupations and health for *Once a Week* (1860–61); and articles promoting Nightingale's nursing programme (*Chambers' Journal* and *Cornhill Magazine*, 1865).

If the absence of immediate military conflict dulled the impact of *England and her Soldiers*,[54] the book found new purpose through its application to the American Civil War. 'Our book . . . is . . . quoted largely & incessantly in American medical Journals,' Martineau wrote to Nightingale, 'as a guide . . . [for] military management in the Northern States.'[55] Of the reports and books sent to America by Nightingale and Martineau she notes: 'I will write . . . to the secretary at war at Washington, to prepare him for what is coming.'[56] Emphasizing the significance of the gift, she assures Secretary Simon Cameron that Nightingale's 'labours have reduced the mortality in the army to one seventh of what it once was.'[57] Although an abolitionist, she regrets the lack of comparable contacts in the South, where lives are just as precious, regardless of the politics. To her cousin Henry Reeve, she reports: 'I have been very hard at work . . . about the health of the American army. I found that my volume about our soldiers was eagerly studied & discussed over there.'[58] Although there are many examples illustrating the overlap of Martineau's private correspondence with her published texts, it is those marked by transatlantic socio-political exchanges that prove to be most rich and fruitful.

Rewriting the 'dull & muddled'

There are some exceptions to Martineau's reluctance to rewrite material, and these were justified primarily in the interest of narrative consistency. Chambers Publishers, who purchased *History of the Peace* from Knight, proposed extending the original scope (1816–1846) to incorporate 1800 through 1854. To Mary Estlin, Martineau wrote: 'I made a stipulation which I hardly expected them to agree to, – that I should rewrite the first 5 years . . . which were written by various hands, & are, on the whole so dull & "muddled" as to be a most serious disadvantage to the rest. . . . if . . . I am allowed to make the work complete & sound, as my own, I have no excuse for declining.'[59] A curious aspect of the work's chequered publishing history is that it was not published until 1864, and then only in America. Chapman notes: 'the author was entreated by the American publishers to furnish them with a preface of warning against the policies that have ruined nations in old times, and that should be accordingly avoided by the statesmen of today. She immediately consented.'[60] In this instance, the suggestion to tailor the work to a particular audience for a specific purpose – one of her favorite projects being to instruct the Americans – was one she found acceptable.

A similar claim for rewriting applies to the *Autobiography*, early attempts of which remained unfinished until 1855. According to Martineau's hand-list of writing between 1822 and 1834, she 'Began own Life' in November 1831, after which there is no further mention of the project;[61] it is likely that this premature 'Life' was an early draft of 1833's 'Some Autobiographical Particulars of Miss Harriet Martineau,' published in *Monthly Repository.*[62] The project languished until 1843, when she wrote to W. J. Fox: 'I tell you a secret, . . . I expect to leave behind me perhaps the amplest account of a life ever written. I have taken measures to prevent my private letters being ever printed: but I shall leave otherwise the fullest possible revelation of myself. . . . When I see what the amount is up to 8 years old, I wonder what the whole mass will come to.[63]

Less than two years later, HM's dramatic release from the sickroom into one of the most physically active and prolific decades of her life caused the urgency of the autobiography to recede. But when diagnosed with fatal heart disease in winter 1855, she determined to complete the much-delayed project – beginning, interestingly, with rewriting: 'I thought it best to rewrite the early portion, that the whole might be offered from one point of view, and in a consistent spirit.'[64] Perhaps because of the pre-writings, the autobiography 'went off like a letter,' its two volumes completed with extreme rapidity; in September 1855 she invited Milnes for a visit to 'see the whole Memoir'.[65] By December 1855 it had been 'printed, under my own eye'[66] by a local printer, who 'most kindly undertook the privacy: & he alone actually read the book'.[67] The American edition being slated for simultaneous release with the English, the manuscript was entrusted to Chapman, to be given to the publisher 'immediately when the time came' – which, as it turned out, was twenty-one years later.[68]

That the *Autobiography* was not only written but printed and stored in 1855 attests to Martineau's determination to exert control over an uncontrollable medium – private words made public through print. One irony of such control is that the last two decades of her life are accounted for only in the *Memorials* and, with far less coherence and accessibility, by the widespread extant letters preserved by correspondents.[69] Such timing speaks eloquently for her determination to complete the book before dying and, above all, to prevent unauthorized versions of her life and legacy from compromising the authenticity of her own account. Aside from such material concerns, her undiminished confidence in the intellectual clarity underpinning what is one of the great achievements of her literary life, produced in record time, printed and thus beyond revision, attests to a remarkable determination to speak for herself, in her own words, without *interference* or *meddling*.

Controlling her posthumous image further extends to her self-authored obituary, 'Harriet Martineau. An Autobiographic Memoir,' also written in 1855 and filed with the *Daily News* editor, who published it on June 29, 1876, two days after her death. Written in third-person voice (a mannerism some critics – Margaret Oliphant, for one – deemed insincere and pretentious), the memoir presents a microcosm of the *Autobiography*, the release of which was delayed until 1877 to accommodate Chapman's completion of the *Memorials*. The memoir's trailing last words – 'Her disease was deterioration and enlargement of the heart, the fatal character of which was discovered in January, 1855. She declined throughout that and subsequent years, and died __' are melodramatically concluded by Chapman: ' – And died in the summer sunset of her home amid the Westmoreland mountains, on the 27th of June, 1876, after twenty-one more diligent, devoted, suffering, joyful years.'[70] In terms of having the last word, this unusual vehicle is of a piece with Martineau's 1869 preface to *Biographical Sketches*, a collection of obituaries written earlier in her career: '[. . .] it was evident to me at the first glance over my material that the Sketches must be presented unaltered' so as not 'to tamper with the truth of the sketch, and to produce something more misleading.' Only by preserving the original perspective can these biographies of the 'distinguished dead':

> convey the impression which the completed life left in each case upon my own mind, and . . . the society of its time. As the impression was final, the first record of it should remain untouched in order to remain faithful. . . . The records are true to my own impressions . . . I have no misgiving in offering them to readers.[71]

Applied to the category of life writing (self or other), the 'first record' is also the definitive 'impression' – unalterable, and thus consistent with her resistance to revising, which to her sacrificed accuracy for style and objectionable literary mannerisms. 'Her object . . . was to be true to what she had known and observed,' wrote Chapman: 'Nothing to extenuate and nothing to overcharge was her will. To copy the portrait her subject had himself painted was her endeavor'[72] – a value Martineau applied to herself as well as to others.

Given the absence of certain primary materials (such as those comprising the *Memorials*), reconciling the contradictions between what Martineau said with what she did is speculative at best. As the one person with access to those materials, Chapman regrets 'inexpressibly that Miss Martineau's long journalising letters of this period cannot . . . be made public. . . . one cannot help wishing this whole collection came within the terms she has laid down. Every letter is full of charm and instruction. . . . they might all go to the press as they stand, without a word of omission.'[73] For author James Payn, it is the letters that best reveal the woman, and their loss 'is a great pity, for she discussed people and things that have an interest for everybody. . . . I regret this veto the more, since but for it I could cull many an extract illustrative of a side of her character the least understood and appreciated – namely, its tenderness and domesticity.'[74] On a more professional note, Richard Garnett, biographer of W. J. Fox, attributes the decline in Martineau's intellectual legacy directly to the 'Letter doctrine' and the autobiographical substitution intended to speak for her. 'Never was there a sadder miscalculation' than presenting the *Autobiography* in place of the letters:

> The simple publication of every word she ever wrote to Fox . . . would . . . restore her to the place she ought to occupy, and which she would always have enjoyed had she been content to refrain from a posthumous control over her correspondence . . . [N]o one would gain so much from their publication as the writer. They would rectify the false impression which she has given of herself in her autobiography.[75]

Whereas Garnett could not then have envisioned an era when that correspondence would be retrieved, and a significant literary reputation along with it, such is no longer the case. The extent to which Martineau conveyed a 'false impression' through the very endeavour designed to control her posthumous legacy finds rectification through those 'traitors' who held alternative views about which impressions are 'final.' Both betrayed and redeemed by her own words, Martineau's assertion that first impressions 'should remain untouched' inadvertently and inevitably establishes that the 'first record' is to be found, ironically, in her own letters.

Notes

1 Deborah Logan (ed.), *Memorials of Harriet Martineau by Maria Weston Chapman* (Bethlehem: Lehigh University Press, 2015), p. 193.
2 Deborah Logan (ed.), *The Collected Letters of Harriet Martineau*, 5 vols. (London: Pickering and Chatto, 2007) (CL) 1: xvii.
3 Rosemarie Bodenheimer's commentary on the 'generic crossing' of female conduct books written in epistolary format is relevant to Martineau: the combination of 'personal

contact and . . . public revelation' shaped a domesticated counterpart to the formal essay associated with male authors, in effect feminizing writing designed to instruct and inform. Rosemarie Bodenheimer, *The Real Life of Mary Ann Evans* (Ithaca: Cornell UP, 1994), p. 10.

4   HM to Mary Estlin, 12 June 1855 (Logan, *Memorials*, p. 473).

5   See *Autobiography* II period IV, sections 3, 5–7.

6   Logan, *Memorials*, p. 278.

7   For a listing of HM's writing in *Monthly Repository*, see Francis E. Mineka, *The Dissidence of Dissent* (Chapel Hill: University of North Carolina Press, 1972). During the mid-1850s, HM's interest in philosophy shifted to 'my political work' (*Autobiography*, p. 34), including such current events as the Crimean War, Indian Uprising, and American Civil War, as reflected in her periodicals writing.

8   See also *Autobiography*, ed. Peterson, p. 127 and *CL* 1:53.

9   *Autobiography*, p. 125.

10 HM's letters to Fox are in the Speck Collection, University of California, Berkeley, and published in *Collected Letters* (2007).

11 'The "articulation of illness" in correspondence served to explain various circumstances, from the vicissitudes of invalidism (chronic or occasional) to periods of physical activity and well-being, constructing a rhetorical common ground that shifted individuals' 'personal myth' into a broader 'societal one' (Bodenheimer, p. 20).

12 *Collected Letters* 2, p. 149.

13 *Collected Letters* 2, p. 153.

14 See also HM to Robinson, 20 July 1843 (*CL* 2: 180–1).

15 HM's letters to Robinson are at Dr. Williams's Library, London; the last extant letter was 6 July 1850 (*CL* 3:162).

16 *Collected Letters* 2, p. 213.

17 The fate of the original 192 letters is unknown; both shorthand and paraphrased versions are at Harris Manchester College library, the paraphrases published in *Further Letters* ed. Deborah A. Logan (Bethlehem: Lehigh University Press, 2012). Unaccounted for in that collection is HM's letter to Helen (Mrs. James) Martineau (Sept. 1843): 'I have your letter. You are aware that it is impossible to *answer* it, & will not suppose I agree in its views & comments because I let them pass. . . . the next time you are about to administer one of your severe censures (of wh I have had so many) you remember how keenly you feel a very slight one. So here it ends' (*CL* 2:190). HM continued to write to Helen (see *CL* vols. 2 and 3, *passim*) through 1854, her commentary attesting to Helen's ongoing ambivalence.

18 *Autobiography*, ed. Peterson, p. 34.

19 According to William Dawson, the letter writer 'must be resolutely sincere, for the moment he begins to pose . . . he becomes tedious and offensive,' producing essays rather than letters; indeed, 'the first aim of a true letter [is] self-revelation' to the individual addressee, not to (an anticipated) broader public (qtd. Bodenheimer, p. 13). Alternatively, eighteenth-century letter-writing manuals (with which HM was likely familiar) highlight the formulaic conventions comprising a shared discourse based on categories of letters (form: business, friendship) and rhetorical constructions (content). The expectations underpinning this discourse were shared by writers and recipients/respondents, requiring both to observe the decorum of epistolary conduct (see Alain Kerhave (ed.), *The Ladies Complete Letter-Writer (1763)* (Newcastle: Cambridge Scholars, 2010); Linda Mitchell, 'Women's Roles in the English Epistolary Tradition,' *Huntington Library Quarterly* 66.3–4 (2003): 331–47; and Eve Bannet (ed.), *British and American Letter Manuals, 1680–1810*, 4 vols. (London: Pickering & Chatto, 2008).

20 Logan, *Memorials*, pp. 268–9.

21 *Autobiography*, ed. Peterson, p. 35.

22 Logan, *Memorials*, p. 137.

23 Written in 1855, printed in *Daily News* (June 29, 1876) and in Logan, *Memorials*, pp. 405–14.
24 *Autobiography*, ed. Peterson, p. 155.
25 Ibid., p. 157. All succeeding quotations on her working practices are from the *Autobiography*, unless otherwise stated.
26 *Memorials*, ed. Logan, p. 90.
27 *Autobiography*, ed. Peterson, p. 326.
28 Such letters 'intersect [with] diaristic genres,' rendering them 'not simply a vehicle of communication but of self-expression' unintended for publication (see Catherine Golden, *Posting It: The Victorian Revolution in Letter Writing* (Gainesville: UP Florida, 2009), p. 199). HM's 'long, journalising letters' represent 'unselfconscious sources of cultural history' by recording 'major political, economic, and social developments,' along with personal reactions; they also represent early drafts of materials subsequently released for public consumption.
29 Harriet Martineau, *Eastern Life, Present and Past* (1848), in *Harriet Martineau's Writing on the British Empire*, vols. 2–3. ed. Deborah Logan (London: Pickering & Chatto, 2004), p. 2.
30 *Memorials*, ed. Logan, p. 179.
31 Ibid., p. 179.
32 *Memorials*, ed. Logan, pp. 192, 186.
33 Ibid., p. 188.
34 *Autobiography*, pp. 442–7.
35 HM to Tom Martineau (*Memorials*, ed. Logan, p. 437). See also *CL* 1:143; 1:8 & 13; and *FL* 405.
36 *Autobiography*, p. 442.
37 *Autobiography*, pp. 444–5.
38 *Autobiography*, p. 447.
39 *Memorials*, ed. Logan, p. 305.
40 *Autobiography*, p. 441.
41 *Collected Letters* 2: p. 196.
42 Ibid., p. 208.
43 *Memorials*, ed. Logan, p. 424.
44 Ibid., p. 305.
45 HM charged that France and Liberia collaborated to perpetuate the international slave trade, thus fueling the American market. Reeve was threatened with libel suits, but HM's evidence precluded their moving forward.
46 *Collected Letters* 4: pp. 118–19.
47 3 Dec. 1858: *CL* 4: p. 138.
48 4 Dec. 1858: *CL* 4: p. 142.
49 9 Jan. 1859: *CL* 4:p. 146.
50 9 Jan. 1859: *CL* 4: p. 146.
51 15 Jan. 1859: *CL* 4: pp. 148–9.
52 19 Jan. 1859: *CL* 4: pp. 150–1.
53 Harriet Martineau, *England and Her Soldiers* (London: Smith, Elder & Co, 1859), p. 5.
54 HM's suggestion that the book be distributed to barracks libraries for the edification of soldiers was rejected for its potential to incite dissatisfaction with the ineptitude of military bureaucracy – which was, of course, the point.
55 20 Sept. 1861: *CL* 4: p. 288.
56 25 Sept. 1861: *CL* 4: p. 289.
57 30 Sept. 1861: *CL* 4: p. 290.
58 2 Oct. 1861: *CL* 4: p. 292.
59 HM to Miss Estlin, 21 Aug. 1854 (*Memorials*, ed. Logan, p. 468).

60 *Memorials*, ed. Logan, p. 306.
61 *CL* 1: p. 353.
62 'Some autobiographical particulars of Miss Harriet Martineau,' *Monthly Repository* (1833), pp. 612–15.
63 *CL* 2: p. 147.
64 *Autobiography*, p. 35.
65 *CL* 3: p. 368.
66 *CL* 3: p. 379.
67 *CL* 4: p. 266.
68 The British edition was published in three volumes, the third being Chapman's *Memorials*. The American edition contained the same material but printed the three volumes in a two-volume set.
69 For extant letters, see Elisabeth Arbuckle, *Harriet Martineau's Letters to Fanny Wedgwood*; Valerie Sanders, *Harriet Martineau, Selected Letters*; Deborah Logan, *Collected Letters of Harriet Martineau*, 5 vols.; *Harriet Martineau, Further Letters*; and Appendix A of *Memorials of Harriet Martineau* (Lehigh UP 2015). See also *Autobiography*, 'Introduction,' and 'Publication of Letters' (*DN* 22 March 1859).
70 *Memorials*, ed. Logan, p. 414.
71 Harriet Martineau, *Biographical Sketches* (London: Macmillan, 1869), p. vi.
72 *Memorials*, ed. Logan, p. 311.
73 Ibid., p. 50.
74 James Payn, *Some Literary Recollections* (New York: Harper, 1884), p. 95.
75 Richard Garnett, *The Life of W. J. Fox* (London: J. Lane, 1910), pp. 77–80.

Afterword

Harriet Martineau and the disciplines

Valerie Sanders and Gaby Weiner

> It is not credible that Miss Martineau should be generally read to-day, at least
> as an author. Her life and her letters, for the sake of literary history, may be well
> enough . . . But there is probably no one left to take her "Eastern Life" as a worthy
> guide to the Holy Land, or to teach political economy, as it was understood fifty
> years ago, by means of her stories written to that end, or even to be bored by the
> dullness of her Norwegian tale for the sake of the alien poetry that is lodged in it.[1]

Alice Meynell's 1895 dismissal of Harriet Martineau encapsulates what might
be regarded as the low point of Martineau's reputational history. At the same
time it distinguishes between works already seen as irrecoverable, in terms of
relevance to readers, and the exceptional life story that accompanied the production of these works. More recently Alexis Easley has also considered Martineau's
'somewhat remarkable' life to be, for some readers at least, 'a replacement for
her work' – now often dismissed as 'ephemeral'.[2] By any account Martineau's
life was extraordinarily varied between the extremes of obscurity and public
notoriety, and as a woman's life specifically, it broke numerous boundaries. As
with many nineteenth-century writers the appeal of whose tumultuous biographies threatens to overtake the effort of reading their works, her achievements as
a woman who stood up for the rights of slaves, women, children, the blind and
deaf sometimes seem easier to applaud than the torrents of dedicated prose that
fuelled those campaigns.

Martineau's late-twentieth-century return to prominence as an outspoken critic
of her age has made the task of evaluating the exact nature of her permanent
worth an exciting and rewarding exercise. We ended our introduction articulating
three aims for this collection: making sense of Martineau's seemingly fragmented
career, seeking to recuperate her for the 'disciplines', and identifying which of
the many genres, subject areas, fields and disciplines with which she has been
associated, she will best be remembered for – in other words, the extent of her
intellectual legacy.

With regard to the first aim, we hope that this collection has provided some sort
of cohesion to, or overview, of Martineau's intellectual output. We have seen the
extent of her life writing, in her autobiographical texts and correspondence. We

have learnt of her initiation into Political Economy which allowed her to spring-board into other disciplines and forms of writing, although she herself, we have been told, had little impact on what was an established, prestigious and male-dominated field. The collection suggests that she fared better in newly emergent disciplines such as sociology, history, realist fiction and psychology, where she was able to insert herself into disciplinary debates with relative ease. She also made her mark in several sub-disciplines, such as women's studies (particularly studies of feminism and women's movements) and travel writing, using both to press her arguments on social justice and anti-slavery. As a prolific journalist – she was one of many, mainly men but some women in the mid-nineteenth century – she often displayed a passion and excitement for things that belied her so-called objectivity.

The issue of Martineau's role in journalism in itself opens up the question of how we measure her achievements, and on what basis we judge her success in the numerous fields she entered over the course of her long career. She herself was not always a reliable judge of her own strengths, as summarised in her *Autobiography* and self-authored *Daily News* obituary, where, for example, she cites her most popular works as *Household Education* and her condensation of Comte. The latter especially she commended as 'her last considerable work; and there is no other, perhaps, which so well manifests the real character of her ability and proper direction of her influence.'[3] Important as it was at the time, however, Martineau's Comte no longer seems her most distinctive work, while *Household Education*, as Ruth Watts indicates in her chapter, was superseded in its essentials by educational reforms later in the century. While Martineau accurately identified her skills as a populariser, she downplays her ability to originate ideas, 'discover' or 'invent', which our essays have revisited in each of the designated disciplines.[4]

If we turn to (her) contemporary responses, what now seems an inflated, even incomprehensible response to her political economy tales in the 1830s offers little help to modern literary historians in evaluating her lasting impact; nor do most of her contemporaries' evaluations of her subsequent works as they were published. While many of her early reviewers, such as Croker and Lockhart, were misogy-nistic and spiteful, subsequent enthusiasms can seem exaggerated or off-kilter in the longer perspective of literary history. Her children's stories in *The Playfellow* are a case in point. Undoubtedly path-breaking in their choice of settings and the autonomy given her child heroes, they have disconcerted many adult readers with their depiction of extreme mental and physical trials. For Margaret Oliphant, how-ever, these were the works of Martineau's 'on which, perhaps, her most lasting title to fame will rest, the "Settlers at Home," and the ever-delightful "Feats on the Fiord."' Her *History of England*, by contrast, 'goes slowly, and drags on its way, and its movements are conducted in a kind of atmosphere of mild preachment, which the ordinary reader will find somewhat enervating.'[5] As Alexis Easley has argued in this collection, however, Martineau's achievements as a contemporary historian make significant advances towards a more democratic, inclusive notion of history, challenging its dominance by a white male majority. Fashions change, and with them come new critical approaches, which in the last twenty years have found much to admire in Martineau works previously overlooked or underrated.

It would be easy to continue enumerating the different historical claims to fame proposed over nearly two centuries on Martineau's behalf. What this essay collection has attempted to do is examine the case for each of the major disciplines in which she participated. Each of our contributors has both contextualized the discipline under scrutiny and identified Martineau's specific contribution to the field. The project has been by no means straightforward, in that her impact on each field has often been difficult to measure. In some cases (e.g., political economy), it was briefly powerful but only in terms of popularising an existing discipline; in others (such as abolitionism) her influence lasted longer, and she became an iconic figurehead for a movement, but in conjunction with others. For Lesa Scholl, Martineau's *Autobiography* is more than a radicalising of the genre: it brings together all the disciplines, and attaches her own mental progress to the intellectual development of the nation, while for Valerie Sanders her acclaimed achievements as a journalist are nevertheless difficult to define in terms of direct influence on such a broad field. For Gaby Weiner, it is Martineau's acute understanding of women's position in society, historically, socially and sexually, that marks her out as an important nineteenth-century feminist. Our contention is that Martineau was essentially in constant dialogue with her own culture, responding rapidly to its latest obsessions and concerns, both high and low, from slavery to the crinoline, and Crimean nursing to somnambulism. Perhaps her greatest achievement was to maintain this dialogue with her contemporaries and their times throughout the duration of her writing life, but can the same be said of her legacy beyond her own lifetime?

Undoubtedly, her dedication to writing as a profession may be seen as a key aspect of her legacy. On the one hand we have her huge literary input; on the other, we can see, say, from her collected letters[6] that she was someone thoroughly engaged in the literary world: a genuine woman of letters. If she was not writing about her own works and/or about payment, she was reading someone else's, often as a means of collecting material for the next book, or asking for books to be sent to her, or giving thanks for books. Her writing was admired for its clarity and accessibility, and her reputation for delivering manuscripts on or before the due date drew much appreciation from her publishers. For much of her life, she had a good sense of the publishing market, and what might be sufficiently controversial or innovative to widen her appeal – in Britain and elsewhere.

Her writing was deeply political in the sense that she wanted to persuade readers that her ideas about morals, values and social organisation, for instance, were the right ones to create a better world. She believed in a harmony rather than a conflict of interests in work relations, because she was optimistic about people's ability to cooperate. Her commitment to laissez-faire, which has been seen by some as uncompromising, did not stop her advocating government intervention when she thought it necessary: for example, in provision of public services, leisure activities, education and public works. Her conception of work whether undertaken by male or female, working-class or middle-class, manual or white collar worker, was both as a right and duty – people should not be denied access to jobs and the professions because of their gender, social origin or religious affiliation, but also that workers had responsibilities too. When she set out, say in *Society in America*, to examine the moral state of society, today her approach might be described as seeking to establish the extent of democracy and human rights. Thus Martineau's so-called didactic moralism which sounds so nineteenth century and reminiscent of middle-class do-gooding, might be better understood today as an indication of her social consciousness and will to activism. Her edict to friends to destroy her letters, as John Warren and Deborah Logan reiterate, was mainly to allow her 'perfect freedom' to write anything she wanted, including her own authentic story, unfettered by worry about what it might do to her historic reputation. Ironically, her 'Letters doctrine' as Deborah Logan terms it, meant a decline of her legacy in the last decades of the nineteenth century and first decades of the twentieth, because only her public writing remained after her death. It is only relatively recently that her correspondence and its illumination of the context in which her work took shape, have come to light. This provides a much-needed insight into the personality behind the Victorian tomes and newspaper journalism.

Martineau has been portrayed as a formidable didact: yet, in her writing on children, for instance, she kept to no ideological or intellectual straitjacket, but rather was sympathetic to children's powerlessness and wholly opposed to the violent disciplining of them. Children for Martineau were seen as a valuable and cherished component of society rather than apart or outside of it, and the same could be said of all the other underprivileged groups, from slaves to the disabled, whom she saw as lacking a voice in her contemporary society. If much of what Martineau wrote now seems obviously right, then this must to some extent be because she was instrumental in permanently changing the nation's values, and showing her readers how to become personally engaged in improving their society. Her strong support for domestic servants, nurses, and the other professions she addressed in her journalism, helped her contemporaries to *see* them as 'professions', for example, through her collaborations with Florence Nightingale and her accounts of her own household management. Above all, perhaps, Martineau was a *practical* writer: from start to finish her writing had an applied function. It was meant to change things. Her 'legacy', in our view, is therefore many-sided, but because of its pervasiveness through many disciplines, all the harder to sum up. For the current generation we suggest her legacy is strongest in feminism, sociology, life writing and journalism, but because all these disciplines are present in her other writings – her history, letters, travel writing, child psychology and fiction – the selection of one field more than another can seem to construct artificial boundaries. Martineau's variety and richness as a chronicler of her times, if once slow to be acknowledged, now opens up many more avenues for exponents of the multiple disciplines she represented. We hope this essay collection will help Martineau scholars to discover other places where her work made a difference, and above all continue to celebrate the extraordinary energy and enjoyment she brought to the profession of writing.

Notes

1 [Alice Meynell], 'A Woman of Masculine Understanding,' *Pall Mall Gazette* (October 11, 1895), p. 4. The 'Norwegian tale' referred to here is *Feats on the Fiord* (1841), one of Martineau's *Playfellow* stories for children.
2 Martineau, *Autobiography*, ed. Peterson (2007), p. 34; Alexis Easley, *First Person Anonymous: Women Writers and Victorian Print Media, 1830–70* (Farnham and Burlington: Ashgate Publishing, 2004), pp. 178–9.
3 Martineau, *Autobiography*, ed. Peterson, p. 670.
4 *Autobiography*, p. 670.
5 Margaret Oliphant (with Francis Romano Oliphant), *The Victorian Age of English Literature*, 2 vols. (New York: Lovell, Coryell and Company, 1892), Vol I, pp. 183–4.
6 Logan (ed.), *The Collected Letters of Harriet Martineau*, 2007.

Selective bibliography

Amigoni, David, 'Victorian Life Writing: Genres, Print, Constituencies', in *Life Writing and Victorian Culture*, ed. David Amigoni (Aldershot: Ashgate, 2006), pp. 1–19.

Arbuckle, Elisabeth Sanders, 'Carlyle Looks Askance at a Hero: Harriet Martineau's Toussaint L'Ouverture', *Carlyle Studies Annual* 19 (1999), pp. 23–31.

———— ed., *Harriet Martineau's Letters to Fanny Wedgwood* (Stanford: Stanford University Press, 1983).

————, *Harriet Martineau in London's 'Daily News'* (New York: Garland, 1994).

Bannet, Eve Tavor, ed., *British and American Letter Manuals, 1680–1810*, 4 vols. (London: Pickering, 2008).

Barros, Carolyn A., *Autobiography: Narrative of Transformation* (Ann Arbor: University of Michigan Press, 1998).

Belasco, Susan, 'Harriet Martineau's Black Hero and the American Antislavery Movement', *Nineteenth-Century Literature* 55, no. 2 (2000), pp. 157–194.

Bending, Lucy, 'Self-presentation and Instability in Harriet Martineau's *Autobiography*', in *Harriet Martineau: Authorship, Society and Empire*, ed. Ella Dzelzainis and Cora Kaplan (Manchester: Manchester University Press, 2010), pp. 63–73.

Bennett, Scott, 'The Editorial Character and Readership of *The Penny Magazine*: An Analysis', *Victorian Periodicals Review* 17 (1984), pp. 127–141.

Berg, Maxine, *The Machinery Question and the Making of Political Economy 1815–1848* (Cambridge: Cambridge University Press, 1980).

Blaug, Mark, *Economic Theory in Retrospect* 4th ed. (Cambridge: Cambridge University Press, 1985).

————, *Ricardian Economics: A Historical Study* (New Haven: Yale University Press, 1958).

Bodenheimer, Rosemarie, *The Real Life of Mary Ann Evans* (Ithaca: Cornell University Press, 1994).

Bohrer, Susan F., 'Harriet Martineau: Gender, Disability and Liability', *Nineteenth-Century Contexts* 25, no. 1 (2003), pp. 21–37.

Booth, Alison, *How to Make It as a Woman: Collective Biographical History from Victoria to the Present* (Chicago: University of Chicago Press, 2004).

————, 'Men and Women of the Time: Victorian Prosopographies', in *Life Writing and Victorian Culture*, ed. David Amigoni (Aldershot: Ashgate, 2006), pp. 41–66.

Bourne Taylor, Jenny and Sally Shuttleworth, eds., *Embodied Selves: An Anthology of Psychological Texts, 1830–1890* (Oxford: Oxford University Press, 1998).

Braid, James, *Neurypnology, or the Rationale of Nervous Sleep Considered in Relation with Animal Magnetism* (London: John Churchill, 1843).

Broomfield, Andrea and Sally Mitchell, *Prose by Victorian Women: An Anthology* (New York and Oxford: Routledge, 1996).

Buckingham, J. S., *America: Historical, Statistic, and Descriptive* (London: Fisher, Son, & Co, 1841).

Burrow, J. W., *A Liberal Descent: Victorian Historians and the English Past* (Cambridge: Cambridge University Press, 1981).

Bushnan J. Stevenson, *Miss Martineau and Her Master* (London: John Churchill, 1851).

Butler, Josephine, *Personal Reminiscences of the Great Crusade* (London: Horace, Marshall & Son, 1896).

Caine, Barbara, 'Feminism, Journalism and Public Debate', in *Women and Literature in Britain 1800–1900*, ed. Joanne Shattock (Cambridge: Cambridge University Press, 2001), pp. 99–118.

Carpenter, Lant, *Principles of Education, Intellectual, Moral, and Physical* (London: Hurst, Rees, Orme and Brown, 1820).

Carpenter, W. B., 'Mesmerism, Odylism, Table-Turning and Spiritualism, Considered Historically and Scientifically', *Fraser's Magazine* 95 (February 1877), pp. 135–157.

Carpenter, W. B., *Principles of Mental Physiology* 4th ed. (New York: D. Appleton and Co., 1883).

Carpenter, William Benjamin, *Principles of Human Physiology* 5th ed. (London: John Churchill, 1855).

Celikkol, A., *Romances of Free Trade: British Literature, Laissez Faire, and the Century*, (Oxford: Oxford University Press, 2011).

Chapman, Maria Weston ed., *Memorials of Harriet Martineau* (London: Smith, Elder, 1877).

Claggitt, Shalyn, 'Harriet Martineau's Material Rebirth', *Victorian Literature and Culture* 38, no. 1 (2010), pp. 53–73.

Colby, Vineta, *Yesterday's Woman. Domestic Realism in the English Novel* (Princeton: Princeton University Press, 1974).

Conway, Jill Ker, *When Memory Speaks: Reflections on Autobiography* (New York: Alfred A. Knopf, 1998).

Cooter, Roger, *The Cultural Meaning of Popular Science: Phrenology and the Organization of Consent in Nineteenth-Century Britain* (Cambridge: Cambridge University Press, 1984).

———, 'Dichotomy and Denial: Mesmerism, Medicine and Harriet Martineau', in *Science and Sensibility: Gender and Scientific Enquiry, 1780–1945*, ed. Marina Benjamin (Oxford: Blackwell, 1991), pp. 144–173.

Crabtree, Adam, *From Mesmer to Freud: Magnetic Sleep and the Roots of Psychological Healing* (New Haven: Yale University Press, 1993).

Craik, George, *The Pictorial History of England: Being a History of the People, as well as a History of the Kingdom* (London: Knight, 1849).

Croker, John Wilson, 'Miss Martineau's Monthly Novels', *Quarterly Review* 49 (April 1833), pp. 136–152.

Cunningham, Hugh, *Children and Childhood in Western Society Since 1500* 2nd ed. (London: Routledge, 2005).

Curthoys, Mark, ' "Secret organisation of trades": Harriet Martineau and "free labour" in Victorian Britain', in *Harriet Martineau: Authorship, Society and Empire*, ed. Ella Dzelzainis and Cora Kaplan (Manchester: Manchester University Press, 2010), pp. 138–150.

David, Deirdre, *Intellectual Women and Victorian Patriarchy: Harriet Martineau, Elizabeth Barrett Browning, George Eliot* (Ithaca, NY: Cornell University Press, 1993).

Durkheim, Emile, *The Division of Labour in Society*, trans. W. D. Halls (New York: The Free Press, 1893).

Dzelzainis, Ella, 'Feminism, Speculation and Agency in Harriet Martineau's *Illustrations of Political Economy*', in *Harriet Martineau: Authorship, Society and Empire*, ed. Ella Dzelzainis and Cora Kaplan (Manchester: Manchester University Press, 2010), pp. 118–137.

Dzelzainis, Ella and Cora Kaplan, eds., *Harriet Martineau: Authorship, Society and Empire*, (Manchester: Manchester University Press, 2010).

Easley Alexis, *First-Person Anonymous: Women Writers and Victorian Print Media, 1830–1870* (Farnham, Surrey: Ashgate, 2004).

———, 'Harriet Martineau: Gender, National Identity, and the Contemporary Historian', *Women's History Review* 20, no. 5 (2011), pp. 765–784.

———, *Literary Celebrity, Gender, and Victorian Authorship* (Newark: University of Delaware Press, 2011).

———, 'Victorian Women Writers and the Periodical Press: The Case of Harriet Martineau', *Nineteenth-Century Prose* 24, no. 1 (1997), pp. 39–50.

Edgeworth, Maria, 'Angelina; or, l'amie inconnue'; 'Forester'. *Moral Tales for Young* edition published in 1803 with the variora of 1806, 1807, 1817 and 1826; edited by PEditions, Peterborough, ON.

Franklin, Caroline, 'Introduction' *to Illustrations of Political Economy, Taxation, Poor Laws and Paupers* (Bristol: Thoemmes Continuum, 2001).

Freedgood, Elaine, 'Banishing Panic: Harriet Martineau and the Popularization of Political Economy', *Victorian Studies* 39, no. 1 (Autumn 1995), pp. 33–53.

Garnett, Richard, *The Life of W. J. Fox* (London: J. Lane, 1910).

Gauld, Alan, *A History of Hypnotism* (Cambridge: Cambridge University Press, 1992).

Gilman, Charlotte Perkins, *Women and Economics* (1898: rpt New York: Harper & Row, 1966).

Golden, Catherine, *Posting It. The Victorian Revolution in Letter Writing* (Gainesville, FL: University Press of Florida, 2010).

Goodlad, Lauren, *Victorian Literature and the Victorian State: Character and Governance in a Liberal Society* (Baltimore: Johns Hopkins University Harlow: Longman, 2005).

Greenwell, Dora, 'Our Single Women', *North British Review* 36 (February 1862), pp. 62–87.

Haac, Oscar A., ed. and trans., *The Correspondence of John Stuart Mill and Auguste Comte* (New Brunswick and London: Transaction Publishers, 1995).

Hall, Catherine, 'White, Male and Middle Class. Explorations in Feminism and History', in *Harriet Martineau: Authorship, Society and Empire*, ed. Ella Dzelzainis and Cora Kaplan (Manchester: Manchester University Press, 2010), pp. 74–87.

Hall, Spencer T., *Mesmeric Experiences* (London: H. Baillière, 1845).

Halsey, A. H., *A History of Sociology in Britain: Science, Literature, and Society* (Oxford: Oxford University Press, 2004).

Hamilton, Susan, 'Women's Voices and Public Debate', in *The Cambridge Companion to English Literature 1830–1914*, ed. Joanne Shattock (Cambridge: Cambridge University Press, 2010), pp. 91–107.

Henderson, W., *Economics as Literature* (Routledge, London and New York, 1995).

Herstein, Sheila, '*The English Woman's Journal* and the Langham Place Circle: A Feminist Forum and Its Women Editors', in *Innovators and Preachers: The Role of the Editor in Victorian England*, ed. Joel Weiner (Westport, CT: Greenwood, 1985), pp. 61–76.

Hill, Michael R., "Harriet Martineau," in *Women in Sociology*, ed. Mary Jo Deegan (New York: Greenwood, 1991), pp. 289–297.

———, ed., *How to Observe Morals and Manners* (New Brunswick and Oxford: Transaction Books, 1989).

———, ed., *An Independent Woman's Lake District Writings* (New York: Humanity Books, 2004).

Hill, Michael R. and Susan Hoecker-Drysdale, eds., *Harriet Martineau: Theoretical and Methodological Perspectives* (New York: Routledge, 2001, 2003).

Hoecker-Drysdale, Susan, 'Harriet Martineau', in *The Blackwell Companion to Major Social Theorists*, ed. George Ritzer (Malden: Blackwell, 2000), pp. 53–80.

———, *Harriet Martineau: First Woman Sociologist* (Oxford: Berg, 1992).

———, 'The Nobleness of Labor and the Instinct of Workmanship: Nature, Work, Gender, and Politics in Harriet Martineau and Thorstein Veblen', in *Thorstein Veblen's Contribution to Environmental Sociology: Essays in the Political Economy of Wasteful Industrialism*, ed. Ross E. Mitchell (Lewiston, NY: The Edwin Mellen Press, 2007) pp. 161–197.

Hollander, S., *The Economics of David Ricardo* (Heinemann: Toronto, 1979).

Holmes, Richard, *The Age of Wonder: How the Romantic Generation Discovered the Beauty and Terror of Science* (London: HarperCollins, 2008).

Holt, Raymond V., *The Unitarian Contribution to Social Progress in England* (London: Lindsay Press, 1938).

Hunter, Shelagh, *Harriet Martineau: The Poetics of Moralism* (Aldershot: Scolar, 1995).

Huzel, J. P., *The Popularization of Malthus in Early Nineteenth Century England: Martineau, Cobbett and the Pauper Press* (Aldershot: Ashgate, 2006).

James, Felicity, ' "Socinian and political-economy formulas": Martineau the Unitarian', in *Harriet Martineau: Authorship, Society and Empire*, ed. Ella Dzelzainis and Cora Kaplan (Manchester: Manchester University Press, 2010), pp. 74–87.

Jann, Rosemary, *The Art and Science of Victorian History* (Columbus: Ohio State University Press, 1985).

Johnson, Samuel, *Dictionary of the English Language* (London: Strahan, 1775)

Kerherve, Alain, ed., *The Ladies' Complete Letter-Writer (1763)* (Newcastle: Cambridge Scholars, Lecture Society, 1877).

Ketabgian, Tamara, 'Spending Sprees and Machine Accidents: Martineau and the Mystery of Improvidence', in *Harriet Martineau: Authorship, Society and Empire*, ed. Ella Dzelzainis and Cora Kaplan (Manchester: Manchester University Press, 2010), pp. 151–162.

Klaver, C. C., *A/Moral Economics: Classical Political Economy and Cultural Authority in Nineteenth-Century England* (Columbus: Ohio State University Press, 2003).

Kuper, A., *Incest & Influence. The Private Life of Bourgeois England* (Massachusetts and London: Harvard University Press, 2009).

Lacey, Candida, ed., *Barbara Leigh Smith Bodichon and the Langham Place Group* (1986; rept., London: Routledge, 2001).

Landow, George, *Elegant Jeremiahs: The Sage from Carlyle to Mailer* (Ithaca, NY: Cornell University Press, 1986).

Lawrence, Karen R., *Penelope Voyages: Women and Travel in the British Literary Tradition* (Ithaca, NY: Cornell University Press, 1994).

Lepenies, Wolf, *Between Literature and Science: The Rise of Sociology* (Cambridge: Cambridge University Press, 1985)

Lipset, Seymour Martin, 'Harriet Martineau's America: Introductory Essay', Harriet Martineau, *Society in America* [edited, abridged and with introductory essay] (Gloucester, MA: Peter Smith, 1968), pp. 5–42.

Logan Deborah A., ed., *Collected Letters of Harriet Martineau*, 5 vols. (London: Pickering and Chatto, 2004).

244 *Selective bibliography*

——, ed., *Harriet Martineau and the Irish Question: Condition of Post-famine Ireland* (Lehigh University Press, 2012).

——, *Harriet Martineau, Victorian Imperialism and the Civilizing Mission* (Aldershot: Ashgate, 2010).

——, ed., *Harriet Martineau's Writing on British History and Military Reform*, 6 vols. (London: Pickering and Chatto, 2005).

——, ed., *Harriet Martineau's Writing on the British Empire.* 5 vols. (London: Pickering and Chatto, 2004).

——, *The Hour and the Woman: Harriet Martineau's 'Somewhat Remarkable Life'* (Dekalb, IL: Northern Illinois University Press, 2002).

——, '"I Am, My Dear Slanderer, Your Faithful Malignant Demon": Harriet Martineau and the *Westminster Review's* Comtist Coterie', *Victorian Periodicals Review* 42, no. 2 (Summer 2009), pp. 171–191.

——, ed., *Illustrations of Political Economy: Selected Tales* (Peterborough, ON: Broadview Press, 2004).

——, 'Introduction' Martineau's *Writings on Slavery and the American Civil War* (DeKalb: Northern Illinois University Press, 2002).

L.U.G.E., 'Miss Martineau and her Traducers', *Zoist* 3, no. 9 (April 1845), pp. 86–96.

Maitzen, Rohan, Gender, Genre, and Victorian Historical Writing (New York: Garland, 1998).

Malthus, T.R. An Essay on the Principle of Population; or A View of its Past and Present effects, (London: J. Johnson, 1798), rpt. Manchester: Manchester University Press, 1989).

Marcet, Jane Haldimand, *Conversations on Chemistry, in which the Elements of that Science are Familiarly Explained, and Illustrated by Experiments*, 2 vols. (London: Longman, Hurst, Rees, Orme and Brown, 1806).

——, *Conversations on Political Economy, in which the Elements of that Science are Familiarly Explained* (1816) 2nd ed. (London: Longman, Hurst, Rees, Orme and Brown, 1817).

Marsh, Jan, ed., *Black Victorians. Black People in British Art: 1800–1900* (London: Lund Humphries Publishers, 2005).

Marx, Karl, *The Economic and Philosophic Manuscripts of 1844* (Moscow: Foreign Languages Publishing House, 1961).

Maudsley, Henry, *The Physiology and Pathology of the Mind* (London: Macmillan, 1867).

McCaw, Neil, *George Eliot and Victorian Historiography: Imagining the National Past* (London: Palgrave, 2000).

McCrone, Kathleen, 'The National Association for the Promotion of Social Science and the Advancement of Victorian Women', *Atlantis* 8 (1982), pp. 44–66

Midgley, Clare, 'The Dissenting Voice of Elizabeth Heyrick: An Exploration of the Links between Gender, Religious Dissent, and Anti-Slavery Radicalism', in *Women, Dissent and Anti-Slavery in Britain and America 1790–1865*, ed. Elizabeth J. Clapo and Julie Roy Jeffrey (Oxford: Oxford University Press, 2011), pp. 88–110.

Mill, James, *Elements of Political Economy* (London: Baldwin, Cradock, and Joy, 1821).

Mill, J.S., *Autobiography* (London: Longmans, Green, Reader, and Dyer, 1873).

——, *The Earlier Letters of John Stuart Mill*, 1812–1848, *Collected Works*, ed. Francis E. Mineka (University of Toronto Press, 1963).

——, *Essays on Economics and Society*, Volumes IV and V of *Collected Works*, edited J.M. Robson, 33 vols. (University of Toronto Press, 1963).

——, *Principles of Political Economy*, Volume III of *Collected Works*, ed. J. M. Robson, 33 vols. (University of Toronto Press, 1963).

Miller, Florence Fenwick, *The Lessons of a Life: Harriet Martineau: A Lecture Delivered 11 March 1877* (Whitefish, MT: Kessinger Publishing, 2010).

Mineka, Francis E., *The Dissidence of Dissent: The Monthly Repository 1806–1838* (1944: rept. Chapel Hill: University of North Carolina Press, 1972).

Mitchell, Rosemary, *Picturing the Past: English History in Text and Image, 1830–70* (Oxford: Clarendon, 2000).

More, Hannah, *Strictures on the Modern System of Female Education* 2 vols. (London: T. Cadell, 1799).

Mullan, John, *How Novels Work* (Oxford: Oxford University Press, 2006).

Oliphant, Margaret, 'Harriet Martineau', *Blackwood's Magazine* 121 (April 1877), pp. 472–496.

——, 'Modern Novelists Great and Small', *Blackwood's Magazine* 77 (May 1855), pp. 554–568.

Oražem, Claudia, *Political Economy and Fiction in the Early Works of Harriet Martineau* (Frankfort: Peter Lang, 1999).

Payn, James, *Some Literary Recollections* (New York: Harper, 1884).

Peterson Linda H, ed., *Becoming a Woman of Letters: Myths of Authorship and Facts of the Victorian Marketplace* (Princeton: Princeton University Press, 2009).

——, 'Harriet Martineau: Masculine Discourse, Female Sage', in *Victorian Sages and Cultural Discourse: Renegotiating Gender and Power*, ed. Thaïs Morgan (New Brunswick: Rutgers University Press, 1990), pp. 171–186.

——, *Harriet Martineau's Autobiography* (Peterborough, ON: Broadview Press, 2007).

——, *Victorian Autobiography: The Tradition of Self-Interpretation* (New Haven and London: Yale University Press, 1986).

Phillips, Patricia, *The Scientific Lady: A Social History of Woman's Scientific Interests 1520–1918* (London: Weidenfeld and Nicolson, 1990).

Phillipson, Nicholas, 'Language, Sociability, and History: Some Reflections on the Foundations of Adam Smith's Science of Man', in *Economy, Polity and Society: British Intellectual History 1750–1950*, ed. Stefan Collini, Richard Whatmore and Brian Young (Cambridge: Cambridge University Press, 2000), pp. 70–84.

Pichanick, Valerie Kossew, 'An Abominable Submission: Harriet Martineau's Views on the Role and Place of Women', *Women's Studies* 5, no. 1 (1977), pp. 13–32.

——, *Harriet Martineau: The Woman and Her Work, 1802–1876* (Ann Arbor: University of Michigan Press, 1980)

Plotz, Judith, *Romanticism and the Vocation of Childhood* (Basingstoke: Palgrave, 2001).

Porter, George, *The Progress of the Nation, in Its Various Social and Economical Relations, from the Beginning of the Nineteenth Century to the Present Time* (London: Knight, 1836–1843).

Postlethwaite, Diana, *Making It Whole: A Victorian Circle and the Shape of Their World* (Columbus: Ohio State University Press, 1984).

Priestley, J., *The Theological and Miscellaneous Works of Joseph Priestley*, ed. J. T. Rutt, 25 vols. (London: G. Smallfield, 1817–1835).

Qualls, Barry, *The Secular Pilgrims of Victorian Fiction* (Cambridge: CUP, 1982).

Ray, Sangeeta, *En-Gendering India: Woman and Nation in Colonial and Postcolonial Narratives* (Durham: Duke University Press, 2000).

Rees, Joan, *Writings on the Nile: Harriet Martineau, Florence Nightingale, and Amelia Edwards* (London: Rubicon Press, 1995).

Reichenbach, Karl von, *Researches on Magnetism, Electricity, Heat, Light, Crystallization, and Chemical Attraction, in Their Relations to the Vital Force*, trans. William Gregory (London: Taylor, Walton, and Maberly, 1850).

Rendall, Jane, *The Origins of Modern Feminism. Women in Britain, France and the United States 1780–1860* (Houndmills, Basingstoke: Macmillan, 1985).

Ricardo, David, *An Essay on the Influence of a Low Price of Corn on the Profits of Stock* (1815), Vol. IV of *The Works and Correspondence of David Ricardo* (Cambridge: Cambridge University Press, 1951).

———, *Principles of Political Economy* (1817), Vol. I of *The Works and Correspondence of David Ricardo* (Cambridge: Cambridge University Press, 1951).

———, *The Works and Correspondence of David Ricardo*, ed. P. Sraffa, 3rd edition 1821 (Cambridge: Cambridge University Press, 1951).

Richards, Graham, *Mental Machinery: The Origins and Consequences of Psychological Ideas, 1600–1850* (Baltimore: Johns Hopkins University Press, 1992).

Roberts, Caroline, *The Woman and the Hour: Harriet Martineau and Victorian Ideologies* (Toronto: University of Toronto Press, 2002).

Robertson, Donald, ed., *The Discovery of Hypnosis: The Complete Writings of James Braid* (London: National Council for Hypnotherapy, 2008).

Robinson, Solveig, ' "Amazed at Our Success" The Langham Place Editors and the Emergence of a Feminist Critical Tradition', *Victorian Periodicals Review* 29, no. 2 (1996), pp. 159–172.

Ryall, Anka, 'Medical Body and Lived Experience: The Case of Harriet Martineau', *Mosaic* 33, no. 4 (2000), pp. 35–53.

Rylance, Rick, *Victorian Psychology and British Culture, 1850–1880* (Oxford: Oxford University Press, 2000).

Sahar Sobhi, Abdel-Hakim, 'Gender Politics in a Colonial Context: Victorian Women's Accounts of Egypt', in *Interpreting the Orient: Travellers in Egypt and the Near East*, ed. Paul and Janet Starkey (Reading: Garnet, 2001), pp. 111–122.

Sanders, Valerie, ed., *Harriet Martineau: Selected Letters* (Oxford: Clarendon Press, 1990).

———, *The Private Lives of Victorian Women: Autobiography in Nineteenth-Century England* (New York and London: Harvester Wheatsheaf, 1989).

———, *Reason Over Passion: Harriet Martineau and the Victorian Novel* (New York: St Martin's, 1986).

———, 'Sibling Performances: HM and JM as Autobiographers' in *A Harriet Martineau Miscellany* (Oxford: Harris Manchester College, 2002).

Scheff, Thomas, 'Getting Unstuck: Interdisciplinarity as a New Discipline', *Sociological Forum* 28, no. 1 (2013), pp. 179–185.

Scholl, Lesa, 'Provocative Agendas: Martineau's Translation of Comte', in *Harriet Martineau: Authorship, Society and Empire*, ed. Ella Dzelzainis and Cora Kaplan (Manchester: Manchester University Press, 2010), pp. 88–99.

Senior, Nassau, *Two Lectures on Population* (London: John Murray, 1829).

Shuttleworth, Sally, *Charlotte Brontë and Victorian Psychology* (Cambridge: Cambridge University Press, 1996).

———, *The Mind of the Child: Child Development in Literature, Science, and Medicine 1840–1910* (Oxford: Oxford University Press, 2010).

Simon, Brian, *The Two Nations and the Educational Structure 1789–1870* (London: Lawrence and Wishart, 1976).

Smith, Adam, *An Inquiry into the Nature and Causes of the Wealth of Nations* (London: W. Strahan and T. Cadell, 1776).

——, *The Theory of Moral Sentiments* (London: A Millar, 1759).

Smith, Bonnie, 'The Contribution of Women to Modern Historiography in Great Britain, France, and the United States, 1750–1940', *American Historical Review* 89, no. 3 (1984), pp. 709–732.

Smith, Sidonie, *A Poetics of Women's Autobiography: Marginality and the Fictions of Self-Representation* (Bloomington and Indianapolis: Indiana University Press, 1987).

Somerville, Mary, *On the Connexion of the Physical Sciences* (London: John Murray, 1834).

——, *Physical Geography*, 2 vols. (London: John Murray, 1848).

Spencer, Peter, *Hannah Greg (nee Lightbody) 1766–1828* (Styal: Quarry Bank Mill Trust, 1985)

Spongberg, Mary *Writing Women's History since the Renaissance* (Basingstoke: Palgrave, 2002).

Taussig, F. W., *Wages and Capital* (London: Macmillan, 1896).

Thomson, Dorothy Lampen, *Adam Smith's Daughters: Six Prominent Economists from the Eighteenth Century to the Present* (New York: Exposition Press, 1973)

Todd, Barbara, *Harriet Martineau at Ambleside* (Carlisle: Bookcase, 2002).

Tong, Rosemarie, *Feminist Thought. A Comprehensive Introduction* (Sydney, Australia: Allen & Unwin, 1989).

Veblen, Thorstein, *The Theory of the Leisure Class: An Economic Study of Institutions* (The Modern Library, 1899, 1934).

Vint, John, *Capital and Wages* (Aldershot: Edward Elgar, 1994).

Walkowitz, Judith, *Prostitution and Victorian Society* (Cambridge: Cambridge University Press, 1980).

Warren, John, 'Harriet Martineau and the Concept of Community: Deerbrook and Ambleside', *Journal of Victorian Culture* 134, no. 2 (2008), pp. 223–246.

——, ' "Now try and recollect if you have done any good today". Household, Individual and Community in the Early Fiction of Harriet Martineau, c. 1825–41' (Oxford Doctoral Thesis, 2014).

Waterfield, Robin, *Hidden Depths: The Story of Hypnosis* (New York: Brunner-Routledge, 2003).

Watts, Ruth E., *Gender, Power and the Unitarians in England, 1760–1860* (London: Longman, 1998).

——, 'The Unitarian Contribution to the Development of Female Education (1790–1850)', *History of Education* 9 (1980), pp. 273–286.

——, *Women in Science. A Social and Cultural History* (London: Routledge, 2007).

Webb, R. K., *The British Working Class Reader, 1790–1848* (London: Allen and Unwin, 1955).

——, *Harriet Martineau: A Radical Victorian* (London: Heinemann, 1960).

Weber, Max, *The Protestant Ethic and the Spirit of Capitalism* (George: Allen and Unwin, 1904–1905).

Weiner, Gaby, ed., *Harriet Martineau, Deerbrook* (London: Virago, 1983).

——, ed., *Harriet Martineau's Autobiography* (London: Virago, 1983)

Whitehead, Alfred North, *Science and the Modern World* (New York: Macmillan, 1962)

Winch, Donald ed., *James Mill: Selected Economic Writings* (Edinburgh: Published for the Scottish Economic Society by Oliver and Boyd, 1966).

——, *Riches and Poverty: An Intellectual History of Political Economy in Britain, 1750–1834* (Cambridge: Cambridge University Press, 1996).

Winter, Alison, 'Harriet Martineau and the Reform of the Invalid in Victorian England', *The Historical Journal* 38, no. 3 (1995), pp. 597–616.

————, *Mesmerized: Powers of Mind in Victorian Britain* (Chicago: University of Chicago Press, 1998).

Woollacott, Angela, *Gender and Empire* (Basingstoke, Hampshire: Palgrave Macmillan, 2006).

Yates, Gayle Graham, *Harriet Martineau on Women* (New Brunswick, NJ: Rutgers University Press, 1985).

Index

Note: Page numbers in italics indicate figures.

Abbott, Edith 71
'Account of Toussaint L'Ouverture'
    (Martineau) 102, 103–6
'Achievements of the Genius of Scott,
    The' (Martineau) 122
Adams, W. H. Davenport 21–2
Addams, Jane 69
agency, centrality of 88
America, Martineau travel writings about
    172–9; on American press and social
    progress 175–8; on Clay, Henry 174;
    How to Observe Morals and Manners
    172; on Niagara Falls 174–5; *Retrospect
    of Western Travel* 172, 173; on river
    systems 173–4; *Society in America* 172,
    175, 177; on Unitarian leaders 178–9;
    writing stance used in 172–3
American Sociological Association (ASA)
    71, 72–3
Amigoni, David 18
apologetics approach to disciplines 25–7
Arbuckle, Elisabeth Sanders 103
Arrowsmith, Jane 142, 147
Associationism 203–4, 212–13
Athenaeum, The 126, 128, 136, 137
Atkinson, Henry 221
Austen, Jane 125, 126–7
'Autobiographic Memoir, An'
    (Martineau) 222
autobiographies, described 20
Autobiography (Martineau) 17–28, 102,
    108, 179; apologetics approach of 25–7;
    assessments of 18; categorisation and
    18–19; critics of 17–18; defining nation
    through 27–8; intellectual development
    and 19–22; interference episodes
    noted in 226; self-engineering through
    intellectual engagement and 22–5

*Autobiography: Narrative of
    Transformation* (Barros) 21

Barbauld, Anna 34, 41, 86, 202–3
Barrett, Elizabeth 142
Barros, Carolyn 21
Bauman, Zygmunt 75
Bell, Charles 135
Bellenden-Ker, Elizabeth 226–7
Bending, Lucy 17, 20
Bentham, Jeremy 85
Berry, Laura 213
'Biographical Memoranda'
    (Martineau) 206
Biographical Sketches (Martineau) 43, 87
Birney, James 106
'Black Giles The Poacher' (More) 203
Blackwood's Edinburgh Magazine
    126, 188
Blasi, Tony 73
Blaug, Mark 49, 54
Bodichon, Barbara 157
Bohrer, Susan F. 7
Bonser, Helen 71
Booth, Alison 27, 113
Bottomore, Tom 71
Boucherett, Jessie 157
Braid, James *138*, 138–40, 142, 145
Briery Creek (Martineau) 35–6, 207
British Association for the Advancement
    of Science 33, 87
British Rule in India (Martineau) 115
Brontë, Charlotte 6, 125, 132, 222–3
Brougham, Lord 57
Brown, Betty 202
Burney, Fanny 111
Bushnan, J. Stevenson 143
Butler, Josephine 157, 164–6

Dresser, Amos 106
Durkheim, Émile 70, 73
Dzelzainis, Ella 7

Easley, Alexis 18, 22, 28, 160, 187, 190, 198
Eastern Life, Present and Past (Martineau) 42, 70, 77, 115, 171, 224
Eastlake, Lady 190
Edgeworth, Maria 37, 87, 202
Edinburgh Review, The 146, 156, 162, 188, 190, 196, 225
education, Martineau and 31–43; on consumption 35–6; over-population themes 36; overview of 31; philosophy and psychology of 31–3; of public 33–8, 42; on slavery 36–8; of women 40–2; of working class 38–40
Elements of Political Economy (Mill) 49–50
Eliot, George 21, 87, 125, 198
Ella of Garveloch (Martineau) 123–4, 204, 209
Elliotson, John 139
employment conditions/opportunities for women 162–4
Empson, William 63–4, 225
England and Her Soldiers (Martineau) 70
epistolary format 217–18
'Essays on the Art of Thinking' (Martineau) 34
Estlin, Mary 229
Evans, Mary Ann 189
Evenings at Home (Barbauld and Aikin) 202–3

'Factory Boy, The' (Martineau) 203
False Key, The (Franklin) 202
Farrers of Budge-Row, The (Martineau) 204
Fawcett, Millicent Garrett 87
Feagan, Joe 72, 77
Female Anti-Slavery Society 107
Female Industry 156, 164, 167
'Female Writers on Practical Divinity' (Martineau) 3, 34, 155, 202–3
feminism, Martineau and 155–68; Contagious Diseases Acts and 156; divorce legislation and 156; *Female Industry* 156; Martineau's brand of 155; overview of 155–7; 'the Political Non-Existence of Women' 156; Wollstonecraft and 155; 'Woman

Question' and 155–6; women's political rights and 158–68
fiction writings of Martineau 121–33; Austen comparisons with 126–7; critics of 123; *Deerbrook* 124–32; *For Each and For All* 124; *Ella of Garveloch* 123–4; heroines in 125; from hobby to career 122–3; *Oliver Weld* 132–3; overview of 121
Five Years of Youth (Martineau) 207, 209
Flower, Eliza 156
'Flower Shows in a Birmingham Hot-House' (Martineau) 192
For Each and For All (Martineau) 62, 124
Forest and Game-Law Tales (Martineau) 70
Fox, Caroline 87
Fox, Charles 50
Fox, William J. 35, 86, 179, 189, 218, 229
Fraser's Magazine 147, 189
Fry, Elizabeth 111

Gall, Franz Joseph 142, 143
Garnett, Richard 231
Garrison, William Lloyd 106
Gauld, Alan 139
gender and class relations 95
Gerth, Hans 71
Gibbon, Edward 108
Giddens, Anthony 75, 77
Gilman, Charlotte Perkins 69
Godwin, William 32, 86, 91
Gouldner, Alvin 77
Greenwell, Dora 125
Greg, Hannah 33
Grimke, Angelina 107
'Guides to Service' (Martineau) 4, 196

Hall, Catherine 2
Hall, Spencer T. 139
Hamlets, The (Martineau) 58
Harriet Martineau: First Woman Sociologist (Hoecker-Drysdale) 72
'Harriet Martineau: Masculine Discourse, Female Sage' (Peterson) 183
Harriet Martineau Sociological Society 9, 72
Harrison, Frederic 144
Hartleian Associationism, *Monthly Repository* and 209–14
Hartley, David 32–3, 201
Hayward, Abraham 190
Hazlitt, William 115

For Product Safety Concerns and Information please contact our EU representative GPSR@taylorandfrancis.com, Taylor & Francis Verlag GmbH, Kaufingerstraße 24, 50667 München, Germany